A

COLLECTION

OF

ESOTERIC WRITINGS

OF

T.SUBBA ROW

A COLLECTION OF ESOTERIC WRITINGS OF T.SUBBA ROW

GYAN

Published by

Gyan Publishing House
5, Ansari Road
Daryaganj, New Delhi-110002
Phone: 011-47034999, 9811692060
E-mail: books@gyanbooks.com

Distribution Network
gyanbooks.com
India, USA, Canada, UK, Australia

ISBN: 978-93-6433-673-4 (PB)
First Published, 1910

2nd Impression 2024

Printed at: Gyan Press, Delhi.

A COLLECTION OF ESOTERIC WRITINGS OF T. SUBBA ROW
Author: T.SUBBA ROW

A COLLECTION OF ESOTERIC WRITINGS

OF

T. SUBBA ROW, F.T.S., B.A., B.L.

PUBLISHED FOR THE BOMBAY THEOSOPHICAL PUBLICATION FUND

BY

RAJARAM TOOKARAM.

Bombay.

PRINTED AT "THE TATVA-VIVECHAKA" PRESS.

1910.

CONTENTS.

PREFACE.

WHILST presenting this little volume to the public, we cannot but pay due tribute to the memory of one who had done such good service to the cause of Occult Science. The late lamented Mr. T. Subba Row, B.A., B.L., of the Madras University, was one of the highest Occultists of Southern India. We tried our utmost to collect as many facts relating to his life as we could possibly get from his relatives and friends, to enable us to write a short sketch of his life to go with this book. But, we regret to say, that our endeavours in this direction have been without fruit. We have, therefore, had no alternative but to reproduce the notice of his death taken by Col. H. S. Olcott, in the "Theosophist," in its place.

Mr. Subba Row was a member of the Theosophical Society, and was highly respected not only by all its members, but also by Madame H. P. Blavatsky, for his great erudition and proficiency in almost all the branches of Occult Science. Madame Blavatsky used always to consult him whenever there were difficult and intricate problems to be solved. And we know she had, at one time, sent the manuscripts of her most valuable work, "The Secret Doctrine," to him for correction and alteration; but he declined to undertake the work because he believed the world was not yet prepared to accept the disclosures of those secrets which had been, for good reason, hitherto kept within the knowledge of the sacred few.

Mr. T. Subba Row had written no book on Occult Science, but he has left behind him a series of lectures and articles which he used every now and then to contribute to the "Theosophist," and which display the real depth of his knowledge, and his worth as an Occultist. He, in the year 1887, at the Convention of the Theosophical Society, held at Adyar, Madras, gave a course of lectures to assist Theosophists and others in their study of the Philosophy of Bhagwad Gita. We all know how difficult to understand is the Philosophy of the Gita, notwithstanding the commentaries written thereon in Sanskrit as well as in many modern Eastern and even Western languages. The reason of this is obvious. Every-one acquainted with the description of the great war between the Pândavas and the Kauravas knows that the Bhagwad Gita was preached by Bhagwan Shri Krishna to his friend and disciple Arjun, because of the disinclination expressed by the latter to fight on the battlefield. This description, as a matter of course, as there was no time to be lost, must have been recited in a short space of time, in the form of Aphorisms in short sentences, conveying a deep hidden meaning. Shri Krishna knew that Arjun was able accurately to comprehend in all its fullness the significance of this teaching.

Mr. Subba Row has written a commentary on this Philosophy, and has done his best to make it as elucidative, consistent, and clear as possible. We have printed these lectures in a separate book, and the readers will find on its study what an amount of learning the lecturer must have had.

These very lectures are conspicuous for the fact of having created between Mr. Subba Row and Madame Blavatsky a difference of opinion regarding the Koshas (कोश) or principles of which the human being is formed. This resulted in a written controversy between them, which the reader will find reprinted in this book.

Though most of the articles reproduced here are of controversial character, the reader will find them of sterling worth and merit on account of the originality of thought displayed and the able treatment of the various points controverted. And, moreover, they teem with learned and useful suggestions for progress of the students of Occult Science. Those who had read and studied these articles in the various numbers of the "Theosophist," as they appeared from time to time, had more than once requested us to reprint them in a collected form for the benefit to students of Occult learning.

Besides these articles, we are in possession of several notes of a miscellaneous character, regarding the private instructions given by Mr. T. Subba Row to the "chosen few" who had the good fortune to be in close contact with him. But we are sorry to say that they are incomplete, and were given by him only under the pledge of secrecy. It has, therefore, been thought desirable not to publish them. Mr. T. Subba Row had also made contributions to the local newspapers and magazines, but we think it unnecessary to reprint these, as they are solely on questions political and social.

Here we cannot help thanking our respected brother, the Hon'ble Mr. Subramaniyar for the valuable help, pecuniary and otherwise, he has rendered us in publishing some of our works.

Bombay, 1st April 1895. T. T.

A SKETCH OF THE LIFE OF THE LATE T. SUBBA ROW, B. A., B. L., F. T. S.

THE announcement, I am now compelled to make of the death of this brilliant young Indian mystical philosopher, will shock the Theosophical reading public. Wherever our work has extended, there has his reputation spread. He was an intellectual phenomenon, and his mental history goes as far as anything conceivable to support the theory of palingenesis. The facts bearing upon the case, as I derived them from his venerable mother on the day of the cremation, will presently be given. When he last visited the Head-quarters, the first week in April last, the mysterious cutaneous disease to which he ultimately succumbed, had begun to show itself in an outbreak of boils. Neither he nor either of us dreamt that it was at all serious. But shortly after he had to keep to his room, then to his lounge, and he never went out again save once, when he was taken to a different house for change of air. In the beginning of June he sent me a touching request to come and see him, which of course, I did. He was a piteous sight: his body a mass of sores from crown to sole, and he not able to bear even a sheet over him, nor to lie in any comfortable position, not get sound sleep. He was depressed and despairing, and begged me to try if I could not help him a little by mesmerism. I did try with all my will, and it seemed with some success, for he began to mend from that evening, and at my third visit he and I thought he was convalescent, and so informed his unhappy family. But suddenly there came a relapse, his disease finished its course rapidly, and, on Tuesday, the 24th June, at 10 P. M., he expired, without a word or a sign to those about him.

The last wordly business he attended to was to declare on the morning of 24th idem in the presence of his relatives and friends, among them, Dewan Bahadur P. Shrinivasa Rao, that he had authorized his wife to adopt a son after his death—there being no issue of his marriage.

At noon on that day, he said his Guru called him to come, he was going to die, he was now about beginning his *tâpas* (mystical invocations), and he did not wish to be disturbed. From that time on, he spoke to no one. When he died, a great star fell from the firmament of Indian contemporary thought. Between Subba Row, H. P. Blavatsky, Damodar and myself there was a close friendship. He was chiefly instrumental in having us invited to visit Madras in 1882, and in inducing us to choose this city as the permanent Head-quarters of the Theosophical Society. Subba Row was in confidential understanding with us about Damodar's mystical pilgrimage towards the North, and more than a year after the latter crossed into Tibet, he wrote him about himself and his plans. Subba Row told me of this long ago, and reverted to the subject the other day at one of my visits to his sick-bed. A dispute—due in a measure to third parties—which widened into a breach, arose between H. P. B. and himself about certain philosophical questions, but to the last he spoke of her, to us and to his family, in the old friendly way. When we last saw each other we had a long talk about esoteric philosophy, and he said that as soon as he could get out, he should come to Head-quarters and draft several metaphysical questions that he wished Mr. Fawcett to discuss with him in the *Theosophist*. His interest in our movement was unabated to the last, he read the *Theosophist* regularly and was a subscriber to H. P. B.'s *Lucifer*.

Our great Vedantin was of the Niyogi caste of the Smartha (Advaita) Brahmans. He was born on the 6th July 1856. At the time of his death he was aged but nearly 34 years. His native country was the Godavery District on the Coromandal Coast of India ; his vernacular tongue the Telugu. His grandfather was the Sheristedar of the District, and his maternal uncle was Dewan (Prime Minister) to the Rajah of Pittapur. His father died when he was but six months' baby, and the uncle brought him up. He first attended the Coconada Hindu School, where he was not at all suspected of possessing any surprising talent. He passed his first Matriculation examination at the Hindu School, Coconada, then under the direction of Mr. J. Kenny. From thence he passed in 1872, into the Madras Presidency College, where his career was a brilliant one, and ended in his passing B. A. in 1876 as the first of the University in his class. In the latter part of the same year that astute satesman, Sir T. Madhava Row, then Dewan of Baroda, offered him the Registrarship of the High Court of that State, and Subba Row stopped there about a year, but then returned to Madras and prepared himself for and passed the B. L. examination, number 4 in the class. Having adopted the law as his profession, he served his apprenticeship under Messrs. Grant and Laing and was enrolled a Vakil (Pleader) of the High Court in the latter part of 1880. His practice became lucrative, and might have been made much more so had he given less attention to philosophy ; however, as he told me, he was drawn by an irresistible attraction. As an example of his extraordinary cleverness, his friends cite his successful passing of the examination in geology for the Statutory Civil Service in 1885, though it was a new subject to him, and he had had only a week for preparation. He leaves a young widow of 24 years, and an aged mother—herself a learned Brahman lady—who mourns ths loss of her great son, the pride of her soul, most bitterly. The cremation took place at 9 o'clock on the morning after his death. Our brother, Judge P. Sreenivas Row, was with him at the last, and T. Vijiaraghava Charlu saw him two hours before the event occurred.

It is remarked above that T. Subba Row gave no early signs of possessing mystical knowledge : even Sir T. Madhava Row did not suspect it in him while he was serving under him at Baroda. I particularly questioned his mother on this point, and she told me that her son first talked metaphysics after forming a connection with the Founders of the Theosophical Society : a connection which began with a correspondence between himself and H. P. B. and Damodar, and became personal after our meeting him, in 1882, at Madras. It was as though a storehouse of occult experience, long forgotten, had been suddenly opened to him ; recollection of his last preceding birth came in upon him; he recognized his Guru, and thenceforward held intercourse with him and other Mahatmas; with some, personally at our Head-quarters. with others elsewhere and by correspondence. He told his mother that H. P. B. was a great Yogi, and that he had seen many strange phenomena in her presence. His stored up knowledge of Sanskrit literature came back to him, and his brother-in-law told me that if you would recite any verse of Gita, Brahma-Sutras or Upanishads, he could at once tell you whence it was taken and in what connection employed. Those who had the fortune to hear his lectures on Bhagvad Gita before the T. S. Convention of 1886 at Adyar, can well believe this, so perfect seemed his mastery of that peerless work. For a man of his abilities, he left scarcely any monument the paper she contributed to these pages and the one-volume Report of his four Adyar Lectures being almost his entire literary remains. As a conversationalist he was most brilliant and interesting ; an afternoon's sitting with him was as edifying as the reading of a solid book. But this mystical side of his character he showed only to kindred souls. What may seem strange to some is the fact that, while he was obedient as a child to his mother in wordly affairs, he was strangely reticent to her, as he was to all his relatives and ordinary acquaintances, about spiritual matters. His constant answer to her importunities for occult instruction was that he "Dared not reveal any of the secrets entrusted to him by his Guru." *He lived his occult life alone.* That he was habitually so reserved, gives the more weight to the confidential statements he made to the members of his own household.

H. S. O.

The above, having been considered in family-council, was endorsed as follows :—"Read and found correct.—D. T. R., Brother-in-Law of T. Subba Row."

—*Theosophist.*

COLLECTION OF ESOTERIC WRITINGS

OF

T. SUBBA ROW, F.T.S., B.A. B.L.

THE TWELVE SIGNS OF THE ZODIAC.

The division of the Zodiac into different signs dates from immemorial antiquity. It has acquired a world-wide celebrity and is to be found in the astrological systems of several nations. The invention of the Zodiac and its signs has been assigned to different nations by different antiquarians. It is stated by some that, at first, there were only ten signs, that one of these signs was subsequently split up into two separate signs, and that a new sign was added to the number to render the esoteric significance of the division more profound and at the same time to conceal it more perfectly from the uniniti-ated public. It is very probable that the real philosophical conception of the division owes its origin to some particular nation, and the names given to the various signs might have been translated into the languages of other nations. The principal object of this article, however, is not to decide which nation had the honour of inventing the signs in question, but to indicate *to some extent* the real philosophical meaning in-volved therein and the way to discover the rest of the meaning which yet remains undisclosed. But from what is herein stated, an inference may fairly be drawn that, like so many other philosophical myths and allegories, the invention of the Zodiac and its signs owes its origin to ancient India.

What then is the real origin of these signs, the philosophical conception which the Zodiac and its signs are intended to represent? Do the various signs merely represent the shape or configuration of the different constellations included in the divisions, or, are they simply masks designed to veil some hidden meaning ? The former supposition is altogether untenable for two reasons, *viz.* :—

1. The Hindoos were acquainted with the precession of equinoxes as may be easily seen from their works on Astronomy and from the almanacs published by Hindu astronomers. Consequently they were fully aware of the fact that the constellations in the various Zodiacal divisions were not fixed. They could not, therefore, have assigned particular shapes to these shifting groups of fixed stars with reference to the divisions of the Zodiac. But the names indicating the Zodiacal signs have been allowed to remain unaltered. It is to be inferred, therefore, that the names given to the various signs have no connection whatever with the configurations of the constellations included in them.

II. The names assigned to these signs by the ancient Sanskrit writers and their esoteric or literal meanings are as follows :—

	The names of the signs.	The esoteric literal meanings.
1	Mésham	Ram or *Aries.*
2	Rishabham	Bull or *Taurus.*
3	Mithunam	Twins or *Gemini*(male and female).
4	Karkátakam	Cancer or Crab.
5	Simham	Lion or *Leo.*
6	Kanya	*Virgo** or Virgin.
7	Tula	*Libra* or Balance.
8	Vrischikam	Scorpion.
9	Dhanus	Sagittarius or Archer.
10	Makaram	Capricornus or Crocodile.
11	Kumbham	Aquarius or Waterbearer.
12	Meenam	Pisces or Fish.

* Virgo-Scorpio, when none but the initiates knew there were 12 signs. Virgo-Scorpio was then followed (for the profane) by *Sagittarius.* At the middle or junction-point where now stands *Libra* and at the sign now called *Virgo*, two mystical signs were inserted which remained unintelligible to the profane.—ED. THEOS.

The figures of the constellations included in the signs at the time the division was first made do not at all resemble the shapes of the animals, reptiles and other objects denoted by the names given them. The truth of this assertion can be ascertained by examining the configurations of the various constellations. Unless the shape of the crocodile* or the crab is called up by the observer's imagination, there is very little change of the stars themselves suggesting to his idea that figure, upon the blue canopy of the starry firmament.

If, then, the constellations have nothing to do with the origin of the names by which the Zodiacal divisions are indicated, we have to seek for some other source which might have given rise to these appelations. It becomes my object to unravel a portion of the mystery connected with these Zodiacal signs, as also to disclose a portion of the sublime conception of the ancient Hindu philosophy which gave rise to them. The signs of the Zodiac have more than one meaning. From one point of view they represent the different stages of creation up to the time the present material universe with the five elements came into phenomenal existence. As the author of "Isis Unveiled" has stated in the second volume of her admirable work, "the key should be turned *Seven times*" to understand the whole philosophy underlying these signs. But I shall wind it only once and give the contents of the *first Chapter* of the History of Creation. It is very fortunate that the Sanskrit names assigned to the various divisions by the Aryan philosophers contain within themselves the key to the solution of the problem. Those of my readers who have studied to some extent the ancient "Mantra" and the "Tantra Sâstrâs" † of India, would have seen that very often Sanskrit words are made to convey a certain hidden meaning by means of certain well-known pre-arranged methods and a tacit convention, while their literal significance is something quite

* This constellation was never called Crocodile by the Western ancient astronomers who described it as a horned goat and called it so—*Capricornus*, —Ed. Theos.

† Works on Incantation and Magic.

different from the implied meaning. The following are some of the rules which may help an enquirer in ferreting out the deep significance of the ancient Sanskrit nomenclature used in the old Aryan myths and allegories:—

1. Find out the synonyms of the word used which have other meanings.
2. Find out the numerical value of the letters composing the word according to the methods given in ancient Tântrik works.
3. Examine the ancient myths or allegories, if there are any, which have any special connection with the word in question.
4. Permute the different syllables composing the word and examine the new combinations that will thus be formed and their meanings, &c., &c.

I shall now apply some of the above given rules to the names of the twelve signs of the Zodiac.

I. *Mésham.* One of the synonyms of this word is *Aja* Now, *Aja* literally means that which has no birth and is applied to the Eternal Brahmam in certain portions of the Upanishads. So the first sign is intended to represent *Parabrahmam*, the self-existent, eternal, self-sufficient cause of all.

II. *Rishabham.* This word is used in several places in the Upanishads and the Vêda to mean *Pranava* (Aum). Sankarâchârya has so interpreted it in several portions of his commentary.*

III. *Mithunam.* As the word plainly indicates, this sign is intended to represent the first androgyne, the *Ardhanâreeswara*, the bisexual Sephira-Adam Kadmon.

IV. *Karkatakam.* When the syllables are converted into the corresponding numbers according to the general

* Example "Rishâbhasyâ—Chandasam Rishâbhasya Pradhanasya *Pranavasya*."

mode of transmutation so often alluded to in Mantra Shastra, the word in question will be represented by ////. This sign then is evidently intended to represent the sacred *Tetragram*; the Parabrahma-thárakam ; the Pranava resolved into four separate entities corresponding to its *four Mâtras ; the four Avasthâs* indicated by Jágrath (waking) Avastha, Swapna (dreamy) Avastha, Shushupti (deep sleep) Avastha, and Turiya (the last stage, *i. e.* Nirvana) Avastha, (as yet in potentiality); *the four states of Brahma* called Vaiswánara, Taijasa (or Hiranya-garbha), Pragna, and Eśwara and represented by Brahma, Vishnu, Mahéswara, and Sadásiva; *the four aspects of Parabrahmam* as Sthoolam, Sookshmam, Beejam and Sakshi ; *the four stages or conditions of the Sacred word* named Para, Pasyanti, Madhyama and Vykhari ; *Nadam, Bindu, Sakti and Kala.* This sign completes the first quaternary.

V. *Simham.* This word contains a world of occult meaning within itself ; and it may not be prudent on my part to disclose the whole of its meaning in this article. It will be sufficient for the purpose of this article to give a general indication of its significance.

Two of its synonymous terms are *Panchásyam* and *Hari*, and its number in the order of the Zodiacal divisions (being the fifth sign) points clearly to the former synonym. This synonym—Panchásyam—shows that the sign is intended to represent the *five Brhamas, viz.,*—Esánam, Aghôram, Tatpurusham, Vámadêvam, and Sadyojátam—*the five Buddhas.* The second synonym shows it to be Náráyana, the Jeevàtma, or Pratyagátma. (The Sukarahasy Upanishad will show that the ancient Aryan philosophers looked upon Náráyana as the Jeevátma.* The Vaishnavites may not admit it. But as

* In its lowest or most material state, as the life-principle which animates the material bodies of the animal and vegetable worlds, &c.,—ED. THEOS.

an Advaiti, I look upon Jeevátma as identical with Paramátma in its real essence when stripped of its fictitious attributes created by Agnánam or Avidya—ignorance.) The Jeevátma is correctly placed in the fifth sign counting from Mêsham, as the fifth sign is the *putrasthânam* or the son's house according to the rules of Hindu Astrology. The sign in question represents Jeevátma—the son of Paramátma as it were. (I may also add that it represents the real Christ, the anointed pure spirit, though the missionaries may frown at this interpretation.)* I will only add here that unless the nature of this sign is fully comprehended it will be impossible to understand the real order of the next three signs and their full significance. The elements or entities that have merely a potential existence in this sign become distinct, separate entities in the next three signs. Their union into a single entity leads to the destruction of the phenomenal universe, and the recognition of the pure spirit, and their separation has the contrary effect. It leads to material earth-bound existence and brings into view the picture gallery of *Avidya* (Ignorance) or Mâya (Illusion). If the real orthography of the name by which the sign in question is indicated is properly understood it will readily be seen that the next three signs are not what they ought to be. Kanya or Virgo and Vrischikam or Scorpio should form one single sign, and Tula must follow the said sign if it is at all necessary to have a separate sign of the name. But a separation between Kanya and Vrischikam was effected by interposing the sign Tula between the two. The object of this separation will be understood on examining the meaning of the three signs.

---

* Nevertheless it is a true one. The *Jiv-âtma* in the (*Microcosm* man) is the same spiritual essence which animates the *Macrocosm* (universe), the differentiation, or specific difference between the two *Jivâtmâs* presenting itself but in the two states or conditions of the same and one Force. Hence "this son of Paramâtma" is an eternal correlation of the Father-Cause. Purusha manifesting himself as Brahma of the "golden egg" and becoming Viradja—the universe. We are "all born of Aditi from the water" (hymns of the Maruts X 632) and "Being was born from not-being" (*Rig-Veda*, Mandala 1, Sûkta 166),—Ed. Theos.

VI. *Kanyá* means a virgin and represents Sakti or Mahámáya. The sign in question is the 6th Rási or division and indicates that there are six primary forces in nature. These forces have different sets of names in Sanskrit philosophy. According to one system of nomenclature they are called by the following names:—(1) Parásakti ; (2) Gnánastaki; (3) Itchásakti (will-power); (4) Kriyásakti; (5) Kundalinisakti; and (6) Matrikásakti.* The six

---

* *Parásakti*:—Literally the great or supreme force or power. It means and includes *the powers of light and heat.*

Gnânasakti:—Literally the power of intellect or the power of real wisdom or knowledge. It has two aspects :

I. The following are some of its manifestations *when placed under the influence or control of material conditions* :—

(*a*)The power of the mind in interpreting our sensations. (*b*) its power in recalling past ideas (memory) and raising future expectations. (*c*) Its power as exhibited in what are called by modern psychologists "the laws of association " which enables it to form *persisting* connections between various groups of sensations and possiblities of sensations and thus generate the notion or idea of an external object. (*d*) Its power in connecting our ideas together by the mysterious link of memory and thus generating the notion of self or individuality.

II. The following are some of its manifestations *when liberated from the bonds of matter*:—

(*a*) Clairvoyance. (*b*) Psychometry.

Itchâsakti:—Literally, *the power of the will*. Its *most ordinary manifestation* is the generation of certain nerve currents which set in motion such muscles as are required for the accomplishment of the desired object.

Kriyâsakti:—The mysterious power of thought which enables it to produce external, perceptible, phenomenal result by its own inherent energy. The ancients held that any idea will manifest itself *externally* if one's attention is deeply concentrated upon it. Similarly an intense volition will be followed by the desired result.

A Yogi generally performs his wonders by means of Itchásakti and Kriyasakti.

Kundalinisakti:—Literally, the power or force which moves in a serpentine or curved path. It is the universal life-principle which everywhere manifests itself in nature. This force includes in itself the two great forces of attraction and repulsion. Electricity and magnetism are but manifestations of it. This is the power or force which brings about that " continuous

forces are in their unity represented by the *Astral light.**

VII. *Tula.* When represented by numbers according to the method above alluded to, this word will be converted into 36. This sign, therefore, is evidently intended to represent *the 36 Tatwams.* (The number of Tatwams is different according to the views of different philosophers; but by Sâktêyás generally and by several of the ancient Rishis such as Agastya, Doorwása and Parasurâma, &c., the number of Tatwams has been stated to be 36). Jeevátma differs from Paramátma, or to state the same thing in other words, "Baddha" differs from "Mukta" † in being encased as it were within these 36 Tatwams, while the other is free. This sign prepares the way

---

adjustment of *internal relations to external relations*" which is the essence of life according to Herbert Spencer and that "continuous adjustment of *external relations to internal relations,*" which is the basis of transmigration of souls or punarjanman (re-birth) according to the doctrines of the ancient Hindu philosophers.

A Yogi must thoroughly subjugate this power or force before he can attain Môksham. This force is, in fact, the great serpent of the Bible.

Mâtrikâsakti :—Literally, the force or power of letters or speech or music. The whole of the ancient Mantra Shâstra has this force or power in all its manifestations for its subject-matter. The power of The Word which Jesus Christ speaks of is a manifestation of this Sakti. The influence of music is one of its ordinary manifestations. The power of the mirific ineffable name is the crown of this Sakti.

Modern science has but partly investigated the first, second and fifth of the forces or powers above-named, but it is altogether in the dark as regards the remaining powers.

* Even the very name of *Kanyá* (Virgin) shows how all the ancient esoteric systems agreed in all their fundamental doctrines. The Kabalists and the Hermetic philosophers call the Astral Light the "heavenly or celestial Virgin." The Astral Light in its unity is the 7th. Hence the seven principles diffused in every unity or the 6 and ONE—two triangles and a crown—ED. THEOS.

† As the Infinite differs from the Finite and the Unconditioned from the conditioned.—ED. THEOS.

to earthly Adam, to Nara. As the emblem of Nara it is properly placed as the seventh sign.

VIII. *Vrischikam.* It is stated by ancient philosophers that the sun when located in this Rási or division is called by the name of *Vishnu* (see the 12th Skandha of Bhâgavata). The sign is intended to represent Vishnu. Vishnu literally means *that which is expanded*—expanded as *Viswam or Universe.* Properly speaking, Viswam itself is Vishnu (see Sankaráchârya's commentary on Vishnusahasranâmam). I have already intimated that Vishnu represents the *Swapnávastha* or the *Dreamy State.* The sign in question properly signifies the Universe in thought or the universe in the divine conception.

It is properly placed as the sign opposite to Rishabham or Pranava. Analysis from Pranava downwards leads to the Universe of Thought, and synthesis from the latter upwards leads to Pranava (Aum). We have now arrived at the ideal state of the universe previous to its coming into material existence. The expansion of the Beejam or primitive germ into the universe is only possible when the 36 "Tatwams"* are interposed between the Máya and Jeevátma. The dreamy state is induced through the instrumentality of these "Tatwams." It is the existence of these Tatwams that brings *Hamsa* into existence. The elimination of these Tatwams marks the beginning of the synthesis towards Pranava and Brahmam and converts *Hamsa* into *Sóham.* As it is intended to represent the different stages of creation from Brahmam downwards to the material universe, the three signs Kanya, Tula, and Vrischikam are placed in the order in which they now stand as three separate signs.

IX. *Dhanus (Sagittarius).* When represented in numbers, the name is equivalent to 9, and the division in question is the 9th division counting from Mêsham.

---

* 36 is three times 12, or 9 Tetraktis, or 12 Triads, the most sacred number in the Kabalistic and Pythagorean numerals.—Ed. Theos.

The sign, therefore, clearly indicates the 9 *Brahmâs*—the 9 Parajâpatîs who assisted the Demiurgus in constructing the material universe.

X. *Makaram.* There is some difficulty in interpreting this word; nevertheless it contains within itself the clue to its correct interpretation. The letter Ma is equivalent to number 5 and *Kara* means hand. Now in Sanskrit *Tribhujam* means a triangle, bhujam or karam (both are synonymous) being understood to mean a side. So, Makaram or Panchakaram means a *Pentagon.**

Now, Makaram is the tenth sign and the term "Dasadisa" is generally used by Sanskrit writers to denote the faces or sides of the universe. The sign in question is intended to represent the faces of the universe and indicates that the figure of the universe is bounded by *Pentagons.* If we take the pentagons as regular pentagons (on the presumption or supposition that the universe is symmetrically constructed) the figure of the material universe will, of course, be a *Dodecahedron*, the geometrical model imitated by the Demiurgus in constructing the material universe. If *Tula* was subsequently invented and if, instead of the three signs "Kanya," "Tula" and "Vrischikam," there had existed formerly only one sign combining in itself Kanya and Vrischikam, the sign now under consideration was the eighth sign under the old system, and it is a significant fact that Sanskrit writers generally speak also of "Ashtadisa" or eight faces bounding space. It is quite possible that the number of *disa* might have been altered from 8 to 10 when the

* See the article in the August (1881) number "the Five-Pointed Star," where we stated that the five-pointed star or pentagram represented the five limbs of man.—Ed. Theos.

formerly existing Virgo-Scorpio was split up into three separate signs.

Again, *Kara* may be taken to represent the projecting triangles of the five-pointed star. This figure may also be called a kind of regular pentagon (see, Todhunter's Spherical Trigonometry, p. 143). If this interpretation is accepted, the Rasi or sign in question represents the "Microcosm." But the "microcosm" or the world of thought is really represented by *Vrischikam*. From an objective point of view the "microcosm" is represented by the human body. *Makaram* may be taken to represent simultaneously both the microcosm and the macrocosm, as external objects of perception.

In connection with this sign I shall state herein a few important facts which I beg to submit for the consideration of those who are interested in examining the ancient occult sciences of India. It is generally held by the ancient philosophers that the macrocosm is similar to the microcosm in having a *Sthoola Sariram* and a *Sookshma Sariram*. The visible universe is the Sthoola Sariram of Viswam; the ancient philosophers held that as a substratum for this visible universe, there is another universe—perhaps we may call it the universe of Astral Light—the real universe of Noumena, the soul as it were of this visible universe. It is darkly hinted in certain passages of the Vêda and the Upanishads that this hidden universe of Astral Light is to be represented by an *Icosahedron*. The connection between an Icosahedron and a Dodecahedron is something very peculiar and interesting though the figures seem to be so very dissimilar to each other. The connection may be understood by the undermentioned geometrical construction. Describe a Sphere about an Icosahedron; let perpendiculars be drawn from the centre of the Sphere on its faces and produced to meet the surface of the Sphere. Now, if the points of intersection be joined, a Dodecahedron is formed within the Sphere. By a similar process an Icosahedron may be constructed from a Dodecahedron. (See Todhunter's Spherical Trigonometry, p. 141, art. 193). The figure constructed as above described will represent the universe of matter and the universe of Astral Light as they actually exist. I shall not now, however, proceed to show how the universe of Astral Light may be considered in the light of an Icosahedron. I shall only state here that this conception of the Aryan philosophers is not to be looked upon as mere "theological twaddle" or as the outcome of wild fancy. The real significance of the conception in question can, I believe, be explained by reference to the psychology and the physical science of the ancients. But I must stop here and proceed to consider the meaning of the remaining two signs.

XI. *Kumbham* (*or Aquarius*). When represented by numbers, the word is equivalent to 14. It can be easily perceived, then, that the division in question is intended to represent the "Chaturdasa Bhuvanam" or the 14 lôkams spoken of in Sanskrit books.

XII. *Meenam* (*or Pisces*). This word again is represented by 5 when written in numbers and is evidently intended to convey the idea of *Panchamahabhûtams* or the 5 *elements*. The sign also suggests that water (not the ordinary water, but the universal solvent of the ancient alchemists,) is the most important amongst the said elements.

I have now finished the task which I have set to myself in this article. My purpose is not to explain the ancient theory of creation itself, but to show the connection between that theory and the Zodiacal divisions. I have herein brought to light but a very small portion of the philosophy imbedded in these signs. The veil that was dexterously thrown over certain portions of the mystery connected with these signs by the ancient philosophers *will never be lifted up for the amusement or edification of the uninitiated public.*

Now to summarize the facts stated in this article, the contents of the first chapter of the history of this universe are as follows :—

(1). The Self-existent, eternal Brahmam.

(2). Pranava (Aum).

(3). The androgyne Brâhma, or the bisexual Sephira-Adam Kadmon.

(4). The Sacred Tetragram—the four mâtras of Pranava—the four avasthâs—the four states of Brahma—the Scared Thárakam.

(5). The five Brahmas—the five Buddhas—representing in their totality the Jeevâtma.

(6). The astral light—the holy virgin—the six forces in nature.

(7). The thirty-six Tatwams born of Avidya.

(8). The universe in thought—the Swapna Avastha—the miscrocosm looked at from a subjective point of view.

(9). The nine Prajápatis—the assistants of the Demiurgus.*

(10). The shape of the material universe in the mind of the Demiurgus—the DODECAHEDRON.

(11). The fourteen lôkams.

(12). The five elements.

The history of creation and of this world from its beginning up to the present time is composed of *Seven* chapters. The *Seventh* chapter is not yet completed.

TRIPLICANE, Madras, 14*th September*, 1881.

---

* The nine Kabalistic Sephiroths emanated from Sephira, the 10th, and the head Sephiroth are identical. Three trinities or triads with their emanative principle from the Pythagorean mystic *Decad*, the sum of *all* which represents the whole *Kosmos*:—ED. THEOS.

*THE ARYAN-ARHAT ESOTERIC TENENTS ON THE SEVENFOLD PRINCIPLE IN MAN.**

. . . Probably the Aryan (we shall for the present call it by that name) and the Chaldeo-Tibetan esoteric doctrines are fundamentally identical and the secret doctrine of the Jewish Kabalists merely an offshoot of these. Nothing, perhaps, can be more interesting now to a student of occult philosophy than a comparison between the two principal doctrines above mentioned. H. P. B.'s letter seems to indicate two divisions in the Chaldeo-Tibetan doctrine: (1) that of the so-called Lamaists; and (2) that of the so-called Arhats, (in Buddhism Arahat, or Rahats) which has been adopted by the Himalayan or Tibetan Brotherhood. What is the distinction between these two systems? Some of our ancient Brahmanical writers have left us accounts of the main doctrines of Buddhism and the religion and philosophy of the Arhats—the two branches of the Tibetan esoteric doctrine being so called by them. As these accounts generally appear in treatises of a polemical character, I cannot place much reliance upon them.

It is now very difficult to say what was the real ancient Aryan doctrine. If an enquirer were to attempt to answer it by an analysis and comparison of all the various systems of esotericism prevailing in India, he will soon be lost in a maze of obscurity and uncertainty. No comparison between our real Brahmanical and the Tibetan esoteric doctrines will be possible unless one ascertains the teachings of that so-called "Aryan doctrine," . . . . and fully comprehends the *whole range* of the ancient Aryan philosophy. Kapila's "Sankhya," Patanjali's "Yoga philosophy," the different systems of "Saktaya" philosophy, the various *Âgamas* and *Tantrâs* are but branches of it. There is a doctrine though, which is their real foundation and which is sufficient to explain the secrets of these various systems of philosophy and

* Extracts from the letter of T. Subbha Rao to H. P. B.—Ed.

harmonize their teachings. It probably existed long before the Vedas were compiled, and it was studied by our ancient Rishis in connection with the Hindu scriptures. It is attributed to one mysterious personage called Maha*. . . .

The *Upanishads* and such portions of the Vedas as are not chiefly devoted to the public ceremonials of the ancient Âryans are hardly intelligible without some knowledge of *that doctrine.* Even the real significance of the grand ceremonials referred to in the Vedas will not be perfectly apprehended without its light being thrown upon them . . The Vedas were perhaps compiled mainly for the use of the priests assisting at public ceremonies, but the grandest conclusions of our real secret doctrine are therein mentioned. I am informed by persons competent to judge of the matter, that the Vedas have a distinct dual meaning—one expressed by the literal sense of the words, the other *indicated by the meter and the swara* which are, as it were, the life of the Vedas . . . Learned Pundits and philologists, of course, deny that *Swara* has any thing to do with philosophy or ancient esoteric doctrines. But the mysterious connection between *Swara and light* is one of its most profound secrets.

Now it is extremely difficult to show whether the Tibetans derived their doctrine from the ancient Rishis of India, or the ancient Brahmans learned their occult science from the adepts of Tibet; or again whether the adepts of both countries professed originally the same doctrine and derived it from a common source.† If you were to go to the Sramana Balagula and question some of the Jain Pundits there about the authorship of the Vedas and the origin of the Brahmanical esoteric doctrine, they would probably tell you that the Vedas were composed by *Râkshasâs*‡ or *Daityas* and that the

---

* The very little of the present chief of the Esoteric Himalayan Brotherhood.—ED.

† See *Appendix*, Note 1—ED.

‡ A kind of demons—*Devil*.ED.

Brahmans had derived their secret knowledge from them.* Do these assertions mean that the Vedas and the Brahmanical esoteric teachings had their origin in the lost Atlantis—the continent that once occupied a considerable portion of the expanse of the Southern and the Pacific oceans ? The assertion in "Isis Unveiled" that Sanskrit was the language of the inhabitants of the said continent, may induce one to suppose that the Vedas had probably their origin there,—wherever else might be the birth-place of the Aryan esotericism.† But the real esoteric doctrine as well as the mystic allegorical philosophy of the Vedas were derived from another source again, whatever that source may be—perchance, from the divine inhabitants (gods) of the sacred Island which once existed in the sea that covered in days of old the sandy tract now called Gobi Desert. However that may be, the knowledge of *the occult powers of nature* possessed by the inhabitants of the lost Atlantis was learnt by the ancient adepts of India and was appended by them to the esoteric doctrine taught by the residents of the sacred Island.‡ The Tibetan adepts, however, have not accepted this addition to their esoteric doctrine. And, it is in this respect that one should expect to find a difference between the two doctrines.§

The Brahmanical occult doctrine probably contains everything that was taught about *the powers of nature* and their

---

* And so would the Christian pâdris. But they would never admit that their "fallen angles" were borrowed from the *Râkshdsâs*; that their "Devil" is the illegitimate son of *Dewel*—the Sinhalese female demon, or that the "War in Heaven" of the *Apocalypse*—the foundation of the Christian dogma of the "Fallen Angles"—was copied from the Hindu story about Siva hurling the *Târakâsura* who rebelled against Brahma into *Andhakâra*,—the Abode of Darkness, according to Brahmanical *Shâstrâs*.—Ed.

† Not necessarily.—See *Appendix*, Note II. From rare MSS. just received we will shortly prove Sanskrit to have been spoken in Jâva and adjacent islands from remote antiquity.—Ed.

‡ A locality which is spoken of to this day by the Tibetans and called by them "Scham-bha-la" the *Happy Land*.—See Appendix, Note III.—Ed.

§ To comprehend this passage fully, the reader must turn to Vol. I., pp. 589-594, *Isis Unveiled*.—Ed.

laws either in the mysterious Island of the North, or in the equally mysterious continent of the South. And, if you mean to compare the Aryan and the Tibetan doctrines as regards their teachings about the occult powers of nature, you must beforehand examine all the classifications of these powers, their laws and manifestations and the real connotations of the various names assigned to them in the Aryan doctrine. Here are some of the classifications contained in the Brahmanical system :

I.	Classification	of the occult powers as	appertaining to *Parabrahmam* and existing in the MACROCOSM.
II.	do.	do.	as appertaining to man and existing in the MICROCOSM.
III.	do.	do.	for the purposes of *Târaka Yôga* or *Pranava Yôga.*
IV.	do.	do.	for the purposes of *Sânkhya-Yôga* (where they are, as it were, the inherent attributes of *Prakriti*).
V.	do.	do.	for the purposes of *Hata Yôga.*
VI.	do.	do.	for the purposes of *Koula Âgama.*
VII.	do.	do.	for the purposes of *Sâkta Âgama.*
VIII.	do.	do.	for the purposes of *Siva Âgama.*
IX.	do.	do.	for the purposes of *Sreechakram.* (The *Sreechakram* referred to in "Isis Unveiled" is not *the real esoteric Sreechakram* of the ancient adepts of Aryâvarta).*
X.	do.	do.	in *Atharvana Vêda, &c.*

* Very true. But who would be allowed to give out the "real esoteric one"?—ED.

In all these classifications, subdivisions have been multiplied indefinitely by conceiving new combinations of the Primary Powers in different proportions. But I must now drop this subject and proceed to consider the article headed the "*Fragments of Occult Truth*" (since embodied in "Esoteric Buddhism.")

I have carefully examined it, and find that the results arrived at (in the Buddhist doctrine) do not seem to differ much from the conclusions of our Aryan philosophy, though our mode of stating the arguments may differ in form. I shall now discuss the question from my own stand-point, though following for facility of comparison and convenience of discussion the sequence of classification of the *seven-fold* entities or Principles constituting man which is adopted in your article. The questions raised for discussion are: (1) whether the *disembodied spirits* of human beings (as they are called by Spiritualists) appear in the séance-rooms and elsewhere; and (2) whether the manifestations taking place are produced wholly or partly through their agency.

It is hardly possible to answer these two questions satisfactorily unless the meaning intended to be conveyed by the expression "*disembodied spirits of human beings*" be accurately defined. The words *Spiritualism* and *Spirit* are very misleading. Unless English writers in general, and Spiritualists in particular, first ascertain clearly the *connotation* they mean to assign to the word *spirit* there will be no end of confusion, and the real nature of these so-called spiritualistic phenomena and their *modus occurrendi* can never be clearly defined. Christian writers generally speak of only two entities in man—the body, and the *soul* or *spirit* (both seeming to mean the same thing to them). European philosophers generally speak of *Body* and *Mind*, and argue that soul or spirit cannot be anything else than mind. They are of opinion that any belief in *Lingasariram** is entirely unphilosophical. These views are certainly incorrect, and are based on

* The Astral Body—so called.—Ed.

unwarranted assumptions as to the possibilities of nature, and on an imperfect understanding of its laws. I shall now examine (from the stand-point of the Brahmanical esoteric doctrine) the Spiritual constitution of man, the various entities or principles existing in him, and ascertain whether either of those entities entering into his composition *can* appear on earth after his death; and, if so, *what it is that so appears.*

Professor Tyndall in his Excellent papers on what he calls the "Germ Theory" comes to the following conclusions as the result of a series of well-planned experiments :—Even in a very small volume of space there are myriads of protoplasmic germs floating in ether. If, for instance, say,—water (clear water) is exposed to them and if they fall into it, some form of life or other will be evolved out of them. Now, what are the agencies for the bringing of this life into existence? Evidently :—

I. *The water*, which is the field, so to say, for the growth of life.

II. The protoplasmic germ, out of which life or a living organism is to be evolved or developed. And, lastly—

III. The power, energy, force or tendency which springs into activity at the touch or combination of the protoplasmic germs and the water, and which evolves or develops life and its natural attributes.

Similarly, there are three primary causes which bring the human being into existence. I shall call them for the purpose of discussion by the following names :—

(1) *Parabrahmam*—The Universal Spirit.

(2) *Sakti* (The crown of the astral light combining in itself all the powers of nature).

(3) *Prakriti*, which in its original or primary shape is represented by *Akasa* (really, every form of matter is finally reducible to *Akasa*).*

* The Tibetan esoteric Buddhist doctrine teaches that *Prakriti* is cosmic matter, out of which all visible forms are prouduced; and *Akasa* that same cosmic matter,—but still more subjective, its spirit, as it were, "*Prakriti*" being the body or *substance*, and "Akasa-Sakti" its soul or energy.—ED.

It is ordinarily stated that *Prakriti* or *Akasa* is the *Kshetram* or the basis which corresponds to water in the example we have taken : *Brahmam* the *germ*, and *Sakti* the power or energy that comes into existence at their union or contact.*

But this is not the view which the *Upanishads* take of the question. According to them, *Brahmam* † is the *Kshetram* or basis, Akasa or *Prakriti*, the germ or seed, and *Sakti* the power evolved by their union or contact. And this is the real scientific, philosophical mode of stating the case.

Now, according to the adepts of ancient Aryavarta, *seven principles* are evolved out of these *three* primary entities. Algebra teaches us that the number of *combinations* of *n* things taken *one* at a time, *two* at a time, *three* at a time and so forth$=2n-1$.

Applying this formula to the present case, the number of entities evolved from different combinations of these three primary causes amounts to $2^3-1=8-1=7$.

As a general rule, whenever seven *entities* are mentioned in the ancient occult science of India, in any connection whatsoever, you must suppose that those seven entities came into

---

* Or, in other words, "*Prakriti* Swabhâvât or *Akasa* is—SPACE as the Tibetans have it; Space filled with whatsoever substance or no substance at all; *i.e.* with substance so imperceptible as to be only metaphysically conceivable. *Brahmam*, then, would be the germ thrown into the soil of that field, and *Sakti* that mysterious energy or force which develops it, and which is called by the Buddhist Arahats of Tibet—FO-HAT. "That which we called form (Rupa) is not different from that which we call space (Sûnyata) . . Space is not different from Form. Form is the same as Space; Space is the same as form. And so with the other skandhas, whether vedana, or sanjna or sanskara or vijnana, they are each the same as their opposite" . . . (Book of *sin-king* or the "Heart Sutra,". Chinese translation of the "Maha-Prajna-Paramita-Hridaya-Sutra." (Chapter on the "Avalokiteshwara," or the *manifested Buddha.*) So that, the Aryan and Tabetan or Arhat doctrines agree perfectly in substance, differing but in names given and the way of putting it. A distinction resulting from the fact that the Vedantin Brahmans believe in Parabrahman, a *deific* power impersonal though it may be, while the Buddhists entirely reject it.—ED.

† See *Appendix*, Note IV,—ED.

existence from *three primary entities* and that these three entities, again, are evolved out of a *single* entity or MONAD. To take a familiar example, the *seven* coloured rays in the solar ray are evolved out of *three primary coloured* rays; and the three primary colours co-exist with the four secondary colours in the solar rays. Similarly, the three primary entities which brought man into existence co–exist in him with the *four secondary* entities which arose from different combinations of the three primary entities.

Now these seven *entities* which in their totality constitute man, are as follows :—I shall enumerate them in the order adopted in the "Fragments" as far as the two orders (the Brahmanical and the Tibetan) coincide :—

		Corresponding names in Esoteric Buddhism.
I.	*Prakriti.*	*Sthûlasarîram* (Physical Body).
II.	The entity evolved out of the combination of *Prakriti* and *Sakti.*	*Sûkshmasarîram* or *Lingasarîram* (Astral Body).
III.	*Sakti.*	*Kâmarûpa* (the *Perisprit*).
IV.	The entity evolved out of the combination of *Brahmam, Sakti and Prakriti.*	*Jivâtmâ* (*Life—Soul*).
V.	The entity evolved out of the combination of *Brahmam and Prakriti.*	Physical Intelligence (or animal soul).
VI.	The entity evolved out of the combination of *Brahmam and Sakti.*	Spiritual Intelligence (or Soul).
VII.	*Brahmam.*	The emanation from the ABSOLUTE, &c. (or pure spirit).

Before proceeding to examine the nature of these seven entities, a few general explanations are indispensably necessary.

I. The secondary principles arising out of the combination of primary principles are quite different in their nature from the entities out of whose combination they came into existence. The combinations in question are not of the nature of mere mechanical juxtapositions, as it were. They do not even correspond to chemical combinations. Consequently no valid inferences as regards the nature of the combinations in question can be drawn by analogy from the nature [variety?] of these combinations.

II. The general proposition that when once a cause is removed its effect vanishes, is not universally applicable. Take, for instance, the following example:—if you once communicate a certain amount of momentum to a ball, velocity of a particular degree in a particular direction is the result. Now, the cause of this motion ceases to exist when the instantaneous sudden impact or blow which conveyed the momentum is completed; but, according to the *first Law of Motion,* the ball will continue to move on for ever and ever with undiminished velocity in the same direction unless the said motion is altered, diminished, neutralized or counteracted by extraneous causes. Thus, if the ball stop, it will not be on account of the absence of the cause of its motion, but in consequence of the existence of extraneous causes which produce the said result.

Again, take the instance of *subjective phenomena.*

Now the presence of this ink-bottle before me is producing in me or in my mind a mental representation of its form, volume, colour and so forth. The bottle in question may be removed, but still its mental picture may continue to exist. Here, again, you see, the effect survives the cause. Moreover, the effect may at any subsequent time be called into conscious existence, whether the original cause be present or not.

Now, in the case of the fifth principle above-mentioned—the entity that came into existence by the combination of *Brahmam and Prakriti,*—if the general proposition (in the "Fragments of Occult Truth") is correct, this principle which corresponds to the *Physical intelligence* must cease to exist whenever the *Brahmam* or the seventh principle should cease to exist for the particular individual; but the fact is certainly otherwise. The general proposition under consideration is adduced in the "Fragments" in support of the assertion that whenever the seventh principle ceases to exist for any particular individual, the sixth principle also ceases to exist for him. The assertion is undoubtedly true though the mode of stating it and the reasons assigned for it are to my mind objectionable.

It is said that in cases where tendencies of a man's mind are entirely material, and all spiritual aspirations and thoughts were altogether absent from his mind, the seventh principle leaves him either before or at the time of death, and the sixth principle disappears with it. Here, the very proposition that the tendencies of the particular individual's mind are *entirely* material, involves the assertion that there is no spiritual intelligence or spiritual *Ego* in him. It should then have been said that, whenever spiritual intelligence ceases to exist in any particular individual, the seventh principle ceases to exist for that particular individual for all purposes. Of course, it does fly off anywhere. There can never be anything like a change of position in the case of Brahmam.* The assertion merely means that when there is no recognition whatever of *Brahmam*, or spirit, or spiritual life, or spiritual consciousness, the seventh principle has ceased to exercise any influence or control over the individual's destinies.

---

* True—from the standpoint of Aryan *Esotericism*, and the Upanishads; not quite so in the case of the *Arahat* or Tibetan esoteric doctrine; and it is only on this solitary point that the two teachings disagree, as far as we know. The difference is very trifling though, resting, as it does, solely upon the two various methods of viewing the one and the same thing from two different aspects—See *Appendix*, Note IV.—Ed.

I shall now state what is meant (in the Aryan doctrine) by the seven principles above enumerated.

I.—*Prakriti.* This is the basis of *Sthûlasarîram* and represents it in the above-mentioned classification.

II. *Prakriti* and *Sakti.*—This is the *Lingasarîram*, or astral body.

III. *Sakti.*—This principle corresponds to your *Kâmarupa.* This power or force is placed by ancient occultists in the *Nâbhîchakram.* This power can gather *akâsa* or *prakriti* and mould it into any desired shape. It has very great sympathy with the fifth principle, and can be made to act by its influence or control.

IV. *Brahmam, Sakti,* and *Prakriti.*—This again corresponds to your second principle, *Jîvâtmâ.* This power represents the universal life-principle which exists in nature. Its seat is the *Anâhatachakram* (heart). It is a force or power which constitutes what is called *Jîva*, or life. It is, as you say, indestructible, and its activity is merely transferred at the time of death to another set of atoms, to form another organism. But it is not called *Jîvâtmâ* in our philosophy. The term *Jîvâtmâ* is generally applied by our philosophers to the seventh principle when it is distinguished from *Paramâtmâ* or *Parabrahmam.**

V. *Brahm* and *Prakriti.*—This, in our Aryan philosophy, corresponds to your fifth principle, called the *Physical Intelligence.* According to our philosophers, this is the entity in which what is called *Mind* has its seat or basis. This is the most difficult principle of all to explain, and the present discussion entirely turns upon the view we take of it.

---

* The impersonal Parabrahmam thus being made to merge or separate itself into a *personal* "Jivâtma" or the personal god of every human creature. This is, again, a difference necessitated by the Brahmanical-belief in a God whether personal or impersonal, while the Buddhist Arahats, rejecting this idea entirely, recognise *no* deity apart from man.—See *Appendix*, Note V.—Ed.

Now, what is mind? It is a mysterious something which is considered to be the seat of consciousness—of sensations, emotions, volitions and thoughts. Psychological analysis shows it to be apparently a congeries of mental states, and possibilities of mental states, connected by what is called memory, and considered to have a distinct existence apart from any of its particular states or ideas. Now in what entity has this mysterious something its potential or actual existence? *Memory* and *expectation* which form, as it were, the real foundation of what is called *individuality*, or *Ahankâram*, must have their seat of existence somewhere. Modern psychologists of Europe generally say that the material substance of *Brain* is the seat of mind; and that past *subjective experiences*, which can be recalled by memory, and which in their totality constitute what is called *individuality*, exist therein in the shape of certain unintelligible mysterious impressions and changes in the nerves and nerve-centres of the cerebral hemispheres. Consequently, they say, the mind—the individual mind—is destroyed when the body is destroyed; so there is no possible existence after death.

But there are a few facts among those admitted by these philosophers which are sufficient for us to demolish their theory. In every portion of the human body, a constant change goes on without intermission. Every tissue, every muscular fibre and nerve-tube, and every ganglionic centre in the brain is undergoing an incessant change. In the course of a man's lifetime there may be a series of *complete transformations* of the substance of his *brain*. Nevertheless the memory of his past mental states remains unaltered. There may be additions of new subjective experiences and some mental states may be altogether forgotten, but no individual mental state is altered. The person's *sense of individuality* remains the same throughout these constant alterations in the brain substance.* It is able to survive all these changes,

* This is also sound Buddhist philosophy, the transformation in question being known as the change of the *skandhas*. —Ed.

and it can survive also the complete destruction of the material substance of the brain.

This individuality arising from mental consciousness has its seat of existence, according to our philosophers, in an *occult power or force* which keeps a registry, as it were, of all our mental impressions. The power itself is indestructible, though by the operation of certain antagonistic causes its impressions may in course of time be effected, in part or wholly.

I may mention in this connection that our philosophers have associated seven *occult* powers with the seven principles or entities above-mentioned. These seven occult powers in the microcosm correspond with, or are the counterparts of the occult powers in the macrocosm. The mental and spiritual consciousness of the individual becomes the general consciousness of *Brahmam* when the barrier of individuality is wholly removed, and when the seven powers in the microcosm are placed *en rapport* with the seven powers in the macrocosm.

There is nothing very strange in a power or force, or *sakti* carrying with it impressions of sensations, ideas, thoughts, or other subjective experiences. It is now a well-known fact, that an electric or magnetic current can convey in some mysterious manner impressions of sound or speech with all their individual peculiarities; similarly, I can convey my thoughts to you by a transmission of energy or power.

Now this fifth principle represents in our philosophy, *the mind*, or, to speak more correctly, the power or force above described, the impressions of the mental states therein, and notion of individuality or *Ahankâram* generated by their collective operation. This principle is called merely *physical intelligence* in the "Fragments." I do not know what is really meant by this expression. It may be taken to mean that intelligence which exist in a very low state of development in the lower animals. *Mind* may exist in different stages of development, from the very lowest forms of organic life, where the signs of its existence or operation can hardly be distinctly realised, up to man, in whom it reaches its highest state of development.

In fact, from the first appearance of life* up to *Thureeya Avastha,* or the state of Nirvana, the progress is, as it were, continuous. We ascend from that principle up to the seventh by almost imperceptible gradations. But four stages are recognised in the progress where the change is of a peculiar kind, and is such as to arrest an observer's attention. These four stages are as follows:—

(1) Where life (fourth principle) makes its appearance.

(2) Where the existence of mind becomes perceptible in conjunction with life.

(3) Where the highest state of mental abstraction ends, and *spiritual consciousness* commences.

(4) Where spiritual consciousness disappears, leaving the seventh principle in a complete state of *Nirvana,* or nakedness.

According to our philosophers, the fifth principle under consideration is intended to represent *the mind in every possible state of development, from the second stage up to the third stage.*

VI. *Brahmam* and *Sakti.*—This principle corresponds to your "spiritual intelligence." It is, in fact, *Buddhi* (I use the word *Buddhi* not in the ordinary sense, but in the sense in which it is used by our ancient philosophers); in other words, it is the seat of *Bôdha* or *Âtmabôdha.* One who has *Âtma-bôdha* in its completeness is a *Buddha. Buddhists know very well what this term signifies.* This principle is described in the "Fragments" as an entity coming into existence by the combination of *Brahmam and Prakriti.* I do not again know

* In the Aryan doctrine which blends *Brahmam, Sakti,* and *Prakriti* in one, it is the fourth principle, then; in the Buddhist esotericism the second in combination with the first.—ED.

in what particular sense the word *Prakriti* is used in this connection. According to our philosophers it is an entity arising from the union of *Brahm* and *Sakti.* I have already explained the connotation attached by our philosophers to the words *Prakriti* and *Sakti.*

I stated that *Prakriti* in its *primary* state is *Akâsa.**

If *Akâsa* be considered to be *Sakti* or Power,† then my statement as regards the ultimate state of *Prakriti* is likely to give rise to confusion and misapprehension unless I explain the distinction between *Akâsa* and *Sakti. Akâsa* is not, properly speaking, the *Crown of the Astral light,* nor does it *by itself* constitute any of the *six primary forces.* But, generally speaking, whenever any *phenomenal result* is produced, *Sakti* acts in *conjunction with Akâsa.* And, moreover, *Akâsa* serves as a basis or *Adhisthanum* for the transmission of force currents and for the formation or generation of force or power correlations.‡

In *Mantrasastra* the letter "*Ha*" represents *Ákása,* and you will find that this syllable enters into most of the sacred, formulæ intended to be used in producing phenomenal results.

---

* According to the Buddhists in *Akâsa* lies that eternal, potential energy whose function it is to evolve all visible things out of itself.—ED.

† It was never so considered, as we have shown it. But as the "Fragments" are written in English, a language lacking such an abundance of metaphysical terms to express every minute change of form, substance and state as found in the Sanskrit, it was deemed useless to confuse the Western reader untrained in the methods of Eastern expression more than necessary, with a too nice distinction of proper technical terms. As "*Prakriti* in its primary state is *Akâsa,* and *Sakti*" is an atribute of "AKASHA," it becomes evident that for the uninitiated it is all one. Indeed, to speak of the "Union of Brahmam and Prakriti" instead of "Brahmam and Sakti" is no worse than for a theist to write that "man has come into existence by the combination of spirit and matter," whereas, his words framed in orthodox shape, ought to read "man as a living soul was created by the *power* (or breath) of God over matter"—ED.

‡ That is to say, the Aryan *Akâsa* is another word for Buddhist SPACE (in its metaphysical meaning)—ED.

But by itself it does not represent any *Sakti*. You may, if you please, call *Sakti*, an attribute of *Akâsa*.

I do not think that as regards the nature of this principle there can, in reality, exist any difference of opinion between the Buddhist and Brahmanical philosophers.

Buddhist and Brahmanical initiates know very well that mysterious circular mirror composed of two hemispheres which reflects as it were the rays emanating from the "burning bush" and the blazing star—the Spiritual sun shining in CHIDÂKÂSAM.

The spiritual impressions constituting this principle have their existence in an occult power associated with the entity in question. The successive incarnations of Buddha, in fact, mean the successive transfers of this mysterious power or the impressions thereon. The transfer is only possible when the *Mahatma** who transfers it, has completely identified himself with his seventh principle, has annihilated his *Ahankâram*, and reduced it to ashes in CHIDAGNIKUNDAM and has succeeded in making his thoughts correspond with the eternal laws of nature and in becoming a co-worker with nature. Or to put the same thing in other words, when he *has attained the state of Nirvâna, the condition of final negation, negation of individual or separate existence.*†

VII. *Atma.*—The emanation from the absolute ; corresponding to the seventh principle. As regards this entity there exists positively no real difference of opinion between the Tibetan Buddhist adepts and our ancient Rishis.

We must now consider which of these entities can appear after the individual's death in sèance-rooms and produce the so-called spiritualistic phenomena.

Now, the assertion of the Spiritualists that the "disembodied spirits" of particular human beings appear in séance-rooms

---

* The highest adept—ED.

† In the words of a gâthâ in the "Mahâ-pari-Nirvâna Sûtra"—

" We reach a condition of Rest."

" Beyond the limit of any human knowledge"—ED.

necessarily implies that the entity that so appears bears the stamp of some particular individual's *individuality.*

So, we have to ascertain beforehand in what entity or entities individuality has its seat of existence. Apparently it exists in the person's particular formation of body, and in his subjective experiences, (called his mind in their totality). On the death of the individual his body is destroyed ; his *lingasarîram* being decomposed, the power associated with it becomes mingled in the current of the corresponding power in the macrocosm. Similarly, the third and fourth principles are mingled with their corresponding powers. These entities may again enter into the composition of other organisms. As these entities bear no impression of individuality, the Spiritualists have no right to say that the "*disembodied spirit*" of the human being has appeared in the séance-room, whenever any of these entities may appear there. In fact, they have no means of ascertaining that they belonged to any particular individual.

Therefore, we must only consider whether any of the last three entities appear in séance-rooms to amuse or to instruct Spiritualists. Let us take three particular examples of individuals and see what becomes of these three principles after death.

I. One in whom spiritual attachments have greater force than terrestrial attachments.

II. One in whom spiritual aspirations do exist, but are merely of secondary importance to him, his terrestrial interests occupying the greater share of his attention.

III. One in whom there exist no spiritual aspirations whatsoever, one whose spiritual Ego is dead or non-existent to his apprehension.

We need not consider the case of a *complete Adept* in this connection. In the first two cases, according to our supposition, spiritual and mental experiences exist together ; when spiritual consciousness exists, the existence of the seventh principle being recognised, it maintains its connections with the fifth and sixth principles. But the existence of terrestrial attachments creates the necessity of *punarjanmam*, the latter signifying the evólution of a new set of objective and subjective experiences, constituting a new combination of surrounding circumstances or, in other words, a new world. The period between death and the next subsequent birth is occupied with the preparation required for the evolution of these new experiences. During the period of incubation, as you call it, the spirit will never of its own accord appear in this world, *nor can it so appear.*

There is a great law in this universe which consists in the reduction of subjective experience to objective phenomena and the evolution of the former from the latter. This is otherwise called "cyclic necessity." Man is subjected to this law if he does not check and counterbalance the usual destiny or fate, and he can only escape its control by subduing all his terrestrial attachments completely. The new combination of circumstances under which he will then be placed may be better or worse than the terrestrial conditions under which he lived. But in his progress to a new world, you may be sure he will never turn around to have a look at his spiritualistic friends.*

In the third of the above three cases there is, by our supposition, no recognition of spiritual consciousness or of spirit. So they are non-existing so far as he is concerned. The case is similar to that of an organ or faculty which remains unused for a long time. It then practically ceases to exist.

These entities, as it were, remain his or in his possession, when they are stamped with the stamp of recognition. When such is not the case, the whole of his individuality is centered in his fifth principle. And after death this fifth principle is the *only representative* of the individual in question.

By itself it cannot evolve for itself a new set of objective experiences, or to say the same thing in other words, it has no

* As M. A. (Oxon) will, see the Spiritualists have still less chance of having their claims recognised by Brahmanical than by Buddhist occultists. —ED.

punarjanmam. It is such an entity that can appear in séance-rooms; but it is absurd to call it a *disembodied spirit.** It is merely a power or force retaining the impressions of the thoughts or ideas of the individual into whose composition it originally entered. It sometimes summons to its aid the *Kámarúpa* power, and creates for itself some particular ethereal form (not necessairly human).

Its tendencies of action will be similar to those of the individual's mind when he was living. This entity maintains its existence so long as the impressions on the power associated with the fifth principle remain intact. In course of time they are effaced, and the power in question is then mixed up in the current of its corresponding power in the MACROCOSM, as the river loses itself in the sea. Entities like these may afford signs of there having been considerable intellectual power in the individuals to which they belonged; because very high intellectual power may co-exist with utter absence of spiritual consciousness. But from this circumstance it cannot be argued that either the spirits or the spiritual Egos of deceased individuals appear in séance-rooms.

There are some people in India who have thoroughly studied the nature of such entities (called *pisacham*). I do not know much about them experimentally, as I have never meddled with this disgusting, profitless, and dangerous branch of investigation.

Your Spiritualists do not know what they are really doing. Their investigations are likely to result in course of time either in wicked sorcery or in the utter spiritual ruin of thousands of men and women.†

The views I have herein expressed have been often illustrated by our ancient writers by comparing the course of a man's life or existence to the orbital motion of a planet round

---

* It is especially on this point that the Aryan and Arahat doctrines quite agree, the teaching and argument that follow are, in every respect, those of the Buddhist Himalayan Brotherhood.—ED.

† We share entirely in this idea.—ED.

the sun. Centripetal force is spiritual attraction and centrifugal, terrestrial attraction. As the centripetal force increases in power in comparison with the centrifugal force, the planet approaches the sun—the individual reaches a higher plane of existence. If, on the other hand, the centrifugal force becomes greater than the centripetal force, the planet is removed to a greater distance from the sun, and moves in a new orbit at that distance—the individual comes to a lower level of existence, These are illustrated in the first two instances I have noticed above.

We have only to consider the two extreme cases.

When the planet in its *approach* to the sun passes over the line where the centripetal and centrifugal forces completely neutralize each other and is only acted on by the centripetal force, it rushes towards the sun with a gradually increasing velocity and is finally mixed up with the mass of the sun's body. This is the case of complete *Adept.*

Again, when the planet in its *retreat* from the sun reaches a point where the centrifugal force becomes all-powerful it flies off in a tangential direction from its orbit, and goes into the depths of void space. When it ceases to be under the control of the sun, it gradually gives up its generative heat and the creative energy that it originally derived from the sun, and remains a cold mass of material particles wandering through space until the mass is completely decomposed into atoms. This cold mass is compared to the fifth principle under the conditions above noticed, and the heat, light, and energy that left it are compared to the sixth and seventh principles.

Either after assuming a new orbit or in its course of diviation from the old orbit to the new, the planet can never go back to any point in its old orbit, as the various orbits lying in different planes never intersect each other.

This figurative representation correctly explains the ancient Brahmanical theory on the subject. It is merely a branch of what is called the Great Law of the Universe by the ancient mystics. . . . .

APPENDIX

BY

MADAME H. P. BLAVATSKY.

NOTE I.

IN this connection it will be well to draw the reader's attention to the fact that the country called "Si-dzang" by the Chinese, and Tibet by Western geographers, is mentioned in the oldest books preserved in the province of Fo-kien (the chief head-quarters of the aborigines of China)—as the great seat of occult learning in the archaic ages. According to these records, it was inhabited by the "Teachers of Light," the "Sons of Wisdom" and the "Brothers of the Sun." The Emperor Yu the "Great" (2207 B. C.), a pious mystic, is credited with having obtained his occult wisdom and the system of theocracy established by him--for he was the first one to unite in China ecclesiastical power with temporal authority—from Si-dzang. That system was the same as with the old Egyptians and the Chaldees; that which we know to have existed in the Brahmanical period in India, and to exist now in Tibet; namely, all the learning, power, the temporal as well as the secret wisdom were concentrated within the hierarchy of the priests and limited to their caste. Who were the aborigines of Tibet is a question which no ethnographer is able to answer correctly at present. They practise the Bhon religion their sect is a pre—andanti—Buddhistic one, and they are to be found mostly in the province of Kam—that is all that is known of them. But even that would justify the supposition that they are the greatly degenerated descendants of mighty and wise forefathers. Their ethnical type shows that they are not pure Turanians, and their rites—now those of sorcery, incantations, and nature-worship, remind one far more of the popular rites of the Babylonians, as found in the records preserved on the excavated cylinders, than of the religious practices of the Chinese—sect of Tao-sse—a religion based upon pure reason and spirituality—as alleged by some. Generally, little or no differnce is made even by the Kyelang missionaries who mix greatly with these people on the borders of British Lahoul—and ought to know better—between the Bhons and the two rival Buddhist sects, the Yellow Caps and the Red Caps. The latter of these have opposed the reform of Tzong-ka-pa from the first and have always adhered to old Buddhism so greatly mixed up now with the practices of the Bhons. Were our Orientalists to know more of them, and compare the ancient Babylonian Bel or Baal worship with the rites of the Bhons, they would find an undeniable connection between the two. To begin an argument here, proving the origin of the aborigines of Tibet as connected with one of the three great races which superseded each other in Babylonia, whether we call them the Akkadians (invented by F. Lenormant,) or the primitive Turanians, Chaldees and Assyrians—is out of question. Be it as it may, there is reason to call the trans-Himalayan esoteric doctrine Chaldeo-Tibetan. And, when we remember that the Vêdâs came—agreeably to all traditions—from the Manssorowar Lake in Tibet, and the Brahmins themselves from the far North, we are justified in looking on the esoteric doctrines of every people who once had or still has it—as having proceeded from one and the same source: and, to thus call it the "Aryan-Chaldeo-Tibetan" doctrine, or Universal Wisdom Religion. "Seek for the Lost Word among the hierophants of Tartary, China and Tibet," was the advice of Swedenborg, the seer.

Note II.

Not necessarily—we say. The Vedas, Brahmanism, and along with these, Sanskrit, were importations into what we now regard as India. They were never indigenous to its soil. There was a time when the ancient nations of the West included under the generic name of India, many of the countries of Asia now classified under other names. There was an Upper, a Lower, and a Western India, even during the comparatively late period of Alexander; and Persia (Iran) is called Western India in some ancient classics. The countries now named Tibet, Mongolia, and Great Tartary were considered by them as forming part of India. When we say, therefore, that India has civilized the world and was the *Alma Mater* of the civilizations, arts and sciences of all other nations (Babylonia, and perhaps even Egypt, included) we mean archaic, pre-historic India, India of the time when the great Gobi was a sea, and the lost "Atlantis" formed part of an unbroken continent which began at the Himalayas and ran down over Southern India, Ceylon, Java, to far-away Tasmania.

Note III.

To ascertain such disputed questions, one has to look into and study well the Chinese sacred and historical records—a people whose era begins nearly 4,600 years back (2697 B. C.). A people so accurate and by whom some of the most important *inventions* of modern Europe and its so much boasted modern science, were anticipated—such as the compass, gun-powder, porcelain, paper, printing, &c.—known, and practised thousands of years before these were rediscovered by the Europeans,—— ought to receive some trust for their records. And from Lao-tze down to Hiouen-Thsang their literature is filled with allusions and references to that island and the wisdom of the Himalayan adepts. In the *Catena of Buddhist Scriptures from the Chinese* by the Rev. Samuel Beal, there is a chapter "On the Tian-Ta'i School of Buddhism" (pp. 244-258) which our opponents ought to read. Translating the rules of that most celebrated and holy school and sect in China founded by Chin-che-K'hae, called Che-chay (the wise one) in the year 575 of our era, when coming to the sentence which reads; "That which relates to the one garment (seamless) worn by the Great Teachers of the Snowy Mountains, the school of the Haimavatas" (p. 256) the European translator places after the last sentence a sign of interrogation, as well he may. The statistics of the school of the "Haimavatas" or of our

Himalayan Brotherhood, are not to be found in the General Census Records of India. Further, Mr. Beal translates a Rule relating to "the great professors of the higher order who live in mountain depths remote from men," the *Aranyakâs*, or hermits.

So, with respect to the traditions concerning this island, and apart from the (to them,) *historical* records of this preserved in the Chinese and Tibetan Sacred Books: the legend is alive to this day among the people of Tibet. The fair Island is no more, but the country where it once bloomed remains there still, and the spot is well-known to some of the "great teachers of the snowy mountains," however much convulsed and changed its topography by the awful cataclysm. Every *seventh* year, these teachers are believed to assemble in SCHAM-CHA-LO, the "happy land." According to the general belief it is situated in the north-west of Tibet. Some place it within the unexplored central regions, inaccessible even to the fearless nomadic tribes; others hem it in between the range of the Gangdisri Mountains and the northern edge of the Gobi Desert, South and North and the more populated regions of Khoondooz and Kashmir, of the *Gya-Pheling* (British India), and China, West and East, which affords to the curious mind a pretty large latitude to locate it in. Others still place it between Namur Nur and the Kuen-Lun Mountains—but one and all firmly believe in Scham-bha-la, and speak of it as a fertile, fairy-like land, once an island, now an oasis of incomparable beauty, the place of meeting of the inheritors of the esoteric wisdom of the god-like inhabitants of the legendary Island.

In connection with the archaic legend of the Asian Sea and the Atlantic Continent, is it not profitable to note a fact known to all modern geologists—that the Himalayan slopes afford geological proof, that the substance of those lofty peaks was once a part of an ocean floor?

NOTE IV.

We have already pointed out that, in our opinion, the whole difference between Buddhistic and Vedantic philosophies was that the former was a kind of *Rationalistic* Vedantism, while the latter might be regarded as *Transcendental* Buddhism. If the Aryan esotericism applies the term *Jivâtmâ* to the seventh principle, the pure and *per se* unconscious spirit—it is because the Vêdânta postulating three kinds of existence—(1) the *paramârthika*,—(*the true, the only real one*,) (2), the *vyavahârika* (the practical,) and (3) the *pratibhasika* (the apparent or illusory life)—makes the first *life* or *Jîva* the only truly existent one. Brahma or the ONE'S SELF is its only representative in the universe, as it is the *universal Life in toto,* while the other two are but its "phenomenal appearance," imagined and created by ignorance, and complete illusions suggested to us by our blind senses. The Buddhists, on the other hand, deny either subjective or objective reality even to that one Self-Existence. Buddha declares that there is neither Creator nor an ABSOLUTE Being. Buddhist rationalism was ever too alive to the insuperable difficulty of admitting one absolute consciousness, as in the words of Flint—"wherever there is consciousness there is relation, and wherever there is relation there is dualism." The ONE LIFE is either "MUKTA" (absolute and unconditioned) and can have no relation to anything nor to any one; or it is "BADDHA" (bound and conditioned), and then it cannot be called the ABSOLUTE; the limitation, moreover, necessitating another deity as powerful as the first to account for all the evil in this world. Hence, the Arahat secret doctrine on cosmogony admits but of one absolute, indestructible, eternal, and uncreated UNCONSCIOUSNESS (so to translate), of an element (the word being used for want of a better term) absolutely independent of everything else in the universe; a something ever present or ubiquitous, a Presence which ever was, is and will be, whether there is a God, gods, or none; whether there is a universe, or no universe; existing during the eternal cycles of Maha Yugs, during the *Pralayas*; as during the periods of *Manvantara*: and this is SPACE, the field for the operation of the eternal Forces and natural Law, the *basis* (as Mr. Subba Row rightly calls it) upon which take place the eternal intercorrelations of Akâsa-Prakriti, guided by the unconscious regular pulsations of *Sakti*—the breath or power of a conscious deity, the theists would say,—the eternal energy of an eternal, unconscious Law, say the Buddhists. Space then, or "Fan, Bar-nang" (Mâha Sûnyatâ) or, as it is called by Lao-tze, the "Emptiness" is the nature of the Buddhist Absolute. (See Confucius' "*Praise of the Abyss.*") The word *jîva*, then could never be applied by the Arahats to the *Seventh* Principle, since it is only through its correlation or contact with matter that *Fohat* (the Buddhist active energy) can develop active *conscious* life; and that to the question "how can *Unconsciousness* generate *consciousness* ?" the answer would be "Was the seed which generated a Bacon or a Newton self-conscious?"

NOTE V.

To our European readers: Deceived by the phonetic similarity, it must not be thought that the name "Brahman" is identical in this connection with Brahma or *Iswara*—the personal God. The *Upanishads*—the Vedânta Scriptures—mention no such God and one would vainly seek in them any allusions to a conscious deity. The Brahmam, or Parabrahm, the ABSOLUTE of the Vedantins, is neuter and unconscious, and has no connection with the masculine Brahmâ of the Hindu Triad, or *Trimûrti*. Some Orientalists rightly believe the name derived from the verb "Brih," to *grow* or *increase*, and to be in this sense, the *universal expansive force of nature*, the vivifying and spiritual principle, or power, spread throughout the universe and which in its collectivity is the one Absoluteness, the one Life and the only Reality.

"THE PHILOSOPHY OF SPIRIT.'

The book bearing the above title, and professing to expound "the philosophy of spirit" contained in the *Bhagavatgita*, has already been introduced to the readers of the "THEOSOPHIST" by the review that appeared in the December number, and the author's reply thereto published in the copy of March. Considering the importance of the issues raised by the author's publication, and the two articles above referred to, I persuade myself that I shall be justified in sifting, with some minuteness, the conclusions arrived at by the author regarding the authorship and philosophy of the *Bhagavatgita* and its esoteric basis or foundation. As the author has not merely published his own speculations regarding the subjects dealt with in that ancient work, but informs the public that his speculations are in perfect accordance with the ancient philosophy of Vyasa, I believe I have a right, as a Hindu, to object to the position taken by him, if, in my humble opinion, his views should be at variance with those of the orthodox pundits and the initiates of ancient Aryavarta, as much as with those of modern India. And I hope the learned gentleman will be good enough to excuse me, if, in this article, I may be under the painful necessity of dwelling longer on what I conceive to be the defects of his work than on its merits. Though the author does not seem to be a Spiritualist in the sense in which that term is used by the so-called modern professors of that name, still he has attempted to give a philosophical shape to their crude notions about "disembodied spirits"; and any intelligent and profitable discussion of the real points of difference between Theosophy and Spiritualism is only possible with writers like Mr. Oxley.

In this article I shall first examine the author's theory about the real origin of sacred writings in general and of the *Bhagavatgita* in particular, and next, in his remarks, scattered throughout the book, about what he calls the Astro-Masonic basis of the said treatise, and his views about some of the doctrines therein explained.

At the outset, it is necessary to apprehend correctly Mr. Oxley's opinions about the constitution of man and the progress of what the learned author is pleased to call "life-principle" after death. The author recognizes the trinity of man, and names the three entities that constitute him—body, spirit and soul. He calls "*Soul*" the "inmost of all," "eternal, incorruptible, unchangeable and inseparable from the grand Life, called God," while describing "*Spirit*" as the "inner or intermediate active agent which guides, propels and uses as its instrument the body, or that covering which is exterior to itself" (p. 221). From these explanations it is apparent that the author means by "soul" and "spirit" the same entities as are denoted by the two Sanskrit terms *Atma* (7th principle) and *Sookshmasariram*, or *Lingasariram*, respectively. The author is at liberty to attach any connotations he pleases to these words, as no definite meaning has yet been attached to them by English writers. But I do not think he has used the word *Spirit* in the sense above indicated *throughout* his book; for, he further says that there are 12 degrees or stages of ascent (p. 40), which the life-principle in man has to pass through in its spiritual progress; and we are also informed that, on reaching the 12th stage, man becomes an *angel*. Further progress from angel-hood upwards or inwards is admitted, though the author does not undertake to describe it. He further proceeds to say (pp. 53, 56, 181, &c.,) that particular individuals are in some mysterious way connected with particular spiritual communities "receiving their life-influx" from them and imbibing their influence. And every human being will, in the course of his progress, become an angel of some particular description or other.

Now I beg to submit, with all due respect to the author's *guru*, that these views do not harmonize with the teachings of Vyasa and the other Rishis of ancient Aryavarta. The difference between the doctrines of the ancient Aryan esoteric science and the propositions above laid down, will not be properly appreciated unless the meaning attached by the author to the word *angel* is first ascertained. Though the said word is no-where defined in his book, yet from a foot-note in page 93, it can be easily seen that an angel means *Dêvata.* Those, who are acquainted with Sanskrit mythology, know very well that there are several classes of *Dêvata*; that these classes perish at the end of each *Manwantara,** and that new classes or tribes (*Ganams*) come into existence at the beginning of every subsequent *Manwantara.* It will also be seen, from the Hindu *Puranas* and the *Mahabharata* itself, that neither the individuals of these various tribes, nor yet the tribes collectively, undergo any change, transmigrations or translations into a higher state, or a higher plane of existence. No Hindu has ever heard of a *Yaksha* or *Gandharva*† becoming a *Deva,* and of a *Deva* becoming a higher being. The really important difference, however, between the author's theory and the doctrines of the ancient Rishis, consists in the view taken of the various degress or "states-being" in a man and their esoteric significance. The author's desire to find some reference to the 12 signs of the Zodiac in almost everything connected with the ancient Aryan religion and philosophy, has probably led him to the belief that there are 12 degrees in man corresponding to the 12 signs of the Zodiac; and it would also, appear that such was his *guru's* teaching. The author, however, has no right, it seems to me, to import into the Aryan doctrine either his *guru's* teaching or his own fancies, unless he is in a position to show that they are in accordance with the teachings of the ancient Rishis. I shall now state what the Aryan doctrine really teaches as regards these states or degrees, as far, of course, as I am permitted to say in an article intended for publication.

The *seven-fold* classification in man was already prominently brought to the notice of the readers of the "THEOSOPHIST" in

---

* The period of Regeneration, or the active life of the universe between two *Pralayâs* or universal Destruction: the former being called the "*day*" and the latter the "*night*" of Brahma—ED.

† Yaksha, the earth-spirit or Gnome; the *Gandharva*, akin to the Christian cherub or singing seraph. There are, says *Atharva Veda* (XI, 5, 2,), 6,333, Gandharvas in their *Loka*.—ED.

the article headed "Fragments of Occult Truth,"* and in a subsequent article, referring to and completing it, published in the January number of the said journal.† These seven entities in man represent the 7 principles that constitute him. But the Rishis also recognized 16 stages of ascent—not 12 as the author has erroneously supposed--from *Prithwi Tatwam* up to " the eternal and infinite monad"—the *augoides* that overshadows every man, the blazing star at the end of *Skodasantum* (end of the 16th stage of ascent). Busiris himself, when in human form *as Krishna Dwypâyana* (!), spoke of *Shodasántum*, as may be seen from the many sacred writings attributed to Vyasa. From the stand-point of Aryan philosophy, the author is right in saying that a man becomes perfect on reaching the 11th stage, but he is wrong in saying that, on attaining the next higher step, he becomes an "angel" or *Deva.* The nature of the last 5 stages, spoken of by the ancient Rishis, is not clearly understood even by the *ordinary initiate.*‡ It is not surprising, then, that an author, like Mr. Oxley, who attempts to interpret the ancient Aryan doctrine without knowing either the Sanskrit language, the Hindu systems of mythology, the Eastern modes of allegorizing spiritual truths, or the physiology and psychology as taught by the ancients, should have misunderstood the meaning of the 12th stage. No one, who correctly understands the meaning of the 8th Adhyaya (chapter) of the *Bhagavatgita*, and compares the original with the author's translation of the said chapter, will be inclined to doubt the correctness of our assertion. In that chapter, Krishna, speaking of the future state of the human being after death, says that, generally speaking, "the life-principle" in man (the *Karanasariram* probably ?) assumes the shape and nature of that being or entity on whom, or on which, the human being concentrates his attention deeply. Therefore, and as it is not desirable for a human being to

---

* "THEOSPHIST," October, 1881.

† " The Aryan-Arhat Esoteric Tenets on the Seven-Fold Principle in Man.

‡ An initiate of the preliminary degrees.

contemplate any other spiritual entity or being than Krishna himself, he advises Arjuna to centre his thoughts in him. But, who is Krishna? The *Bhagavatgita* does not leave us in any doubt about this question. In giving an account of his *Vibhuti* (as it is called in Sanskrit) Krishna commences by saying "Ahamatma"* (I am Atma—the 7th principle in man). To use the author's phraseology, he is the "soul" —the inmost principle in man. The author admits this view in certain portions of his book, though, for the purpose of establishing the claims of Busiris to the authorship of the "Mahabharata," a different interpretation would perhaps be necessary. And, in recommending the contemplation or *Dhyan* of one's own atma, Krishna points out two different modes of doing it, in the 9th, 12th and 13th *Slokams* of the chapter above mentioned. The author's translation of the 9th Slokam is enough to convince me that he has no defininte idea about the esoteric meaning therein found, and that he mistook the spiritual being or entity described in the said Slokam for his favourite angel. He translates the significant Sanskrit adjective—*Puranam*, as if it meant '*The Ancient Angel.*' I shall be very happy indeed to learn in what Sanskrit Lexicon is this meaning given, or what are the Sanskrit words used in the *Slokam* that could ever suggest that idea of an "angel." From this instance of mis-translation, as well as from other similar instances, which will be noticed further, I am justified in thinking that the author's theories were formed before he had carefully ascertained the esoteric meaning of the *Bhagavatgita*; and that he simply attempted to find support for his individual speculation in it, and to identify modern Spiritualism (however advanced) with what he is pleased to call "Ancient Yoginism" (P. 87).

In fact, in the *Slokam*, or verse in question, there is no reference whatsoever to any angel, Deva or God. The last five stages in the ladder of ascent have exactly the same meaning

---

* The "I AM, THAT I AM" of the Biblical Jehovah, the "I AM WHO I AM," or Mazdao" of Ahuramazda in the Zend Avesta, &c. All these are names for the 7th principle in man.—ED.

that is given by the esoteric Buddhism to the four celestial "Dhyan-Buddhas" and "Adi-Buddha." Krishna significantly alludes to the Dhyan-Buddhas in the 9th and 10th Slokas, and speaks of "Adi-Buddha"—the state or condition represented by *Pranava*—in the succeeding verses.* While he applies the wore *Purusha* to these "Dhyan-Buddhas" he speaks of Adi-Buddhas, as if it were merely a state or condition.† The two expressions, *Anusasitarum* and *Aditya-Varnam*, in the 9th verse may give the author a clue to the mystery connected with these "Dhyan-Buddhas." I am not permitted to state in an article the views of the ancient Rishis concerning these 5 stages—the spiritual counterparts of *the* 5 *chambers of construction* above the King's chamber in the great Pyramid of Egypt —or the phliosophy underlying the Buddhist doctrine regarding these 5 Buddhas. But it is enough for my present purpose to state that these celestial "Dhyan-Buddhas" came into existence (according to Vyasa) before the last work of creation or evolution commenced, and consequently, before any Deva or Angel was evolved. Therefore, they are to be regarded as occupying a higher position (in a spiritual sense) than even Brahma, Vishnu and Ishwara, the three highest gods of the Hindu Pantheon—as they are *the direct emanations* of *Parabrahman.* The author will understand my meaning clearly, when he examines the accounts of "creation" given in the Hindu Puranas, and comes to comprehend what the ancient Rishis meant by *Sanaka*, *Sanandana*, *Sanatkumara*, *and Sanatsujata.*

From the teachings of Krishna himself, as disclosed in the chapter under examination, it is clear that the transformation

---

* Hence, the great veneration of the Buddhists for *Bhagavatgita.*—Ed.

† "Adi-Buddha" *creates* the four celestial Buddhas or "Dhyans," in our esoteric philosophy. It is but the gross misinterpretation of European Orientalists, entirely ignorant of the Arhat-doctrine, that gave birth to the absurd idea that the Lord Gautama Buddha is alleged to have created the five Dhyan or celestial Buddhas. Adi-Buddha, or, in one sense, Nirvana, "creating" the four Buddhas or degrees of perfection—is pregnant with meaning to him who has studied even the fundamental principle of the Brahmanical and Arhat esoteric doctrines.—Ed.

into an angel after death (even into a Busiris, *the light-giver*) is not a state or position which is so devoutly to be wished for, by any true Yogi. The ancient Rishis of Aryavarta have taken considerable pains to impress upon the minds of their followers that *the human spirit* (7th principle) has a dignity, power and sacredness which cannot be claimed by any other God, Deva or angel of the Hindu Pantheon; * and human beings are stated in the Puranas to have performed actions which all the 33 crores of Devas in Swarga were unable to perform. Rama *in human shape*, conquers Ravana, a giant, who drove before him all the angel-bands of Heaven. Krishna again, *in human form*, conquers Narakasura, and several other Rakshasas whom even Indra was unable to oppose. And again Arjuna—a man significantly calld by Vyasa "Nara," —succeeds in destroying the "Kalakayas" and the "Nivatakavachas" (two tribes of *Rakshas* or demons) who were found invincible by the "Devas," and actually defeats Indra himself with the help of his friend, Krishna. If the learned author is pleased to read between the lines of our Puranas and to ascertain the grand idea which found expression in such myths and allegories, he will be in a better position to know the opinion of our ancient teachers regarding *the human spirit* (7th principle) and its supremacy over all the angels of Swarga. Even on "this mundane plane of existence a Hindu "Yogi" or a Buddhist "Arhat" aims at a result immeasurably higher than the mere attainment of *Swargam*:—namely, a state of *eternal rest*, which even the *devas* do not comprehend. And I can safely assure the author that an eastern adept would not consider it a compliment if he were told that he would reach *Swargam* after death or that he would become an "angel." Krishna goes to the length of saying (chap. 8)

---

* In view of this, Gautama Buddha, after his inititation into the *mysteries* by the old Brahman, *His Guru*, renouncing gods, Devas and personal deity, feeling that the path to salvation lay not in vain glorious dogmas, and the recognition of a deity *outside* of oneself, renounced every form of theism and—became BUDDHA, the one *enlightened*. "Aham eva param Brahma," I am myself a Brahma (a god), is the motto of every Initiate. —ED.

that even residence in *Brahma Loka* is not desirable for a man who cares for *Swaswarupagnanâm*—the KNOWLEDGE OF SELF.

Under such circumstances, it is with considerable astonishment that every Hindu will receive the author's astounding assertion that "Busiris, the angel"—(viewing him absolutely in the sense that the author would have us view him)—made an announcement sometime ago in a seance-room at Manchester or London to the effect that he was the author of the *Mahabharata* ? If the author's declaration or announcement means the entity or life "life-principle," which was represented by Vyasa on the mundane plane of exsitence 5,000 years ago, is now represented by Busiris on the Angelic plane of existence, or, to express the same thing in other words, that Vyasa is now an angel called Busiris—his Hindu readers will not be able to reconcile it with the teachings of their ancient Rishis; unless they are willing to admit that Vyasa, insted of being, during his life-time, a great Rishi on earth, was neither an adept, not even an *initiate*, but merely a worshipper of a particular Angel or Deva, who spent his life-time in the contemplation of that Deva longing all the while for "angelhood," a dwelling in *Swargam* (or paradise) after death.

With these preliminary remarks, I shall now proceed to consider the claims of Busiris to the authorship of the *Mahabharata.* The various passages, referring to this subject, in Mr. Oxley's book, may point to either of the following conclusions:—

(1) That Vyasa is now an angel, called "Busiris," as explained in the foregoing, and that, in writing his epic poem, he was inspired by the angel—collectively called Busiris.

(2) That, even supposing Vyasa has already attained *Moksha*, or Nirvana, and reached a higher plane of existence than that of an angel, still he is changed with having composed the *Mahabharata* and the *Bhagwatgita*, through inspiration received from the band of angels or *Devagnanam*, now collectively represented by "Busiris," the *light-giver*.

Taking either of those two propositions, one may naturally expect that some evidence will be found either in the BHAGAVATGITA or the remaining portions of the BHARATA in support of them. And, as the author assures us (p. 181) that the individuals, who collect the utterances of angelic intelligences and reduce them to written form, very "wisely keep their own personalities in the shade," we are led to believe that this expectation is likely to be realised. But the whole of the internal evidence, gathered by the author on behalf of his angelic hero, amounts only to this :—

1. Vyasa means a "Recorder:" therefore the word was purposely applied to Krishna Dwapayana to indicate his real position as regards the authorship as the MAHABHARATA.

Now I beg to submit, in reply to this argument, that Vyasa does not exactly mean *a recorder*; but that it means *one who expands or amplifies.* The thing or doctrine explained or amplified by him, is a *mystery* to the uninitiated public. This term was applied to the HIGHEST Guru in India in ancient times; and the author will be able to find in the "Linga Puran" that the author of the MAHABHARATA *was the 28th Vyasa in the order of succession.* I shall not now attempt to explain the real meaning of the 28 incarnations therein mentioned,† but I shall only say that the entity, amplified

---

* In no case can the term be translated as "Recorder," we should say. Rather a "Revealer," who explains the mysteries to the neophyte or candidate for initiation by *expanding* and amplifying to him the meaning.—ED.

† To one, who has even a vague notion how the mysteries of old were conducted, and of the present Arhat system in Tibet vaguely termed the "Re-incarnation System" of the Dalai-Lamas, the meaning will be clear. The chief Hierophant who imparted the "word" to his successor *had to die* bodily. Even Moses dies after having laid his hands upon Joshua, who thus became "*full of the spirit of wisdom of Moses,*" and—it is the "Lord" who is said to have buried him. The reason why "no man knoweth of his sepulchre unto this day," is plain to an Occultist who knows anything of the supreme initiation. There cannot be *two* "Highest" Gurus or Hierophants on earth, living at the same time.—ED.

and expanded by these MAHATMAS* for the instruction of their highest circle of disciples was PRANAVA (see "Kurma Purana"). The author will be able to learn something about this mysterious *amplification* of PRANAVA *only* in the sacred region where Swedenburg advised his readers to search for the "Lost Word," and in a few unexplored and unknown localities in India.

II. *Sanjaya*—according to Mr. Oxley—was purposely introduced into the story to give to the reader an indication of the way in which divine truths were communicated by "Busiris" to Vyasa. On page 61 the author writes, in this connection, as follows :—"*Sanjaya* means a *messenger*, (and, if interpreted by modern Spiritualist experiences, refers to the communicating spirit or angel) who is gradually absorbed into the individuality of the organism of the recorder who assumes the name or title of Krishna."

It will be very interesting to know on whose authority the author says that *Sanjaya* in Sanskrit means *a messenger*? No one would feel inclined to quarrel with him, if he only gave fanciful names to imaginary angels. But is it fair, on the author's part, to misconstrue Sanskrit names without possessing any knowledge of that language, and to represent, to the English and Indian public, that the "crude notions" of modern Spiritualists and his own speculations completely harmonize with the teachings of the sacred books of the Aryans? The author says (p. 55) that—

"An understanding of the grand Law of Influx (but little dreamt of and still less comprehended by the mass), enables us to receive the statement of the *new* Angel Busiris, *that he* was the author of the Mahabharata."

Though I do not know much about the author's "grand Law of Influx," I know of a particular Law of *efflux* (but little dreamt of by authors and still less comprehended by their

* "Grand Souls" in literal translation; a name given to the great adepts.—ED.

readers) which enables me to perceive that mere fancies are often mistaken for realities, especially when the said authors think that they are "inspired."

If Sanjaya really represented the angelic intelligence which communicated the truths embodied in the Bhagvatgita to Vyasa, it is surprising to find in the last chapter—the very chapter, in fact, which, in the opinion of the author, contains the key for the clear understanding of the whole philosophy—Sanjaya informing Dhritarashtra that *by favour of Vyasa* (Vyasa prasadana) he was able to hear the mystic truths revealed by Krishna. Sanjaya's meaning would be rendered clear by the account of the arrangement made by the Vyasa for getting information of the war between the Pandavas and the Kouravas to the blind Dhritarashtra given at the commencement of Bheeshmaparva. Vyasa, in fact, endowed Sanjaya, for the time being, with the powers of *Dooradrishti* and *Doorasravanam*, and made him invulnerable, so that he might be present on the battle-field and report everything to the blind old man. These facts recorded in the "Mahabharata" are quite inconsistent with the author's theory unless we are prepared to admit that Vyasa has published deliberate falsehoods, with the intention of concealing the real authorship of the "Mahabharata." But the author informs us that "recorders," like Vyasa, "very wisely keep their own personalities in the shade." I must, therefore, assume that the author's suppositions about Sanjaya and angelic intelligences are erroneous until the facts are proved to be incorrect.

III. Again in page 54 of his book, in giving his interpretation of the words *Krishna* and *Dwypayana*, he says that *Krishna* means black, and Dwypayana, *difficult to attain*, which "spiritually interpreted symbolises the states of mankind to whom the revelation was made."

The author evidently means to suggest, by this passage, that the appellation given to Vyasa contains some evidence of the revelation made by Busiris. And here, again, the author is misinterpreting the Sanskrit word " Dwypayana " to create a fresh evidence for his favourite theory. This name was given to Vyasa, because he was borne in a Dweepam or island (on the Ganges) as will be seen from the "Bharata" itself. Unless the author can successfully demonstrate that all the Sanskrit words he has misconstrued really belong to the mysterious language to which the two words she has selected—" Osiris " and " Busiris "—belong, and which he alone can understand, mistakes, like these, cannot but produce an unfavourable impression upon the mind of the Hindu reader.

This is the whole of the internal evidence brought to light by the learned author in support of the claims of Busiris. If such evidence is really worse than useless, for the reasons above-mentioned, on what other grounds are we to admit the truth of the alleged declaration made by Busiris in England ? The author is likely to take up his stand on his theory about the composition of sacred books in general, and on the direct evidence supplied by the claimant himself.

As regards the first of the two propositions above-mentioned, I have already shown that, to the Hindu mind, the fact that Vyasa was an adept and a MAHATMA in his life-time, and that other fact that he is now an angel or Deva—are irreconcilable. I admit that there is no *primâ facie* improbability in the fact of an angel giving information to a mortal, although my opinions, regarding the nature of so-called "angels," differ vastly from those of the author. But no one, I venture to affirm, who is acquainted with Eastern adepts and the powers possessed by them, will be willing to admit that an adept like Vyasa would ever be under the necessity of learning spiritual truths from an angel or a Deva. The only infallible source of inspiration with respect to the highest spiritual truths, recognized and respected by an Eastern adept, is the eternal and infinite MONAD—his own *Atma,* in fact. He may make use of the assistance of the elementals and the semi-intelligent powers of nature whenever he is pleased to do so. But his own inherent powers can give him all the information, or instruction which angels like Busiris can ever give him. I do not profess to say anything about the way in which spiritual truths are being learnt by the "adepts" of France, the "adepts" of America, and, probably, also the adepts of Patagonia and Zululand alluded to by "Alif" in his review of the author's book in the "Psychological Review,"; but Vyasa was an Eastern adept; and, it must be presumed that he possessed at least the powers now exercised by adepts in Tibet and India. In the Hindu *Puranas*, there are, no doubt, instances recorded of initiates having received information and instruction through the assistance of intelligent powers of nature. But there is very little resemblance between such powers and angels like Busiris. When the author succeeds in finding out the mode in which an adept communicates with these powers, and obtains a clue to construe the *cipher* which nature herself uses, he will be in a better position to understand the difference between spirit communion in a séance-room and the way in which initiates of Ancient Aryavarta gathered their information on various subjects. But what necessity was there for anything like special revelation in the case of the MAHABHARATA? As regards the facts of history mentioned therein, there could not be any need for Vyasa's interiors being opened;" as he had merely to record the events occurring before his very eyes. He was, in fact, the "father" of Pandu and Dhritarashtra, and all the events mentioned in the Mahabharata took place during his lifetime. As regards the various philosophical discourses such as BHAGVATGITA in "Bheeshmaparvam," "Sanat Sujatyam" in "Udyogaparvam" and *Uttaragita* in "Amsasanikaparvam," many of the learned Pundits of India are of opinion that orginally they were not included in the MAHABHARATA. Whatever may be the strength of the reasons given by them for saying so, it is clear to those, who are acquainted with the real history of Aryan thought, that all the esoteric science and philosophy contained in the MAHABHARATA existed long before Vyasa was born. This work did not mark the advent of a new era in Aryan philosophy or introduce into the Aryan world a new Dispensation, as the author has imagined. Though Vyasa is generally spoken of as the founder of the Vedantic Doctrine, it was not for the Mahabharata, or anything contained in it, that he obtained this title, but on account of his celebrated *Brahmasutras* which are supposed to contain a complete exposition of the doctrines taught by the Vedantic school. This book is particularly referred to in the 5th verse of the 13th chapter of the BHAGVATGITA, where Krishna informs Arjuna, that the nature of *Kshatram* and *Kshatragna* has been fully defined in the *Bhrahmasutras*. Not knowing anything about the exsitence of this great philosophical work, the author thought that the Sanskrit expression *Brahmasutras* merely meant "precepts taught of truths divine." If the author had known anything about the importance of the work in question, Busiris would, no doubt, have announced himself by this time the author of the *Brahmasutras* also. If these *Sutras* were composed by Vyasa before Krishna revealed the truths of the BHAGVATGITA to Arjuna, as we are led to infer from the words used in this Slokam, there was no necessity whatsoever for the assistance of Busiris in composing the BHAGVATGITA, as the "philosophy of spirit" contained in it was already fully contained in the said *Sutras*.

The author will probably say : "I see no reason why I should not believe the statement made by Busiris." He may argue that he knows for certain that "it was made by an angel ; and as an angel cannot, under any circumstances, utter a falsehood," he has to believe that "the Mahabharata is really the production of Busiris."

The learned author has informed the public in page 51 of his book, that, after making the important declaration that he was the author of the Mahabharata, Busiris proceeded "to give an interesting account of the civilization and manners and customs of the inhabitants in his day, *long antecedent* to the system of caste which now prevails in India." Unfortunately we do not find the whole of this interesting account published by the learned author for the benefit of the public.

But the only statement of an historical importance contained in the sentence above quoted—that the system of caste did not prevail at the time when Busiris was in India in human form—is such as to make everyone who is acquainted with Indian history doubt the veracity of Busiris. Rig-veda speaks of the four castes of the Hindus (see MaxMuller's Lectures, &c.), and, as the author admits that Rig-veda existed long before the composition of the Mahabharata, the system of caste must have also existed before Busiris had appeared in human form in this country. Again, "Santiparvam" and "Anusasanika-parvam" of the MAHABHARATA will distinctly show to the author that the system of caste existed when Busiris was living here as Vyasa. And, moreover, in the 13th verse of the 4th chapter of the *Bhagvatgita* itself, Krishna says that he had already created the four divisions of caste ("Chaturvarnam maya sreshtam"). This statement of Busiris, then, is clearly wrong. It is very surprising that an angel should lose his memory in the course of his transformation from man to angel, or should wilfully make false statements with reference to well-known facts of history. Under such circumstances, no one will be prepared to admit that Busiris was the author of the great poem, if there is no other evidence in support of it, but the value of his own statements.

We have thus seen the degree of reliance that can be placed on the revelation from angels, who delight in giving now and then sensational news to the public through their friends and admirers in séance-rooms. So long as the so-called celebrated "Historical Controls" continue to give incorrect information regarding the events and facts in history, the public in general, and the Hindus in particular, ought to be excused for not giving credence to all that is claimed by Spiritualists on behalf of the "disembodied spirit" and "spirit communion."

I have purposely abstained from saying anything about the real agency at work in producing the so-called spirit manifestations, and from testing Busiris and his pretensions by examining the very basis of modern Spiritualism from its first principles. Unless the real points of divergence between Spiritualism and Theosophy in their fundamental doctrines are first settled, there will be little or no profit in stating merely the conclusions arrived at by Theosophists about the séance-room phenomena. Conclusions based on the systematic investigation and discoveries made by the brightest intellects of Asia, for thousands of years, are liable to be often mistaken for idle speculations and whimsical hypotheses, if the ground, on which they rest, is masked from view. I can hardly be expected to undertake a complete discussion of the subject within the limits of one article. I have already given a brief and general statement of my views about Spiritualism in a paper published in the "*Theosophist.*"

As the present review has already reached an inordinate length, I shall now bring it to a close. The author's views about the Astro-Masonic basis of the BHAGVATGITA and his elucidation of some of its imporatant doctrines will be examined in my next paper.

An article by Mr. W. Oxley, under the above heading, has appeared in the *Theosophist.* It is intended to be a reply to the strictures contained in my review of "The Philosophy of Spirit," published in the *Theosophist*; but a considerable portion of it is devoted to the exposition of some of the important doctrines of what is termed "Hierosophy and Theosophy," as understood by the author. I shall first examine the author's defence of Busiris and the statements contained in his treatise on "The Philosophy of Spirit" regarding the authorship of Mahabharata, and then proceed to point out his misconceptions of the real doctrines of "Theosophy," and the fanciful nature of his speculations on the doctrines of the new system of Esoteric Philosophy and Science, which, it is confidently predicted, will soon supplant the existing systems of Eastern Brotherhoods, and which is hereafter to be known under the name of "Hierosophy."

Mr. Oxley is pleased to state at the commencement of his article, that whatever may be the views of "*orthodox Bramhins*," regarding his theories and speculations, "enlightened Buddhists" would not be unwilling to sympathize with and receive him as an ally in the work of reform.

Buddhists may not be very much interested either in Bhagavatgita, its authorship, or its correct interpretation, and consequently they may not take the trouble of arriving at any particular conclusions about the correctness of the authors' interpretation of its philosophy, or the justness of his views concerning its authorship. But if the author would publish another small treatise to explain the philosophy of spirit contained either in the Tripitakas, or in the Dharma Chakkra Pravartana Sutra, and assert that the real authors of these works were better known to certain mediums in England than to all the Buddhist Lamas and Arhats put together, that they were, in fact, certain angels called by names which they never heard in their lives, and that Gautama Buddha's interiors were opened to let in spiritual light and wholesome life influx from the sphere of solar angels, he will have an opportunity of ascertaining the opinion of "enlightened Buddhists" on the real value of his speculations and the extent of their usefulness in promoting the cause of Buddhist philosophy and Buddhist reform. I hardly ever expected that a philosopher of Mr. Oxley's pretensions would think it proper to attack orthodox Bramhinism and inform the public that his reading of the doings of orthodox people in past history and observations of their spirit and action in present times has not left a very favourable impression on his mind, when the said statement is perfectly irrelevant to the argument in question. Busiris must, indeed, have been reduced to desperate straits when this counter-attack on "orthodox Bramhinism" is considered necessary to save him from annihilation. But what does Mr. Oxley know of "orthodox Bramhins?" So far as I can see, his knowledge of the doctrines of orthodox Bramhinism is all derived from the perusal of a few incorrect English translations of Bhagavat-Gita; he is confessedly ignorant of the Sanskrit language, and is, therefore, unable to derive information from any of our Sanskrit works. He must have based his assertion, perhaps, on the statements of some interested missionaries, who are generally fond of abusing orthodox Brahminism when they find themselves unable to convert Hindus to their creed by fair argument. Under such circumstances, what is the good of informing his readers that he does not patronize "orthodox Brahminism," when he is not prepared to point out in what respects orthodox Brahminism is bad, and how far my connection with it has tended to vitiate my arguments against the claims of Busiris to the authorship of Mahabharata? I beg to inform the author that if there is reason to condemn any of the rites, ceremonies, or practices of modern Brahmins, their Brahminism would be heterodox Brahminism, and not orthodox Brahminism. The true orthodox Brahmins are the children of the mysterious *Fire-mist* known to Eastern Occultists. The two Sanskrit words, Badaba and Badabaya, generally applied to Brahmins, will reveal to the author the real basis of orthodox Brahminism, if he can but understand their significance. The real orthodox Brahmin is the *Astral man* and his religion is the only true religion in the world; it is as eternal as the mighty law which governs the Universe. It is this grand religion which is the foundation of Theosophy. Mr. Oxley is but enunciating a truism—a truism to Theosophists, at least,—when he says that "esoteric truth is one and the same when divested of the external garb in which it is clothed." It is from the stand-point of this esoteric truth, that I have examined the theories of the author explained in his book, and arrived at the conclusion that they were mere fancies and speculations, which do not harmonize with the doctrines of the ancient WISDOM-RELIGION which, in my humble opinion, is identical with the real orthodox Brahminism of ancient Aryavarta and the pre-Vedic Buddhism of Central Asia. I shall now request my readers to read my review of "The Philosophy of Spirit" in connection with the article under consideration fully to appreciate the relevancy of Mr. Oxley's arguments.

8

I stated in my review that as regards the *facts of history* mentioned in Mahabharata, there could not be any need for Vyasa's "interiors being opened," and that as regards the philosophy contained therein, there was no necessity for anything like a special revelation by angels like Busiris. The learned author objects to this statement for two reasons which may be stated as follows :—

I.—*Vedic* allegories have about as much literal historical truth in them as the Hebraic allegories, &c.

Therefore, *Mahabharata* does not contain any *facts of history.* It is hardly necessary for me to point out the fallacy and worthlessness of such an argument. Argument No. II. is still more ridiculous; when stated in plain language, it stands thus :—

Orthodoxy insists on a literal interpretation of such books as Mahabharata.

Mr. Oxley is not favourably disposed towards "Orthodoxy."

And, therefore, it necessarily follows that Mahabharata contains no facts of history, and that Vyasa's "interiors were opened" to let in light from Busiris.

Having urged these two useless arguments in defence of Busiris, the learned author proceeds to notice the *sixteen states* mentioned in my review, after giving me due warning, that I should meet him as a Theosophist, and not as an orthodox Brahmin. He says that as his twelve states are qualities, he has, in fact, twenty-four states when I have only sixteen, and treating these latter, according to his own method, he asserts that Eastern Theosophists have not gone beyond his eighth stage of ascent. If I were to tell him in reply to this statement, that my states are also dualities, he will probably say that his twelve states are so many *trinities.* Any how, Mr. Oxley's number must be greater than my number; and this is the grand result to be achieved at any cost. Mr. Oxley will do well to remember that just as a geometrical line may be divided into parts in an infinite number of ways, this line of ascent may similarly be divided into various stages in an innumerable number of ways. And, in order to astertain whether the very last stage reached by Eastern adepts in higher or lower than the last stage conceived by Mr. Oxley he ought to examine carefully the characteristics of our last stage, instead of merely comparing the number of stages without knowing anything about the basis of our division. I beg to submit that the existence of any state or condition beyond the Shodasanthnm (sixteenth state) emntioned in my review is altogether inconceivable. For, it is the Thureeya-kala which is *Nishkala* ; it is the *Grand Nothing* from which is evolved, by the operation of the external law, *every existence*, whether physical, astral, or spiritual; it is the condition of Final Negation—the Maha Sunyam, the Nirvana of the Buddhists. It is not the *blazing star* itself, but it is the condition of perfect unconciousness of the entity thus indicated, as well as of the "*Sun*," which is supposed to be beyond the said star.

The learned author next points out that there cannot be any difficulty or objection "to accepting as a *possibility*, that the actual author of Mahabharata should put in, not an objective, but a subjective, appearance in London, or elsewhere *if he chose so to-do*." Quite true; but he will never choose to do so. And consequently, when such subjective appearance is stated to have taken place, very strong grounds will be required to support it. So far as I can see, all the evidence is against the said statement. Subjective appearances like these are generally very deceptive. The mischievous pranks of Pisachams or elementals may be often mistaken for the subjective appearances of solar angles or living adepts. The author's statement about the supposed astral visits of "the venerable Koot-Hoomi" is now contradicted by Koot-Hoomi's chela under the orders of his Master. Unfortunately, Busiris has no chela in human form to contradict Mr. Oxley's statements. But the account of Koot-Hoomi's visits will be sufficient to show how very easily the learned author may be deceived by devils and elementals, or by his own uncontrolled imagination. I respectfully beg to suggest to Mr. Oxley that it may be argued in conformity with his own mighty "law of influx," that the Pisacham or elemental, whom he mistook for Vyasa, might have put forth a false statement, being unable to maintain "concurrent consciousness at both ends of the line," or for the same reason, and labouring under a similar difficulty (for we are told by the author that even the highest Deva cannot transcend "the law of conditions"), Busiris might have mistaken himself for the author of Mahabharata, having lost the consciousness of what he really was before he had put in the subjective appearance in question.

The learned author reminds me that Krishna Dwypayana "is only the supposed author of Mahabharata," and confidently asserts that "no man living knows who were the authors of the Hindu sacred records, or when and where they were written and published," relying upon the authority of Professor Monier Williams, who stated in his book on "Hinduism" that Sanskrit literature is wholly destitute of trustworthy historical records.

This assertion does not prove that Busiris was the real author of Mahabharata for the following reasons:—

I. With all due respect to the learned Professor, I venture to affirm that the general proposition relied upon is not correct. We have got trustworthy historical records which no Europeon has ever seen; and we have, besides, the means of finding out any historical fact that may be wanted, or of reproducing in its entirety any work that might have been lost. Eastern occult science has given us these powers.

II. Even if the general proposition is correct, it cannot reasonably be inferred therefrom, that, when the names of the authors of Sanskrit works are mentioned in the said works themselves or in other books, which may be considered an authoritative, no reliance should be placed on such statements.

III. Even if such inference were permissible, it cannot be contended, in the absence of any reliable independent evidence, that, because the author of a certain Sanskrit book is not known, it should be presumed to be the production of an angel.

The following statement is to be found in the author's book, p. 51 :—"Busiris expressly declared: 'I am the author of Mahabharata, and I can answer for five thousand years of time, for I was then on earth'; and he goes on to give an inteaesting account of the civilization, and manners and customs of the inhabitants of his day, long antecedent to the system of caste which now prevails in India." We are now informed by Mr. Oxley that the words, "long antecedent to the system of caste which now prevails in India," were not uttered by Busiris, but that they were written by himself. Even then, Busiris has undoubtedly some connection with the statement. "The interesting account of the civilization, and manners and customs of the inhabitants of his day,'' given by Busiris, is either consistent with the existence of caste at that time, or it is not. If it is, the author's statement does not harmonize with the account of Busiris, and I do not suppose that the author will venture to contradict the statements of an angel. I should, therfore, assume that the account given by Busiris is incosistent with the existence of caste at the time he appeared in human form.

If so, the account in question flaty contradicts all the statements in Mahabharata itself, which refer to the system of caste (see Santiparvam and Anusasnikaparvam). The author's quotation of Professor Williams' opinion regarding Purusha Sukta does not show that it does not properly form a portion of Rig-Veda, and no reasons are given for holding that the system of caste mentioned in Bhagvat-Gita is not properly speaking a system of caste. And here again the author thinks it necessary to condemn orthodox Brahminism for the purpose of enforcing his arguments. If the author really thinks that he will gain his cause by abusing "orthodox Brahminism," he is entirely mistaken.

After giving us a brif account of the progress of the United States and predicting the future downfall of orthodox Brahminism, the learned author informs his readers that it would be better not to notice what in his opinion might be urged to prove that my criticisms are from a mistaken stand-point. Certainly, the author has acted very prudently in making this declaration ; any attempt on his part to answer the main arguments urged by me would have ended in a disastrous failure.

It is always difficult for a foreigner to understand our religious philosophy and the mysteries of our Puranas, even when he devotes a considerable portion of his time and energy to the study of Sanskrit literature and the real secrets of Eastern occult science can only be revealed by an INITIATE. So long as Europeans treat the opinions of Hindus with contempt and interpret our religious books according to their own fancies, the sublime truths contained therein will not be disclosed to Western nations. Mr. Oxley evidently thinks that there is no initiate in India, who can interpret our religious books properly, and that the real key to esotoric Hinduism is in his possession. It is such unreasonable confidence that has hitherto prevented so many European enquirers from ascertaining the real truth about our ancient religious books.

Mr. Oxley means to assume a certain amount of importance by putting forth the following astounding assertion. He says in his article:—"What, if I State to my reviewer that perchance—following the hint and guidance of Swedenbourg—I and some others may have penetrated into that sacred region (Central Asia) and discovered the 'Lost Word'" !

If I had not seen the author's book and his articles in the *Theosophist*, I would have refrained from saying anything against such a statement on the assumption that no man's statement should be presumed to be false, unless it is proved to be so. But from the following considerations, I cannot help coming to the conclusion that the author knows nothing about the "Lost Word".

(1.) Those who are in possession of it are not ignorant of the "art of dominating over the so-called forces of Nature".

The author confesses that he and his associates are ignorant of the said art.

(2.) Those who are acquainted with the Mighty Law embodied in the "Lost Word" will never affirm that the "Infinite Monad receives influx of energy from the Planetary Spirits" as stated by the author.

(3.) The author's assertion about the flow of energy from solar angles shows that he is not acquainted with the real source of creative energy indicated by the Name.

Here ends Mr. Oxley's reply to my criticisms. He then proceeds to explain the doctrines of Hierosophy. I shall examine the author's theories in the continuation of this article which will appear in the *Theosophist*.

In continuation of my article on the "Philosophy of Spirit," published in the October issue of the *Theosophist*, I shall now examine Mr. Oxley's notions of Theosophy and Hierosophy. It is not easy to understand his definitions of the two systems of philosophy thus indicated; and no definite issue or issues can be raised regarding the important distinction between the said systems from the meaning conveyed by these definitions. But he has explained some of the important doctrines of theosophy and hierosophy from his own stand-point for the purpose of comparing the two systems. Though he believes that "it will be admitted" that he has "not either under-or over-stated the case for theosophy," I respectfully beg to submit that he has entirely misunderstood the main doctrines inculcated by it.

The learned writer says that theosophists teach that in the instance of wicked and depraved people, the spirit proper at death takes its final departure. This statement is certainly correct; but the conclusions drawn from it by Mr. Oxley are clearly illogical. If this doctrine is correct, says the author, then it will necessarily follow that to all intents and purposes to *plain* John Brown "life eternal is out of the question." He then expresses his sympathy for pariahs, vagabonds, and other unfortunate poor people and condemns the doctrine for its partiality to "Rajahs, Maharajahs, plutocrats, aristocrats," &c., &c., and rich Brahmins, and its want of charity towards others who constitute the greater portion of humanity. Here it is quite clear that the fallacy in Mr. Oxley's argument consists in the change of adjectives. From the main doctrine in question it follows that "life eternal is out of the question" not to *plain* John Brown, but to *wicked* and *depraved* John Brown; and I can hardly see any reason why the author should so bitterly lament the loss of immortality so far as utterly wicked and depraved natures are concerned. I do not think that my learned opponent will be prepared to maintain that all pariahs, vagabonds, and other poor people, are all depraved and wicked, or that all Rajahs, Maharajahs, and other rich people are always virtuous. It is my humble opinion that utterly wicked and depraved people are in the minority; and loss of immortality to such persons cannot seriously be made the ground of an objection to the Theosophical doctrine under consideration. Properly speaking theosophy teaches not "conditional immortality," as the author is pleased to state, but conditional mortality if I may be permitted to use such a phrase. According to theosophy, therefore, annihilation is not the common lot of mankind unless the learned author is in a position to state that the greater portion of the human race are wicked and depraved—beyond redemption. Theosophists have never stated, so far as I know, that adepts alone attain immortality. The condition ultimately reached by ordinary men after going through all the planetary rounds during countless number of ages in the gradually ascending order of material objective existence is reached by the adept within a comparatively shorter time, than required by the uninitiated. It is thus but a question of time; but every human being, unless he is utterly "wicked and depraved," may hope to reach that state sooner or later according to his merits and Karma.

The corresponding hierosophic doctrine is not fully and definitely stated in the article under review, but the views of the author regarding the same may be gathered from his treatise on the philosophy of spirit. They may be summarized as follows:—

(1.) The four discreeted degrees in the human being "called animal, human, angelic, and deific," show that *every* human being (however wicked and depraved) will ultimately reach immortality.*

(2.) There is no re-birth in the material human form, there is no retrogression at any time.

And there is this interesting passage in the author's book:—

(3.) "The thread of life is broken up at the point where it appeared to be broken off by physical dissolution, and every one will come into the use and enjoyment of his or her own specific life, *i. e.*, whatever each one has loved the most, he or she will enter into the spirit of it, not using earthly material or organisms for the same but spiritual substances, as distinct from matter as earth is from at atmospheric air; thus the artist, musician, mechanic inventor, scientist, and philosopher will still continue their occupations but in a spiritual manner."

Now as regards the first proposition, it is not easy to understand how the existence of four discreeted degrees in human being or any number of such degrees necessarily leads to unconditional immortality. Such a result may follow if deific or angelic existence were quite consistet with, or could reconcile itself to, a depraved and wicked personality or individuality or the recollection of such personality. The mere existence of an immortality principle in man can never secure to him unconditional immortality unless he is in a position to purify his nature, either through the regular course of initiations or successive re-births in the ordinary course of nature according to the great cyclic Law, and transfer the purest essence of his individuality and the recollection of his past births and lives

---

* Had Mr. Oxley said instead—"every human monad" which changes its personalities and is in every new birth, a new "human being," then would his statement have been unanswerable.

to his immortal Atma and the developed and purified spiritual Ego in which they inhere.

The second proposition above stated is opposed to all the ancient traditions of Eastern nations and the teachings of all the Eastern adepts, and I do not think that any passage in support of it can be found in Bhagavat-Gita.

The last statement above-quoted is certainly a very extraordinary proposition; and I shall be very happy it the author can point out any authority for it in the Bhagavat-Gita or in the other portions of Mahabharata.

Whatever may be the nature of the purely ideal or subjective existence experienced in Devachan after death and before the next birth, it cannot be held that the artist or musician carries on his "occupations" except by way of ideation.

I shall now leave it to the readers to say whether this assertion is really "based upon foundations more substantial than mere fancies and speculations".

The second doctrine of Theosophy which Mr. Oxley notices in his article is that "occult powers and esoteric wisdom can only be attained by the severest asceticism and total abstention from the use of the sensual degrees in nature in their physical aspect." If this doctrine is universally admitted, he says, physical embodiment would be impossible. I can safely assure him that this contingency is not likely to happen under the present conditions of our planet; and I am unable to understand how physical embodiment is desirable in itself. It yet remains to be proved that "occult powers and esoteric wisdom" can be acquired from the teachings of Hierosophy without the restrictions imposed by esoteric Theosophy.

The learned author further adds that under the conditions abovementioned "the powers of adept life cannot be perpetuated by hereditary descent". He evidently thinks that this fact discloses a very great defect in the theosophical system. But why should adept life be perpetuated necessarily by hereditary descent? Occult wisdom has been transmitted from

Guru to disciple without any serious break of continuity during thousands of years in the East. And there is no danger of adept life ceasing to exist from want of transmission by hereditary descent. Nor is it possible to bring into existance a race of hierophants in whom occult knowledge will be acquired by birth without the necessity of special study or initiation. The experiment was tried, I believe, long ago in the East, but without success.

The author will be in a position to understand the nature of some of the difficulties which are to be encountered in making any such experiment from a perusal of Bulwer Lytton's "Zanoni."

The world has yet to see whether "under the sway of Solar Angels," the adepts trained under the system of Hierosophy, can retain their powers and knowledge after having renounced "asceticism, abstinence and celibacy," and transmit the so-called "adept life" to their descendants.

Speaking of the attitude of Theosophists towards spiritualism, Mr. Oxley observes that they hold that the so-called spiritualistic phenomena are due to the "intervention of enlightened living men, but not disembodied spirits." I shall be very glad if the learned author can point out any foundation for this statement in the utterances of Theosophists. Strangely enough, he says further on that, in the opinion of the Theosophists, such phenomena are due to "wandering shells and decaying *reliquiœ* of what was once a human being." This is no doubt true in the case of some of the phemomena at least: and the author should not presume to say that any one of these phenomena has its real origin in the action of *disembodied living conscious beings*," unless he is fully prepared to state exactly who these mysterious beings are, and demonstrate, by something weightier than mere assumption, the fact of their real existence. He is entirely mistaken in supposing that the *modus operandi* in the case of the socalled spiritualistic phenomena are precisely the same as in the phenomena produced by Eastern adepts. However I do not mean to say anything further about this subject here as it has been already fully discussed in the columns of the *Theosophist*.

Mr. Oxley objects to my statement that "the human spirit (7th principle) has a dignity, power, and sacredness which cannot be claimed by any other God, Deva or Angel of the Hindu Pantheon". Although I had taken care to inform my readers that by *human spirit*, I meant the immortal and unborn 7th principle or Atma in man, he construed the expression to mean the spirit or life principle in the human degree of his peculiar classification. It would have been better if he had taken the pains to understand my language before venturing to assert that my statement was against the doctrine taught by Krishna. So far as I can see, his notions about the seven principles in man so often mentioned in this journal are utterly confused and incorrect. As the English language is deficient in the technical phraseology required for expressing the truths of Aryan philosophy and science, I am obliged to use such English words as can be got to convey my meaning more or less approximately. But to preclude the possibility of any misunderstanding on the part of my readers I clearly intimated in the passage in question that by human spirit I meant the 7th principle in man. This principle, I beg to submit, is not derived from any angel (not even from Busiris) in the universe. It is unborn and eternal according to the Buddhist and Hindu philosophers. The knowledge of its own *Sivarupam* is the highest knowledge of self: and according to the doctrines of the Adwaita school of Aryan philosophy, to which I have the honor to belong, there is in reality no difference between this principle and Paramatma.

Mr. Oxley believes that the claims of the Spiritualists have virtually been admitted by the Theosophists, inasmuch as in the opinion of the latter "communications may be established with other spirits." But the learned author fails to percieve that by the word "Spirit" Theosophists mean something quite different from the so-called "disembodied spirits" of the Spiritualists. The belief in question does not therefore amount to any concession to the claim of the Spiritualists as is supposed by him.

The esteemed author then proceeds to explain some of the important doctrines of Hierosophy, which, he takes particular care to add, are not to be considered "by his readers as mere" fancies and speculations. Hierosophists seem to believe that the influx of life flows from the "Infinite monad" mentioned by me in the first part of my review on "The Philosophy of Spirit." Mr. Oxley's conceptian of this monad is not, then, quite consistent with the views of Eastern occultists. Properly speaking, this monad or centre is not the source of cosmic energy in any one of its form, but it is the embodiment of the great Law which nature follows in her operations.

The learned author then asserts that "Esoteric Theosophists" and their great leaders have admitted that there is an "influx" of energy from the planetary spirits to the manad abovementioned. Here, again, I am sorry to say, Mr. Oxley is misrepresenting the views of Theosophists according to his own imagination. And the statement itself is thoroughly unphilosophical. This transmission of energy from the planetary spirits to the Great Law that governs the Universe, is inconcievable to every ordinary mortal. It does not appear that the monad referred to by Mr. Oxley is a different entity from the monad alluded to in my article. He himself says that it is not so. Then the only conclusion to which I can come under the circumstances of the case is, that Mr. Oxley has put forward these strange and groundless statements about the action and reaction of cosmic energy between the Infinite Monad and the planetary spirits without having any clear and definite ideas about these entities. The truth of this statement will be confirmed on examining his views about the nature of the work done by the planetary spirits. These spirits, it would appear, "detain myriads of elementals in the spheres of interior Nature, *i. e.*, the next plane of life immediately contiguous to this ; and compel them in the most tyrannical manner to obey their commands and produce effects which are calculated to perpetuate their own peculiar qualities in the plane of material existence. I confess I do not know anything about the beings who exercise such despotical functions. They are not the planetary spirits of the Theosophists; and if they have any existence outside the region of Mr. Oxley's fancy, I beg to request he will be kind enough to enlighten the public about the nature of these mysterious and dreadful tyrants. I can assure him that the orthodox Brahmins, whom he is so very unwilling to patronize, have nothing to do with such planetary spirits; nor do they know anything of them. I am really delighted to hear from my learned opponent that the Solar Angels are fully prepared to fight for the liberty of our unfortunate elementals and put an end to this abominable tyranny within a very short time; and if, among other beautiful and useful occupations, arts, and sciences that exist in the world inhabited by these angels, (since we are told that, the artist, musician, mechanic, minister, scientist, philosopher will "still continue their occupations" in this world of spirit)—a Society for the Prevention of Cruelty to Animals will have its place along with other associations, than the Solar Angels would surely deserve to be nominated as its most honorary and honoured members.

The learned author concludes his interesting exposition of the principles of Hierosophy by proclaiming to the world at large that "under the sway of Solar Angels, neither asceticism, abstinence, nor celibacy, as such, will find place, but the perfection of life's enjoyment will be found in the well regulated use of all the faculties to which humanity is heir".

Whether this novel system of philosophy and ethics is really "rhapsodical and utopian," or not, the public—especially the Indian—will have to decide. But I can affirm without any fear of contradiction that this system has not the slightest foundation in anything that is contained in the Bhagavat-Gita or in any other religious or philosophical book of the Hindus. It is simply the result of the author's independent speculations and must rest upon its own strength. In my humble opinion it is clearly erroneous and unphilosophical.

I shall now take leave of Mr. Oxley and request him to kindly excuse me for the adverse criticism contained in my artictes. I shall be very glad if my strictures can Induce him to re-examine carefully the philosophy of spirit contained in Bhagavat-Gita and scrutinize the reasons for the conclusions arrived at by him in his book on the fundamental questions of occult philosophy and ethics. With his intuition and intelligence, he will no doubt be in a position to open out for himself a way to understand the mysteries of the Eastern arcane sciences,—if he only avoids the temptation to leap to general conclusions from insufficient data, and draw inferences prematurely before the whole range of our ancient science and philosophy is carefully explored by him.

I am very happy to hear that my learned antagonist has joined our Theosophical association, and I hope he will henceforth work in fraternal concord with his Eastern brothers for recovering the grand truths taught by the ancient Hierophants and promoting the cause of Universal Brotherhood.

RETROGRESSION IN RE-BIRTH.

In his able review of Mr. Oxley's "Philosophy of Spirit," Mr. Subba Row, criticising the author's views of the hierosophic doctrine, remarks :—

" The second proposition (there is no re-birth in the materail " human form, *there is no retrogression at any time*) is opposed " to all the ancient traditions of Eastern nations and the *teach-* " *ing of all the Eastern adept.*"

The italics are mine. The proposition is certainly not in union with "all the ancient traditions of Eastern nations," but is the portion of it which I have italicised (there is no retrogression at any time), though certainly opposed to ancient Hindu traditions, really at variance with the "teaching of all the Eastern adepts"? Unless I am mistaken, you have all along strenuously maintained it as one of the truths of occult philosophy that re-birth in a *lower* state is impossible, that there is no *going back* in the scale of existence, that "nature invariably shuts the door behind her :" in other words, that there is no retrogression. Exactly the proposition advanced by Mr. O. and objected to by Mr. S. R. !

Will you or the learned reviewer kindly explain this ?

H.

BOMBAY, *2nd December* 1883.

EDITOR'S NOTE.—We have "strenuously maintained," and still maintain, that there is no "retrorgression" in the dead-letter sense as taught by exoteric Hinduism—*i. e.*, that the re-birth of a man in the *physical* form of an animal was impossible on this earth. But, we never affirmed that there was no *moral* retrogression,—especially in the interplanetary spheres ; and that is what is combated by Mr. T. Subba Row, for Mr. Oxley means "retrogression" in that very sense, we believe.

ESOTERIC SPIRITUALISM.

THE LAW OF "INFLUX" AND "EFFLUX".

BY WILLIAM YEATES,

Fellow of "the British Theosophical Society".

[IN giving room to the following clever paper, it is but just that its several points should be answered by Mr. T. Subba Row, against whom it is directed, now and here, and without having to postpone the reply for another month. Most of the foot-notes, therefore, are his.—*Ed.*]

The October number of the *Theosophist* for 1882 contains strictures on Mr. William Oxley's article (in the September number) by a respected Eastern Brother, Mr. T. Subba Row. In the latter, quoting from the former's words to the effect "that there cannot be any difficulty or objection 'to accepting as a *possibility*, that the actual author of the Mahabharata should put in, not an objective but a subjective appearance in London, or elsewhere, *if he chose so to do*". Mr. Subba Row remarks :—"Quite true ; but he will never choose to do so."

After making the admission of the possibility is there not an inconsistency in adding the latter clause, coming as it does from a defender of the true faith in Orthodox Brahmanism ?* It sounds like a claim on Mr. Row's part to a perfect knowledge of the motives which actuate the exalted one. On what grounds does Mr. Row claim his right to the knowledge as to what the real author of the Mahabharata "chooses to do" ?†

From the Bhagavatgita, I learn that the one who (in a certain state) is described as the "Lord of all created beings," used this language, "Having command over my nature, I am made manifest by my own power: and as often as there is a decline of virtue, and an insurrection of vice and injustice in the world, I make myself manifest: and thus I appear from age to age". Through thus taking command over his own nature, and all men, I hold that for all practical purposes, he does choose "*a chela in human form*:" *i. e.*, one who takes on the clothing of *The Sun*, by means of the divine ray in which he makes Himself evident: and more, that there are *chelas in human form*, through whom the powers of The Grand Spirits Identity will be unfolded in due order ; even as it has been in past ages. What is true in regard to the Great one, is true in regard to spirits of lesser degree ; who also can have chelas of a degree corresponding with them.

According to *The Theosophist*, a Raja Yogee Brother has the power to assume whatever form he pleases, and to communicate with spirits either in, or the body. Why then should

* Our esteemed correspondent and brother is wrong here. We say again—Mr. T. Subba Row is no "defender of the true faith in orthodox Brahmanism," for the present "orthodox Brahmanism" is rather *heterodox* than orthodox. Our brother Mr. T. Subba Row is a true Vedantic Adwaitee of the esoteric, hence genuine Brahman faith and—an occultist—*Ed.*

† On the *grounds* of the genuine and authentic teachings of the true "exalted one" himself *as* correctly understood, on the grounds of the esoteric teaching of the "real author of the Mahabharata," rightly comprehended by the *initiated* Brahmins alone.—T. S. R.

it be deemed incredible that one, such as undoubtedly was Vyasa, can take command of his own life and nature in the forms beneath him, and assume the name of "Busiris," in order to make himself manifest through a medium ?* Does not the greater include the less ?

"If I pass entirely under the dominion of my highest, or seventh principle," I can, while in that state, receive a communication from spirits of that degree, and translate the substances to other ; just as *a chela in human form* would do with a message, or communication received from the Brothers. The modes of manifestation may be diverse, but the same law is operative in both instances ; surely, then, Mr. Subba Row must be mistaken in his assertion that "Busiris has no *chela* in human form". For most certainly, He, who has seconded to such an altitude, has command over his own nature in all those who subsist in the atomic life of his Spiritual Body; for it is only such that he can command, or "control". Likewise the Brothers themselves, they are able to command the unseen atoms who subsist within, or beneath, their own order; but can they so command the interior lives of life atoms which form the Spiritual Body of another of different order, and it may be suprrior to their own ? Herein lies the difficulty of any attempt to mould the new order of the modern Spiritualistic movement, according to the genius of the order of Eastern Occultism. Before this can be accomplished, command over the invisible heads of the Spirit Bands must first be obtained.

The inner Voice of the Angel of God speaks through the intuitions to all men and women who belong to this order of life, and who form the body, Church, or system, telling each one in their own order, the way to the Resurrection of the life; (some

* For the simple reason that the alleged teachings and esoteric interpretations of "Busiris" clash entirely with the teachings and interpretations of both Vyasa and the initiates of the esoteric school. The "Spirit" of Vyasa cannot well contradict, and without giving any reasons for it, the teachings of the latter when alive.—T. S. R.

partake of the life of more than one order) and everyone who perceives a ray of light, should follow it, for it will lead them to the summit of the Mount to which they are called whether it be that of a Planetary or Solar order Adeptship.*

As matter is within matter; spirit within spirit; atom within atom: and as Influx is within Efflux: even so there are orders within orders of Intelligences, both of a Planetary and Solar nature. From these we derive our life, and from them (mediately,) we receive that which form the higher qualities of our life. It matters little how the life quality is divided in its descent or ascent to the atom from whence it came and returns; the line may be extended until the atom becomes invisible to the external man; but invisibility becomes visible in the lives of the whole body of atom who came out from that ONE which can never be divided into less than one. Even so, it is possible for us to be inducted into a perceptive knowledge of the direct presence of the Angelic parents who gave us birth into the inmost quality of their life, and in which we live, and move, and have our being. By means of such outbirths, we partake of the differentiations of every Father and Mother through whom we came besides that of our own, and these augmented qualities will take eternity to unfold themselves; and in view of such a truth, there can be no place found for annihilation; inasmuch as the annihilation of one atomic quality in the child's life would be the the annihilation of him who gave it birth.† Can a part of God be

---

* I confess to my inability to distinguish between the two kinds of adeptship, called "Solar" and "Planetary" since the terminology is not in vague among Asiatic Occultists, but belongs, most likely, to the new Western "hierosophy."—T. S. R.

† Eastern esoteric philosophy denies the theistic idea that "the whole body of atoms" came out from some "ONE atom," and teaches that there is no difference between the 7th principle of man and that of universal nature. "Hence a child may be annihilated as a *personality*, whereas his 6th and 7th principles, the one *divine monad*, remain unaffected by this disintegration of freed atoms of still *particled* matter known as Soul."—T. S. R.

destroyed ?* In the universal life, I maintain, that not one single atom can be lost.†

Creation is infinite, with an endless capacity for growth and development. But if only the law of Efflux were operative there could be no improvement. Like produces Like, and although there might be an endless procession of variations—they would be but a mere repetition of the series of like to like again, and no improvement in the forms evolved from the parent stock.‡ But with the Law of Influx in operation, the forms are respective of new and higher qualities, which when evolved produce new and living forms of a higher and more interior order. It is only the recognition of this that can account for the development and manifestation of new forms of life of all kinds. To produce these, it must be evident that the germs of this new order of life were begotten from above

---

* "A part of God!" Before we venture to talk of a *part*, we ought to make sure of the existence of the *whole*; or at least learn to know something more than we do of the Essence of that "God" people are so freely discussing about. The Adwaita philosophy teaches to believe in one universal Principle it calls Parabrahm and to eschew *idols*. Hence it rejects the idea of a personal God, whether called by the latter name or that of ONE ATOM the Father and *Creator* of all other atoms.—T. S. R.

† "Atom lost?" No atom is ever lost but atoms combine in transitory groups which are entities, which are atomic congeries. So that if one personality is "annihilated," this is but a breaking up of an atomic group, and the freed atoms are drawn into new combinations—the 6th and the 7th principles being of course excluded—T. S. R.

‡ "*Creation* infinite." For "creation" read *universe*, and then the "endless capacity for growth and development" would fit in better, and there would be no contradiction to comment upon. As here written it reads like a theological paradox. For if the whole *creation* is "infinite" and there is still in it "an endless capacity for growth and development," then it becomes the antithesis of "creation". And if the writer means that cosmic matter was created and infused with a law of "growth and development," then cosmic matter must have been created out of nothing which is scientifically absurd. "Efflux" and "Influx" sound here like words without meaning. It is *Influx* that brings into being everything, and it is *Efflux* that changes conditions and obliterates all temporary forms, to evolve out of them the one *Eternal Reality*.—T. S. R.

within the transformed soul; and in no case is it a repetition from the "old seed after its kind". Hence it is, that the new order of spiritual life appearing in the West so diverse in its manifestation to that of the East, is scarcely comprehended by the latter, in the light as I have shown it. In the Hebrew Record we read that the *young* Sampson "as yet, knew not his strength". Neither, as yet, is the spiritual power of the child of the Occident known or comprehended by his elder Brother of the Orient. Will the Brothers of the Orient take to the stripling by recognising him as the "Heir of the Inheritance," and send down a little of the hoarded stores to nature the new-born life in the valley below?

The *Theosophist* admits that notwithstanding the vantage ground of the possession of ancient stores of occult knowledge the Oriental system has, from time to time, declined: and in spite of repeated revivals at different epochs, every effort to restore it to the traditional pristine glory of the Golden Age has failed.*

Now assuming that one section of the Brothers succeed in resuscitating their order on the old lines, what security can we have that, at best, it would be but a sprouting out from the decaying trunk of the old tree of knowledge: as is proved by the history of the past.

The ancient Hindu, Brahminical, Buddhistic, Egyptain, Hebrew or Arabic, Christian and Mahomedan systems are mere variations from the same stock, and all of which were best at their beginnings. How comes it, that notwithstanding the more immediate presence, influence, and tutelage of the

---

* We beg to be permitted to emphatically deny the statement. Neither the *Theosophist—i.e.*, its editor nor any one of the Founders, has ever admitted anything of the sort about the "Oriental System," whatever some of its contributors may have remarked upon the subject. If it has degenerated among its votaries in India (a fact due entirely to the cunning of its dead letter interpretation by the modern *orthodox* Brahmin who has lost the key to it) it flourishes as high as ever in the Himalayan retreats, in the ashrum of the initiated Brahmin, and in all the "pristine glory of the Golden Age."—*Ed.*

Brothers to the Indian populations, that these confessedly have become degraded, and have lost their own spirituality and power.*

What other fate can befall us, as a Theosophical Society, if the very roots of our life, as such, draw their vitality from a decaying Tree, whose fruits, leaves, and branches are of "efflux" growth, and that of a descending order; inasmuch as it ignores the inmost "Law of Influx" from the Tree of Life of an inner causation ? All outgrowth in that direction must, of necessity, sooner or later exhaust their vitality.

It is the new influx from the Grand Central Sun of all existences, that causes of the soul to rise to higher states and forms of consciousness; and by means of this, the newly evolved states therefrom, form a new series of a system—on an ascending scale which will never retrograde, as have done and do, the grades of a purely Planetary Cycle of incarnations, whose occultations shut out the direct light of Grand Eternal Sun.

The teachings of 'Theosophy' appear to imply that there is latent power possessed of self-sufficient energy, sufficient in itself for the evolvement of a new species, without the intervention of a still higher power.

For instance, can this alleged self-sufficient energy from an object without existing materials ? Can it create a thought

---

* The "tutelage of the Brothers to the Indian populations" is a fancy based on a misconception. Ever since Buddhism with its esoteric interpretations of the *Vedas* and other sacred books was driven out of the country by the ambition and jealousy of the Brahmins, the *truths* of esotericism began to fade out of the memory of those populations until there now remains hardly one Brahmin in ten thousand who understands the Shastras at all. Hindus were degraded for the same reason that life and spirit have gone out of Christianity. The increase of wealth-bred sensuality, quenched spiritual aspiration and intuition, plugged the ears that once listened and shut the eyes that once saw the teachers. And at last by gradual deterioration of species, multiplications of war, and increased scarcity of food supply, the prime question became that of a struggle for life to the obliteration of spiritual yearnings.—T. S. R.

or an idea of a new form, absolutely independent of that which comes into the mind from the ideal realm of being from whence all germs are derived?*

It it were possible to sever the lines of the subtile—but externally invisible—thread of life which extends from the Parent Tree of life in the midst of the universal Garden to the external circumference of its physical manifestation; and to maintain such severed lives vitality; then, I admit, the Law of Efflux would be an all-sufficient cause for the appearance and perpetuation of those new and higher forms of life which have been evolved and manifested at different epochs.

If any order,—dependent solely on the traditional observances of those who ages ago derived their light at first and second hand from the fountain of all light,—should deny us the privilege of using their stores of ancient experimental knowledge by interposing impractical barriers; yet no order can prevent our access to the Grand Fountain of Light and Love, where we may drink freely of the waters of Life.† Is not this better than being confined to partake of a descending stream of wisdom which silts up its outlets with the stands of ages,—leaving a portion of its strength and power at every stage of its descent, until, at length, it is lost in the desert waste, where so many famish; and who cannot reach the purer water higher up the stream? Nor is it so with those systems which are on the ascending plane and order. By virtue of their being ever subject to the direct energy of the

* Most assuredly not. Both this neither proves existence of the *one* Atom, separated from and differentiated by, its unity from all other atoms, nor does it point to the necessity of one. At any rate, even our English Brother's "one atom" or God can hardly create "an object" without existent materials or matter.—T. S. R.

† The "Grand Fountain of Light and Love" is a very poetical metaphor—and no more, when applied to an unproved abstraction. We admit of such a fountain but not outside of, independent from, past, present and future humanity, (the crown of the evolution on our globe) every individual atom of which is a drop of that "Water of Life" the agglomeration of the drops of which forms that "*one* Fountain."—T. S. R.

Divine Solar ray, they have power to do that which other systems never could accomplish.

How can a system impart that which it admits it does not possess, viz., the *dual* states of adeptship? Where there are no feminine adepts in the order, it must ultimately yield to that dual power which is able to polarise and prepare both male and female atoms for the state in which they are fitted to be drawn up into the 'Celestial Marriage'. When intromitted into this state these wedded atoms act and re-act until every quality of their united being rotates and vibrates up and down the *seven* sides of the ray until becoming all radiant with light and heat in themselves, they are able to project the new born germs of a higher and purer life into the souls of those beneath them, who are drawn into the same state, and who, in their turn, may give out their several degrees of light and heat, and life to all around; and so on *ad infinitum.**

By these intermediates the mass of mankind receive the new order of life *unconsciously* according to their respective deeds, but the dual adepts will receive it consciously by direct influx. In order that new life-forms may be generated, the new life-force of a higher and purer order, must inflow into prepared atoms to receive the same both on this and other earths.

---

* Again an unwarranted assertion whichever way we see it. There *are* "female" adepts in the Brotherhood, and of a very high order. Therefore, there being such, in fact, the deductions drawn from a mistaken premise fall. And if our opponent had in mind in writing the above sentence, something more abstract and vague than a more physical difference of sexes, then he will allow me perhaps, to tell him that our esoteric philosophy *proves* that outside of the world of gross matter there is no such difference, the latter itself occurring (even on our earth) as an accident due to gestation and not as a result of such or another male or female germ. Even the Christian Bible, the youngest of the many attempts to religious philosophy, teaches him that in the resurrection the people "neither marry not are given in marriages". So that "Celestial marriage, whatever this may mean in modern Esotericism, appears to be but a figure of speech. Our readers might also be benefited were they explained what it meant by a "Dual Adept."—T. S. R.

How, except through the Divine Solar state of a wedded pair, can this higher and purer life be generated? With this in view, it can be seen that the 'Brothers'—with their celibate conditions of adeptship—cannot possibly beget a higher, or purer, order of life than their own; hence it follows that a system, based on such a principle, cannot perpetuate itself.*

It is at the culmination of a seventh cycle—a symbol of the Celestial Sun-day—that another Ray is shot forth across the universal Earth, and those who are prepared to receive its influence, and give birth, or ultimation, to higher forms of life, upon the respective earths they inhabit, according to its degree of development in the series; for as so ably shown by the writer of "Fragments of Occult Truth," the varied earths of a system, all differ as to states of mental and spiritual development; and yet not one could suffer deprivation of this Cyclic action from the 'Grand Sun,' without all the rest suffering from such loss to any specific member of the Solar family. Here comes in the distinction and difference between the guidance and teaching of the Planetary and Solar *Guru*. The one is the Forerunner, and prepares the way for the other; and it is the later one who leads his Chelas—both masculine and feminine—beyond the Tree of Knowledge, even to the Tree of Life itself.†

* Not necessarily. One critic seems to forget,—or perchance never know—that an adept has means of *inbreathing*, into his chosen "chela" besides his own "high order of life," to use his own expression, that of one still higher than himself, *i. e.*, of the highest Bhodisatva living or dead, provided the purity of his own life permits to him the performance of the mysterious assimilation. But we can assure our Brother, that without that "celibate" mode of life, against which he seems to protest so strongly, no adept could ever reach such a degree of power. Souls as well as spirits are sexless, and it is a great mistake to say that no "male monad" (?) can incarnate in a female body or *vice versa*. Mental and moral characteristics or idiosyncracies as met daily in life contradict the statement. It is owing to previous Karma that we discover so often masculine traits in weak female bodies and feminine tenderness and nervousness in strong men.—T. S. R.

† Does our Brother, who speaks so often of the "Tree of Life," know *its real esoteric significance*? Let him prove it, by hinting at the grand mystery, and if he does show his knowledge—then verily will our Mahatmas *be at his orders*!—T. S. R.

It is the leaves of this Tree--the life-giving power which are to be given for the "healing of the nations," and by this means the long-lost, and neglected ones, which the Occult system would hopelessly consign to annihilation, are to be gathered up and untilted by the great Economiser; so that there shall be nothing lost; and thus the fragments of the (apparently) long-lost Orb shall be collected and form a shining Sun to enlighten the still denser darkness of the neither realms.

In the above few hints, (for your space would not permit of more) I have shown *a use* for the elementals, *reliquæ*, etc., etc., which Occult science does appear to recognise; and did your space permit I should be glad to show the necessity for these in the formation of earths, and sustenance of life-forms thereon, and the position they occupy in the Cosmos; but I content myself with this bare outline.

Modern spiritualism, when viewed as an entirely new and diverse (from all that preceded) order of life,—which, instead of being the best at its beginning, commences at Zero,—is a factor which is overlooked in this respect by the *Theosophist* in its response to Mr. Terry, of Australia—(who is a personal acquaintance of my own) and is hardly satisfactory to those who accept the higher aspects of a more advanced spiritualism. Occultists say that the only safe and right way in dealing with unseen forces, entities, intelligences, or whatever else, is according to *their* method: and that to seek for or allow 'Controls' to use the human organism, is wrong, if not positively dangerous to the morals of those who permit it; but to my view, the right or wrong of this depends upon the use we make of it, and we must not be forgetful, that this "Controlling power and influence" sometimes comes with a resistless force and the sensitives are completely helpless to withstand.*

* Exactly; and since in this mad inrush of controls the poor sensitive may at any time be knocked off his moral feet down the precipice of spiritual degradation, why tamper with so dangerous a gift? Adepts never encounter a "resistless force," since adeptship means *self*-control first and then control over all forces of nature external to himself.—T. S. R.

Even the 'invocation' of spiritual beings, if the modern practice of Seance-holding can be so called, which affords conditions for spiritual manifestations—is quite in conformity with the rituals and ceremonials of the ancient Indian system; as, for instance, the *Sama Veda* says, "Come, O Father, *along with the spirits of our Fathers*."* If this practice was observed, and formed an integral part of religious worship,—and if this was done under the ægis of the Church itself in far back ages; surely with our increase of knowledge, and, we may hope, with improved morals, we may now safely engage in it with safety to both sides, provided the motives are pure and worthy. Are there not any adept "Brothers" of British or European extraction in sufficient sympathy with the efforts of their own countrymen to open up a direct correspondence with those who are striving to attain to a higher order of Life?†

[A full reply is left over for a future article.]

A PERSONAL AND AN IMPERSONAL GOD.

VARIOUS remarks that I have noticed in the *Arya* lead me to believe that, as is so commonly the case, differences in interpretations of terms, are leading to *apparent* antogonisms between persons whose views are in reality identical.

Attacks are made on those who deny the existence of a personal God, and we are told that such persons, even the believing in an Impersonal God, are in reality Atheists.

---

* We invite our brother's attention, in reference to this quotation, to what Manu says (IV. 123, &c.,) of this practioe. The *Sama Veda* dealing with the Spirits of the dead, he says that "even the sound of it (the Sama Veda) *is impure*."—T. S. R.

† This seems hardly a fair question. Our correspondent first assumes that our adepts are of an inferior order, and neither living nor capable of showing a way to "a higher order of life," and then despairingly asks if there are no adepts to teach him. What talented beings there may be in the "Solar" and "Planetary" orders—we cannot say, our experience having been confined to human adepts. But among these, we should certainly say that on the terms stated there is not one among our Brothers, whether of British or Asiatic extraction, who would volunteer for the service.—T. S. R.

Now this is simply, in my humble opinion, a mistake, resulting from differences in the significations attached by different persons to the terms Personal and Impersonal God.

Let me at the outset, however, explain, that I am not here seeking to defend the THEOSOPHIST or yourself, you are quite able to defend yourself, and I am in no way empowdered or competent to express your views or those of the Himalayan Brotherhood whose representative you are, as to the nature of the First Cause—nor do I desire to enter into any controversy with any man; I desire to live in peace and brotherly love with all men; I have my own views, which satisfy *my* head and heart, in which I firmly believe, and which I hope all other men will respect in me; and I do not doubt that others who differ from me have equally seized the views that satisfy their heads and hearts, are equally justified in holding these and have an equal claim on me to respect these their views.

Looking round the universe nothing so strongly impressed me, as the system of division of labour which pervades it. Practical results never spring from solitary causes; they are ever the resultants of the more or less divergent effects of an inextricable plexus of diverse causes. It is from contrasts, that all the joys and beauties of the world arise; it is from the equilibrium of antagonistic forces that the Universe subsists. All progress springs from difference; all evolution is the result of differentiation; as in the great, so in the spiritual; as in the visible so in the unseen universe.

How, then, can men fail to see that differences of opinion on matters spiritual are parts of the necessary mechanism of the spiritual organism that everywhere underlies (as the bones underlie the flesh and skin) the physical or visible world? How can they find fault with others for holding views different from their own? How fail to realise that those others are as truly working in harmony with the pervading design or law of the ALL as themselves? Night is as needful to our mundane economy as day; shall the night revile the day, for its glare, its noise, its heat, or the day reproach the night for its dusky stillness?

So then it is no spirit of finding fault with those who differ from me, but only in the hope of clearing away imaginary differences which being *unreal* work harm, not good as *real* differences do), that I desire to say a few words as to belief in a Personal God, in an Impersonal God and in No-God.

The three beliefs are very different and *pace* our brethren of the *Arya*, who seem to think differently, the believer in an Impersonal God is not only no Atheist, but actually in many cases holds the exact tenets of the Upanishads.

It is in the meaning of the word Person that the misconception originates.

The *Arya* says, "By personal we understand the attribute of being an individual—the essence of personality is consciousness—the knowledge of the fact that I AM." But this, if the writer will pardon my so saying, is really not a tenable position. *Persona*, or a mask, refers only to the mask of flesh and blood and bones and the associated powers that conceal, the spirit, soul or whatever it pleases men to call that portion of the human entity which survives the dissolutions of the physical body. For materialists, who believe that with this latter the entire man perishes, it *may* be correct to say that the essence of personality is consciousness, but certainly, no Vedantist could ever say this if he really understood what personality signified. The essence of *individuality* is consciousness; it is the individuality which feels "I AM," not the *personality*, which no more feels, *of itself*, I AM, than does the suit of clothes in which it is arrayed.

Now there are many good men who believe in a Personal God, a radiant, glorified man, with head and body and limbs; and they draw pictures of him (those who have haunted the galleries of Europe only know what glorious idealizations of the "human form divine" this belief has inspired), and they attribute to him human feelings, anger, repentance and the like, and they picture him to themselves, and love him as a veritable "Father who is in Heaven." But there are others (who cannot accept these conceptions which to them seem derogatory to the Infinite and absolute) who believe in an Impersonal God. They hold that God is not a mere magnified man; that he has no form or PERSONA, at any rate that we can conceive, that he is a spirit, all pervading, all sustaining, neither liable to anger, repentance or change, and hence panic (having always known from all eternity what was right and therefore what he willed), always working through immutable laws. Many of these (but by no means all) hold further that he is not *conscious* or *intelligent*, in OUR sense of the word, because both these terms imply duality, an entity to cognize and a thing to be cognized, whereas He is All in All and in Him, we and all things, move and live and have our being, but still that He is *All* consciousness and all intelligence. The believers therefore in an Impersonal God are some of them Theists, some Panthesists, but can by no means truly be designated Atheists.

Lastly there are the so-called Atheists, who *say* they believe in no God, Personal or Impersonal, who affirm that the universe is an infinite aggregation of substance, its undifferentiated condition, neither conscious nor intelligent, expanding and contracting by the inherent laws of its own being, and subject in accordance with these to alternate periods of day and night, activity and rest; who maintain that during such periods of activity in accordance still with these inherent laws, all things human and divine differentiate out of, and are evolved from, this primal all-pervading substance, to disintegrate, once more, into it as the night of rest supervenes.

These *call* themselves Atheists; and if there *be* such, they probably have the best right to assume the title, but I confess that I doubt whether even these are really Atheists.

In the first place, when they talk of laws, they overlook, it seems to me the fact, that a law postulates a law-giver—a will at any rate that has impressed a course of action—and so it seems to me that, admitting an inherent law, they cannot logically escape a will that orginated that law, and such a will in such a case *must* be what mankind understands as God.

But in the second place, though they deny this primary will, they do not really deny all Gods. For they say that in accordance witht the inherent laws, develop, not only all we see and know, but incredibly and inconceiveably higher spiritual beings, who guide and direct all things in the visible universe, and to whose power and love are due all the beauties and wonders of the world that so impress us with a sense of design.*

So then, though they may call these, Dhyan Chohans or Elohim, these exalted spiritual beings are really their Gods, and they are

* Reference is here made to the Tibetan Arhats—our Masters.—ED.

Polytheists rather than Atheists. Only it must be remembered that these, their Gods, are neither infinite nor absolute. They are finite; billions on billion of years as they subsist, they pass into non-*existence* (but whether into non-*being* or not the holders of these tenets are not agreed) with the close of the great day, and they are conditioned by the eternal inherent law of the infinite substance one of whose developments they are.

Why, they have preferred finite and conditioned Gods to one Infinite and Absolute God is clear. On the former hypothesis, the origin of evil, the *existence* of sin and suffering offer no difficulty; the Gods do their best; but there are laws of opposite polarity, of antagonistic, opposites, to which the universe owes its origin, and with it they themselves, which are above them and which they are powerless to *control*, although they can largely modify their results. They do their best; if there still remain misery and evil, it is because not being omnipotent, they cannot cure without medicine, cannot make light apparent without darkness.

Why, too, they deny the primal Will as giving with to the so-called inherent laws is also clear. So long as these are blind laws, self-existing, no one is responsible for all the sin and sorrow and suffering that these laws entail. But admit the will, then this as (*exhypothese*) Omnipotent becomes responsible for all the evil that evolves from its behests and could not therefore apparently be perfectly beneficent. Whichever way we turn, then there are difficulties. No solution of the fundament problem of the universe that in all these thousands of thousands years the mind of man has been able evolve is altogether unimpeachable.

Let us then each take the solution that best suits our mental and spiritual constitution, and let us leave our neighbours an equal freedom of choice; let us never hesitate to state and defend our own views and oppose those other views that we think wrong, but let us do all this as we would defend our own and oppose our opponent's game at chess, with no more feeling against our opponents than we have against an adversary at the noble game.

Above all let us remember that in this present life, the high theoretical questions of Personal, Impersonal, and No-God, are of less concern to us than our own everyday life about the right conduct of which no similar difficulties exist.

That we should all try to love our neighbours as ourselves, that we should forgive our enemies, that we should do good to those who do evil to us, that we should value purity of life, truth and goodness far above wealth or place or personal enjoyment,—these are truths admitted *ubique, semper et ab omnibus*, and surely these furnish a wide enough platform on which we can all, whether Bramhins, Christians, Theosophists, Aryans or what not, meet and labour in one universal being Brotherhood.

H. X.

I.

Replied by T. Subba Rao, B.A., B.L., F.T.S.

A letter signed by "H. X." has appeared in the December issue of the *Theosophist* under the heading abovementioned containing some observations on "the Theoretical Questions of Personal, Impersonal, and No-God." Anything like an intelligent discussion of these questions is beset with almost insurmountable difficulties; and it is not likely that any one, who has not exactly defined to himself what is knowable to man and what is unknowable, by a careful examination of the nature of man and his latent powers, will ever be profited by devoting any portion of his time to speculations concerning these subjects. Jesus declared that nobody had ever seen the Father; Buddha was silent when he was questioned about the nature of the Absolute and the Infinite, and our Sankaracharyar said that all that was written on these questions only revealed the depth of human ignorance. But mankind have never ceased to speculate on these questions. Thousands of conflicting hypotheses have come into existence by reason of these speculations: disputants have never ceased quarrelling about them and the human race has divided itself into hundreds of warring sects on account of their differences of opinion in theoretical Metaphysics. If, as is stated by "H.X.," differences of opinion on matters "Spiritual" are inevitable, there must be an irrepressible desire in the human being to grapple desperately with the unknowable and unknown without knowing anything about the real capabilities of his own powers.

The generality of the public (at least in this country) are accustomed to associate every religious and social movement with some particular belief regarding the subject under consideration. In their opinion every system of philosophy, science, or ethics which does not inculcate some particular doctrine with respect to the problems in question is necessarily imperfect. The importance of every religious movement, the usefulness of every association and the value of every philosophical system, is always estimated by them in connection with such belief or doctrine. An association, like the Theosophical Society, composed of various religionists and established for the purposes of religious and scientific enquiry, is a novelty to them. Consequently, enquiries are constantly being made regarding the views of the founders of the Theosophical Society and our great Teachers of the Himavat about the questions under consideration. It is represented to them by some people that they are *Nastikas*. When the great mass of the people are unaccustomed to philosophical enquiry and precise modes of thinking, the charge of Atheism is sufficient to lower in their estimation any particular individual or association. When any man's Atheism is condemned almost without hearing, no particular connotation hardly ever attached to the word; but it is associated with a large cluster of vices and deformities. It is highly desirable therefore to state to the public in clear language the doctrine of the Arhat philosophy regarding the problem in question and point out such misconceptions as are likely to arise from a perusal of the letter under review. Before proceeding further, I beg to inform my readers that in his letter "H. X." speaks of the Adwaita doctrine under the heading of impersonal God and introduces the Arhat doctrine under that of Atheism. It would have been better if he had referred to these two systems of philosophy under their proper designations. The general public have not yet accepted any one difinition of the so-called impersonal God, and the word atheism, as above stated, conveys but a very vague idea. Without attempting, therefore, to ascertain the significance of the same, I shall state the general principles of the Adwaita and the Arhat doctrines on the subject under consideration, and leave it to my readers to decide whether they indicate a belief in a *personal* or an *impersonal* God, or whether they amount to Atheism.

I shall here request my readers (such of them at least as are not acquainted with the Cosmological theories of the Idealistic thinkers of Europe) to examine John Stuart Mill's Cosmological theory as explained in his examination of Sir William Hamilton's philosophy, before attempting to understand the Adwaita doctrine; and I beg to inform them beforehand that in explaining the main principles of the said doctrine I am going to use, as far as it is convenient to do so, the phraseology adopted by English psychologists of the Idealistic School of thought. In dealing with the phenomena of our present plane of existence John Stuart Mill ultimately came to the conclusion that matter or the so-called external phenomena are but the creation of our mind; they are the mere appearances of a particular phase of our subjective self, and of our thoughts, volitions, sensations and emotions which in their totality constitute the basis of that Ego. Matter, then, is the permanent possibility of sensations; and the so-called Laws of matter are, properly speaking, the Laws which govern the succession and co-existence of our states of consciousness. Mill further holds that properly speaking there is no noumenal Ego. The very idea of a mind existing separately as an entity distinct from the states of consciousness which are supposed to inhere in it, is in his opinion illusory, as the idea of an external object which is supposed to be perceived by our senses.

Thus the ideas of mind and matter, of subject and object, of the Ego and external world are really evolved from the aggregation of our mental state which are the only realities so far as we are concerned.

The chain of our mental states of consiousness is "a double-headed monster" according to Professor Bain, which has two distinct aspects, one objetive and the other subjective.

Mr. Mill has paused here confessing that psychological analysis did not go any further, the mysterious link which connects together the train of our states of consciousness and gives rise to our Ahankaram in this condition of existence, still remains an incomprehensible mystery to Western psychologists, though its existence is but dimly perceived in the subjective phenomena of memory and expectation.

On the other hand, the great physicists of Europe are gradually coming to the conclusion* that mind is the product of matter, or that it is one of the attributes of matter in some of its conditions. It would appear, therefore, from the speculations of Western psychologists that matter is evolved from mind and that mind is evolved from matter. These two propositions are apparently irreconcilable. Mill and Tyndal have admitted that Western science is yet unable to go deeper into the question. Nor it is likely to solve the mystery hereafter, unless it calls Eastern occult science to its aid and takes a more comprehensive view of the capabilities of the real subjective self of man and the various aspects of the great objective universe. The great Adwaitee philosophers of ancient Aryavarta have examined the relationship between subject and object in every condition of existence in this solar system in which this differentiation is presented. Just as a human being is composed of 7 principles, differentiated matter in the solar system exists in 7 different conditions. These different states of matter do not all come within the range of our present objective consciousness. But they can be objectively perceived by the spiritual Ego in man. To the liberated spiritual monad of man, or to the Dhyan Chohans, every thing that is material in every condition of matter is an object of perception. Further *pragna*, or the capacity of perception, exists in 7 different aspects corresponding to the 7 conditions of matter. Strictly speaking, there are but 6 states of matter, the so-called 7th state being the aspect of Cosmic matter in its original undifferentiated condition. Similarly there are 6 states of

* See Tyndall's Belfast Address.—S. R.

differentiated Pragna, the seventh state being a condition of perfect unconsciousness. By differentiated Pragna, I mean the condition in which Pragna is split up into various states of consciousness. Thus we have 6 states of consciousness, either objective or subjective, for the time being as the case may be, and a state of perfect unconsciousness which is the beginning and the end of all conceivable states of consciousness, corresponding to the states of differentiated matter and its original undifferentiated basis which is the beginning and the end of all Cosmic evolutions. It will be easily seen that the existence of consciousness is necessary for the differentiation between subject and object. Hence these two phases are presented in 6 different conditions, and in the last state there being no consciousness as above stated, the differentiation in question ceases to exist. The number of these various conditions is different in some systems of philosophy. But whatever may be the number of divisions, they all lie between perfect unconsciousness at one end of the line and our present state of consciousness or *Bahipragna* at the other end. To understand the real nature of these different states of consciousness, I shall request my readers to compare the consciousness of the ordinary man with the consciousness of the astral man, and again compare the latter with the consciousness of the spiritual Ego in man. In these three conditions the objective Universe is not the same. But the difference between the Ego and the non-Ego is common to all these conditions. Consequently, admitting the correctness of Mill's reasoning as regards the subject and object of our present plane of consciousness, the great Adwaitee thinkers of India have extended the same reasoning to other states of consciousness, and came to the conclusion that the various conditions of the Ego and the non-Ego were but the appearances of one and the same entity—the ultimate state of unconsciousness. This entity is neither matter nor spirit; it is neither Ego nor non-Ego; and it is neither object nor subject. In the language of Hindu philosophers it is the original and eternal combination of Purusha and Prakriti. As the Adwaitees hold that an external object is merely the product of our mental state, Prakriti is nothing more than illusion, and Purush is the only reality; it is the *one* existence which remains eternal in this universe of Ideals. This entity then is the Parabrahmam of the Adwaitees. Even if there were to be a personal God with any thing like a material *upadhi* (physical basis of whatever form), from the stand-point of an Adwaitee there will be as much reason to doubt his nominal existence as there would be in the case of any other object. In their opinion conscious god cannot be the origin of the universe, as his Ego would be the effect of a previous cause, if the word conscious conveys but its ordinary meaning. They cannot admit that the grand total of all the states of consciousness in the universe is their deity, as these states are constantly changing and as Cosmic idealism ceases during Pralaya. There is only one permanent condition in the universe which is the state of perfect Unconsciousness, bare *chidakasam* in fact.

When my readers once realize the fact that this grand universe is in reality but a huge aggregation of various states of consciousness, they will not be surprised to find that the ultimate states of unconsciousness is considered as Parabrahmam by the Adwaitees.

The idea of a God, Deity, Iswar, or an impersonal God [if consciousness is one of his attributes] involves the idea of Ego in some shape or other, and as every conceivable Ego or non-Ego is evolved from this primitive element [I use this word for want of better one] the existence of an extra-cosmic god possessing such attributes prior to this condition is absolutely inconceivable. Though I have been speaking of this element as the condition of unconsciousness, it is, properly speaking, the *chidakasam* or *chinmatra* of the Hindu philosophers which contains within itself the potentiality of every condition of "Pragna," and which results as consciousness on the one hand and the objective universe on the other, by the operation of its latent *chichakti* (the power which generates thought).

Before proceeding to explain the definition of *Parabrahmam* with which my last article closes, I beg to inform my readers that in the opinion of *Adwaitees*, the *Upanishads* and the *Brahmasutras* fully support their views on the subject. It is distinctly affirmed in the *Upanishads* that *Parabramam* which is but the bare potentiality of *pragna*,* is not an aspect of *pragna* or ego in any shape and that it has neither life nor consciousness. "H. X." will be able to ascertain that such is really the case on examining the *Mundaka* and *Mundukya Upanishads*. The language used here and there in the Upanishads is apt to mislead one into the belief that such language points to the existence of a conscious *Iswar*. But the necessity for such language will be perceived on examining the following remarks.

From a close examination of Mill's Cosmological theory as explained in my last article, it will be clearly seen that it will be extremely difficult to account satisfactorily for the generation of conscious states in any human being from the standpoint of the said theory. It is generally stated that sensations arise in us from the action of the external objects around us: they are the effects of impressions made on our senses by the objective world in which we exist. This is simple enough to an ordinary mind, however difficult it may be to account for the transformation of a cerebral nerve-current into a state of consciousness.

But from the stand-point of Mill's theory we have no proof of the existence of any external object ; even the objective existence of our own senses is not a matter of certainty to us. How, then, are we to account for and explain the origin of our mental states, if they are the only entities existing in this world ? No explanation is really given by saying that one mental state gives rise to another mental state as may be shown to a certain extent by the operation of the so-called psychological "Laws of Association." Western psychology honestly admits that its analysis has not gone any further.

* The power or the capacity that gives rise to perception.

It may be inferred, however, from the said theory that there would be no reason for saying that a material *Upadhi* (basis) is necessary for the existence of mind or states of consciousness.

As is already indicated in my last article, the Aryan psychologists have traced this current of mental states to its source—the eternal *Chinmatra* existing everywhere. When the time for evolution comes this germ of *Pragna* unfolds itself and results ultimately as *Cosmic ideation.* Cosmic ideas are the conceptions of all the conditions of existence in the Cosmos existing in what may be called the universal mind (the demiurgic mind of the Western Kabalists).

This *Chinmatra* exists as it were at every geometrical point of the infinite *Chidakasam.* This principle then has two general aspects. Considered as something objective it is the *eternal Asath—Mulprakriti* or *Undifferentiated Cosmic matter.* From a subjective point of view it may be looked upon in two ways. It is *Chidakasam* when considered as the field of Cosmic ideation; and it is *Chinmatra* when considered as the germ of Cosmic ideation. These three aspects constitute the highest Trinity of the Aryan *Adwaitee* philosophers. It will be readily seen that the last mentioned aspect of the principle in question is far more important to us than the other two aspects; for, when looked upon in this aspect the principle under consideration seems to embody within itself the great Law of Cosmic evolution. And therefore the *Adwaitee* philosophers have chiefly considered it in this light, and explained their cosmogony from a subjective point of view. In doing so, however, they cannot avoid the necessity of speaking of a universal mind (and this is *Brahma,* the Creator) and its ideation. But, it ought not to be inferred therefore that this universal mind necessarily belongs to an Omnipresent living conscious Creator, simply because in ordinary parlance a mind is always spoken of in connection with a particular living being. It cannot be contended that a material *Upadhi* is indispensable for the existence of mind or mental states when the objective universe itself is, so far as we are concerned, the result of our states of consciousness. Expressions implying the existence of a conscious *Iswar* which are to be found here and there in the *Upanishads* should not therefore be literally construed.

It now remains to be seen how *Adwaitees* account for the origin of mental states in a particular individual. Apparently the mind of a particular human being is not the Universal mind. Nevertheless Cosmic ideation is the real source of the states of consciousness in every individuals. Cosmic ideation exists everywhere; but when placed under restrictions by a material *Upadhi* it results as the consciousness of the individual inhering in such *Upadhi*. Strictly speaking, an *Adwaitee* will not admit the objective existence of this material *Upadhi*. From his stand-point it is *Maya* or illusion which exists as a *necessary condition of pragna*. But to avoid confusion, I shall use the ordinary language; and to enable my readers to grasp my meaning clearly the following simile may be adopted. Suppose a bright light is placed in the centre with a curtain around it. The nature of the light that penetrates through the curtain and becomes visible to a person standing outside depends upon the nature of the curtain. If several such curtains are thus successively placed around the light, it will have to penetrate through all of them: and a person standing outside will only perceive as much light as is not intercepted by all the curtains. The central light becomes dimmer and dimmer as curtain after curtain is removed the light becomes brighter and brighter until it reaches its natural brilliancy. Similarly Universal mind or Cosmic ideation becomes more and more limited and modified by the various *Upadhis* of which a human being is composed; and when the action or influence of these various *Upadhis* is successively controlled, the mind of the individual human being is placed *en rapport* with the Universal mind and his ideation is lost in Cosmic ideation.

As I have already said these *Upadhis* are strictly speaking the conditions of the gradual development or evolution of *Bahipragna*—or consciousness in the present plane of our existence—from the original and eternal *Chinmatra* which is the 7th principle in man and the *Parabrahmam* of the *Adwaitees.*

This, then, is the purport of the *Adwaita* philosophy on the subject under consideration and it is, in my humble opinion, in harmony with the *Arhat* doctrine relating to the same subject. The latter doctrine postulates the existence of Cosmic matter in an undifferentiated condition throughout the infinite expanse of space. Space and time are but its aspects, and *Purush,* the 7th principle of the Universe, has its latent life in this Ocean of Cosmic matter. The doctrine in question explains Cosmogony from an objective point of view. When the period of activity arrives, portions of the whole differentiate according to the latent Law. When this differentiation has commenced, the concealed Wisdom or latent *Chichakti* act in the Universal mind and Cosmic energy or *Fohat* forms the manifested universe in accordance with the conceptions generated in the Universal mind out of the differentiated principles of Cosmic matter. This manifested universe constitutes a solar system. When the period of *pralaya* comes, the process of differentiation stops and cosmic ideation ceases to exist; and at the time of *Brahmapralaya* or *Mahapralaya* the particles of matter lose all differentiation and the matter that exists in the solar system returns to its original undifferentiated condition. The latent design exists in the one unborn eternal atom, the centre which exists everywhere and nowhere; and this is *the one life* that exists everywhere. Now, it will be easily seen that the undifferentiated Cosmic matter, *Purush* and the ONE LIFE of the *Arhat* philosophers are the *Mulaprakriti, Chidakasam* and *Chinmatra* of the *Adwaitee* philosophers. As regards Cosmogony, the *Arhat* stand-point is objective, and the *Adwaitee* stand-point is subjective. The *Arhat* Cosmogony accounts for the evolution of manifested solar system from undifferentiated Cosmic matter, and *Adwaitee* Cosmogony accounts for the evolution of *Bahipragna* from the original *Chinmatra*. As the different conditions of differentiated Cosmic matter are but the different aspects of the various conditions of *pragna*, the *Adwaitee* Cosmogony is but the complement of the *Arhat* Cosmogony. The eternal Principle is precisely the same in both the systems and they agree in denying the existence of an extra-Cosmic God.

"H. X." is pleased to inform his readers that the *Arhats* call themselves *Atheists*. They will be justified in doing so if *theism* inculcates the existence of a conscious God governing the Universe by his will-power. Under such circumstance the *Adwaitees* will come under the same denomination. Atheism and theism are words of doubtful import and until their meaning is definitely ascertained, it would be better not to use them in connection with any system of philosophy.

WILL.

"Sors de l'enfance ami, reveilles toi."

—*(Schopenhauer's motto.)* ROUSSEAU.

It is with the greatest interest that I read the profound article by T. Subba Row, "A Personal and an Impersonal God,"—logically arriving at a condition of unconsciousness, though containing the potentiality of every condition of "Pragna," the only permanent state in the universe.

The theory of the Idealistic thinker John Stuart Mill is metnioned in connection, who is certainly the type of Western Idealistic philosophy.

But there is another Idealist, another Western thinker, who has expressed the same long before J. S. Mill in other words, but with a candid reference to Asiatic philosophy, and given these ideas at the same time a far more palpable objectivity, as far as regards our conscious world.

Perhaps for the latter reason your readers may find an interest in his thoughts, which I allow myself to render as follows :—

"The world is my mental perception,"—this is a self-evident truth for every living and discerning being, although man alone can bring it into a reflecting abstract consciousness, and when he does do so, in fact, then philosophical reflection has begun in him. Then also it becomes a clear certainty to him, that what he knows is no Sun, no Earth, but only an eye that sees a Sun, a hand that touches an Earth, that the surrounding world is there only as a mental representation, *i.e.*, absolutely in relation to something else, which something else is himself. If any truth can be pronounced *a priori*, then it is this one, the statement of that form of all possible and thinkable experiences, more universal than all others, more so than time, space and causality. All these, in fact, presuppose already the former ; it is only the division in object and subject that makes possible and imaginable phenomena of whatsoever kind, abstract or intuitive, pure or empirical. Therefore, no truth is more certain, more independent of all others, or requiring less proof than that everything that exists in our perception is only Object in relation to Subject, the perception of that which perceives: in a word,—our own mental representation.

"And this applies as much to all Past as to the Present, and all Future; to what is most distant, and to what is most near, because it applies to time and space themselves, in which alone the relations can exist.

"This is by no means a new truth. It was already contained in the sceptical premises from which Descartes proceeded. Berkeley, however, was the first to give it an absolute form, and has thereby deserved much of philosophy, though his other doctrines cannot bear criticism. The principal mistake of Kant was his neglect of this axiom.

"*How long ago, however this 'fundamental truth has been acknowledged by the Sages of India, appearing as the funda-*

mental principle of the Vedanta philosophy, ascribed to Vyasa, is demonstrated by Sir W. Jones, in his work "On the Philosophy of the Asiatics."—(*Asiatic Researches*, Vol. IV, p. 164). The fundamental tenet of the Vedanta school consists not in denying the existence of matter, that is of solidity, impenetrability, and figure (to deny which would be lunacy), but in correcting the popular notion of it, and in contending that it has no essence independent of mental perception: that existence and perceptibility are convertible terms."

"These words express sufficiently the co-existence of empirical reality with transcendental Idealism.

"Thus only and from this aspect of the world as mental perception, can we begin to contemplate it. That such a contemplation, however, without any detriment to its truth. is one-sided, and therefore, the result of some arbitrary abstraction, is nevertheless felt by everybody and proved by that internal revolt, with which one accepts the world as one's mere mental perception, and of which, on the other hand, one can yet never entirely rid himself. Later on, however, we will make up for the one-sidedness of this consideration, by the enunciation of a truth, not so directly certain as that one from which we now proceed, but the only one to which a profounder injury can lead; still more difficult as an abstraction, the division of what is different, and union of that which is identical; a most important truth, which, if not dismaying, yet must appear critical to everyone, the following one in fact; that we can as well say, and must say—

'THE WORLD IS MY WILL.'"*

We must begin to consider not only the world, but even our own body as mere perception. That from which we are now abstracting shall presently clearly show itself as Will, of which alone the world in its other aspect consists, for that

* See Schopenhaur's chief work *Die welt als Wille und Verstallung.* *Isis Unveiled,* II. pp. 159 and 261.—L. A. S.

aspect is in one respect exclusively MENTAL PERCEPTION, but on the other absolutely WILL!*

L. A. SANDERS, F. T. S.

BORNEO, 18*th March* 1883.

EDITOR'S NOTE.—For the benefit of those of our readers in India, who, although excellent Vedantic scholars, may have never heard of Arthur Schopenhauer and his philosophy, it will be useful to say a few words regarding this German Metaphysician, who is ranked by many among the world's great philosophers. Otherwise, the above translated fragment, picked out by our brother, Mr. Sanders, for the soul purpose of showing the great identity of view, betwween the Vedanta system—the *archaic* philosophy (we beg Professor Max Müller's pardon) and the comparatively modern school of thought founded by Schopenhauer,—may appear unintelligible in its isolated form. A student of the Göttingen and Berlin Universities, a friend of Goethe and his disciple initiated by him into the mysteries of colour (See A. Schopenhauer's Essay *Ueber Sehen und Farben*, 1816,) he evoluted, so to say, into a profoundly original thinker without any seeming transaction, and brought his philosophical views into a full system before he was thirty. Possessed of a large private fortune, which enabled him to pursue and develope his ideas uninterruptedly, he remained an independent thinker and soon won for himself, on account of his strangely pessitimistic view of the world, the name of the "misanthropic sage." The idea that the present world is radically evil, is the only important point in his system that differs from the teachings of the Vedanta. According to his philosophical doctrines, the only thing truly real, original, metaphysical and absolute, is WILL. The world of objects consists simply of appearances; of *Maya* or illusion—as the Vedantins have it. It lies entirely in, and depends on, our representation. Will is the "thing in itself" of the Kantian philosophy, "the substratum of all appearances and of nature herself. It is totally different from, and wholly independent of, cognition, can exist and manifest itself without it, and actually does so in all nature from animal beings downward." Not only the voluntary actions of animated beings, but also the organic frame of their bodies, its form

---

* *An entity, however that would be none of either, but an Object for itself,* to which Kant's "*Ding an sich*" degenerated under his treatment, *is a phantasm, and its recognition a will-o'-the-whisp in* "*philosophy.*" Arthur Schopenhauer (Vol. I, p. 35,) edited in 1818, at a period when the knowledge of Sanskrit in Europe was very meagre. Schopenhauer's "Objectivation of Will" throws light upon the other side of the universe. —L. A. S.

and quality, the vegetation of plants, and in the inorganic kingdom of nature, crystallization and every other original power which manifests itself in physical and chemical phenomena, as well as gravity, are something outside of appearance and identical with what we find in ourselves and call—WILL. An intuitive recognition of the identity of will in all the phenomena separated by individuation is the source of justice, benevolence, and love; while from a non-recognition of its identity spring egotism, malice, evil and ignorance. This is the doctrine of the Vedantic *avidya* (ignorance) that makes of *Self* an object distinct from Parabrahm, of Universal Will. Individual soul, physical self, are only imagined by ignorance and have no more reality and existence than the objects seen in a dream. With Schopenhauer it also results from this original identity of will in all its phenomena, that the reward of the good and the punishment of the bad are not reserved to a future heaven or a future hell, but are ever present (the doctrine of *Karma*, when philosophically considered and from its esoteric aspect). Of course the philosophy of Schopenhauer was radically at variance with the systems of Schelling, Hegel, Herbert and other contemporaries, and even with that of Fichte, for a time his master, and whose philosophical system while studying under him, he openly treated with the greatest contempt. But this detracts in nothing from his own original and profoundly philosophical though often too pessimistic views. His doctrines are mostly interesting when compared with those of the Vedanta of "Sunkar-charya's" school, inasmuch they show the great identity of thought arriving at the same conclusions between men of two quite different epochs, and with over two milleniums between them. When some of the mightiest and most puzzling problems of being are thus approximately solved at different ages and by men entirely independent of one another, and that the most philosophically profound propositions, premises and conclusions arrived at by our best modern thinkers are found on comparison nearly, and very often entirely, identical with those of older philosophers as enunciated by them thousands of years back, we may be justified in regarding "the heathen" systems as the primal and most pure sources of every subsequent philosophical development of thought.

ADWAITA PHILOSOPHY.

[As the subjoined letter comes from such a learned source, we do not feel justified in commenting upon it editorially, our personal knowledge of the Adwaita doctorine being unquestionably very meagre when contrasted with that of a Paramahamsa. Yet we felt a strong suspicion that, whether owing to a mistranslation or an "original misconception" there was an error with regard to Tadpada, called herein the 8th principle. Hence—the foot-notes by our learned brother T. Subba Row, to whom we turned over the MS. for reply. We know of no better authority in INDIA in anything concerning the esotericism of the Adwaita philosophy.—*Ed.*]

The following few lines are from an Indian Hermit in the Himalayas—and these convey a mere hint which may help to eradicate by means of your valuable journal a very serious *error* which has been misleading the Western Philosophers for the past (nearly) nineteen hundred years—we mean the historical sense in which the Bible has been accepted by the Orthodox Christians of the day. We are surprised to find that the modern spiritualists in the West have ignored this very important subject and are sitting quite apathetic—while they profess to have pledged themselves to the establishment of truth.

We see that the British Government makes now and then a sudden and spasmodic effort to have the English version of the Bible revised and corrected; and still the good people of Christendom—(we mean that portion which is seeking after truth—and not the selfish and handsomely paid missionaries) —fail to reap the fruit they so long for. Now and again we find some correspondence on this subject in the THEOSOPHIST, but it does not seem to end in any tangible result. Up to this time we have been reading and hearing of only the literal Bible, but not a single word of the esoteric spirit to enliven it do we find therein. If the Bible, as interpreted by the bigoted missionaries, is really a book of history, or even of morality, then, it cannot be a book of divine inspiration; hence but little fit to form the foundation of State-religions. Unless a full view be taken of the Bible from different stand-points, it cannot be decided whether it be true or not. We will try to put its credibility to a test by a few points quoted from the New Testament, and see :—

1.—Whether the Bible speaks symbolically or literally, *i.e.*, whether the Bible is Theosophy or History ?

2.—Whether the guiding star which appeared to the wise men from the East was really a star or only a metaphor for something higher and nobler ?

3.—Whether the powers ascribed to Christ in the Bible were physical, metaphysical, (supersensuous ?) or spiritual ?

4.—Whether a *gijnasu* (seeker after truth and salvation) can derive the smallest benefit from ths said Biblical history of the physical and incarnate Christ ?

5.—What is the proper time to practise the teachings of the Bible? And who are the persons most fit to study the New Testament ?

These are the few points in which the Bible ought to be examined.

On behalf of our sister Theosophy, we give our personal solutions upon the questions as above raised. We call upon all the spiritually inclined, right-thinking, pious and impartial men and Theosophists throughout the four quarters of the Globe to judge of, and to criticise, our answers, and to give their verdict in the matter. The subject is one of the greatest importance, and if need be, will be decided by appealing even to the verdict of the SPIRIT itself.

1.—As a book of Revelation the Bible cannot and ought not to be a book of history.

2.—Its utterances are almost entirely allegorical : and a spiritual commentary is urgently needed to make them acceptable to the students of Theosophy. Vedanta and the New Testament, if properly understood, mean the same thing in the abstract.

3.—The guiding star does by no means mean a real objective star ; such a version is quite against the laws of Nature, Reason and Theosophy. Vedantists regard this star as PRANAVA, or *Jivatma*, the witness soul or *Sakshi Chaitanya*.

It is the seventh principle of the Theosophists,* Yoga-Acharyas, *Tantrikas* and Shivas, called in Brahmavidya or Mahavidya.† The Mahomedan Theosophists believe and teach of the existence of this star before Creation, or before *Táus* (peacock) was produced. Temples dedicated to this allegorical Star are yet to be found among several nations of Asia; and some great Theologians speak of this star as "Spirit." We hermits—if any value be attached to our words—regard it as *kutastha* and liable to be merged into the eighth principle or *Tatpada*‡ as such. We do not understand, how it can

---

* Strictly speaking *Pranava* is not *Jivatma* or the 7th principle in man. It represents the condition or the aspect of the 7th principle in the highest state of Nirvana—T. SUBBA ROW.

† The 7th principle itself can never be called by either of those names, though it may be the subject of BRAHMAVIDYA OR MAHAVIDYA.—T. S. R.

‡ The statement is not quite in accordance with the doctrines of Adwaita philosophy. If the star in question is taken to indicate the 7th principle in man as above stated,—it is not *Kutastha* from the standpoint of a real Adwaitee. As is well-known to learned Adwaitee a clear line of distinction is drawn between *Kutastha* and *Uttamapurusha* (otherwise called Paramatma) in a well-known Sloka of Bhagavat-Gita:—

द्वाविमौ पुरुषौ लोके क्षरश्चाक्षर एव च ॥
क्षरः सर्वाणि भूतानि कूटस्थोऽक्षरउच्यते ॥

अध्या० १५ श्लो० १६.

Now if *Kutastha* means the 7th principle in man, the distinction thus drawn will really be a distinction between Paramatma and Jeevatma. This distinction or separation is denied by *real* Adwaitees. Hence, as is clearly pointed out by Sankaracharia in his able Commentary on the above-mentioned Sloka, as well as in the other portions of his "Bhashyam," *Kutastha* is not the 7th principle in man. It is merely called *Vignanatma* by Sankaracharia and corresponds with the 7th spiritual Ego or the 6th principle of the Theosophists.

It is absurd to say that the "Tatpada" is the 8th principle. Now, this *Tatpada* is either identical with the 7th principle or it is not. If it is really identical with the *Tawampada* of the Mahavakya it is impossible to understand why it should be described as the 8th principle. If it is not, the views of the learned Hermit are opposed to the fundamental doctrine of the Adwaita philosophy and the grand truth indicated by the Samaveda Mahavakyam alluded to. I invite the great Paramahamsa Swami of Almora to explain what he really means.

T. SUBBA ROW.

appear as a material substance to some particular persons (wise men) when it has existed from the unknown and *unknowable* time! How can it be possible that a material thing, unless compelled and then drawn back by some living-force, should stop of itself as described in the Bible? We are of opinion that the star in question is nothing but spirit and is identical with the entity meant in the Revelation. It is as if it were a condensed spirit (*viz.* Soul); and this star ought to be taken as the real Christ, the Saviour and the guide.

4.—To call the powers ascribed to Christ, physical or metaphysical, is sheer ignorance and an insult to Spirit. Hitherto many adepts have been seen and heard of, to possess extraordinary powers of various kinds, more marvellous than those described in the Bible; and these were all spiritual. The Tantras, Yoga and other Aryan occult works will tell how they can be acquired. We have already stated that, unless a spiritual commentary is added to the Bible, it is worse than useless to a follower of Theosophy; and no spiritual benefit whatever can ensure from it, except perhaps the idea of an imaginary and external "Heaven and Hell."

5.—The Old Testament is the Karma Kanda; and the New Testament, the Gyana Kanda of Theosophy. Those only who have prepared themselves after going through the routine of the Old Testament are entitled to practise the teachings of the New Testament; and not the schoolboys or the low castemen to whom it is now-a-days offered by the missionaries. The former, *i. e.*, boys and low castes, are not fit persons for it.

In conclusion, we earnestly request Mr. Oxley, who have been so good as to take such a kind notice of the *Bhagavat-Gita*, and who is so eminently qualified for the task; and also appeal to the fellows of the Theosophical Society, who have spiritual Gurus to consult, and with whom they ought to communicate on the subject, to take in hand this arduous task of interpreting the Bible esoterically. For, nothing will better help the growth of Theosophy in both East and West.

Firstly, we make an appeal to the "Comforter" (the Holy Ghost of the Bible) itself, to decide whether the Bible has an allegorical, spiritual or a literal dead-letter meaning. We may also remark here that some of the Brothers whom we find occasionally mentioned in the *Theosophist*, and whom we have the pleasure of knowing by another name,* would approve of our plan if asked. But the star itself—our every-day guide—has directed us to write this. All the seekers of truth ought to enquire into this solemn subject, without the least prejudice or bias. Millions of generations are interested in this question; and to solve it for the good of humanity should be the aim of every true Theosophist.†

ALMORA, PATALDEVI,
12th *December* 1882. } PARAMAHAMSA SWAMI.

"*H. X.*" *AND GOD PERSONAL AND IMPERSONAL.*

"H. X." in the above named article writes about the so-called Atheists: "In the first place while they talk of laws, they overlook, it seems to me, the fact that a law postulates a law-giver—a will at any rate that has impressed a course of action —and so it seems to me that admitting an inherent law, they cannot logically escape a will that originated that law, and such a will in such a case *must* be what mankind understands as God."

---

* Not that of "refined Tantrikas"—we hope, as they were once called?—T. S. R.

† Those who have any knowledge of the "Brothers" are well aware that they have ever and most emphatically insisted upon the esoteric interpretation of the ancient Scriptures of every great religion. "Isis Unveiled," by H. P. Blavatsky, is full of the real meaning—as interpreted by the Kabalists—of the Jewish and Christian Bible. And now, there has just been published that wonderfully clever book written by two English seers—"The Perfect Way," a work of which it can be truly said that it is more inspired than the book it interprets. But, why should the learned Swami of Almora insist upon the esoteric interpretation of the Bible alone without any concern for the Vedas, the *Tripitakas* and the *Upanishads*, all three far more important, is something we fail to comprehend.—T. S. R.

If I am allowed to paraphrase this freely, it can be rendered thus:—

One of the fundamental laws of the Universe is that there *can* be no law without a law-giver.

Now, I find this assumption in Mill, if I am not mistaken, in what is appropriately called his 'Carpenter's theory of the Universe.' Mr. Joseph Cook in his Boston lectures, and subsequently at Bombay, uses the same argument; and doubtless many men take this for an axiom, as I did only a little while ago. But on investigation I find it not true in all cases. Their deduction from this is inconsistent with the axiom; and this delusion arises from the fact that human laws *created* by human beings are confounded with universal laws; and by analogy it is inferred, that those latter also must have been created by a law-giver. I proceed to show what, I believe, is an inconsistency in those who argue in this fashion. Just on account of its inconsistency with itseif, the argument will not be clear, but may be intelligible on reflection.

If, then, 'That there can be no law without a law-giver' is a *universal* law, then, by this very law, which, to avoid confusion of ideas, I shall call the *Law* of laws, it must itself have a *law-giver*. This very *giving* of law implies that there was a time when the law did not exist,—*i. e.*, before the will of the Giver 'impressed the course of action.' If this is admitted, then, there was a time when laws did not require a law-giver; is it not *possible* to conceive they may have existed then? They may have, or they may not, but it is, at least, a *possible* conception. If, on the other hand, anybody would say that this 'giving' does not imply any limit of time (which is a very audacious suggestion, to say the least,) even then he does not gain much by it. For, if the law were eternal, it was co-eternal with the giver, *it had no birth*; in fact, *it was not given* and there was no *giver*.

Having shown this difficulty in the way of accepting "H. X.'s" hypothesis, I have only to remark that his idea of 'personal' God is not without difficulties to me.

B. J. P.

IN RE *ADWAITA PHILOSOPHY.*

WILL the Editor satisfy us by moving the assertion that "matter is as eternal and indestructible as spirit?" The assertion was made in the Editor's note to a correspondent's letter on 'Karma' (*vide* page 89 of the *Theosophist* for January 1883). You should bear in mind that we are speaking of matter and spirit beyond the present developed form, or in the stage of perfect *Laya** according to Patanjali's second and third *Sûtras*, or, from the stand-point of the Esoteric Theosophy. Could you kindly explain what is meant by *Satta Samanya* (सत्तासामान्य) and *Parampadam* (परमपदम्) of the Aryan adepts, Nirvana of the Buddhas, and the Philosopher's stone of the votaries of other occult philosophies? As far as we understand the Aryan Theosophy, when the *Mahapralaya* takes place, matter is absorbed by, or dissolved into, *Mahat-tattwam* (महत् तत्त्वम) and the same again into *Prakriti*, and the Prakiti finally into *Pûrûsha* or *Parampadam.*

In the same way of the components of the mysterious letter Om (अ) A (अ) is dissolved into U (उ) and the *raja* part of U (उ) into M (म्) You will thus see that matter and force can both be *layed* (or dissolved) ultimately into the Spirit which alone remains as "True," and should be called Eternal—which term neither matter nor force deserve—being liable to evolution from, and dissolution into, Spirit—or the Absolute. As you are well acquainted with the doctrines of the Adwaita Vedanta, it is needless to write more on this subject.

We would, however, call your attention to page 99 of the same number of the *Theosophist,* and entreat you to remove our doubt by establishing scientifically a certain point. Who was it that died as stated in the article "Can the Double murder?" According to our belief man exists in a three-fold way; 1st, externally; 2nd, internally; and 3rd, spiritually.

---

* *Laya*, or a state of absolute dissolution, *annihilation* of all substance.—*Ed.*

(1) By externally we mean in gross body (स्थूलशरीरम्) or Annamaya(अन्नमय). (2) The internal fold is the astral body formed of the three koshas or cases, viz. :--Pranamaya (प्राणमय), Manamaya (मनमय), and Vignyanmaya (विज्ञानमय). (3) The spiritual fold is the Pragna state or Anandmaya (आनन्दमय). You say "* * * that a mortal wound may be inflicted upon the inner man, &c., &c." Now what do you mean by the inner man here? The question to be settled is whether the double murdered the double or treble. In our opinion the double murdered the treble and not the double--and in no case the spiritual--one. Our object in writing this is to ask you to kindly ascertain what is the extent of a human will's influence, or in other words. Can the *Mayavi Rupa* be also annihilated by mesmeric force or the material body only?

ALMORA PATALDEVI,
20*th January* 1883.

SWAMI OF ALMORA.

EDITOR'S NOTE:—To our utter amazement, we are called upon to prove that matter is indestructible; at any rate, that "matter is as eternal and indestructible as spirit!" Though the question and proofs as to the eternity and indestructibility of matter alone, might be safely left to the Royal Society to answer, yet we are fully prepared to satisfy our learned correspondent, and, with his permission, will answer all his queries.

We are asked to bear in mind that the *entities* in question are "matter and spirit beyond the present developed form, or in the stage of perfect *Laya*."

We are unable to understand what is really meant by "spirit beyond the present developed form." The sentence presents no sense to our mind, trained as it has been by our great Masters to think of "Spirit" as of something formless and entirely beyond the ken of our sensual perceptions, and, therefore, not to be considered apart from, or independently of, corporeal existence. UNIVERSAL INTELLIGENCE and the ONE LIFE, as we call it, conceived of, apart from any physical organization, becomes vital essence, an energy of force; and none of these we believe can be considered as a distinct entity, a substance, or, as having a being or even a form separate from matter. Locke's definition, that "Spirit is a *substance*, in which thinking; knowing, doubting and a power of moving do subsist"—would hardly be accepted by the average Vedantee, and would find itself absolutely rejected by every true Adwaitee and Eastern Occultist. The latter would answer that "matter alone is a substance, in which thinking, knowing, doubting, and a power of moving, are *inherent*, whether as a latent or active potentiality—and whether that matter is in a differentiated, or an undifferentiated state.

Thus, in our humble opinion, the something, or rather the *no*-thing, called Spirit, has by itself, no form or forms in either progressive or stationary "states of development;" and we say again that the expression is perfectly unintelligible to every real Adwaitee. Even supposing that the qualifying clause refers only to matter, the meaning conveyed by the expression "matter and spirit beyond the present developed form" is the same as conveyed by that of—"matter and spirit in the stage of perfect *Laya*"? We fail to see the point made, or even any sense in such a sentence as "matter and spirit in the stage of perfect *Laya*," implying as it does the possibility of spirit, a pure abstraction, being dissolved and annihilated—we will not say—as matter— since the latter in its primordial, cosmic state can be no more annihilated or even dissolved than spirit—but as a *thing* of matter having substance and form. Can a *void* be annihilated? And what is pure, *absolute* spirit but the "void" of the ancient Greek philosophers? Well, says Lucretius, "there can be no third thing besides body and void; for if it be to the smallest extent tangible—it is *body*; if not,—it is void." And let it not be urged, on the strength of this quotation, that because we quote the words of a great "Atheist," a *materialist*, as an authority, we are therefore a materialist and an atheist (in the usual sense of both terms) ourself. We object to the very term "materialism" if it is to be made indentical with, or a synonym of "corporealism," that is to say, an antithesis of, "Spiritualism." In the light we, Occultists, regard matter, we are all materialists. But it does not at all stand to reason that because of that, we should be, at the same time, "corporealists," denying in any sense or way the reality of the so-called spiritual existence, or of any being or beings, living on another plane of life, in higher and far more perfect worlds than ours, having their being in *states* of which no untrained mind can have the smallest conception. Hence our objection to the idea and possibility of "matter and spirit, in the stage of perfect *Laya*" unless it can be shown that we have misunderstood the latter word. According to the doctrines of the Arhat philosophy there are *seven* states of matter, the 7th state being the sum total, the condition or aspect of *Mulaprakriti*.*

Consequently the state of Cosmic matter beyond its "present developed form" may mean any of the other six states in which it exists; and

* Undifferentiated cosmic matter.

hence it cannot necessarily mean "matter in a stage of perfect Laya." In what sense, then, does the learned querist want us to interpret the words "matter" and "spirit"? For, though we are aware that there exist, even in the present age of science and enlightenment, persons who, under the pretext of religion, teach the ignorant masses that there was a time when matter *did not exist* (since it was *created*) implying thus that there will come a moment when it will be annihilated, we have never yet met any one, whether atheist or deist, materialist or spiritualist, who would presume to say that spirit—whether we call it "void" or "divine breath"—can ever be *annihilated*; and if the word *Laya* means *annihilation*, the very expression used by the respected Swami involves an assumption that "spirit" can be destroyed in course of time. In such a case, we are evidently called upon to demonstrate that matter and spirit are eternal on the supposition that both have a period of *Laya*." If we are to avoid this extremely *awkward* conclusion, what is the purport of the Swami's question? Verily, it would have been better if he had allowed us the privilege of interpreting our own statements. Moreover, our learned opponent is not satisfied with merely giving us his own—begging his pardon—incomprehensible definition of matter and spirit, to enable us to prove our "assertion," but we are asked to answer the question "according to Patanjali's second and third *Sutras*, or, from the stand-point of esoteric theosophy." How or why should the Swami think or know, that we made the statement in question on the authority of Patanjali's treatise? Or is Patanjali's philosophy identical with esoteric theosophy in his opinion? If not, why should our statement be *sine qua non* proved only "according" to that philosopher's *second and third Sutras*? It would be just as reasonable to call upon us to prove the proposition under consideration from the stand-point of the Salvationists. As it is almost hopeless for us to understand his definition, or satisfy his curiosity under the extraordinary restrictions imposed, we shall, with the venerable Swami's permission, interpret our "assertion" in our own way and *prove it* agreeably to esoteric theosophy, and we hope, in accordance with the Adwaita philosophy, that our corrrespondent knows so well.

Our "assertion" then means the following Undifferentiated cosmic matter or *Mulaprakriti*, as it is called in Hindu books, is *uncreated* and eternal. It would be impossible to prove this assertion from *à priori* reasons, but its truth can be tested by the ordinary inductive method. In every objective phenomenon perceived, either in the present plane of consciousness or in any other plane requiring the exercise of spiritual faculties, there is but change of cosmic matter from one form to another. There is not a single instance, or the remotest suspicion of the annihilation of an atom of matter ever brought to light either by Eastern Adepts or Western scientists. When the common experience of generations of

Adepts in their own spiritual or psychic field of observation, and of the ordinary people in theirs—(*i. e.*, in the domain of physical science) points to the conclusion that there never has been utter annihilation of a single material particle, we are justified we believe, in saying that matter is in destructible though it may change its forms and properties and appear in various degrees of differentiation. Hindu and Buddhist philosophers have ages ago recognised the fact that *Purush* and *Prakriti* are eternal, co-existent, and not only correlative and interdependent, but positively one and the same thing for him who can read between the lines. Every system of evolution commences with postulating the existence of *Mulaprakriti* or *Tamas* (primeval darkness). Leaving aside the great authority of Kapila on the subject, we may refer to the celebrated Rik of *Rigveda* describing this Primeval Chaos, and using such expression as :—

"*Tama eva purasthath abhavath viswarupam*" and "*Asthwa ithamagra Asith,*"* etc.—

scattered throughout the *Veda* and the *Upanishads* in support of our assertion. All those Great philosophers of India who have added the ancient wisdom-religion of Agasthya, Thoorwasa and other Rishis to the pure Adwaita philosophy of Vasishta, Vyasa and Suka, have recognized this fact. Gaudapatha and Sankaracharya have given expression to their views on the subject in their works, and those views are in perfect accordance with their doctrines of the Arhat philosophy. The authority of the latter two great philosophers will, we believe, be sufficient to show to the learned Swami, since he is an Adwaitee, that our statement is correct. And primeval Cosmic matter, whether called Asath or Tamas, or Prakriti or Sakti, is ever the same, and held to be eternal by both Hindu and Arhat philosophers, while *Purusha* is inconceivable, hence non-existent, save when manifesting through Prakriti. In its undifferentiated condition, some Adwaitees refuse to recognize it as matter, properly so called. Nevertheless this entity is their PARABRAHMAM, with its dual aspect of Purush and Prakriti. In their opinion it can be called neither; hence in some passages of the *Upanishads* we find the expression "PRAKRITI-*layam*" mentioned; but in all such passages the word "Prakriti" means, as we can prove—*matter in a state of differentiation*, while *undifferentiated* Cosmic matter in conjunction with, or rather in its aspect of *latent* spirit is always referred to as "MAH-ISWARA," "Purusha" and "Parampada." The description given by our learned correspondent and the very words used by him when he says, "when the Mahapralaya takes place, matter is *absorbed* by, or *dissolved* into, *Mahat-tatwa*, and the same again into PRAKRITI, and the Prakriti finally into *Purusha* or *Parampadam*"—show that he is either waging a war of words, or seeking to draw us out

---

* "Primeval darkness resulted as the manifested universe" and "Asath or Prakriti existed first."—*Ed.*

(whether for friendly purposes, or otherwise, he knows himself best) for neither the words "*absorbed* by," or "*dissolved* into," can mean *annihilated*. Why should he then use against his own argument the term "*Laya*," since if he once calls himself an Adwaitee, he *must* know the doctrine, and therefore understand the various senses in which such specific terms are used. Thus, we shall feel grateful to our learned correspondent if he can quote to us a few authorities in support of *his* statement about the dissolution of *Mahat-tatwa** and *Prakriti* at the time of MAHAPRALAYA. We shall then be able to see what the Aryan philosophers really meant by such an assertion.

In reference to the real meaning of *Satta Samanya* and *Parampada*† of the Aryan Adepts, Nirvana of the Buddhas and the "Philosopher's stone," their meanings are identical in both the Aryan and Arhat secret doctrines. *Satta Samanya* sometimes means *latent spirit*. It also means "Guna *Samyapadhi*," or the undifferentiated condition of SATWAGUNA, RAJAGUNA and TAMAGUNA‡. As to *Parampada* and Nirvana, both mean the same thing. From an objective point of view it is the condition of Purusha-Prakriti as above described; from the subjective—it is a state of perfect unconsciousness resulting as bare *Chidakasam*.

If the Swami is desirous to learn more about the "Philosopher's stone" of "the votaries Of other Occult Philosophies," then we may refer him to our foot-notes to the articles "Gleanings from Eliphas Levi," published in the January number of the *Theosophist*, and other sundry articles. If the " other Occult Philosophies " are worthy of their name, then the doctrines taught in them must not differ save in the names given to identical things. Truth is but one, and of two different versions one must be necessarily false. We are not prepared to accept the interpretation given of the world *Aum*, since the above interpretation is not quite consistent with the doctrines of the Adwaitee Vedanta philosophy. We shall feel grateful, nevertheless, if the learned Swami can refer us to any great Adwaitee philosopher as an authority in support of his explanation.

No less puzzling are his curious ideas about our *supposed* meaning and views about the potentialities and nature of the human double.

---

* *Mahat-tatwa* corresponds to the spiritual Light, or the *Sephira* of the Jewish Kabalists.—*Ed.*

† Literally—*the most sacred places*, means Nirvana or the condition of *Moksha*—*Ed.*

‡ *Satwaguna*—the quality of passivity, or absence of any cause of disturbance; *Rajaguna*—the quality of activity, or that which induces to action; *Tamguna*—the quality of ignorance, inactivity of mental and spiritual faculties arising from that ignorance.—*Ed.*

The question is not "whether the double murdered the double or the treble," for neither the "double" nor the higher "treble" (if, as we suppose the 5th, 6th and 7th principles are meant) can be *murdered* by living man or ghost. The fact we suppose to be that by the concentrated energy of implacable hate [of Prince Obrenovitch's foster-mother against his assassin], and through the agency of the clairvoyant's double, "*the* silver cord" of life was snapped and the inner-man *driven* out of its physical covering. The wound which destroyed life, *i. e.* broke up the relationship between the *Sthoolsariram*, with its informing *Jiva*, and those other component parts of the entire personality, was inflicted upon the lower "treble"—if the Swami of Almora must use the clumsy term, even in sarcasm—without first transpiercing the physical body. In a case of natural death the citadel of life is captured, so to speak, only by gradual approaches; in deaths of violence it is taken with a rush. If fright, or joy, or the lethal current of hatred be the cause, the body will show no wound yet life be extinguished all the same. Sorcerers' victims usually appear as though killed by heart disease or apoplexy; chemical analysis will afford no clue to the assassin's method, nor the surgeon be able to find a suspicious mark upon the *surface* of the cadaver.

THE ALMORA SWAMI.

UPON PHILOSOPHY IN GENERAL AND OUR FAILINGS IN PARTICULAR.

In our February number (see page 118) prefacing the valuable though somewhat hazy contribution by the venerable Swami of Almora on "Adwaita Philosophy," we wrote the following editorial lines :—

"As the subjoined letter comes from such a learned source, we do not feel justified in commenting upon it editorially. Our personal knowledge of the Adwaita doctrine being unquestionably meagre when contrasted with that of a Paramahansa—*hence* THE FOOT NOTES BY OUR LEARNED BROTHER T. SUBBA ROW, TO WHOM WE TURNED OVER THE MS. FOR REPLY."

This notice, we believe, was plain enough to screen us thereafter from any such personal remarks as are now flung at our head by the holy ascetic of Almora in the paper that follows. Some of those rhetorical blossoms having been left by us for the purpose of enlivening the otherwise too monotonous field of his philosophical subject, the reader may judge for himself. We say "some," for, having to satisfy all our contributors, and our space being limited, we cannot consent to crowd out more interesting matter to make room for just 15½ columns of quotations profusely mixed with reprimands and flings of any correspondent, even though the latter be as, we learn from his own words, "a modest hermit of the jungle." Therefore, with all our profound respect for our opponent, we had to curtail his too long paper considerably. We propose, however, to show him his chief mistake, and thus to blunt a few of the most pointed shafts intended to pierce through the points of the editorial harness.

If, after the humble confession quoted above from our February number, the editorial reply that followed another paper from the same ascetic, namely, the *In re* "Adwaita Philosophy," in the March number—was still taken as emanating from one who had just confessed her incompetency to hold a disputation with the learned Swami upon Adwaita tenets—the fault is not ours. This error is the more strange since the Swami had been clearly warned that his points would be disputed and questions answered in future by our brother Mr. T. Subba Row, as learned in Adwaita philosophy as in the esotericism of the sacred books of the East. Therefore we had a right to expect that the *Paramahansa* would have remembered that he was ventilating his not over-kind remarks upon the wrong person, since *we had nothing to do personally* with the replies. Thus the disagreement upon various topics in general, and the abstruse tenets of esoteric Adwaita Philosophy especially, between the "Almora Swami" and Mr. T. Subba Row, can, in no way, or with any degree of justice, be laid by the former at the door of either the "foreigners who have come to India for knowledge," nor of "Western Theosophy;" for, in this particular case he has found an opponent (quite as learned, we love to think as himself) in one of his own race and country—a real Adwaitee Brahmin. To take therefore to task theosophy for it or the conductor of this magazine, expressing dissatisfaction in such very strong terms, does not show either that philosophical equanimity, or tact and discrimination that might be expected from one who has devoted his life exclusively to meditation and the Yoga Philosophy. If pardonable in a person who has to lead that sort of life which in the word of Mr. Max Müller, quoted by the "Almora Swami"—(as an additional hint and a *hit* we suppose)—a life "with telegrams, letters, newspapers, reviews, pamphlets and books"—it is quite unpardonable in a holy ascetic, who is never troubled with anything of the sort, and gets, as we suspect, even his appropriate quotations from European authors ready-made for him by his amanuenses and friends. But, since the article is addressed in the form of a letter to the editor, the humble individual who holds this office hastens to assure the venerable Swami that beyond their appalling length, his letters have never given the said editor one moment of "annoyance and trouble," as he seems to imagine.

In reference to another personal taunt, we agree with him. It is more than likely that some (not all by any means) Vedantists, such as the modern "Aryas" and some Dwaitees and Visishtadwaitees—aftar "hailing Western Theosophy with joy," have ended by comparing it "to the mountain that gave birth to a mouse"—the disenchantment being due to many and various reasons upon which it is needless to enter at present. We can only hope and trust that the lofty Almorian mountain, chosen by our venerable friend as the seat of his contemplation, may not bring forth some day, for India, any worse animal than the humble "black mouse." True we have come to *learn* in this country, and we have learned a good deal already. One fact, among several others, namely, that the learned ascetics of modern India have widely shot off from the original mark when compared with the Rishis of old. Spinoza is quoted against us in this definition of methods of investigation. Our saintly critic fears that his venerable friends have followed the first (or vulgar) method. The proof which with him goes far to justify his "fear," rests chiefly upon a *fallacy and mistake* of ours—(one happily held by us in common with nearly all the great men of science in Europe, *viz.*, our *ignorant* claim—THE MATTER IS INDESTRUCTIBLE, HENCE ETERNAL. We will not understand his ideas, he says, because being fond of absurdities, "our own absurdity would be exposed." If so, we prefer indeed our absurd belief in the indestructibility of matter to any scientific opinion upholding the contrary submitting cheerfully, in this case, "the weakness of our understanding to be laughed at"—even by an ascetic in "the state of Nirvikalpa."

We feel very grateful to the good Swami for his explanation of "Pranava" and other kindred words. Mr. Subba Row will no doubt profit by, and answer them. Personally, however, we respectfully decline to be taught the noble science by any other man, however learned he may be, than him who has originally undertaken the task—namely, our own MASTER: yet, as many of our readers may well benefit by the controversy, we will, with his permission, leave the arena for the present to Mr. Subba Row, a far abler controversialist than we can ever hope to become.

THE SWAMI OF ALMORA TO HIS OPPONENTS.

"WE DO NOT WAGE WAR OF WORDS, BUT SIMPLY SPEAK AND SEEK TRUTH."

WE are sorry to see that we have been the cause of something like irritation to you by our last letter, which perhaps was not suitable to the modesty of a hermit. Therefore, we beg your pardon, if there was in it anything offensive to you, and, at the same time, beg liberty to speak the truth. We are always friendly to every one, but particularly to the foreigners, who have come to India for knowledge. We are friendly in the spiritual sense of the word, therefore, we must be taken as a real friend and not a flatterer, even if we say something disagreeable now and then. . . . Those who seek to find fault with us and become hostile to us are, we think, prejudiced and stubborn, and we desire them to acquire simplicity of heart and an unbiassed mind to enable them to understand *us* thoroughly.* We hermits are a nomadic class of people and generally pass our time in places far away from habitation, and do not much cultivate the language and idioms of the world, nor do we care much for these. To attack us about modes of our expressing our ideas is, therefore, only childish. Our readers are to take our idea only and not our style. Because,--we are neither an M.A., nor a B.A.; neither an Addison, nor a Johnson, nor a Macaulay, but simply a hermit of the jungle.

Let us now see what was the purport of our letter. Our words were, "you should bear in mind that, *we* are speaking of matter and spirit beyond the present developed form or in the state of perfect *laya*, according to Patanjali's 2nd and 3rd Sutras, or from the stand-point of the Esoteric Theosophy." How can this mean that we are asking you to answer the questions according to Patanjali's 2nd and 3rd Sutras, we fail to understand. By the above sentences, we simply meant to show our own stand-point whence our enquiry commences. We referred to Patanjali's Sutras, because we intended to show that our starting point was in perfect accord with the true yoga state, *nirvikalpa*, ecstasy, *i. e.*, the Turya state, and not with ordinary Jagrata, Swapna and Sushupta (for the former, *i. e.*, Turya, state of man is of real awaking and the latter illusory), while you have been pleased to understand us as speaking of ordinary human states. Moreover, by *laya*, we never meant annihilation, as is assumed by you. It is your own version that the word *laya* means "a state of absolute dissolution, annihilation of all substance, differentiated, &c." In some of the former numbers of the *Theosophist* the word laya was explained by you as merging, and in this number you

* Quite so; and therefore, this kind desire is fully reciprocated.—*Ed.*

give another meaning of it.* Why, merely because you require a handle to *ridicule* us. However, we forget all this, and beg to say, that according to Aryan adepts, by laya is meant and understood "absorption or transformation of one thing into another," such as the river is absorbed or transformed, when it loses itself, in the sea. It is a process among the Aryan occultists, by which they can (like the modern scientific Realists and Chemists as you understand them), analyse the different component parts of a compound body, and reduce them to their primary or original condition—and by which they are not only able to ascertain what the substance really is, but they can also penetrate into the mystery of its past and future, to make themselves certain about the cause of the origin and termination of the phenomenon, known as creation or *dwaita* in its present manifested form. It is odd that our phrase "present developed form" has cost you more than a column to comment on it.† We might here explain our meaning. By this we simply meant soul in its Viswa, Taijasha, and Pragna, states, or, the spirit in its impure condition by contact with matter and force, *i. e.*, in a state of duality. But, perhaps, nominal yogees, who are disturbed in head and heart, cannot tranquillize and compose

* No "merging" or absorption can take place without *dissolution*, and an absolute annihilation of the previous form. The lump of sugar thrown into a cup of liquid must be dissolved and its form annihilated before it can be said to have been absorbed by, and in, the liquid. It is a correlation like any other in chemistry. Yet indestructible matter can as in the case of sugar, or any other chemical element, be recalled to life and even to its previous form. The molecule that cannot be divided by any physical means is divided by the universal solvent and resolved into something else. Hence—it is, for the time being, at least, annihilated in its form. This is simply a war on words.—Ed.

† It is still older that a few foot-notes should have cost the venerable Paramahansa over 15 columns of ill disguised abuse, out of which number three or four columns are given. That which was suppressed may be judged by what remains.—*Ed.*

themselves for Nirvikalpa* ecstasy, will not be able to comprehend us, nor also those who confound Prakriti with Purusha, or matter with spirit.† If by "scientifically" be meant curiosity, then not only we, but the whole class of philosophers from Thales to Auguste Comte are only hunters of curiosity, and our respected friends more so, as for this purpose only they have come from the other part of the world and pledged their lives and fortune on this. But to come to the point, we are not attracted by curiosity. Our motives are not shallow. Whatever we ask, we ask for scientific purposes, and for that only we entreated you to kindly ascertain the extent of mesmeric force, whether it influences the outer man only, or the inner one too--you said " * * * that a mortal wound may be inflicted upon the inner man, &c., &c." Now, according to our knowledge the inner man means the *double*, *i. e.*, the Taijasha, prágna being the original or first, and the Anna-maya or the Viswa, the third.‡ To this third, we

---

* Surely our respected correspondent cannot mean to convey the idea that in penning this answer *he* had " composed" himself into the state of Nirvikalpa : unless we take Monier Williams' definition of the term and bear in mind that it is a state " destitute of all reflection." (*See Indian Wisdom*, page 122, foot-note 2.)—*Ed.*

† To this kind thrust we answer that we have never confounded Prakriti with Purusha any more than we have confused the north with the south Pole. As both Poles belong to the same and one earth, so spirit and matter, or Purusha and Prakriti, are the two ends that lose themselves, in the eternity of unmanifested and the cycles of manifested matter. But like some of our distinguished Western metaphysicians, our opponent seems to regard matter and energy as two distinct things, whereas the Esoteric doctrine recognizes but one substratum for everything visible as invisible—" Purush-Prakriti " and *vice versa*. Moreover, we may remind the good Swami, that one need not be a yogee to be a good occultist, nor are there many yogees in India who know anything of real occult sciences.—*Ed.*

‡ In such case, our respected critic ought to criticize and correct Professor Monier Williams and other Sanskritists, who regard *Anna-Maya* as " the covering supported by food, *i. e.*, the corporeal or gross body," calling it the *fourth*, while we name it as the *first* sheath or *Kósa*. (See p. 128 of *Indian Wisdom*.)—*Ed.*

applied the term *treble*, and we are justified in doing so, in the same way as you apply double to the Taijasha,—and we do not see any harm in taking the gross one as third; but those who are fond of absurdities will not understand our ideas.* Why, because their own absurdity will be exposed. We beg your pardon for this outspokenness.† How can you, being a practical theosophist, *say* carelessly that a mortal wound may be inflicted upon the inner man, &c., &c., when in reality the outer one was the victim. You evade our question in an off-hand manner by saying that the question is not whether the *double* murdered the double treble. Now we particularly begged you to remove our doubts by establishing this fact scientifically.‡ Instead of complying with our

---

* We leave it to our readers to judge which is the most *absurd*—to consider our physical body as the *first*, or to call it, as the Swami does—the *treble* or the third; though of course there is "no harm" in either.—*Ed.*

† We willingly forgive the impolite remark under its garb of "outspokenness." We beg our respected correspondent to bear in mind though that it is one thing to be "outspoken," and quite another one to be *rude*.—*Ed.*

‡ It is precisely because we claim to know something of "practical" Occultism in addition to being a Theosophist that we answer without in the least "evading the question" that a mortal wound may be inflicted "not only *upon*, but also by one" inner man upon another. This is the A B C of esoteric mesmerism. The wound is inflicted by neither a real dagger or a hand of flesh, bones and blood, but simply by—WILL. It is the intense will of the "Gospoja" that guided the astral or inner body, the *Mayavi-rupa* of Frozya. It is the passively obedient action of the latter's "double" that scanning space and material obstacles, followed the "trial" of, and found the real murderers. It is again that WILL shaped by the incessant thought of the revenger, that inflicted the internal wounds which, though unable to kill or even to hurt the inner man, yet by reaction of the interior *physical* body proved mortal to the latter. If the fluid of the mesmerizer can cure, it can also kill. And now we have "established the fact as scientifically"—as science which generally disbelieves in and rejects such mesmeric phenomena will permit it. For those who believe in, and know something of, mesmerism, this will be plain. As to those who deny it the explanation will appear to them as absurd as any other psychological claim: as much so as the claims of Yogism with its beatitudes of *Samadhi* and other states, for the matter of that.—*Ed.*

request, you have been gracious enough to make that a matter of humorous jokes, and try to make us ashamed of our question. When we say "* * * the double murdered, the treble, not the double, and in no case the spiritual one," then in the sense, by treble you should have understood the *Annamaya*, but instead of so doing you are disgusted with the sentence, not only this sentence but also another one, in regard to which you say, "why should he then use against his own argument the term laya?" How can we erase the word out of Kosha (dictionary)? It would be better to understand us by our own idea and not through your own interpretations.

"There are two methods of investigation," says Spinoza, "the vulgar and the scientific. The one starts from principles which have been accepted without examination, which are not, therefore, clearly understood. The other starts from principles clearly defined and accurately known. It is the latter only which can lead to true knowledge." We fear, our venerable friends have followed the first method, which we shall try to prove by and by. * * *

Before doing this, however, may we be permitted to ask an answer to our question—Is spirit and matter the same thing? Or whether Prakriti, Shakti, and Spirit are the same things? Unless Prakriti be the same with spirit, how can the former be eternal, since two eternals cannot exist at the same time, and the belief in two eternals is against the fundamental truths of the Adwaita Philosophy,* as embodied in the aphorism *ek meva dwitiyam*. And matter has attributes, such as color, form, sound, touch, sight, taste and smell; but the spirit has none. Matter is dead (jad), Spirit is living (chaitanya); matter is temporary and subject to change, and spirit is eternal; matter is partial, and spirit is universal.† But what is

* This is precisely the question we have been asking; and also the reason why, knowing that matter is indestructible, as also spirit or rather *energy*—we say with all the *esoteric* Adwaitees that matter and spirit are ONE—*Ed.*

† See Mr. Subba Row's reply. While we mean Cosmic, indestructible matter, the Swami speaks of *objective* and *differentiated* matter!—*Ed.*

temporary? That which appears and exists for a certain period of time, or that which has beginning and end. And what is eternal? Eternal means that which exists throughout present, past, and future, and also in Jagrita, Swapna, and Sushupta. Owing to these and various other causes matter cannot be spirit nor *vice versa*. If you say like Vashishtha that the sleeping particles of Chid (spirit) are ignorantly called matter, then we agree with you to a certain extent; but still how can they, for that reason, be called by the erroneous and misleading term *matter* which is inert and spiritually non-exitent. Why do you not call a piece of wood or stone spirit?* Can you prove the existence of matter in sound sleep?† Perhaps you will reply like the Nayayiks that matter exists with Karana in sleep, if so, where does it exist in Turya? You cannot prove that either matter or Prakriti exists in Turya. How then can matter or Prakriti be called eternal? If matter is merely a manifestation of spirit, why call it by the false name of matter instead of its own name spirit?‡ Now having done with the effect, *matter*, we come to its cause, the Mula-Prakriti, which is also called Avidya or ignorance, the mother of Karma and the cause of Bundha. So long as this Prakriti is not *layed* into spirit by dissolving it into Satvaguna, there is no emancipation, Mukti with Prakriti is no Mukti at all. Beyond Prakriti is emancipation. This is the conclusion of the whole of our Aryan Occultism. Let us now see what the Mimansa says. We make a few quotations from the "Saddarshana-Chintanika, or Studies in Indian Philosophy," Vol. V. of 1881. No. 11, page 347§ edited at Bombay. * * *

---

* Because it is not usual to call them by such a name. Nevertheless, we maintain that there is in a piece of wood or a stone as much of latent spirit or life as there is in a weak—old human fœtus.—*Ed.*

† See Mr. T. Subba Row's *reply*.—*Ed.*

‡ For the same good reason that we call a chair by its "false" name of *chair* instead of calling it by that of the "oak" or any other wood of which it was made.—*Ed.*

§ We refer the reader to the pages of the abovenamed excellent monthly magazine.—*Ed.*

· It is not our object, even if we could, to cite all the Aryan books, but we would desire you and your readers to read in continuation of our quotations all the numbers of the sixth Volume of 1882 of the "Saddarshana Chintanika" which will shew that not only Shankaracharya, but also almost all the commentators and reformers and other great Rishis, not to speak of the Upanishads, have rejected the theory of the matter being as eternal as spirit, by which you are misled.* We will now see what other schools of philosophy say about the Prakriti. By other schools we mean the systems of Patanjali. Buddha and Jaina. Let our readers remember that we are speaking of the first class Boudhas, who agreed with Aryans in many essential points, and, particularly, as regards Nirvana, though they disagree in regard to Kriyakanda. The esteemed Editor of the *Theosophist* seems to follow the doctrine of Madhyamica, *i. e.*, middle class Buddhists, or those who are followers of Sugata's doctrines of whom we shall speak afterwards.† We call our reader's attention to the summary, Vol. VI (1882), No. 2, page 106, of the Studies in Indian Philosophy‡ * * * We cite a few lines from Sutras 24 and 25. * * * The Jainas do not believe in the independent power known as delusion to the Vedantists. The spirit is naturally knowing. It is omniscient. Its knowledge is covered over and obscured by an activity or *karma.* The perception of the spirit is also obscured by karma, &c., &c. The Boudhas believe that pure Nirvana alone

---

* We thank the good Swami for his advice. We have read all the monthly numbers of the *Saddarshana Chintanika* with great attention until lately, and advocated it zealously both in America and upon our arrival here. Notwithstanding all that Shankaracharya may be *made to say* in the abovenamed *studies*, we claim to know that he said nothing of the kind, not at any rate in the sense conveyed by our opponent. We leave the question to be settled between him and Mr. Subba Row.—*Ed.*

† The "esteemed Editor" follows but the doctrines of Esoteric Buddhism, which are nearly identical with those of the esotoric Adwaitees—the *true* followers of Shankaracharya.—*Ed.*

‡ We refer the reader to the abovenamed volume of the "Studies in Indian Philosophy."—*Ed.*

exists. Nirvana is a transcendental condition. It is infinitude. It is not subject to being acted upon. Nothing excels it. The great Rishis who are free from all desire, describe it to be so. Besides the Nirvana, karma or activity is also eternal.* Aided by ignorance, activity produces five elements and developes worldliness. These five elements are form or Rupa, sensation or Vedana, perception or Sangna, discrimination or Samascar, and consciousness or Vijnana. Virtue and contemplation destroy the power of ignorance. Activity thus becomes impotent and Nirvana is next attained to.† All these schools are described together in this place, because they represent Indian pessimism, and that the reader may know their points of resemblance and difference.

We now come to your foot-note. "Asat or Prakriti existed first, &c." A brief reply to this is given somewhere in the History of Philosophy. "The pagans said *ex-nihilo nihil.* The Christian father altered it to *ex-nihilo-omnia.*" Still let us see what our Aryan Rishis say. We call your attention to the verses from the second book called *Panch Mahabhuta Viveka* of *Panchadasi*, which speaks in accordance with Upanishads‡ * * * You will please understand the verses according to their commentary, now very ably translated into Hindi.

---

* And if "activity *is also eternal,*" then how can our philosophical antagonist maintain that matter is not so? Can *activity* (in the usual sense of the word), whether physical or mental, manifest itself or exist without, or outside of, *matter*, or to be plainer—outside of any one of its seven states? And how about his contradicting himself? "Activity also eternal." Then there *are* after all *two* eternals, how? And he just saying that "two eternals cannot exist at the same time." (See above).—*Ed.*

† We beg to draw our correspondent's attention to the fact that he is again contradicting himself. Or is it the "Boudhas"? But a few lines above he declares "activity . . . *eternal*" and now he makes it "impotent"—in other words, kills and annihilates that *which is eternal*?—*Ed.*

‡ *The reader is invited to turn to the Sanskrit verses of the abovenamed work, as the additional quotations would again require at least two columns. Our magazine avoids as much as possible the publication of anything that is not original matter.—Ed.*

Mandukya Upanishad says, Prakritis are of two kinds, Apara and Para; the former produces *Karma* and the latter Mukti. The one is Jad, the other Chaitanya. This is also the opinion of Bhagvat Gita, seventh chapter. Mandukya Karika, third chapter, and Prasna Upanishad also speak of Maya and Prakriti—please see the Upanishads with Sankara's commentary. Vasishta, Vyasa, Ashtavakra and all great sages recommend the divorcement of this illusive Prakriti, and nowhere in their works do we find any sentence which says that this illusive Prakriti is to be known with God. If Brahma can, in your opinion, be knwon through *Prakriti*, then why not with all others but *Tamasa* only? According to Indian philosophy and the practical experience of hermits, this Mula-Sakti or Avidya, as you understand it, is not to be known in Brahman. Because it is illusive and false, moreover, it can be dissolved and made inactive. It loses itself in Turya when *layaed*, as the river into the ocean. But as long as you will be ignorant of this process, so long you have liberty to call it a protest of religion; but the thinking class, who understand this mysterious process, will laugh at your weakness of understanding. As you have purposely come to India for true esoteric knowledge, we always pray for your success, and entreat you to understand us a little *hermitically*.* We explained to you Pranava according to the interpretation of Rama Gita, a chapter of esoteric Ramayana, but as you are not well acquainted with the *laya* theory, you could not accept it. It does not, however, matter much; practical Vedantists have accepted it before. We very gladly and without any apology quote a few lines from Max Muller's very able preface to "The Sacred Books of the East," as it bears on our subject. "This concentration of thought, Chagrata or one pointedness as the Hindus called it, is something to us

---

* See Mr. T. Subba Row's reply. We thank again our kind adviser for the interest he displays in our spiritual welfare, and refer him, if he desires to learn the cause of our refusal, to our note at the end of his letter. We can also assure him that we have never and nowhere called *Laya* "a protest of religion."—*Ed.*

almost unknown,—our minds are like kaleidoscopes of thoughts in constant motion : and to shut our mental eyes to everything else, while dwelling on one thought only, has become to most of us almost as impossible as to apprehend one musical note without harmonies. With the life we are leading now, with telegrams, letters, newspapers, reviews, pamphlets and books even breaking in upon us, it has become impossible, or almost impossible, ever to arrive at that intensity of thought which the Hindus meant by *Chagrata*, and the attainment of which was to them the indispensable condition of all philosophical and religious speculation. The loss may not be altogether on our side, yet our loss it is, and if we see the Hindus, even in their comparatively monotonous life, adopting all kinds of contrivances in order to assist them in drawing away their thoughts from all disturbing impressions and to fix them on one subject only, we must not be satisfied with smiling at their simplicity, but try to appreciate the object they had in view.

Below are the few verses on Laya Prakarana from Siva Sanhita, which it is hoped will show you how you mistake our meaning.* . . .

Nowhere throughout Yoga Vasisht and Bhagvat do we find any statement which recommends this Prakriti to be known. On the contrary, every Aryan occultist, particularly Kapila in his lectures to Devhutee speaks against it. Will you be so kind as to point out to us the places where Vasishta, Vyasa, Suka and Shankaracharya have given expression to their views which agree with your doctrines of the Arhat philosophy, otherwise, we might or might not, believe in your explanation.

Purusha, according to Upanishads, is Swayam Prakasha, *i. e.*, self-manifesting ; therefore cannot be dependant on *Prakriti* only, for its manifestation. No *Adwaitee* will take Brahmam with Prakriti or *gun* or duality. Their Brahmam

---

* Reader referred to the abovementioned work.—*Ed.*

is Purusha beyond the Prakriti, or in other words, Akshara. Latent spirit is never referred to as *Maha Iswara*. Please read the verse quoted below, which distinctly states that Maha Iswara is the spirit beyond *Prakriti* when the latter is *layed.**

Void is a fictitious name to the Aryan Rishis, who knew the omnipresence of the soul, and that void they destroyed by filling it up. Moreover, there is no void in nature, vide the maxim "Nature hates vacuum." At present we desist to answer your other points, till we have your reply to this. As the subject is very serious and important, we entreat you to discuss the points calmly and dispassionately ; without this mood of mind, one cannot penetrate into the esoteric philosophy of India. Your present opinions are not esoteric, they are rather exoteric.

SWAMI OF ALMORA.

ALMORA, *22nd April* 1883.

EDITOR'S NOTE.—We sincerely regret that such should be the opinion of the Swami of Almora. But since we know neither himself, nor the religion or school of philosophy he belongs to, we may perhaps repeat with him, " It does not, however, matter much" whether he agrees with us or not, for practical (esoteric and initiated) Vedantists have found our opinions correct and in perfect harmony with their own. There are nearly as many interpretations of the esoteric meaning of certain words we have

* We beg to be explained the hidden meaning of this really incomprehensible sentence. " Latent spirit is never referred to as *Maha Iswara*," (a term *we*, at any rate, never used,) while the Sanskrit verse "states that *Maha Iswara* is the spirit beyond *Prakriti*, when the latter is layed." Now does the learned Swami mean to say that the spirit beyond differentiated matter is *active*? It cannot mean anything else, for otherwise the two assumptions would contradict each other most absurdly and would be suicidal ; and if he *does* mean that which he says—*viz.*, that *Maha Iswara* (if the latter is identified here with Parabrahma), the spirit *beyond*" Prakriti becomes *active* since it is called *Maha Iswara*, which it would not be were it *latent*—then, we are sorry to say to the learned Paramahansa that he does not know what he is talking about. He is *no Esoteric* Adwaitee and—we close the discussion as becoming quite useless.—*Ed.*

to use as there are yogees and sannyasis of various sects in India. A Visishtadwaita *yogi* will contend the correctness of the meaning as given by an Adwaitee-ascetic, and a devotee of Chaitanya or a Bhakti-yogee will never accept the interpretation of the Vedas or Bhagavadgita made by a Brahmo or an Arya. Thus truth is everywhere and may be said to be nowhere. For us it is absolutely and solely in the Arhat esoteric doctrines; and we remain firm in our convictions, all our opponents being quite as free as ourselves to adhere by their own views. We have met in the N. W. P. with an erudite Pundit, a renowned Sanskritist, the most learned authority with, and at the head of the Vaishnavas, and recognized as such by many others; and he wanted us to believe that the culmination of "Raj-yoga" was the practical and absolute powers it conferred upon the Raj-yogee over all the female sex in creation!! Shall we believe every exponent of the Vedas, the Shastree of every sect, only because he may be an authority to those who belong to the same denomination with him, or shall we make a judicious selection, following out the dictates of our reason, which tells us that he is most right and nearer to truth, who diverges the less from logic and—Science? The *occult* philosophy we study, uses precisely that method of investigation which is termed by Spinoza the "scientific method." It starts from, and proceeds only on "principles clearly defined and accurately known," and is therefore "the only one" which can lead to true knowledge. Therefore, be this philosophy, and no other shall we abide. And now we must leave the venerable Swami and his views to the dissecting knife of Mr. T. Subba Row.

PRAKRITI AND PURUSHA.

THE editorial at the head of the article that precedes will explain to the learned Hermit of Almora and the readers of the *Theosophist* the reason for my having undertaken to write the following lines in connection with the controversy raised by the Swami as regards *Prakriti layam* (dissolution of Prakriti).

I am really quite delighted to be informed by the respected ascetic that his "motives are not shallow," and that he has raised the present controversy "for scientific purpose." But it is certainly a very dangerous task to enter into controversy with a disputant who, according to his own candid confession, is unable to give a clear expression to his thoughts, but who, nevertheless, is prepared to declare that "those who seek to find fault with" him "and become hostile to" him "are prejudiced and stubborn." Probably if understood "hermitically" and (we are called upon to construe the Swami's article in this manner) they *may* disclose some other meaning, and I sincerely hope they will. Meanwhile I trust he will not be pleased to consider me as either "prejudiced" or "stubborn" if I venture to defend the position taken up by the editor of this journal (who belongs to the same school as I do) as regards the subject in disputes.

I will begin by respectfully informing the learned hermit that it is not childish "to scrutinize and try to understand the wording of a question before attempting to answer it." Nobody has found fault with his style, nor has any one thought of "attacking" him. On the other hand, every attempt was made to weed out the grammatical errors in his article (the foot-notes to which have provoked his anger) before it was printed. But controversies like the present one can never come to any satisfactory conclusion unless the disputants clearly understand each other. I claim the right to remark that in the shape his articles generally reached the *Theosophist* Office, it became next to impossible to correctly ascertain the real meaning of the "idea" he tried to convey, so long as the latter found itself successfully concealed under what he terms his "style." Philosophical disputations apparently formidable in their appearance have often been found to have their origin in the various meanings attached to a single word; and it will be no exaggeration to say that innumerable creeds and sects have arisen from disputes about mere words. Under such circumstances, it may be humbly submitted that it is extremely improper on the Swami's part to lose his temper in spite of his *Nirvikalpa Samadhi* as soon as an attempt is made to analyse his question and ascertain its real meaning. Even now, after so much discussion, it is not easy to see what the editor is called upon to prove? If the Swami had merely asked the editor to explain more fully the assertion contained in one of the issues of this journal to the effect that Prakriti co-exists eternally with Purusha, there would be no confusion whatever. From the explanations given in his article, it would however appear that the learned hermit requires the editor to prove that Prakriti exists in *Tureeya Avastha.** Even then the question still remains vague and uncertain. I shall now proceed to point out clearly the difficulty involved in the question and explain the doctrines of esoteric theosophy on the subject under consideration, in order to enable the Swami to see that the difficulty is not merely an imaginary one created by the editor for the purpose of giving "evasive replies" to his questions and ridiculing him for his bad English; but that the teachings of esoteric science being, I can assure him, neither absurd and illogical nor as "unscientific" as he has imagined,—one has to thoroughly understand and assimilate before criticising them. Let us trust this may not become a hopeless task with regard to our learned critic !

For the purposes of this contoversy it must be explained that Prakriti may be looked upon from two distinct stand-points. It may be looked upon either as *Maya* when considered as the *Upadhi of Parabrahmam* or as *Avidga* when considered as the *Upadhi of Jivatma* (7th principle in man).† Avidya is ignorance or illusion arising from Maya. The term Maya, though sometimes used as a synonym for Avidya, is, properly speaking, applicable to Prakriti only. There is no difference between Prakriti, Maya and Sakti; and the ancient Hindu philosophers made no distinction whatsoever between Matter and Force. In support of this assertion I may refer the learned hermit to "Swetaswatara Upanishad" and its commentary by Shankaracharya. In case we adopt the four-fold division of the adwaitee philosophers, it will be clealy seen that Jagrata,‡

---

* Condition of the highest *Samadhi* (or trance), or as expressed by the Swami, "in sleep."

† *Upadhi*—vehicle.

‡ *Jagrata*—waking state, or a condition of external perception.

Swapna* and Sushupti Avasthas† are the results of Avidya, and that Vyswanara,‡ Hiranyagarbha§ and Sutratma|| are manifestations of Parabrahmam in Maya or Prakriti. Now I beg to inform the learned hermit that the statement made in the *Theosophist* regarding Prakriti has no connection whatever with Avidya. Undifferentiated cosmic matter or Mulaprakriti eternally co-exists with Purusha, but there is Avidya Layam in Tureeya Avastha. The Editor of the *Theosophist* has never maintained that Avidya, illusion or ignorance, is eternal. Why should, then, the learned hermit require the Editor to prove that which has never been claimed ? I cannot help suspecting that the erudite Swami is confounding Avidya with Prakriti, the effect with its cause. In drawing a distinction between Avidya and Prakriti, I am merely following the authority of all the great Adwaitee philosophers of Aryavarta. It will be sufficient for me to refer the Swami to his favourite book of reference, the first chapter of Panchadasi. If, however, the learned Swami is prepared to say that *Mulaprakriti* itself is not eternal, I beg to inform him that his views are clearly wrong and that his arguments and his *Layaprakarna*, of which he is very proud, do not prove the *Layam* of "Mulaprakriti," whatever meaning he may attach to the word " Laya." Before proceeding to notice his arguments, I shall say a few words about the " murder by the double " which appears so very ridiculous to this, our " practical" Yogi. The hermit is probably aware of the fact

---

* *Swapna*—dreamy state, or a condition of *clairvoyance* in the astral plane.

† *Sushupti*—a state of ecstasis ; and *Avastas*—states or conditions of *Pragna*.

‡ *Vyswanara*—the magnetic fire that pervades the manifested solar system—the most objective aspects of the ONE LIFE.

§ *Hirnyagarbha*—the One Life as manifested in the plane of astral Light.

|| *Sutratma*—the Eternal germ of the manifested universe existing in the field of *Mulaprakriti*.

that, sometimes, a severe mental shock can cause death when the physical body itself remains apparently unhurt. And every practical occultist knows that in several instances when death is caused by recourse to "black magic," the victim's physical body bears no sign of injury. In these cases the blow given, as it were, in the first instance, to the 4th and 5th principles of man which constitute his astral body, is immediately communicated to his *Sthoola-sariram.* And hence there is no absurdity in saying that a wound which proves mortal to the victim's Sthoolasariram can be inflicted on his astral body. The Swami, however, seems to think that the astral body itself is the victim in the Editor's opinion. There is no room whatever for any such misapprehension in the article regarding the subject in question; and I am very sorry that the hermit has thought it fit to abuse the Editor under the plea of outspokenness, having himself carelessly misunderstood the correct meaning. The Swami is at full liberty to call Sthoolasariram the *treble* if he is pleased to do so ; but as the Upadhis are generally named Samharakrama,* the treble would ordinarily be taken to mean Karanasariram† and when the Swami was pleased to name them in a different order, he ought to have expressed himself in less ambiguous manner. Our correspondent seems to be very fond of stale remarks. There seems hardly any necessity for all his wise flings about modes of investigation in general, when he is not fully prepared to show that *our* method of investigation is unscientific.

The Swami now comes forward with another question : Whether matter is indentical with spirit? Our learned hermit is always ready to raise fresh issues without any cause for it. The real question is, whether Mulaprakriti is eternal, and I fail to see the necessity for examining the nature of its relationship to what is ordinarily called spirit in deciding whether it

* *Samharakrama*—order of involution or evolution reversed.

† *Karanasariram*—the germ of *Avidya* (ignorance) which is the cause of rebirth.

is eternal or not. But if the Swami insists upon my giving him a definite answer to his question, I beg to refer him to my article on "Personal and Impersonal God," published in the *Theosophist,* and to Shankaracharya's commentary on the 4th para. of the first chapter of Brahma Sutras. In truth, Prakriti and Purusha are but the two aspects of the same ONE REALITY. As our great Shankaracharya truly observes at the close of his commentary on the 23rd Sutra of the above-mentioned Pada, "Parabrahmam is Karta (Purusha), as there is no other Adhishtatha,* and Parabrahmam is Prakriti there being no other Upadanam." This sentence clearly, indicates the relation between "the One Life" and "the One Element" of the Arhat philosophers. After asking us this question, and quoting the doctrines of the Adwaita philosophy *against* the assumption that matter is not spirit, the learned Swami proceeds to show on his own authority that matter is *not* Spirit, in fact. If so, is the Swami's doctrine consistent with the doctrines of the Adwaitee philosophers? Our hermit probably thinks that the quotation will not affect his own statement, inasmuch as *he* holds that matter is *not* enternal. What then is the meaning of the statement soof ten quoted by Adwaitees—"Sarvan khalvitham Brahma" ?† and what is meant by saying that Brahmam is the *Upadanakarnam* of the Universe? It seems to me that the Swami has entirely misunderstood the Adwaitee doctrine regarding the relation between Prakriti and Purusha. If confusion is to be avoided, it is highly desirable that our critic should inform us distinctly what he means by "matter." I shall now examine his arguments or rather his assumptions to show that Prakriti, is not eternal in the order in which they are stated.

I. For certain reasons matter is not Spirit; Spirit is enternal and therefore matter is not eternal.

---

* *Adhishtatha*—That which inheres in another principle—the active agent working in *Prakriti.*

† Everything in the universe is Brahma.

In reply to this argument I beg to state that the major premise is wrong in itself, and does not affect undifferentiated Prakriti, as the grounds on which it is based are not applicable to it for the following reasons :—

(*a*) Mulaprakriti has not the attributes enumerated, as the said attributes imply differentiation and Mulaprakriti is undifferentiated according to our doctrines.

(*b*) Mulaprakriti is not dead or *jadam*, as Purusha—the one life—always exists in it. It is in fact *Chitanya deepta* (shining with life) as stated in Uttaratapani (see also *Goudapatha Kârika*).

(*c*) Mulaprakriti is not temporary but eternal.

(*d*) When subjected to change it always loses its name, reassuming it after returning to its original undifferentiated condition.

(*e*) It is not partial but co-extensive with space.

(*f*) It eternally exists in the universe in whatever Avastha (state or condition) a particular human being may be.

And, moreover, I deny the validity of the inference drawn even if, for the sake of argument, the truth of the premises be granted.

Our Swami's second argument is extremely ridiculous. When stated briefly it stands thus :—

II. The existence of matter is not known either in *Sushupti* or *Tureeya** Avastha, and therefore matter is not eternal.

This is enough to convince me that the Swami of Almora knows as much about *Tureeya Avastha* as of the features of the man in the moon. The learned gentleman is in fact confounding Avidya, with Maya. Indeed, he says that Mulaprakriti is Avidya, I shall be very happy if he can quote any authority in support of his proposition. I beg to inform him

---

* Dreamless sleep, and Tureeya Avastha, or the condition of intimate union with Parabrahm—a stage higher than ecstasis.

again that *Avidya layam* is not necessarily followed by *Prakriti layam.* It is the differentiation of Mulaprakriti that is the cause of *Avidya* or ignorant delusion, and when the differentiated Cosmic matter returns to its original undifferentiated condition at the time of Mahapralaya, *Avidya* is completely got rid of. Consequently, Mulaprakriti, instead of being identical with Avidya, implies the absence of Avidya. It is the highest state of *non-being*—the condition of Nirvana. Mukti, therefore, is beyond differentiated Prakriti and beyond Avidya, but it expresses the condition of undifferentiated Mulaprakriti. On referring to Uttaratapani and its commentary, the learned hermit will be able to see that even the Mahachitanayam at the end of *Shodasanthum* indicated by Avikalpapranava is spoken of as existing in what is described as "*Guru beejopadhi Sakti mandalum.*"* This is the nearest approach to the one undifferentiated element called Mulaprakriti. It will also be seen from the passage above referred to that Mulaprakriti exists even in the highest stage of Tureeya Avastha. The Swami is pleased to ask us why we should call this element matter if it is but an aspect of Purusha. We are obliged to use the word matter as we have no other word in English to indicate it; but if the Swami means to object to the word Prakriti being applied to it, it will be equally reasonable on my part to object to its being called either God, Spirit or Purusha.

Our Swami's lengthy quotations from "Saddarshana Chintanika" happily eliminated by the Editor do not help him much. If the term Avyakta † is applied to Brahman instead of being applied to " the Parkriti of the Sankhyas," how does it prove that undifferentiated Parkriti is not eternal? Shankaracharya merely says that Avidya or ignorance can be exterminated; but he says nothing about the laya of Mulaprakriti. It is

---

* A condition of Prakriti when it has but the germs of the three gunas, viz., Satwa, Rajas, and Tamas.

† *Avyakta*—The unrevealed Cause.

unnecessary for me to say anything about the Swami's views regarding other systems of philosophy. I am only concerned with the esoteric Arhat philosophy and the Advaita philosophy as taught by Shankaracharya. The remaining quotations from the works of various authors, contained in the Swami's article are, in my humble opinion, irrelevant. The chapter on Pancha Mahabhutaviveka in Panchadasi does not show that *Asat* has not existed with *Sat* from all eternity. This is the first time I hear that the Paravidya mentioned in Manduka Upanishad is a kind of Prakriti as stated by our learned hermit. I have reason to think that the entity indicated by the said Paravidya is Parabrahmam. In conjunction with the said entity Shankaracharya speaks of undifferentitated Parkriti as "Akasakhyamaksharam" pervading it everywhere. Our opponent seems to think that as every Yogi is asked to rise above the influence of Avidya, it must necessarily be assumed that Prakriti is not eternal in its undifferentiated condition. This is as illogical as his other arguments. Illusion arises from differentiation or, Dwaitabhavam as it is technically called; and absence of differentiation, whether subjective or objective, is the Nirvana of Adwaita. If the Swami only pauses to consider the nature of "this one element" in its dual aspect, he will be able to see that it is but an aspect of Parabrahmam. All the arguments advanced by him seem to show that he is labouring under the impression that we are contending for the permanancy of this illusive manifested world. If this Mulaprakriti that I have attempted to describe is not noticed in Brahmam according to the "practical experience of hermits," all that I can say is that their experience is different from the experience of Shankaracharya, Vyasa, Goudapada and several other Rishis. The hermit is welcome to "laugh at our weakness of understanding" if it can in the least comfort him; but mere vituperation will bring him very little benefit if he rushes into controversy without clearly understanding the subject under disputation and with worthless arguments and irrelevant quotations as his weapons.

The Editor of this journal is, I think, perfectly justified in rejecting our hermit's interpretation of *Pranava*, as it is not quite consistent with what is contained in Mandukya, Uttaratapane and Naradaparivrajaka Upanishads and other authoritative treatrises on the subject. I do not think that the three mantras in Pranava mean *matter*, *force* and *spirit* respectively, as stated by the Swami. I have seen several interpretations of Pranava in various books; but this explanation is entirely novel to me; and I respectfully submit that it is wrong, inasmuch as no clear distinction is ever drawn between matter and force in our ancient philosophical works. If our Swami is satisfied that Ramagita is a great authority on Esoteric science, I shall not attempt to deprive him of his satisfaction; and as the Esoteric doctrine taught by Shankaracharya and other great Vedantic writers is almost identical with the Esoteric Arhat doctrine as far as it goes, it is impossible for me to enumerate all the similarities between the two systems for our hermit's delectation; but I shall be very glad if he can kindly point out *where* and in *what* they differ.

I beg also to inform him that it is impossible to think of Purusha except in conjunction with Mulaprakriti, since Purusha can act *only through Prakriti*. In support of these views I may refer him to Shankaracharya's *Soundarya lahari* and his commentary on Namakam and Swetaswatara Upanishad. It is quite clear that an *Adhishtatha* can never exist without Upadanam. If, as is stated by Shankaracharya, Purusha is Adishtatha or Karta, and if Prakriti is Upadanam, the necessary co-existence of these two aspects become inevitable. As regards the passage quoted from Taittiriya Upanishad, I have to inform the hermit that the word Prakriti therein mentioned means differentiated Prakriti. Not satisfied with the abusive language contained in the body of his article and his allusion to the "black mouse," (a passage omitted therefrom for decency's sake,) our learned opponent has thought it proper to record an emphatic declaration at the termination of his article that the Editor's views are *Exoteric* and not *Esoteric*. Undoubtedly, as far as they are communicated to him through the medium of this journal, they are exoteric, for if really esoteric they would not be thus made public. But it is a matter of very little consequence to the progress of theosophy whether the Swami of Almora considers them esoteric or exoteric, provided they are reasonable, and in harmony with the doctrines of the great teachers of ancient Aryavarta.

SRI SHANKARACHARYA'S DATE AND DOCTRINE.

It is always difficult to determine with precision the date of any particular event in the ancient history of India; and this difficulty is considerably enhanced by the speculations of European Orientalists whose labours in this direction have but tended to thicken the confusion already existing in popular legends and traditions which were often altered or modified to suit the necessities of sectarian controversy. The causes that have produced this result will be fully ascertained on examining the assumptions on which these speculations are based. The writings of many of these Orientalists are often characterized by an imperfect knowledge of Indian literature, philosophy and religion and of Hindu traditions, and a contemptuous disregard for the opinions of Hindu writers and pundits. Very often, facts and dates are taken by these writers from the writings of their predecessors or contemporaries on the assumptions that they are correct without any further investigation by themselves. Even when a writer gives a date with an expression of doubt as to its accuracy, his follower frequently quotes the same date as if it were absolutely correct. One wrong date is made to depend upon another wrong date, and one bad influence is often deduced from another inference equally unwarranted and illogical. And consequently if the correctness of any particular date given by these writers is to be ascertained the whole structure of Indian Chronology constructed by them will have to be carefully examined. It will be convenient to enumerate some of the assumptions above referred to before proceeding to examine their opinions concerning the date of Shankaracharya.

I. Many of these writers are not altogether free from the prejudices engendered by the pernicious doctrine, deduced from the Bible, whether rightly or wrongly, that this world is only six thousand years old. We do not mean to say that any one of these writers would now seriously think of defending the said doctrine. Nevertheless it had exercised a considerable influence on the minds of Christian writers when they began to investigate the claims of Asiatic Chronology. If an antiquity of 5 or 6 thousand years are assigned to any particular event connected with the Ancient history of Egypt, India or China, it is certain to be rejected at once by these writers without any inquiry whatever regarding the truth of the statement.

II. They are extremely unwilling to admit that any portion of the Veda can be traced to a period anterior to the date of the Pentateuch, even when the arguments brought forward to establish the priority of the Vedas are such as would be convincing to the mind of an impartial investigator untainted by Christian prejudices. The maximum limit of Indian antiquity is, therefore, fixed for them by the Old Testament, and it is virtually assumed by them that a period between the date of the Old Testament on the one side and the present time on the other, should necessarily be assigned to every book in the whole range of Vedic and Sanskrit literature, and to almost every event of Indian History.

III. It is often assumed without reason that every passage in the Vedas containing philosophical or metaphysical ideas must be looked upon as a subsequent interpolation and that every book treating of a philosophical subject must be considered as having been written after the time of Buddha or after the commencement of the Christian Era. Civilization, philosophy and scientific investigation had their origin, in the opinion of these writers, within the six or seven centuries preceding the Christian era, and mankind slowly emerged, for the first time, from "the depths of animal brutality" within the last four or five thousand years.

IV. It is also assumed that Buddhism was brought into existence by Gautama Buddha. The previous existence of Buddhism, Jainism and Arhat philosophy is rejected as an absurd and ridiculous invention of the Buddhists who attempted thereby to assign a very high antiquity to their own religion. In consequence of this erroneous impression on their part every Hindu book referring to the doctrines of Buddhists is declared to have been written subsequent to the time of Gautama Buddha. For instance, Mr. Weber is of opinion that Vyasa, the author of Brahma Sutras, wrote them in the 5th century after Christ. This is indeed a startling revelation to the majority of Hindus.

V. Whenever several works treating of various subjects are attributed to one and the same author by Hindu writings or traditions, it is often assumed, and apparently without any reason whatever in the majority of cases, that the said works should be considered as the production of different writers. By this process of reasoning they have discovered two Badarayanas (Vyasas), two Pantanjalis, and three Vararuchis. We do not mean to say that in every case identity of names is equivalent to identity of persons. But we cannot but protest against such assumptions when they are made without any evidence to support them, merely for the purpose of supporting a foregone conclusion or establishing a favourite hypothesis.

VI. An attempt is often made by these writers to establish the chronological order of the events of ancient Indian history by means of the various stages in the growth or development of the Sanskrit language and Indian literature. The time required for this growth is often estimated in the same manner in which a geologist endeavours to fix the time required for the gradual development of the various strata composing the earth's crust. But we fail to perceive anything like a proper method in making these calculations. It will be wrong to assume that the growth of one language will require the same time as that of another within the same limits. The peculiar characteristics of the nation to whom the language belongs must be carefully taken into consideration in attempting to make any such calculation. The history of the said nation is equally important. Any one who examines Max Müller's estimation of the so-called Sutra, Brahmana, Mantra and Khanda periods, will be able to perceive that no attention has been paid to these considerations. The time allotted to the growth of these four "Srata" of Vedic literature is purely arbitrary.

We have enumerated these defects in the writings of European Orientalists for the purpose of showing to our readers that it is not always safe to rely upon the conclusions arrived at by these writers regarding the dates of ancient Indian history.

In examining the various quotations and traditions selected by European Orientalists for the purpose of fixing Shankaracharya's date, special care must be taken to see whether the person referred to was the very first Shankaracharya who established the Adwaitee doctrine or one of his followers who became the *Adhipatis* of the various *Mathams* established by him and his successors. Many of the Adwaitee *Mathadhipatis* who succeeded him (especially at the Sringeri Matham) were men of considerable renown and were well-known throughout India during their time. They are often referred to under the general name of Shankaracharya. Consequently any reference made to any one of these *Mathadhipatis* is apt to be mistaken for a reference to the first Shakaracharya himself.

Mr. Barth, whose opinion regarding Sankara's date is quoted by the *London Theosophist* against the date assigned to that teacher in Mr. Sinnett's book on Esoteric Buddhism, does not appear to have carefully examined the subject himself. He assigns no reason for the date given and does not even allude to the existence of other authorities and traditions which conflict with the date adopted by him. The date which he assigns to Sankara appears in an unimportant foot-note appearing on page 89 of his book on "The Religions of India," which reads thus: "Shankaracharya is generally placed in the 8th century; perhaps we must accept the 9th rather. The best accredited tradition represents him as born on the 10th of the month 'Madhava' in 788 A. D. Other traditions, it is true, place him in the 2nd and 5th centuries. The author of the Dabistan, on the other hand, brings him as far down as the commencement of the 14th." Mr. Barth is clearly wrong in saying that Sankara is generally placed in the 8th century. There are as many traditions for placing him in some century before the Christian Era as for placing him in some century after the said era, and it will also be seen from what follows that in fact evidence preponderates in favour of the former statement. It cannot be contended that the generality of Orientalists have any definite opinions of their own on the subject under consideration. Max Müller does not appear to have ever directed his attention to this subject. Monier Williams merely copies the date given by Mr. Wilson, and Mr. Weber seems to rely upon the same authority without troubling himself with any further enquiry about the matter. Mr. Wilson is probably the only Orientalist who investigated the subject with some care and attention; and he frankly confesses that the exact period at which "he (Sankara) flourished can by no means be determined" (page 201 of Vol. I of his Essays on the religion of the Hindus). Under such circumstances the foot-note above-quoted is certainly very misleading. Mr. Barth does not inform his readers wherefrom he obtained the tradition referred to and what reasons he has for supposing that it refers to the first Shankaracharya and that it is "the best accredited tradition." When the matter is still open to discussion, Mr. Barth should not have adopted any particular date if he is not prepared to support it and establish it by proper arguments. The other traditions alluded to are not intended, of course, to strengthen the authority of the tradition relied upon. But the wording of the foot-note in question seems to show that all the authorities and traditions relating to the subject are comprised therein, when, in fact, the most important of them are left out of consideration, as will be shown hereafter. No arguments are to be found in support of the date assigned to Sankara in the other portions of Mr. Barth's book, but there are few isolated passages which may be taken either as inferences from the statement in question or arguments in its support, which it will be necessary to examine in this connection.

Mr. Barth has discovered some connection between the appearance of Sankara in India and the commencement of the persecution of the Buddhists which he seems to place in the 7th and 8th centuries. In page 89 of his book he speaks of "the great reaction on the offensive against Buddhism which was begun in the Deccan in the 7th and 8th centuries by the schools of Kumarila and Sankara"; and in page 135, he states that the "disciples of Kumarila and Sankara organized into military bands, constituted themselves the rabid defenders of orthodoxy". The force of these statements is, however, considerably weakened by the author's observations on pages 89 and 134 regarding the absence of any traces of Buddhist persecution by Sankara in the authentic documents hitherto examined and the absurdity of legends which represent him as exterminating Buddhists from the Himalaya to Cape Comorin.

The association of Sankara with Kumarila in the passages above cited is ridiculous. It is well-known to almost every Hindu that the followers of Purva Mimamsa (Kumarila commented on the Sutras) were the greatest and the bitterest opponents of Sankara and his doctrine, and Mr. Barth seems to be altogether ignorant of the nature of Kumarila's views and Purva Mimamsa and the scope and aim of Sankara's Vedantic philosophy. It is impossible to say what evidence the anocher has for asserting that the great reaction against the Buddhists commenced in the 7th and 8th centuries and that the Sankara was instrumental in originating it. There are some passages in his book which tend to show that this date cannot be considered as quite correct. In page 153 he says that Buddhism began persecution even in the time of Asoka.

Such being the case, it is indeed very surprising that the Orthodox Hindus should have kept quiet for nearly ten centuries without retaliating on their enemies. The political ascendency gained by the Buddhists during the reign of Asoka did not last very long ; and the Hindus had the support of every powerful king before and after the commencement of the Christian era. Moreover the author says in p. 132 of his book, that Buddhism was in a state of decay in the seventh century. It is hardly to be expected that the reaction against the Buddhists would commence when their religion was already in a state of decay. No great religious teacher or reformer would waste his time and energy in demolishing a religion already in ruins. But, what evidence is there to show that Sankara was ever engaged at his task ? If the main object of his preaching was to evoke a reaction against Buddhism, he would no doubt have left us some writings specially intended to criticize its doctrines and expose its defects. On the other hand, he does not even allude to Buddhism in his independent works. Though he was a voluminous writer, with the exception of a few remarks on the theory advocated by some Buddhists regarding the nature of perception contained in his commentary on the Brahma-Sutras, there is not a single passage in the whole range of his writings regarding the Buddhists or their doctrines ; and the insertion of even these few remarks in his commentary was rendered necessary by the allusions contained in the Sutras which he was interpreting. As, in our humble opinion these Bramha-Sutras were composed by Vyasa himself (and not by an imaginary Vyasa of the 5th century after Christ evolved by Mr. Weber's fancy) the allusions therein contained relate to the Buddhism which existed previous to the date of Gautama Buddha. From these few remarks it will be clear to our readers that Shankaracharya had nothing to do with Buddhist persecution. We may here quote a few passages from Mr. Wilson's Preface to the first edition of his Sanskrit Dictionary in support of our remarks. He writes as follows regarding Sankara's connection with the persecution of the Buddhists:—"Although the popular belief attributes the origin of the Bauddha persecution to Sankaracharya, yet in this case we have some reason to distrust its accuracy. Opposed to it we have the mild character of the reformer, who is described as uniformly gentle and tolerant, and speaking from my own limited reading in Vedanta works, and the more satisfactory testimony of Ram Mohun Roy, which he permits me to adduce, it does not appear that any traces of his being instrumental to any persecution are to be found in his own writings, all which are extant, and the object of which is by no means the correction of the Bauddha or any other schism, but the refutation of all other doctrines besides his own, and the reformation or re-establishment of the 4th religious order." Further on he observes that "it is a popular error to ascribe to him the work of persecution; he does not appear at all occupied in that odious task, nor is he engaged in particular controversy with any of the Bauddhas."

From the foregoing observations it will be seen that Sankara's date connot be determined by the time of the commencement of the Buddhist persecution, even if it were possible to ascertain the said period.

Mr. Barth seems to have discovered some connection between the philosophical systems of Sankara, Ramanuja and Anandatirtha, and the Arabian merchants who came to India in the first century of the Hejira, and he is no doubt fully entitled to any credit that may be given him for the originality of his discovery. The mysterious and occult connection between Adwaita philosophy and Arabian commerce is pointed out in p. 212 of his book, and it may have some bearing on the present question, if it is anything more than a figment of his fancy. The only reason given by him in support of his theory is, however, in my humble opinion, worthless. The Hindus had prominent example of a grand religious movement under the guidance of a single teacher, in the life of Buddha, and it was not necessary for them to imitate the adventures of the Arabian prophet. There is but one other passage in Mr. Barth's book which has some reference to Sankara's date. In p.207 he writes as follows:– "The Siva, for instance, who is invoked at the commencement of the drama of Shakuntala, who is at once God, priest and offering, and whose body is the universe, is a Vedantic Idea. This testimony apppears to be forgotten when it is maintained, as is sometimes done, that the whole sectarian Veda ntism commences with Sankara." But this testimony appears to be equally forgotten when it is maintained, as is sometimes done by Orientalists like Mr. Barth, that Sankara lived in some century after the author of Shakuntala.

From the foregoing remarks it will be apparent that Mr. Barth's opinion regarding Sankara's date is very unsatisfactory. As Mr. Wilson seems to have examined the subject with some care and attention, we must now advert to his opinion and see how far it is based on proper evidence. In attemping to fix Amara Sinha's date (which attempt ultimatley ended in a miserable failure), he had to ascertain the period when Sankara lived. Consequently his remarks concerning the said period appear in his preface to the first edition of his Sanskrit dictionary. We shall now reproduce here such passages from this preface as are connected with the subject under consideration and comment upon them. Mr. Wilson writes as follows :—

"The birth of Sankara presents the same discordance as every other remarkable incident amongst the Hindus. The Kadali (it ought to be Koodali) Brahmins, who form an establishment following and teaching his system, assert his appearance about 2,000 years since; some accounts place him about the beginning of the Christian Era, others in the 3rd or 4th century after; a manuscript history of the kings of Konga, in Colonel Mackenzie's Collection, makes him contemporary with Tiru Vikrama Deva Chakravarti, sovereign of Skandapura in the Dekkan, A. D. 178; at Sringeri, on the edge of the Western Ghauts, and now in the Mysore Territory, at which place he is said to have founded a College that still exists, and assumes the supreme control of the Smarta Brahmins of the Peninsula, an antiquity of 1,600 years is attributed to him, and common tradition makes him about 1,200 years old. The Bhoja Prabandha enumerates Sankara among its worthies, and as contemporary with that prince; his antiquity will then be between 8 and 9 centuries. The followers of Madhwacharya in Tuluva seem to have attempted to reconcile these contradictory accounts by supposing him to have been born three times; first at Sivuli in Tuluva about 1,500 years ago, again in Malabar some centuries later, and finally at Padukachaytra in Tuluva no more than 600 years since; the latter asscertion being intended evidently to do honor to their own founder, whose date that was, by enabling him triumph over Sankara in supposititious controversy. The Vaishnava Brahmins of Madura say that Sankara appeared in the ninth century of Salivahana or tenth of our era. Dr. Taylor thinks that, if we allow him about 900 years, we shall not be far from the truth, and Mr. Colebrooke is inclined to give him as antiquity of about 1,000 years. This last is the age which my friend Ram Mohun Roy, a diligent student of Sankara's works, and philosophical teacher of his doctrines, is disposed to concur in, and he infers that 'from a calculation of the spiritual generations of the followers of Sankara Swami from his time up to this date, he seems to have lived between the 7th and 8th centuries of the Christian Era,' a distance of time agreeing with the statements made to Dr. Buchanan in his journey through Sankara's native country, Malabar, and in union with the assertion of the Kerala Utpatti, a work giving an historical and statistical account of the same province, and which, according to Mr. Duncan's citation of it, mentions the regulations of the castes of Malabar by this philosopher to have been effected about 1,000 years before 1798. At the same time, it must be observed, that a manuscript translation of the same work in Colonel Mackenzie's possession, states Shankaracharya to have been born about the middle of the 5th century, or between 13 and 14 hundred years ago, differing in this respect from Mr. Duncan's statement—a difference of the less importance, as the manuscript in question, either from defects in the original or translation, presents many palpable errors and cannot consequently be depended upon. The weight of authority therefore is altogether in favour of antiquity of about ten centuries, and I am disposed to adopt this estimate of Sankara's date, and to place him in the end of the 8th and beginning of the 9th centuries of the Christian era."

We will add a few more authorities to Mr. Wilson's list before proceeding to comment on the foregoing passage.

In a work called "The Biographical Sketches of Eminent Hindu Authors," published at Bombay in 1860 by Janardan Ramchanderjee, it is stated that Sankara lived 2,500 years ago, and that, in the opinion of some people, 2,200 years ago. The records of the Combaconum Matham give a list of nearly 66 Mathadhipatis from Sankara down to the present time, and show that he lived more than 2,000 years ago.

The Kudali Matham referred to by Mr. Wilson which is a branch of the Sringeri Matham, gives the same date as the latter Matham, their traditions being identical. Their calculation can safely be relied upon as far as it is supported by the dates given on the places of Samadhi (something like a tomb) of the successive Gurus of the Sringeri Matham; and it leads us to the commencement of the Christian Era.

No definite information is given by Mr. Wilson regarding the nature, origin or reliability of the accounts which place Sankara in the 3rd or 4th century of the Christian era or at its commencement; nor does it clearly appear that the history of the kings of Konga referred to unmistakably alludes to the very first Shankaracharya. These traditions are evidently opposed to the conclusion arrived at by Mr. Wilson, and it does not appear on what grounds their testimony is discredited by him. Mr. Wilson is clearly wrong in stating that an antiquity of 1,600 years is attributed to Sankara by the Sringeri Matham. We have already referred to the account of the Sringeri Matham, and it is precisely similar to the account given by the Kudali Brahmins. We have ascertained that it is so from the agent of the Sringeri Matham at Madras, who has published only a few days ago the list of teachers preserved at the said Matham with the dates assigned to them. And further we are unable to see which "common tradition" make Sankara "about 1,200 years old." As far as our knowledge goes there is no such common tradition in India. The majority of people in Southern India have, up to this time, been relying on the Sringeri account, and in Northern India there seems to be no common tradition. We have but a mass of contradictory accounts.

It is indeed surprising that an Orientalist of Mr. Wilson's pretensions should confound the *poet* named Sankara and mentioned in Bhoja Prabandha with the great Adwaitee Teacher. No Hindu would ever commit such a ridiculous mistake. We are astonished to find some of these European Orientalists quoting now and then some of the statements contained in such books as Bhoja Prabandha, Kathá Sarit Sagara, Raja-tarangini and Panchatantra as if they were historical works. In some other part of his preface Mr. Wilson himself says that this Bhoja Prabandha is altogether untrustworthy, as some of the statements contained therein did not harmonize with his theory about Amarasimha's date; but now he ***misquotes*** its statements for the purpose of supporting his conclusion regarding Sankara's date. Surely, consistency is not one of the prominent characteristics of the writings of the majority of European Orientalists. The person mentioned in Bhoja Prabandha is always spoken of under the name of Sankara *Kavi*, and he is nowhere called Shankara-*charya*, and the Adwaitee Teacher is never mentioned in any Hindu work under the appellation of Sankara *Kavi*.

It is necessary for us to say anything about the Madhwa traditions or the opinion of the Vaishnava Brahmins of

Madura regarding Sankara's date. It is, in our humble opinion, hopeless to expect anything but falsehood regarding Sankara's history and philosophy from the Madhwas and the Vaishnavas. They are always very anxious to show to the world at large that their doctrines existed before the time of Sankara, and that the Adwaitee doctrine was a deviation from their pre-existing orthodox Hinduism. And consequently they have assigned to him an antiquity of less than 1,500 years.

It does not appear why Dr. Taylor thinks that he can allow Sankara about 900 years, or on what grounds Mr. Colebrooke is inclined to give him an antiquity of about 1,000 years. No reliance can be placed on such statements before the reason assigned therefor are thoroughly sifted.

Fortunately, Mr. Wilson gives us the reason for Ram Mohun Roy's opinion. We are inclined to believe that Ram Mohun Roy's calculation was made with reference to the Sringeri list of teachers or Gurus, as that was the only list published up to this time, and as no other Matham, except perhaps the Cumbaconum Matham, has a list of Gurus coming up to the present time in uninterrupted succession. There is no necessity for depending upon his calculation (which from its very nature cannot be anything more than mere guess-work) when the old list preserved at Sringeri contains the date assigned to the various teachers. As these dates have not been published up to the present time, and as Ram Mohun Roy had merely a string of names before him, he was obliged to ascertain Sankara's date by assigning a certain number of years on the average to every teacher. Consequently, his opinion is of no importance whatever when we have the statement of the Sringeri Matham which, as we have already said, places Sankara in some century before the Christian Era. The same remarks will apply to the calculation in question even if it were made on the basis of the number of teachers contained in the list preserved in the Cumbaconum Matham.

Every little importance can be attached to the oral evidence adduced by some unknown persons before Dr. Buchanan in his travels through Malabar; and we have only to consider the inferences that may be drawn from the accounts contained in Kerala Utpatti. The various manuscript copies of this work seem to differ in the date they assign to Shankaracharya; even if the case were otherwise, we cannot place any reliance upon this work for the following among other reasons:—

I. It is a well-known fact that the customs of Malabar are very peculiar. Their defenders have been, consequently, pointing to some great Rishi or some great philosopher of ancient India as their originator. Some of them affirm (probably the majority) that Parasurama brought into existence some of these customs and left a special Smriti for the guidance of the people of Malabar; others say that it was Shankaracharya who sanctioned these peculiar customs. It is not very difficult to perceive why these two persons were selected by them. According to the Hindu Puranas, Parasurama lived in Malabar for some time, and according to Hindu tradition Sankara was born in that country. But it is extremely doubtful whether either of them had anything to do with the peculiar customs of the said country. There is no allusion whatever to any of these customs in Sankara's work. He seems to have devoted his whole attention to religious reform and it is very improbable that he should have ever directed his attention to the local customs of Malabar. While attempting to revive the philosophy of the ancient Rishis, it is not likely that he should have sanctioned the customs of Malabar which are at variance with the rules laid down in the Smritis of those very Rishis; and as far as our knowledge goes he left no written regulations regarding the castes of Malabar.

II. The statements contained in Kerala Utpatti are opposed to the account of Sankara's life given in almost all the Sankara Vijiams (Biographies of Sankara) examined up to this time *viz.*, Vidyaranya's Sankara Vijiam, Chitsukhachary's Sankara Vijayavilasam, Baihat Sankara Vijiam, &c. According to the account contained in these works Sankara left Malabar in his eighth year and returned to his native village when his mother was on her death-bed when he remained there only for a few days. It is difficult to see at what period of his life-time he was engaged in making regulations for the castes of Malabar.

III. The work under consiperation represents Malabar as the seat of Bhattapada's triumphs over the Buddhists, and says that this teacher established himself in Malabar and expelled the Buddhists from that country. This statement alone will be sufficient to show to our readers the fictitious character of the account contained in this book. According to every other Hindu work, this great teacher of Purva Mimansa was born in Northern India; almost all his famous disciples and followers were living in that part of the country, and according to Vidyaranya's account he died at Allahabad.

For the foregoing reasons we cannot place any reliance upon this account of Malabar.

From the traditions and other accounts which we have hitherto examined, Mr. Wilson comes to the conclusion that Shankaracharya lived in the end of the 8th and the beginning of the 9th centuries of the Christian Era. The accounts of the Sringeri, Kudali and Cumbaconum Mathams, and the traditions current in the Bombay Presidency, as shown in the biographical sketches published at Bombay, place Sankara in some century before the Christian Era. On the other hand, Kerala Utpatti, the information obtained by Dr. Buchanan in his travels through Malabar, and the opinions expressed by Dr. Taylor and Mr. Colebrooke, concur in assigning to him an antiquity of about 1,000 years. The remaining traditions referred to by Mr. Wilson are as much opposed to his opinion as to the conclusion that Sankara lived before Christ. We shall now leave it to our readers to say whether, under such circumstances, Mr. Wilson is justified in asserting that "the weight of authority is altogether in favour" of his theory.

We have already referred to the writings of almost all the European Orientalists who expressed an opinion upon the subject under discussion; and we need hardly say that Sankara's date is yet to be ascertained.

We are obliged to comment at length on the opinions of European Orientalists regarding Sankara's date, as there will be no probability of any attention being paid to the opinion of Indian and Tibetian Initiates when it is generally believed that the question has been finally settled by their writings. The Adepts referred to by the London Theosophist are certainly in a position to clear up some of the problems in Indian religious history. But there is very little chance of their opinions being accepted by the general public under present circumstances, unless they are supported by such evidence as is within the reach of the outside world. As it is not always possible to procure such evidence, there is very little use in publishing the information which is in their possession until the public are willing to recognize and admit the antiquity and trustworthiness of their traditions, the extent of their powers and the vastness of their knowledge. In the absence of such proof as is above indicated, there is every likelihood of their opinions being rejected as absurd and untenable; their motives, will no doubt, be questioned and some people may be tempted to deny even the fact of their existence. It is often asked by Hindus as well as by Englishmen why these Adepts are so very unwilling to publish some portion at least of the information they possess regarding the truths of physical science. But in doing so, they do not seem to perceive the difference between the method by which they obtain their knowledge and the process of modern scientific investigation by which the facts of nature are ascertained and its laws are discovered. Unless an Adept can prove his conclusions by the same kind of reasoning as is adopted by the modern scientist, they remain undemonstrated to the outside world. It is of course impossible for him to develope in a considerable number of human being such faculties as would enable them to perceive their truth; and it is not always practicable to establish them by the ordinary scientific method unless all the facts and laws on which his demonstration is to be based have already been ascertained by modern science. No Adept can be expected to anticipate the discoveries of the next four or five centuries and prove some grand scientific truth to the entire satisfaction of the educated public after having discovered every fact and law of nature required for the said purpose by such process of reasoning as would be accepted by them. They have to encounter similar difficulties in giving any information regarding the events of the ancient history of India.

However, before giving the exact date assigned to Shankaracharya by the Indian and Tibetan Initiates, we shall indicate a few circumstances by which his date may be approximately determined. It is our humble opinion that the Sankara Vijiams hitherto published can be relied upon as far as they are consistent with each other regarding the general outlines of Sankara's life. We cannot, however, place any reliance whatever upon Anandagiri's Sankara Vijia published at Calcutta. The Calcutta edition not only differs in some very material points from the manuscript copies of the same work found in Southern India, but is opposed to every other Sankara Vijiam hitherto examined. It is quite clear from its style and some of the statements contained therein that it was not the production of Anandagiri, one of the four chief disciples of Sankara and the commentator on his Upanishad Bhashyam. For instance, it represents Sankara as the author of a certain verse which is to be found in Vidyaranya's Adhikaranaratnamala written in the fourteenth century. It represents Sankara as giving orders to two of his disciples to preach the Visishtadwaitee and the Dwaitee doctrines which are directly opposed to his own doctrine. The book under consideration says that Sankara went to conquer Mandanamisra in a debate followed by Sureshwaracharya, though Mandanamisra assumed the latter name at the time of initiation. It is unnecessary for us here to point out all the blunders and absurdities of this book. It will be sufficient to say that in our opinion it was not written by Anandagiri, and that it was the production of an unknowng author, whc does not appear to have been even tolerably well acquainted with the history of the Adwaitee doctrine.

Vidyaranya's (or of Sayanachary, the great commentator of the Vedas,) Sankara Vijia is decidedly the most reliable source of information as regards the main features of Sankara's biography. Its authorship has been universally accepted and the information contained therein was derived by its author, as may be seen from his own statements, from certain old biographies of Sankara existing at the time of its composition. Taking into consideration the author's vast knowledge and information, and the opportunities he had for collecting materials for his work when he was the head of the Sringeri Matham, there is every reason to believe that he had embodied in his work the most reliable information he could obtain. Mr. Wilson, however, says that the book in question is "much to poetical and legendary" to be acknowledged as a great authority. We admit that the style is highly poetical, but we deny that the work is legendary. Mr. Wilson is not justified in characterizing it as such on account of its description of some of the wonderful phenomena shown by Sankara. Probably the learned Orientalists would not be inclined to consider the Biblical account of Christ in the same light. It is not the peculiar privilege of Christianity to have a miracle-worker for its first propagator. In the following observation we shall take such facts as are required from this work.

It is generally believed that a person named Govinda Yogi was Sankara's Guru, but it is not generally known that this Yogi was in fact Patanjali—the great author of the Mahabhashya and the Yoga Sutras—under a new name. A tradition current in Southern India represents him as one of the chelas of Patanjali; but it is very doubtful if this tradition has anything like a proper foundation. But it is quite clear from the 94th, 95th, 96th, 97th verses of the 5th chapter of Vidyaranya's Sankara Vijia that Govinda Yogi and Patanjali were indentical. According to the immemorial custom observed amongst Initiates, Patanjali assumed the name of Govinda Yogi at the time of his initiation, by Goudapada. It cannot be contended that Vidyaranya represented Patanjali as Sankara's Guru merely for the purpose of assigning some importance to

Sankara and his teaching. Sankarais looked upon as a far greater man than Patanjali by the Adwaitees, and nothing can be added to Sankara's reputation by Vidyaranya's assertion. Moreover Patanjali's views are not altogether identical with Sankara's views; it may be seen from Sankara's writings that he attached no importance whatever to the practices of Hatha Yoga regarding which Patanjali composed his Yoga Sutras. Under such circumstances, if Vidyaranya had the option of selecting a Guru for Sankara he would no doubt have represented Vyasa himself (who is supposed to be still living) as his Guru. We see no reason therefore to doubt the correctness of the statement under examination. Therefore, as Sankara was Patanjali's chela and as Goudapada was his Guru, his date will enable us to fix the dates of Sankara and Goudapada. We may here point out to our readers a mistake that appears in p. 148 of Mr. Sinnett's book on Esoteric Buddhism as regards the latter personage. He is there represented as Sankara's Guru; Mr. Sinnett was informed, we believe, that he was Sankara's Paramaguru, and not having properly understood the meaning of this expression, Mr. Sinnett wrote that he was Sankara's Guru.

It is generally admitted by Orientalists that Patanjali lived before the commencement of the Christian Era. Mr. Barth places him in the second century before the Christian Era, accepting Goldstucker's opinion, and Monier Williams does the same thing. W. Weber, who seems to have carefully examined the opinions of all the other Orientalists who have written upon the subject, comes to the conclusion that "we must for the present rest satisfied with placing the date of composition of the Bhashya between B. C. 140 and A.D. 60, a result which, considering the wretched state of the chronology of Indian Literature generally, is, despite its indefiniteness, of no mean importance." And yet even this date rests upon inferences drawn from one or two unimportant expressions contained in Patanjali's Mahabhashya. It is always dangerous to draw such inferences, and especially so when it is known that, according to the tradition current amongst Hindu grammarians, some portions of Mahabhashya were lost and the gaps were subsequently filled up by subsequent writers. Even supposing that we should consider the expressions quoted as written by Patanjali himself, there is nothing in those expressions which would enable us to fix the writer's date. For instance, the connection between the expression "*Arunad Yavanah Sâketam*," and the expedition of Menander against Ayodhya between B. C. 144 and 120 relied upon by Goldstucker, is merely imaginary. There is nothing in the expression to show that the allusion contained therein points necessarily to Menander's expedition. We believe that Patanjali is referring to the expedition of *Yavanas* against Ayodhya during the lifetime of Sagara's father described in Harivamsa. This expedition occurred long before Rama's time and there is nothing to connect it with Menander. Goldstucker's inference is based upon the assumption that there was no other *Yavana* expedition against Ayodhya known to Patanjali, and it will be easily seen from Harivamsa (written by Vyasa) that the said assumption is unwarranted. Consequently the whole theory constructed by Goldstucker on this weak foundation falls to the ground. No valid inferences can be drawn from the mere names of kings contained in Mahabhashya, even if they are traced to Patanjali himself, as there would be several kings in the same dynasty bearing the same name. From the foregoing remarks it will be clear that we cannot fix, as Weber has done, B. C. 140 as the maximum limit of antiquity that can be assigned to Patanjali. It is now necessary to see whether any other such limit has been ascertained by Orientalists. As Panini's date still remains undetermined the limit cannot be fixed with reference to his date. But it is assumed by some Orientalists that Panini must have lived at sometime subsequent to Alexander's invasion, from the fact that Panini explains in his grammar the formation of the word *Yavanani*. We are very sorry that European Orientalists have taken the pains to construct theories upon this basis without ascertaining the meaning assigned to the word *Yavana* and the time when the Hindus first became acquainted with the Greeks. It is unreasonable to assume without proof that this acquaintance commenced at the time of Alexander's invasion. On the other hand there are very good reasons for believing that the Greeks were known to the Hindus long before this event. Pythagoras visited India according to the traditions current amongst Indian Initiates, and he is alluded to in Indian astrological works under the name of *Yavanacharya*. Moreover it is not quite certain that the word *Yavana* was strictly confined to the Greeks by the ancient Hindu writers. Probably it was first applied to the Egyptians and the Ethiopians; it was probably extended first to the Alexandrian Greeks and subsequently to the Greeks, Persians and Arabians. Besides the *Yavana* invasion of Ayodhya described in *Harivamsa*, there was another subsequent expedition to India by *Kala Yavana* (Black *Yavana*) during Krishna's lifetime described in the same work. This expedition was probably undertaken by the Ethiopians. Anyhow, there are no reasons whatever, as far as we can see, for asserting that Hindu writers began to use the word Yavana after Alexander's invasion. We can attach no importance whatever to any inferences that may be drawn regarding the dates of Panin and Katyayana (both of them lived before Patanjali) from the statements contained in *Katha Sarit Sagara*, which is nothing more than a mere collection of fables. It is now seen by Orientalists that no proper conclusions can be drawn regarding the dates of Panini and Katyayana from the statements made by Hiuan Thsang, and we need not therefore say anything here regarding the said statements. Consequently the dates of Panini and Katyayana still remain undetermined by European Orientalists. Goldstucker is probably correct in his conclusion that Panini lived before Buddha and the Buddhists' accounts agree with the traditions of the Initiates in asserting that Katyayana was a contemporary of Buddha. From the fact that Patanjali must have composed his Mahabhashyam after the composition of Panini's Sutras and Katyayana's Vartika we can only infer that it was written after Buddha's birth. But there are a few considerations which may help us in coming to the conclusion that Patanjali must have lived about the year 500 B.C. Max Müller fixed the Sutra period between 500 B. C. and 600 B. C. We agree with him in supposing that the period probably ended with B. C. 500, though it is uncertain how far it extended into the depths of Indian antiquity. Patanjali was the author of the Yoga Sutras, and this fact has not been doubted by any Hindu writer up to this time. Mr. Weber *thinks*, however, that the author of the Yoga Sutras, might be a different man from the author of the Mahabhashya, though he does not venture to assign any reason for his supposition. We very much doubt if any European Orientalist can ever find out the connection between the first Anhika of the Mahabhashya and the real secrets of Hatha Yoga contained in the Yoga Sutras. No one but an Initiate can understand the full significance of the said Anhika; and the "eternity of the Logos" or Sabda is one of the principal doctrines of the ancient Gymnosophists of India who were generally Hatha Yogis. In the opinion of Hindu writers and Pundits Patanjali was the author of three works, *viz.*, Mahabhashya, Yoga Sutras, and a book on Medicine and Anatomy; and there is not the slightest reason for questioning correctness of this opinion. We must, therefore, place Patanjali in the Sutra period, and this conclusion is confirmed by the traditions of the Indian Initiates. As Shankaracharya was a contemporary of Patanjali (being his Chela) he must have lived about the same time. We have thus shown that there are no reasons for placing Sankara in 8th or 9th century after Christ as some of the European Orientalists have done. We have further shown that Sankara was Patanjali's Chela and that his date should be ascertained with reference to Patanjali's date. We have also shown that neither the year B. C. 140 nor the date of Alexander's invasion can be accepted as the maximum limit of antiquity that can be assigned to him, and we have lastly pointed out a few circumstances which will justify us in expressing an opinion that Patanjali and his Chela Sankara belonged to the Sutra period. We may perhaps now venture to place before the public the exact date assigned to Shankaracharya by Tibetan and Indian Initiates. According to the historical information in their possession he was born in the year B. C. 510 (51 years and 2 months after the date of Buddha's nirvana), and we believe that satisfactory evidence in support of this date can be obtained in India if the inscriptions at Conjeveram, Sringeri, Jaggurnath, Benares, Cashmere and various other places visited by Sankara are properly deciphered. Sankara built Conjeveram, which is considered as one of the most ancient towns in Southren India; and it may be possible to ascertain the time of its construction if proper enquiries are made. But even the evidence now brought before the public supports the opinion of the initiates above indicated. As Goudpada was Shankaracharya's Guru's Guru his date entirely depends on Sankara's date; and there is every reason to suppose that he lived before Buddha. As this article has already become very legngthy we will now bring it to a close. Our remarks about Buddha's date and Shankaracharya's doctrine will appear hereafter.

AGE OF LORD BUDDHA'S DEATH.

INSCRIPTION DISCOVERED BY GENERAL A. CUNNINGHAM.

We have carefully examined the new inscription discovered by General A. Cunningham on the strength of which the date assigned to Buddha's death by Buddhist writers has been declared to be incorrect; and we are of opinion that the said inscription confirms the truth of the Buddhist tradition instead of proving them to be erroneous. The abovementioned archæologist writes as follows regarding the inscription under consideration in the first volume of his report:—"The most interesting inscription (at Gaya) is a long and perfect one dated in the era of the Nirvana or death of Buddha. I read the date as follows:—*Bhagavati Parinirvritlee Samvat* 1819 *Karttike badi* 1 *Budhi*—that is 'in the year 1819 of the Emancipation of Bhagavata on Wednesday, the first day of the waning moon of Kartik.' If the era here used is the same as that of the Buddists of Ceylon and Burmah, which began in 543 B. C., the date of this inscription will be 1819—543= A. D. 1276. The style of the letters is in keeping with this date, but is quite incompatible with that derivable from the Chinese date of the era. The Chinese place the death of Buddha upwards of 1000 years before Christ, so that according to them, the date of this inscription would be about A. D. 800, a period much too early for the style of character used in the inscription. But as the day of the week is here fortunately added, the date can be verified by calculation. According to my calculation the date of the inscription corresponds with Wednesday, the 17th September A. D. 1342. This would place the Nirvana of Buddha in 477 B. C., which is the very year that was first proposed by myself as the most probable date of that event. This corrected date has since been adopted by Professor Max Müller."

The reasons assigned by some Orientalists for considering this so-called "corrected date" as the real date of Buddha's death have already been noticed and criticized in the preceding article;* and now we have only to consider whether the inscription in question disproves the old date.

Major General Cunningham evidently seems to take it for granted, as far as his present calculation is concerned, that the number of days in a year is counted in the Magadha country by Buddhist writers in general on the same basis on which the number of days in a current English year is counted; and this wrong assumption has vitiated his calculation and led him to a wrong conclusion. Three different methods of calculation were in use in India at the time when

---

* See "Replies to Inquiries suggested by *Esoteric Buddhism*," *Theosophist*, vol. v., pp. 35—43.

Buddha lived, and they are still in use in different parts of the country. These methods are known as *Souramanam, Chandramanam* and *Barhaspatyamanam*. According to the Hindu works on Astronomy a Souramanam year consists of 365 days, 15 ghadias and 31 vighadias; a Chandramanam year has 360 days, and a year on the basis of Barhaspatyamanam has 361 days and 11 ghadias nearly. Such being the case, General Cunningham ought to have taken the trouble of ascertaining before he made his calculation the particular *manam* employed by the writers of Magadha and Ceylon in giving the date of Buddha's death and the *manam* used in calculation the years of the *Buddhist era* mentioned in the inscription above quoted. Instead of placing himself in the position of the writer of the said inscription and making the required calculation from that standpoint, he made the calculation on the same basis on which an English gentleman of the 19th century would calculate time according to his own calendar.

If the calculation were correctly made, it would have shown him that the inscription in question is perfectly consistent with the statement that Buddha died in the year 543 B. C. according to Barhaspatyamanam (the only *manam* used in Magadha and by Pali writers in general). The correctness of this assertion will be clearly seen on examining the following calculation.

543 years according to Barhaspatyamanam are equivalent to 536 years and 8 months (nearly) according to Souramanam.

Similarly 1819 years according to the former *manam* are equivalent to 1798 years nearly according to the latter manam.

As the Christian era commenced on the 3102 in the year of Kaliyuga (according to Souramanam) Buddha died in the year 2565 of Kaliyuga and the inscription was written in the year 4362 of Kaliyuga (according to Souramanam). And now the question is whether according to the Hindu Almanac, the first day of the waning moon of Kartik coincided with a Wednesday.

According to Suryasiddhanta the number of days from the beginning of Kaliyuga up to midnight on the 15th day of increasing moon of Aswina is 1,593,072 (the number of Adhikamasansas (extra months) during the interval being 1608 and the number of Kshayathithis 25,323.

If we divide this number by 7 the remainder would be 5. As Kaliyuga commenced with Friday, the period of time above defined closed with Tuesday, as according to Suryasiddhanta a week-day is counted from midnight to midnight.

It is to be noticed that in place where Barhaspatyamanam is in use Krishnapaksham (or the dark half) commences first and is followed by Suklapaksham.

Consequently the next day after the 15th day of the waning moon of Aswina will be the 1st day of the waning moon of Kartika to those who are guided by the Barhaspatyamanam calendar. And therefore the latter date, which is the date mentioned in the inscription, was Wednesday in the year 4362 of Kaliyuga.

The geocentric longitude of the sun at the time of his meridian passage on the said date being 174°—20′—16″ and the moon's longitude being 7°—51′—42″ (according to Suryasiddhanta (it can be easily seen that at Gaya there was Padyamithithi (1st day of waning moon) for nearly 7 ghadias and 50 vighadias from the time of sunrise.

It is clear from the foregoing calculation that "Kartika 1 Badi" coincided with Wednesday in the year 4362 of Kaliyuga or the year 1261 of the Christian era, and that from the standpoint of the person who wrote the inscription the said year was the 1819th year of the Buddhist era. And consequently this new inscription confirms the correctness of the date assigned to Buddha's death by Buddhist writers. It would have been better if Major General Cunningham had carefully examined the basis of his calculation before proclaiming to the world at large that the Buddhist accounts were untrustworthy.

BUDD-HISM AND ANCIENT WISDOM-RELIGION.

[*Note added in reply to a correspondent.*]

We are in a position to state that Mr. Sinnett never intented to maintain that Buddhism, as popularly conceived, is the nearest approach ever made to the ancient Wisdom-Religion. His assertion simply means that the Tibetan from of Exoteric Buddhism is in closer connection at present with the Esoteric Doctrine than any other popular religion on account of the presence of the great Himalayan Brotherhood in Tibet, and their constant guidance, care and supervision. The name given to Mr. Sinnett's book will not be misleading or objectionable when the close identity between the doctrines therein expounded and those of the ancient Rishis of India is clearly perceived. As the writer of the foregoing article seems to be in a state of doubt as to the position occupied by the septenary constitution of man as expounded by Mr. Sinnett, in the Aryan Hindu Occult System, we shall herein below state in a tabular form corresponding principles recognized by the Vedantic teachers :—

Classification in Esoteric Buddhism.	Vedantic Classification.	Classification in Tharaka Raja Yoga.
(1.) Sthula sarira	Annamaya kosa	Sthulopadhi.
(2.) Prana	Pranamaya kosa	
(3.) The Vehicle of Prana		
(4.) Kamarupa	Manomaya kosa	Sukshmopadhi.
(5.) Mind (a) Volutions and feelings, &c.		
(5.) Mind (b) Vignanam	Vignanamaya kosa	
(6.) Spiritual Soul	Anandamaya kosa	Karanopadhi.
(7.) Atma	Atma	Atma.

From the foregoing table it will be seen that the 3rd principle in the Buddhist classification is not seperately mentioned in the Vendantic division as it is merely the vehicle of Prana. It will also be seen that the 4th principle is included in the 3rd kosa, as the said principle is but the vehicle of will power which is but an energy of the mind. It must also be noticed that Vignanamayakosa is considered to be distinct from Manomayakosa, as a division is made after death between the lower part of the mind, as it were, which has a closer affinity with the 4th principle than with the sixth and its higher part, which attaches itself to the latter and which is in fact the basis for the higher spiritual individuality of man.

We may also here point out to our readers that the classification mentioned in the last column is for all practical purposes connected with Raja Yoga, the best and simplest. Though there are 7 principles in man, there are but 3 distinct Upadhis, in each of which his *Atma* may work independently of the rest. These 3 Upadhis can be separated by an adept without killing himself. He cannot separate the 7 principles from each other without destroying his constitution.

THE "OCCULT WORLD."

HAPPY MR. HENRY KIDDLE'S DISCOVERY.

I HAVE been watching with considerable interest the effect produced on the Western Public by Mr. Sinnett's book on "Esoteric Buddhism;" and I have not been disappointed in my expectations. There is nothing surprising in the attitude of the Spiritualists towards Theosophy and its Teachers. Startled by the strange phenomena—erroneously called *spirit* manifestations, which have been witnessed during the last few years, the majority of the so-called Spiritualists have firmly persuaded themselves into the belief that those manifestations indicate a turning point in the history of mankind, that they are destined to introduce into the world a sublime system of religous philosophy which will supplant every other existing system whether in the East or in the West, and that for the first time in the annals of this globe man is being permitted through the instrumentality of the manifestations to have a glimpse into the mysterious inner world. Thy are not probably aware of the fact, or they are extremely unwilling to believe, that these phenomena were known in the East for long ages and that their mysterious causes were carefully studied by esoteric mystics. They are evidently offended at being told that these phenomena are rather stale to the Eastern nations; that there is nothing very profound either in their manifestations or in their immediate causes, that they can never unravel the real mystery of the manifested Cosmos or of the human Spirit (7th principle)! and that all *they* can teach was long ago known to the Eastern Occultists. And probably there is another reason why the Spiritualists and the Teosophists of the West do not treat the teachings embodied in Mr. Sinnett's "Occult World" and "Esoteric Buddhism" with the serions attention that they deserve. Western nations are accustomed to look upon the Esterns as their inferiors in *every respect*. In their opinion, as it seems, muscular strength is always co-existent with intellectual power and spiritual insight; and European political ascendency means and includes intellectual and spiritual superiority. Hence they are too proud to admit that there are mystics in the East who know a good deal more about nature and her laws than all their scientists, philosophers, Spiritualists and religious teachers put together. The discovery of Mahatmas in the East is almost a nightmare to them; and they would feel very happy to get rid of it as soon as possible. Therefore instead of carefully examining the theories propounded in Mr. Sinnett's book, they are trying their best to ferret out a few facts and incidents which will enable them to disprove the existence of our Mahatmas, render it extremely doubtful; or if both these courses be found impracticable, to show the Sadhus extremely inferior to themselves. Several prominent Spiritualists have already been giving absurd, superficial and one-sided accounts of the doctrines contained in Mr. Sinnett's book apparently with a view to allay the fears of orthodox Spiritualists, to soothe their own feelings and to vindicate the importance and incomparable grandeur of the "New Dispensation" ushered into the civilized and enlightened West by spirit-rapping and table-turning; while some other Spiritualists are probably consoling themselves with the idea that even if the Mahatmas should be proved to have an actual existence (outside of Madam Blavatsky) they cannot be anything more than spirits (Pisachas!), or, at best—strong physical mediums. Under such circumstances anything like argument with the Spiritualists is worse than useless. Mere phenomena, however wonderful, can never prove to their satisfaction either the actual existence of Adepts or the nature of true Adeptship. Any phenomena that you may show them will at once be attributed to the agency of spirits (as they are called by them) or elementals as we call them, and classed with their own *seance* room manifestations. Even if we were to effect an impossibility and induce one of our Eastern Adepts to appear in London and prove his existence and knowledge before their eyes, these phenomena-hunters would proclaim him by way of compliment an excellent medium and nothing more. Hence, it is not difficult to foresee that so long as the general body of Spiritualists or their leaders are satisfied with their own illogical and fanciful hypothesis and make no attempt to investigate scientifically their phenomena and their causes in connection with the ancient systems of religious philosophy and occultism, it is impossible to expect them to give a patient hearing to the teachings of our Mahatmas. To a real scientific investigator who is attempting to ascertain the general law governing a particular class of phenomena, even the suggestion of a plausible hypothesis is of considerable value. The Mahatmas have never declared that they would give a systematic and exhaustive exposition of the Occult Science, but only that they intended to place before the general public a few general doctrines which might suggest some reasonable hypothesis by which the experience of ancient mystics and the so-called Spiritualistic phenomena of modern time may be kint together, and brought under one general law, and which may also show to some extent the scientific basis of all ancient religions whose teachings are generally supposed to be diametrically opposed to those of modern science. To every genuine Occultist and every student of science these doctrines are of immense importance; especially at the present time, when old religious systems are dying out from want of real vital strength, when science has as yet found no means of penetrating into the inner world of noumena, and when the strange manifestation taking place in *seance*-rooms are rejected by the majority of the men of science as absurd superstitions, while they are regarded by the Spiritualists as indicative of the existence of disembodied Spirits!

Our Eastern doctrines having been proclaimed by the general body of Spiritualists as impertinent intruders, leaders of that body seem to have discovered at last a very simple means for getting rid of them. Mr. Henry Kiddle has found out that the Mahatma whose instructions are embodied in Mr. Sinnett's publications has committed an act of plagiarism in borrowing certain sentences from one of his lectures without admitting his obligation. He tells us, he wrote to Mr. Sinnett about his discovery more than a year ago; and though Mr. Sinnett distinctly states that he never heard from him, this American discoverer has been very persistently complaining to the public of the great injury done to him. This is considered as a very "grave charge" by the Spiritualists, who suppose that it "strikes at the very root of the pretentions of the Adepts." But if these Spiritualists, "Perplexed Readers," and "Students" who are making such a terrible fuss about the matter were to examine the passage in question carefully, they will, perchance, be able to perceive that there is evidently some confusion and mistake in the whole matter, and that the probabilities of the case are against the truth of Mr. Kiddle's complaint. Upon a closer examination of it I find that—

I. So far as the leading idea in the passage is concerned, if any body has committed literary theft it is the complainant himself and not the accused. I find no reference to Plato in the passages quoted from Mr. Kiddle's lecture in his letter published in *Light*,* and the complainant has very prudently omitted the reference to the Greek philosopher that precedes the passages which he reproduces from the Mahatma's letter.

---

* Nor is there in his now famous lecture at Lake Pleasant, for we have procured and carefully read it.—*Ed.*

II. There seems to be nothing very sublime in the language used by Mr. Kiddle in the passage under consideration; and it may be easily seen from the other letters written to Mr. Sinnett by the Mahatma concerned, that the said Mahatma's English vocabulary is not more limited than his own and that he is not wanting in power of expression. It is, therefore, very difficult to see why the Master should have borrowed Mr. Kiddle's language, unless some good reason can be shown for it.

II. There are certain expressions and certain alterations of Mr. Kiddle's language in the passage in question which show that the Mahatma never intended to borrow Mr. Kiddle's ideas and phrases, but that he rather intended to say something against them. Where the Spiritualistic lecturer says that "the world advances," the Mahatma says that "the world *will* advance" for the purpose of showing that this change in ideas must inevitably take place by reason of the great cyclic Law to which the Universe is subject. Where the lecturer says that "the agency called Spiritualism is bringing a new set of ideas into the world," the Mahatma emphatically affirms that "it is not physical phenomena" that he and his brother Occultists study, but "these universal ideas" which are as it were the noumena underlying all physical manifestations. The contrast between the Mahatma's view of the relationship between these ideas and physical phenomena, and Mr. Kiddle's view is striking. The latter thinks that new ideas are being introduced into the world by physical phenomena, which the former thinks that new physical phenomena have begun to manifest themselves by reason of a change in these general ideas (noumena) which govern all physical phenomena in the objective world. It seems to me that even the word 'idea' has been used in two different senses by the Mahatma and Mr. Kiddle respectively. The former means by the word 'idea' the original form or type according to which the objective manifestation takes place. And this is Plato's meaning which the Spiritualistic lecturer has not properly understood. Mr. Kiddle, on the other hand, uses the same word in the sense it is ordinarily used by English writers. And again, where the lecturer speaks of "the universal reign of law as the expression of the divine will," the Mahatma postulates the existence of "an immutable Law" not depending on any divine will.

But "A Perplexed Reader," writing to *Light*, says that the Mahatma "has omitted inconvenient words and has so distorted the ideas he has borrowed as to divert them from their original intention to suit his own very different purpose." If there is a difference of words and ideas, where is the offence? Or is it a law of plagiarism that the person who borrows from another's writings should do so without making the slightest alteration in the passage extracted? If this "Perplexed Reader" were not also a perplexed thinker, he would have seen that these very alterations in the passage in question go very far to show that there was no intention on the Mahatma's part to borrow Mr. Kiddle's inaccurate language and erroneous ideas, and that there is some misconception—some mistake in all this.

IV. It is quite evident from the wording of the passage under examination that there *is* "something wrong somewhere." Plato is introduced into it rather abruptly and the grammatical construction of the last sentence is by no means clear. Apparently there is no predicate which refers to "ideas larger," &c.

A part of the sentence is thus evidently lost . . . . From the foregoing consideration it will be clearly seen that it could not have been the Mahatma's intention to *borrow* anything from Mr. Kiddle's lecture. On the other hand, the Mahatma's emphatic declaration immediately preceding the passage in question, that Adepts of the "Good Law" do not believe in any other but planetary spirits, his remarks regarding the insufficiency and worthlessness of more physical phenomena in unraveling the mysteries of the noumena world, and his enunciation of the existence of an immutable law in no way subject to the divine will, the existence of which is assumed by the lecturer—all tend to show that the Mahatma's real intention was rather to criticise than adopt the views of the Spiritualists as embodied in Mr. Kiddle's remarks. Therefore, from a careful perusal of the passage and its contents, any unbiassed reader will come to the conclusion that somebody must have greatly plundered over the said passage and will not be surprised to hear that it was unconsciously altered through the carelessness and ignorance of the Chela by whose instrumentality it was "precipitated." Such alterations, omissions and mistakes sometimes occur in the process of precipitation; and I now assert, I know it for certain *from an inspection of the original precipitation proof*, that such was the case with regard to the passage under discussion, I can assure the "Student" who throws out a suggestion in his letter to *Light* that there might be some deep psychological problem involved in the matter in dispute, that there *is* one, and that one is no other psychological mystery than the above indicated. The Mahatma against whom the accusation has been brought will, of course, think it beneath his dignity to offer any explanation in his own defence to Mr. Kiddle or his followers and supporters. But I hope Mr. Sinnett will be good enough to place before the public as soon as possible such explanation or information as he may be permitted by the Mahatma concerned, with regard to the "Mystery" of the passage in question and the manner in which the letter which contains the said passage was received by him.

In conclusion I cannot but regret that some writers in the Spiritualistic organs and other English journals have thought it fit to drag our Mahatma's name into public print without any necessity for doing so, using, moreover, such remarks and insinuations as are fully calculated to be highly offensive to those who have the good fortune to be personally known to, and acquainted with, the Mahatma in question. The reproach contained in the *Protest* of 500 Hindu theosophists—just published in *Light*—may be fairly applied to many a Spiritualists besides "G. W. M. D."

NOTES ON OCCULT PHILOSOPHY.

[The following notes are answers to philosophical questions raised by some of the Delegates at the Convention of the T. S., which were taken up at the time by a member.]

DEVACHAN.

It has been asked why the activity exhibited by a human monad in Devachan should last through a longer period of time than that same monad's activity on the present plane of existence ?

From our present standpoint the difference is a great one, but this is not so from the standpoint of the Devachanee. When a Yogi is in a state of Samadhi, years may pass and seem only months or days to him. Energy exerted on the astral plane produces effects which last for a longer period of time than those produced by an equal amount of energy on the material plane, for the reason that less friction of opposition is encountered on the astral plane.

On the objective plane, the metallic sound produced by the striking of a bell will not last more than five or six minutes, however, finely the bell be made; but after the sound seems dead to the ordinary man, the chela can hear it on the astral plane for one or two hours longer. So we say that the momentum being the same, the period of time occupied by effects differs on the material and on the astral plane.

It is not possible to fix beforehand the definite length of the time passed by a human being or even a race, in Devachan; that depends a great deal upon the nature and development of the spiritual monad in the man, and also on the impulses it has generated in the world of effects and, more or less, on the nature of the man's aspirations. When the element of spirituality appears in the monad, its Devachanic existence will be longer. Perhaps the highest adept, after making a careful psychical analysis of a man, would be able to foretell the length of the latter's stay in Devachan within one or two thousand years, but he could not give the exact duration.

In estimating the influence on a man's Devachanic existence of a particular thought or train of thought, we must enquire into the utility of the latter and its effect on the world at large, and not imagine that everything depends upon whether the thought is subjective or objective.

It is a mistake to suppse that ideation which refers to practical work has less potentiality in this direction than ideation which only relates to the mental plane.

Good work on the physical plane hepls on our spiritual development.

First, by its influence on the formation of habits; a man constantly engaged in doing good works is not likely to fall into bad habits.

Secondly, by its effects on both the astral and the physical plane, a good action has the effect of concentrating good influences on the doer. When a man makes bad Karma, by the very ideation he attracts to himself forces which will lead him from bad to worse. A man, who has good ideas, attracts influences of quite a different kind and these will begin to help him on his way.

On the other hand, actions must not be judged of by their effects alone, because then one element is wanting, the inward impulse prompting the act must also be taken into consideration.

The question of our responsibility for the occurrence of a bad thought must be considered from a purely causal standpoint, so that the introduction of anything like the idea of a judge may be avoided.

The fact that the bad thought has occurred in your mind, makes an impression on the astral plane, though, if the thought is driven away by opposition, the bad effects may be neutralized. But if your will-power gives way to the bad ideas, they will produce evil effects, whereas if a determined will-power controls your thoughts, you will get into the path of virtue.

Devachanic existence does not always begin immediately after death. The period in the case of very good people begins immediately and the transition of Kamaloka is not felt.

There are no doubt a few other cases, such as that of an infant, whose monad has exhausted the results of its Karma, or where there is some physical reason against existence in a particular body, where the reincarnation may take place after a few minutes, or on the other hand it may not do so for a hundred years, during which period the entity is in a profound sleep and there is nothing like ideation.

When an entity reincarnates, the shell is invariably disintegrated.

THE HUMAN MONAD.

A complete explanation of what is meant by the term "human monad" would include the whole range of occult science. It may be said, however, that the human monad is not identical with the seventh principle, the Atma or Logos; it is energy which works through the sixth principle. It is the one energy diffused from the Logos, the one life proceeding from the Logos as an active entity.

What is meant will be best explained in a simile.

Take the sun; according to the occult theory, that which emanates from it is uniformly spread throughout boundless space, the sun, is like a focus in which this matter is concentrated and which it is given off as visible light and heat. The one element is Parabrahm, and whenever the centre of activity called the Logos emerges from it as an active force, this force is the one element in its active condition, the one life, and it is the very same power which Hartmann describes as the one unconscious energy which may be called the will-power of nature, which produces consciousness and every other physical fact in the manifested universe.

We cannot say it comes into existence at any particular time, it seems latent in the one life throughout but at its appearance as an active energy, it is the first germ of consciousness in the whole universe. This is Atma.

This is but one power, it begins to work through all the gradations of the various kingdoms, and on arriving at the plane of human volition, becomes differentiated and acquires a certain kind of individuality and this we call the monad. If this monad were not interconnected with the Logos, immortality would be impossible, but as it has been defused through the Logos, there is a change of its passing back through the Logos again and so gaining immortality.

The experiences of to-day are not those of to-morrow, each day a man may be considered as a different being, but there seems to be something within each of us on which all these varied experiences are strung and by which they have something like a continuity. The monad may be considered as a string on which the experiences of many births are strung. You may consider the Logos as the basis of innumerable monads. These never die out but start into active existence again. All the human beings whose experiences have been brought to the Logos by the travelling monad may be said to have gained immortality, but sometimes the monad becomes so opposed in its magnetic effect to the Logos from which it has emanated, that its absorption is impossible. This happens only in the case of a very wicked man, and then that monad never gains immortality; it may live on till the Pralaya arrives; and is then merged into the ocean of cosmic matter without transferring its impressions to any Logos.

A monad may remain for perhaps millions of years, till the Pralaya comes, this time can be almost called infinity, but it is as nothing in comparison to the existence of the Logos itself.

Is the ego ever really wiped out or effaced ?

The monad is never killed though the man may be. You call the monad by a particular name so long as it retains the owner's subjective experiences, but when the monad is made quite clean, you can say the experiences are wiped out. A monad is only a centre of energy.

Nirvana means the absorption into the Logos, but for the purpose of differentiating, three conditions are intended by the one name. A period of rest not only from objective but also from subjective activity arrives after the completion of each round, but the real Nirvanic condition is only reached when the monad is transferred into the Logos and the man's life becomes part of the life of the Logos.

Many have asked whether after the close of one solar manvantara when a particular monad is absorbed into the Logos if by the activity of the same Logos that monad is again ejected; if so it would be said that even after the absorption birth is possible, but from the stand-point of the Logos there is no birth. Just as I may send my aura to your brain, the Logos emits a ray from itself into matter, the Logos does not suffer, but the ray does. From the stand-point of the Logos there is no rebirth.

The Logos has an objective existence. Beyond Logos there is the unmanifested Parabrahm.

Vishnu is the Logos. Brahma is the universal mind, the Demiurgos.

Each Logos has a consciousness of its own. Consciousness which is non-consciousness, means a state of consciousness unlike the state of consciousness with which we are acquainted.

THOUGHT-TRANSFERENCE.

The only explanation we can give of the phenomena of thought-transference depends upon the existence of the astral fluid,—a fluid which exists throughout the manifested solar system, but which does not extend beyond it.

It must be borne in mind that there is a difference between Âkâsh and the astral light, though the two terms have often been used as being synonymous. Âkâsh is a much higher kind of cosmic ether which exists as a link between one solar system and another, and is as infinite as the original cosmic matter. It is the result of motion in that very cosmic matter. Astral light is not âkâsh, but a different form of cosmic ether. It is simply that entity in the manifested solar system, which corresponds to what we have called the fourth principle in man. It is a manifestation of undifferentiated matter. It is a kind of matter far more ethereal than any with which we are acquainted. Perhaps matter in its ultra-gaseous condition—radiant matter—may help us to a conception of the astral fluid. Though it exists uniformly throughout space in the solar system, it is yet more dense around certain objects by reason of their molecular action, this is especially the case around the brain and spinal cord of human beings, where it forms what is called the aura. It is this aura round the nerve cells and nerve tubes which enables a man to catch the impressions made upon the astral light in the cosmos. If we divide mental phenomena into the three branches of modern psychologists ; intellectual images, emotions and volition, we find that volition always makes itself felt by an increase of vibration in the astral aura. The intellectual image makes itself felt by the impression of the image on the aura; and in other cases there is a change of colour which also corresponds to change of spiritual feelings.

It is asserted that each colour corresponds to a certain emotion, but I am not prepared to say occultists agree with phrenologists in their arrangement.

If I have the idea of a circle, the figure of a circle is formed in the sensitive's odic aura. All mental ideas have their pictures in astral light which are almost similar to the images that afterwards rise in the brain, but the intermediate link between the two, the nerve current in the brain, does not actually describe the picture in the mind. If there were in space no medium to serve as a means of communication between one human being and another, all thought-transference would be impossible, it is impossible so conceive of communication without a medium.

The existence of this astral light can be proved from the fact that certain phenomena can only be explained upon the assumption of such existence, and it is moreover an objcet of direct perception to Adepts. Once let its existence be granted, and also the fact that it concentrates itself more thickly around the brain and nervous system than elsewhere, and you will see that nature has made provision to enable a person to catch the impressions made by others on the astral light.

In thought-reading experiments the best results have generally been obtained from children. The reason of this is that the aura of a child is passive, because it has not generated any active tendencies of its own. This fact can be inferred from the difference in colour between the aura of a child and that of an adult. The aura of a child is milk-white, but in the case of a grown-up person there is always upon this basic colour, another colour as green, yellow, red, &c. These colours denote a particular peculiarity of mental or spiritual organization. Whenever one of these colours is present and shows an absence of sympathy with the characteristics indicated by the colour of the aura of the operator, then a repulsion will be set up; but when there is no such repulsion—whenever the mind is passive, thought-transference is possible.

Every thought is accompanied by another physical phenomenon which may be described as an alteration in the nervous fluid. There is intimate connection between nerve-fluid properly so-called and the aura surrounding it. Nerve-fluid has its own aura like every congregation of molecules in nature, even prime ether has its own aura which is âkâsh. Nerve-fluid has its own aura, called the odic aura of the man. All auras have one base, they are all akin to the magnetic fluid in the cosmos. For every thought there is an affection of the nerve currents of the brain or nerve. This implies vibration which is caught up by the astral aura which communicates with the astral fluid with which it is in contact.

This vibration affects the odic aura round the thinker's brain, and is immediately transmitted to the brain to which the thought is transferred ; it is converted into a particular kind of motion in his aura and then into action in the nerve-fluid and is thus immediately transmitted to his brain.

If the will-power of the operator is not strong enough to give a direction to the vibration generated in the astral fluid, touch is generally required; and where there is magnetic sympathy or at least absence of repulsive tendencies, the vibration immediately reaches its destination and is transferred into a thought in the mind of the sensative, which will be the same thought first generated in the mind of the operator. If a particular sort of motion in nerve-fluid means a certain thing in the mind of one man, it means the same thing in another man's mind.

The ideas of modern scientists about luminiferous ether are hardly sufficiently definite to enable us to express an opinion about their resemblance to our views, but from the manner in which the conclusions have been arrived at, we see certain differences.

First, we see light coming to us from the fixed stars, and they say, admitting the undulatory theory of optics, there must be a medium through which the vibrations pass.

Secondly, they have ascertained from minute mathematical calculations that, owing to friction in this ether, there is a certain amount of retardation in the path of the planets. Admitting the two premises, it will be plain that the ether exists throughout space; now the astral fluid does not exist throughout space, but âkâsh does, and the latter is more likely to correspond with the ether of the scientists.

Their cosmic ether is not peculiarly permanent in connection with any particular organism and does not appear to have any special connection with nerve force, but we hold that whenever there is a specially sensitive organization, the astral fluid is there concentrated, and in other places it exists more or less uniformly diffused, but its uniformity is never continuous like that of the ether of the scientists.

The fact is that the astral fluid only comes into existence when certain kinds of differentiation take place in the original Mulaprakriti.

If the scientists recognize a distinction between "bound ether" and "free ether," it amounts to the same kind of distinction as that between astral fluid and âkâsh, but even as it exists in point of space without any organisms, it differs in its constitution from real cosmic ether.

In the course of ordinary thought-transference there is no mediation of any elemental whatever.

In certain cases we find that a sense of calamity is felt by a person at a distance when his friend is dying; in such instances the impression is actually a picture of the person and sometimes the image is very distinct. But we believe that somehow our mental ideas are connected with the emotions of pleasure and pain; therefore, admitting that some currents are accompanied by feelings without images, we may conceive a case in which the image, being indistinct, is accompanied by a nerve current which is only expressed by an emotion. Sometimes there are variations. It may be that a portion of the picture is lost, or some new elements are introduced, but when there is no picture, but only a kind of vibration, there will be nothing but a vague ideas of grief or calamity.

Again, we sometimes find that the recipient has some token transferred to him, such as, for instance, a coffin when a person is dying.

I believe if we take into consideration the results likely to be produced by the laws of psychological association, the case is that particular groups of ideas are connected, as death with a coffin in the mind of a Christian, &c.

One idea has the effect of recalling other ideas which are associated with it. Any of these ideas may be pictured in the brain and be followed by other ideas, and sometimes it happens that the associations become more prominent than the main idea.

A case is mentioned in which a soldier's wife, travelling with the regiment, one night, while her husband was present and seated on a chair, declared she saw her mother appear, that her mother pressed her shoulders and said : "And I have left you the cream-jug, mind you get it." The husband heard and saw nothing. The figure then vanished, and it was afterwards found that the mother had died and left a cream-jug to her daughter.

This was a case of thought-transference. The woman must have been very anxious to give her daughter this information before her death, anxiety must have increased, when she was dying the thought connected itself with her aura, that thought carried with it, at the time of dissolution, the odic aura of the person herself, but it is not a case of the astral body going to a distance. In all cases except those where Adepts are concerned it is the energy of thought-transference which sometimes takes a portion of a person's aura. Generally this takes place in cases of death ; in other cases, unless the person is clairvoyant, it will not be possible for the astral body to be seen.

Sometimes it happens that when a portion of the aura is thus brought, it will be visible only to the man to whom the thought refers.

When the thought is transferred, the image is transferred. From a more distinct mental subjective image an objective figure, there may be infinite gradations of clearness and visibility.

Another case was as follows : A lady was going to India to her brother, she died on the voyage, and was seen clad, as at the moment of death, by the *brother's wife* three hours after the death occurred.

Here there must either have been strong sympathy between the two, or else the sister must have been a seer, or there must have been some other agency, such as an elemental at work. It is a case of thought-transference, but in the absence of further particulars a detailed explanation cannot be given.

The impression could not have been transferred from the husband to the wife if the former did not see the apparition.

As to the difference of three hours between time of death and of the appearance, generally speaking, the shell may wander about for a time, unless it is a case of a death at which all the principles are immediately separated. If this was so, if the dead body had these two persons in her mind, there is every likelihood that the shell would travel to the place, and not finding the person to whom she wished to communicate sufficiently sensitive, she communicated with the more sensitive person who was present.

There cannot be any delay in the mere transmission of the image. The mind may be sometimes active in cases of insensibility. You may have read accounts of persons under chloroform where the internal man was feeling peculiar sensations though apparently insensible. The delay might be accounted for by supposing the person to whom the image is transmitted did receive the image by means of his odic aura, but his brain being at work at the time did not cognize the impression; it will be sometime before the impression is effaced, so the image may make itself felt at some future time.

The following instance differs in many ways from the previous ones. A man willed his own appearance at a distance to two ladies on a certain occasion. He went to bed and woke up unconscious of anything having taken place, but was afterwards told that on a certain night he had appeared to them and acted in accordance which details previously written down. They had seen him as if in life.

This may be accounted for in various ways. He may have dreamt though ignorant of having done so, and again the astral man may have states of consciousness of his own, of which the physical man is ignorant and which last for some time. Again, it may be possible that this will-power that he should go at a particular time had the effect of producing a particular nerve current in his brain, and it might actually have emanated from his brain at the time he had willed. In such cases I do not know of any instances in which the time set has varied. There are many cases to be disposed of on that supposition, the only way in which we can account for it is, that the astral man generated the impression at a particular moment without the knowledge of the physical brain, or else it was generated in the physical brain according to the impression left by the first determination.

THOUGHTS ON KAMA-LOKA.

*Suggested by Mr. Sinnett's paper on the same subject.**

In considering this subject we must, above all things, take care to realise that the seven principles in man are not several entities or substances that can be separated and each considered as a distinct individuality having definite characteristics peculiar to itself. In Sanskrit the different principles are called *Upadhis*, *i. e.*, the sheaths or seats of the different states of existence of the ONE LIFE.

The seat of consciousness which gives rise to the feeling of individuality and the sense "I am I" is in the fifth principle.

If there is no fifth principle, *i. e.*, if there is no consciousness of individuality, all the other states of existence are non-existent, for without a percipient ego there can be neither perception nor any object of perception. Hence it is said, that without the son (the germ of consciousness in the Logos roused into activity at the time of Cosmic evolution) there is no Father or Mother. The Father and the Holy Ghost come into existence when the Son is born, and this is the true occult explanation of the Trinity in Unity and Unity in Trinity. Perhaps it may be objected that animals can take cognisance of existence although they have no fifth principle; but the reason of this is that, although the fifth principle is not *united* to the lower principles of the animals, it yet *over-*

* *Vide* the *Theosophist*, February 1885, page 106.

shadows them. Thus, properly speaking, it is the fifth principle only which plays a prominent part in the various states of man in life and after death. By its association (no matter how, for the present) with the lower principles, it generates earthly and material tendencies which attract it downwards. At the same time, being *overshadowed* by *its* father, the sixth and seventh principles, it generates higher aspirations which attract it upwards. After physical death, when the entity passes into *Kama-Loka,* the real struggle is confined to the fifth principle alone, that is, to the seat of consciousness, together with the affinities generated in it during its earthly incarnation. In *Kama-Loka,* therefore, the fourth principle or *Kama-Rupa,* which is the *Upadhi* or seat of all earthly desires and passions, &c., drags towards itself those affinities of the fifth principle which are of a material nature, while the higher aspirations are attracted towards the sixth and the seventh principles. The conception may be made clear by remembering that the seventh principle is the source of energy, while the sixth principle is merely the energy radiated by the seventh. The states of existence of man may be divided into three which can be again divided into seven. The first three are :—physical life, astral life and spiritual life. The seven states are:—(1) Physical life, (2) the state between physical and astral life, (3) the astral life, (4) the state between the astral life and the spiritual life, and (5, 6, 7,) the three states of spiritual life. In physical life, all the physical activities are strong while the astral life is exhibited in the temporary cessation of the functions of physical activities, as takes place in sleep, &c. Each life manifests itself only on those spheres to which its organisation is adapted. Thus for manifesation on this physical world a physical organism is essential, and without its help no activity can be manifested in this sphere. In this life we have, as it were, brought with us such an accretion of principles as has been produced by the *effects* of the causes generated in a previous incarnation. At the same time we have an organisation which enables us to generate new causes. When the physical body is worn out by the activities manifested through it, the cohesive force which held its particles together becomes weaker and weaker until physical death takes place. We do not therefore die at once (except in cases of sudden death caused by accidents, &c.), but are gradually dying every moment of our lives. The vital principle, finding its present *Sthulasariram* unfit for habitation, leaves it, to animate some other *Sthulasariram*. The third principle, which is the agglomeration of the magnetic emanations of the physical body, cannot but die at the death of the latter. The fourth principle, however, by its contact with the third in physical life, has gathered round itself some of its essence. But this essence is like the smell of a rose, which lingers only for a time after the rose has been destroyed. Hence it is that the so-called astral body is seen at a distance by the friends or relatives of a dying man. The concentrated thought, an intense desire to see a friend, &c., clothes itself in the fourth principle, which, by the essence of the third gathered around itself, makes itself objective to the distant friend. And such a manifestation is possible, only so long as this essence is still retained. This is the reason for the Hindu custom of burning the dead, for when the body is once burnt, no more astral essence can be drawn out of it. But a buried body, although in the process of decomposition, still furnishes the aura, however feeble it may be, through which the dead entity finds itself able to manifest itself. In the dying man the struggle between the physical and the astral man goes on till it ends in physical death. This result produces a shock stunning the astral man who passes into a state of unconscious sleep until he re-awakens into the *Kama-Loka*. This sleep is the second state of existence. It will thus become apparent why it is that "apparitions" are seen at the time of death. Sometimes it so happens that these "apparitions" are seen some time after the supposed death of the man. But on careful examination it may be found that the man only *appears* to be dead; and although the medical faculty may not be able to detect any signs of life in him, still, in reality, the struggle between the physical and the astral man is not yet ended.

It is because this struggle is sliently going on that the ancients enjoined solemn silence in the awful presence of death. When the man awakens into the *Kama-Loka*, he begins his third state of existence. The physical organisation, which alone enables *man* to produce causes, is not there, and he is, as it were, concerned only with those affinities which he has already engendered. While this struggle in the fifth principle is going on, it is almost impossible for the entity to manifest itself upon earth. And when a dweller on this earth tries to establish a connection with that entity, he only disturbs its peace. Hence it is that the ancients prohibited these practices, to which they gave the name of necromancy, as deadly sin. The nature of the struggle depends upon the tendencies engendered by the individual in his physical life. If he was too material, too gross, too sensual, and if he had hardly any spiritual aspirations, then the downward attraction of the lower affinities causes an assimilation of the lower consciousness with the fourth principle. The man then becomes a sort of astral animal, and continues in that state until, in process of time, the astral entity is disintegrated. The few spiritual aspirations that he might have had are transferred to the *monad*; but the separate *consciousness* being dragged into the animal soul, dies with it and his *personality* is thus annihilated. If a man, on the other hand, is tolerably spiritual, as most of our fellowmen are, then the struggle in *Kama-Loka* varies according to the nature of his affinities; until the *consciousness* being linked to the higher ones is entirely separated from the "astral shell," and is ready to go into *Devachan*. If a person is highly spiritual, his *Kama-Loka* is of a very short duration, for the consciousness is quickly assimilated to the higher principles and passes into *Devachan*. It will thus be seen that in any case intercourse with the *Kama-Loka* entities is detrimental to the progress of those entities and also injurious to the persons indulging in such intercourse. This interruption is just as bad and even far worse than the disturbance in the death-chamber on this physical plane. When it is remembered that the fourth principle by its contact with the fifth has assimilated to itself the *essence* of the latter, it becomes an easy matter to account for those rare phenomena in which a high degree of intelligence has been exhibited by the *Kama-Loka* entities dragged into mediumistic *seances*. Of course there are cases in which an "astral shell" acts merely as a mirror through which the intelligence of the "medium" is reflected, as there are others in which "*elementals*" make use of these "astral shells." But in those cases where the *Kama-Loka* entities actually appear and exhibit a rare intelligennce, it is on account of the *essence* absorbed by the fourth principle during its connection with the fifth. There are again cases in which the *Kama-Loka* entities of "suicides" and of persons dying unnatural and accidental deaths may appear and exhibit rare intelligence, because those entities have to live in *Kama-Loka* the period they would have passed on earth if those accidents had not carried them away—before the struggle between the astral and spiritual affinities commences. The causes engendered by them during earth-life are not yet ripe for fruition and they must wait their natural time. But to recall these into "mediumistic" circles is equally dangerous as in the above-mentioned cases, and for the very same reasons. It may not be positively injurious in all cases, but at any rate the process is fraught with danger and should not be undertaken by inexperienced persons. As regards those good persons, who, it is apprehended, may on account of some unsatisfied desire linger on earth, the Hindus have a peculiar custom which is generally relegated to the limbo of exploded superstitions, because its scientific rationale is not properly understood. If the desire be of a spiritual nature, then of course it is only concerned with the spiritual affinities set up in the *Manas*. But if it be of a material nature, such as some act to be done for the welfare of a friend or family, &c., &c., then only need it be taken into account. In ancient times, an initiate or adept was always present in a death chamber, and attended to the necessary conditions and thus released the dying man from his earthly attractions.

This is the real origin of "extreme unction" in the Roman Catholic Church and the custom of having a priest near the dying man in other religions. Gradually as a meterializing tendency began to assert itself, the Hindus invented a ceremony which is the next best thing they could do under the circumstances. It is a general belief among them that after physical death, the entity lingers on the earth for a period of ten days before passing into any other state of existence. During this period they perform a regular daily ceremony in which they prepare some rice balls and put them before crows. The belief is that crows are so sensitive as to detect any astral figure they see. If the man dies, having some unsatisfied desire, then his astral figure covers the rice balls which the crows cannot touch. If the balls are immediately touched, then it is concluded that the man having no unsatisfied desire is no longer earth-bound. But if they are not, then the relatives of the dead person go on recounting all the wishes of the latter, that they can possibly think of, promising at the same time to fulfil them. When the right thing is hit on, then it is believed the entity immediately goes off to its sphere, and the crows touch the balls. Whatever it may be, the Hindus have a horror of those elementaries, and instead of dragging them into *séances* they try by every possible means to release them from the earth's atmosphere. When the struggle between the lower affinities and the higher aspirations of the man is ended in *Kama-Loka*, astral death takes place in that sphere as does physical death on this earth. The shock of death again throws the entity into a state of unconsciousness before its passage into *Devachan*. The "shell" left behind may manifest itself until it is disintegrated, but it is not the real spiritual man; and the rare intelligence exhibited by it, occasionally, is the radiation of the aura caught by it during its connection with the spiritual individuality. From its fourth state of existence, it re-awakens in *Devachan*, the conditions of which, according to Hindu books are, *Salokata*, *Samipata* and *Sayujata*. In the lowest state, *i.e.*, of *Salokata* the entity is only under the *influence* of the sixth and the seventh principle, while in the second state, *i. e.*, of *Samipata*, it is *fully overshadowed* by the latter. It is in the *Sayujata* state only that it is fully merged into its *Logos* to be thrown again into re-incarnation when it has fully enjoyed the effects of the spiritual aspirations created by it. It is only very highly spiritualised entities that reach this highest state of *Devachan*. Of course, the cases of adepts are here entirely left out of consideration, for as the *Bhagavat Gita* says, the *Gnyani* reaches that state from which there is no re-birth and which is called *Moksha* or *Mukti*. The period of gestation between the *Devachanic* condition and the physical re-birth may be called the eighth state; but in the Hindu books the physical life being the basis of the seven after-states is not included in the category of the *Sapta* higher *lokas*, just as in the septenary principles, *Parabrahma* is not taken into account for the very same reason. From the subjective stand-point, the *Parabrahman*, and from the objective stand-point the *Sthula-sariram*, are not included in the septenary division, as the former is the basis upon which the whole structure is built.

NADIGRANTHAMS AND THEIR INTERPRETERS.

FOR some time past I have been hearing of Nadigranthams and their predictions. But the reports that reached me from various quarters regarding these marvellous books and the answers diocovered therein to a variety of questions put by different people, gave me little or no information regarding their real origin and the plan on which they were constructed. Some said that they were written by Brahma himself, while others attributed their authorship to Vyasa; a third account says that they were written by the presiding deities of the various planets by whose names they are called, while those that have no connection with individual planets are supposed to be the production of a variety of authors, human and divine. Putting together all the various accounts received, it appears there are fifteen different kinds of Nadigranthams:—*viz.* (1) Suryanadi, (2) Chandranadi, (3) Kujanadi, (4) Budhanadi, (5)

Sukranadi, (6) Gurunadi, (7) Saminadi, (8) Rahunadi, (9) Ketunadi,(10) Sarvasangrahanadi,(11) Bhavanadi, (12) Dhruvanadi, (13) Sarvanadi, (14) Sukanadi, and (15) Devinadi. There may be perhaps one or two more nadis, but all those generally referred to are included in the foregoing first. I may mention in this connection that the books attributed to the celebrated Bheemakavi of Vegidesa (Godavery District) may also be considered as another variety of Nadigranthams. It is not possible to say how many volumes of palm-leaf manuscript books are included under each heading as the possessors of these granthams are unwilling to give precise information on this point, but I have not actually seen with them more than one book of each class. It seems incredible, however, that fifteen palm-leaf books of ordinary size should contain detailed information regarding the horoscopes and the lives of every man and woman on this planet for any length of time, or give answers to any question that may be asked regarding events past, present and future. I attempted therefore to ascertain whether the contents of these strange books have anything like limits with reference to time and space. Different astrologers have given me different answers. Those who professed to find in these books answers to any question that might be asked by calculation made with reference to the time of questioning, or "Arudhalagnam" as it is generally called, and other circumstances connected with the question and the incidents appertaining to the act of questioning, found it difficult to assign any reasonable limits to the range of information contained in their books. One of them said that the books referred to the occurrences during four yugas and that there were certain signs given therein to indicate the yuga in which any particular question was asked. Apparently any person coming from any part of the world may have access to the astrologer and ask him any questions he pleases. The authors of these works could not have written the books for the special use and benefit of any particular astrologer and confined their answers to the questions which would be put to him during his lifetime. But it is not admitted by these astrologers that the whole history of the human race for a period of 4,320,000 years is contained in these volumes.

We must therefore assume that the authors foresaw into whose hands their books would come during the four yugas, and knew perfectly well beforehand the circumstances connected with the persons who would put questions to these people, and that they therefore give just so much information in their books as would be actually utilized by the human race. Even if any such achievement were possible, one would naturally expect to find millions of volumes in the hands of these astrologers, as many of them are deriving a pretty large income every month from the fees paid by a large number of questioners during these few years of Kaliyuga. Even if we suppose that all the books which satisfied the requirements of past generations have been destroyed already, there must be a considerable number left for the benefit of future generations that Kaliyuga has yet to run on for nearly 427,000 years more. But these lakhs of volumes are nowhere to be found though stern logic sometimes compels these astrologers to admit that they ought to exist. It so happens, however, that each of these men has in his possession just the number of volumes required to meet the demands of enquirers that flock to him and does not trouble himself about the rest.

The astrologers who profess to find in these Nadigranthams the horoscopes of any people that choose to come to them and the predictions based thereupon, have now and then attempted to set a limit to the pretensions of their granthams, especially when the extravagance of such pretensions appeared to disturb the minds of enquirers and make them assume a sceptical attitude of mind. Some said that the horoscopes of caste people only would be found in these books, while others asserted that only the horoscopes of distinguished men would find a place in their mysterious volumes. One of them is of opinion that only a pious orthodox Hindu can expect to find his horoscope in their leaves, while another hinted that the horoscope defined in these books related to a period of one hundred years, of which a considerable portion had already elapsed. Practically, however, I have ascertained, that every man who can pay handsomely for the search can expect to find his horoscope or some kind of description of it, whether intelligible or otherwise, in these volumes.*

I may further state here that the language used in these books is Sanskrit and that the technical phraseology of Hindu astrology is to be found in almost every Sloka. They are written in every variety of character, Nagri, Telugu, Grantha, Kanarese and Malyalam characters are employed indiscriminately in transcribing these books. Judging from appearance many of these books seem to be very old ; but this fact is of no importance whatsoever. Even if the book is a new one it will always be asserted that it was copied from some old manuscript and no importance whatever is attached to any particular book.

From the foregoing description of the Nadigranthams it is clearly not a very easy thing to account for their existence and examine their foundation to see if they have anything like a scientific basis. A thorough knowledge of all the existing systems of astrology does not enable a person to find out the process by which they could have been written, much less to produce similar works on any limited scale. It is not alleged by these astrologers that they have any occult basis or that any occult powers are needed to interpret them. There is not even room for the supposition that by some mysterious occult process, these so-called astrologers ascertain the horoscope of an enquirer and the past, present and future incidents of his life and only use these Nadigranthams as a veil to hide their real secret and mystify the public. And moreover all the circumstances connected with them are calculated to create

* I am told that one trick of roguish astrologers is to insert in a Nadi extra leaves, specially prepared with reference to the expected client; such facts about his history as are accessible being etched on the leaves and an appearance of age given them by steeping them in muddy-water.

H. S. O.

distrust in the mind of an honest enquirer. However, by a reason of a few exaggerated and incorrect accounts of successful predictions the belief in these books is gradually gaining ground. In an article written by Mr. Chidambaram Iyer, and published in the issue of the *Theosophist* for June 1883, it was stated that these Nadigranthams were of considerable scientific importance and that it would be possible by their help, to fix the first point of Aries from which the Aryanamsam is calculated. Nothing more has been heard since then regarding Mr. Chidambaram Iyer's investigations in this direction. These books have again been prominently brought to the notice of the public by an article on "Indian Sibylline Books," published in the May issue of the *Theosophist*, and some fresh reports of wonderful predictions that have been circulated. I therefore thought it necessary to examine carefully one or two of these astrologers and ascertain the real value of these books—a determination strengthened by the request of my friend, Col. Olcott. The result of my inquiries is given for what it is worth in the following paragraphs.

It will be unnecessary for me to say anything about astrology in general in this connection; and I do not intend to advance now any theoretical considerations to show that these Nadigranthams cannot be genuine and that such books can by no possible means be composed. No such theoretical reasoning, however sound and convincing from a scientific point of view, will produce any impression on an ordinary mind which believes the statements made regarding these books on the strength of the marvellous reports of their predictions. So long as such reports are believed on hearsay evidence, all such considerations will be set aside on the ground that nothing would be impossible for a divine being or a Rishi like Vyasa. The following account will, however, show that these Nadigranthams are not always trustworthy and that a strict investigation is absolutely necessary before they can be relied upon and recommended to the public as authentic sources of information. If these books are the spurious concoctions of men who are trying to derive some anvantage from the credulity and superstition of the uneducated mass of people, every effort must be made to disclose their real nature to the public.

Before proceeding further I may mention here that the Telugu Brahmin astrologer alluded to in the article on "The Indian Sibylline Books" has not yet given me an opportunity of consulting his Bheemakavi's book or his Nadigranthams although I have made several attempts to obtain an interviews

The other astrologer with whom I had an interview on the 16th day of May is known by the name of Auritavak Balakrishnagyosulu and is at present residing in the Mint Street in Black Town. He has been living here for the last four or five years deriving a very good income by means of his Nadigranthams and is reputed to be one of the most celebrated and learned astrologers of Southern India. Hearing of some of his predictions I expected to find out the real truth about these Nadigranthams by visiting him, and proposed to a well-known and respectable native gentleman here that we should both go to the astrologer in question on the date abovementioned to consult his book. My friend sent an intimation to the astrologer that he would come and see him on the next day. We accordingly went to the astrologer's house and requested him to give us an opportunity of putting to him certain questions on payment of the fee usually charged. Not expecting me there with my friend, the astrologer immediately made some enquiries about me and made the necessary preparations for giving us a sitting. The walls of the room in which we sat were covered with pictures of gods and goddesses and a box full of Nadigranthams was placed on the left side of the astrologer. He began his discourse by complimenting us and pointing out the importance of his sacred Nadigranthams. He explained to us that an astrologer had to get by heart and retain in his memory thousands of signs and symbols and several thousands of Sanskrit verses before he could become a competent interpreter of these mysterious books. After favouring us with these remarks he proposed to send away all his servants to ensure privacy except a boy who required to take down our questions. He then enquired about the offerings brought by us which consisted of betel-leafs, areca nuts, bits of saffron and plantains. After counting the number of things brought, with a great show of accuracy and explaining to us the method of selecting the nadi applicable to the enquiry in hand, he ordered the boy above mentioned to enter in a book the address of the questioner, the number of things brought by him and the questions proposed, after answering himself, however, that a currency note of 5 Rupees was placed in his hands which he was pleased to call an "Asurapatram" (paper of the Raksham or demons). He appeared to be very particular about the point of time when the questions were declared though it did not appear what use was made of this fact in finding out the nadi or interrupting the same. He then asked me if I had any questions to put, and when I told him that I would propose my questions after seeing the result of my friend's enquiries he appeared to be dissatisfied and said that it would be very convenient for him if I were to ask my questions also immediately and pay down my fees. I did so and the same process of calculation was gone through in my case. After these preliminary preparations were finisned two books were taken out of the box and placed on a stand called Vyasapeetham. One of these books which appeared to be old was then opened; after looking at it for a while, the astrologer opened his box and took out a third book which appeared to be new, saying that the account in the old book began with the answers, but that the preface required had to be read from another book. My readers will be pleased to notice here that no calculation was needed to select this new book and that in all probability this single book contains the prefatory remarks to every answer given to every enquirer, as no attempt was made by the astrologer to select one book from a number of such books.

When the astrologer began to read from this new book we found that the scene opened in Vykuntham with Narayana sitting there with his three wives and a host of Rishis. A considerable portion of the account was devoted to the description of the dancing of Apsaras and planetary deities. I may here mention that in reply to one of my questions, the astrologer informed me that Yyasa was the author of the book from which he was reading. But Vyasa knew nothing about the third wife of Narayana who was introduced, as is well-known, into the Hindu Pantheon by the Vaishnavite writers of Southern India in later times. The dancing or *nrityam* of Grahams or Planetary deities is a new idea which does not appear in any other Hindu book.

The account then proceeded to state that in the present year of Kaliyuga on the very date on which my friend's questions were asked, certain would be asked by a Madhava Brahmin. The astrologer went on giving lengthy explanations of the meaning of the Sanskrit text until he came to the description of the questioner and the enumeration of the questions. After arriving at this stage he began to propose explanations and tried to discuss the subject with us for the purpose of ascertaining the real meaning of his text. My friend hastily produced his horoscope and placed it before the astrologer for his guidance. Seeing, however, the real difficulties of the astrologer's situation, and estimating at its true worth his anxiety to get his interpretation confirmed and cleared of all its ambiguities by the light of our statements, I requested him to go on reading the text to its end without taking the trouble to explain its meaning to us as we could understand it ourselves. This proposal was not quite agreeable to him, he, however, proceeded to describe my friend and his antecedents. The description was extremely meagre and contained nothing more than what was known about him to a considerable number of people in Madras. The description was wrong, however, in stating that my friend was a follower of Vysarayamatham, while he was a follower of Raghavendaswamy's matham. It was also wrong in stating that his father was married thrice. I found that in four or five distinct and unambiguous statements made two were clearly wrong, and one of the mistakes committed was just the sort of mistake which a hasty enquirer would commit. As the majority of Madhavas are the followers of Vysarayamatham, Vyasa seems to have made a shrewd guess that the questioner would be a follower of the same matham. When he came to that part of the account which described my friend's horoscope, the astrologer had the advantage of having before him the diagram of the same and squeezed out of the senseless Sanskrit text some statements applicable to the horoscope under consideration. But it would be interesting to notice in this connection that nothing was stated which was not clearly visible on the very face of the diagram, and that whenever a word or phrase was detected by me in the obscure text which indicated a reference to the horoscope in question, I found disturbance of the metre of the Sanskrit verse. I then asked him in what metre the text was composed; the reply given is significant. He told me that the verses had no settled metre, but that they were so composed that it would be impossible for even the greatest Pundit to substitute one syllable for another, and that this fact was proved by him in an Assembly of Pundits at Sringeri. I need hardly say that this explanation is more damaging to the Nadigranthams than anything else connected with this interview. After thus defining the questioner in a very unsatisfactory, ambiguous and suspicious manner, Vyasa took the trouble to point out at great length the articles brought by my friend and notice the additional articles which he ought to have brought, but which he had omitted to bring. Vyasa also stated that my friend would bring Rakshasapatram (the same as Ausurapatram), thus showing that he clearly anticipated, five thousand years ago, the introduction of paper currency into India by the British Government, though the name given by him to an English currency note was not quite appropriate. It was further stated in this book that a boy would take down the question proposed by my friend. It is astonishing to find that, while dealing with the history of the human race for several millions of years, the author of these books took the trouble to record such unnecessary details and trifling events.

When we approached expected answers, the old book was opened and the verses therein found were read. The first question related to the Theosophical Society. But unfortunately the astrologer was unable to understand the meaning of the expression. As might be expected under such circumstances, he was not very eager to give lucid explanations and comment upon the text as he did when dealing with the articles brought and the dancing in Vykuntham, in spite of my request that he should proceed with text and not waste his time on such trivial things. The text was the most ridiculous rigmarole that I ever heard. Each verse contained three or four contradictory verbs of various meanings and a number of other words which seemed to refer to a puzzling variety of subjects. Their combination conveyed no meaning whatever and might be made to mean anything and everything, provided the interpreter was allowed to have his own way in the matter. But how could the astrologer interpret it in a manner that would connect his explanation with the question when he was unable to understand the question, though we allowed him a Sanskrit dictionary and grammar of his own choise? He tried his best to catch any remark that we might make and proceeded in a very cautious and guarded manner. I requested my friend, therefore, in English, not to make any remark which would, in the slightest degree, help him. The result, as might be anticipated under such circumstances, was a ridiculous failure. For a few more minutes the astrologer went on reading, now and then catching a word and looking at our faces to see if we would be foolish enough to suggest a meaning and soon dropping his eyes when his expectations were disappointed. I may notice in this connection an interesting incident that occurred. In one of the verses my friend noticed the phrase "Mayasakti" and expecting to find something in it, asked the astrologer what it meant. He interpreted it in the usual manner, but my friend said that it had no connection with his question. The clever astrologer then said that it might have some other meaning in his books; so saying he suddenly opened his box, took out another palm-leaf book, appeared to find the expression in question in the twinkling of an eye and announced to us that it meant something else. He then threw the book aside and I found that it was neither a dictionary nor a glossary and that the pretended search for the proper meaning was merely intended to have a dramatic effect.

Thoroughly disappointed with the answers given, my friend hoped that we might be more fortunate in eliciting answers to my questions. When it came to my turn to get my difficulties solved, I requested the astrologer to omit that portion of the account which related to dancing in Vykuntham or Kailyasam and forthwith begin to read the answers to my questions. He, however, began his account with what appeared to be a description of the question and the position of the planets at the time of questioning. The astrologer said that I must first be assured that the answers related to the very questions proposed by me by the help of the description given of myself and my circumstances. I thanked him for his kind advice so frankly given and waited for the proferred assurance. I was, however, dismayed to find that the account related to somebody else, as it did not at all harmonize with my environment. I pointed this out to the astrologer and suggested that he might not have selected the right portion of the book. He readily accepted the suggestion and after turning over a few more leaves, began to read again. But it appeared to me that so far as the astrologer was concerned the difficulty of getting at my horoscope remained as great as ever. I was asked whether I had my horoscope with me; but I was not willing to repeat my friend's blunder and consequently informed him that I had not my horoscope with me. In sheer despair, the astrologer wanted to get over the difficulty by a bold and fearless asscertion. He then began to read a verse which stated that I was born when Leo was ascending, that my future career would be prosperous, and that I would be a very shrewd and discriminative man or something to that effect.

But here again the Nadigranthams was found to be blundering hopelessly. Leo was not in my ascendant and consequently I informed the astrologer again that he was probably reading from the wrong page. My suggestion was again accepted and a few more leaves were turned over. The time the astrologer did not venture to meddle witch my horoscope, but read something which pretended to indicate the time when I put my questions. He informed me that the horoscope of the questioner would not be given in every case and that, because the time of questioning was properly defined, I must infer that the answers which followed were intended to be replies to my questions. But a fresh difficulty presented itself to my mind. In two separate places in his book, the astrologer appeared to have found an indication of the time when my questions were made known to him, but it was clear that, at that particular instant, I was the only person that questioned him. Why was the same moment noticed, then, in two different places in the Nadigrantham and apparently in connection with two distinct personalities? If it should be asserted that at that very moment, some other person might be proposing questions to a Nadigrantham astrologer at some other place, and that consequently the second account might refer to him, then, it would be necessary to find a correct indication of time as well as a proper description of the questioner to assure one's self that answers were being searched for in the right place. If so, the description of the horoscope would be indispensably necessary in every case; if, on the other hand, it should be admitted that there could be but one questioner at a time, the discovery in two different places of the description of the same moment or Arudhalagnam would be altogether inexplicable and exceedingly suspicious. I plainly pointed out my difficulties to the astrologer and asked him for a satisfactory explanation. He was mute for a few seconds, then grew passionate and told my friend that I had spoiled the whole business. I expected that the affair would come to a disagreeable close if I should insist upon getting an explanation which, from the astrologer's standpoint, was clearly impossible. I therefore mildly told him that in putting such questions to him I was acting in conformity with his own advice and that he might proceed to read the answers without troubling himself about the matter. He then read some gibberish which had no meaning and which he was unable to explain. Fully convinced that we ought not to waste any more time with him and wishing to bring the matter to a speedy conclusion, I asked him to explain the last verse that he had read. He went on saying that the word "lokadhya" meant the people of the world or those who have the world and so forth. I was again obliged to point out to him that the verse had nothing to do with my question. He then looked at my question and found that it had something to do with Shankaracharya. Turning round he said that the word in question meant Shankaracharya; my friend contended that it would be absurd to force such a meaning into the context in an arbitrary manner after looking at the question, and suggested that in the following verses some unequivocal reference might probably be found to that great teacher; of course such reference was immediately found in the very next verse, into which an appropriate expression was introduced in defiance of grammar, logic and metre. When we came to this point even my friend lost all his confidence and was waiting for an opportunity to bring the interview to a decent close. For a few more seconds we had to wait during which time I could hardly suppress my laughter on finding the astrologer inform my friend that I knew "Vatarayana Yogam" and that I was a "Sakya" at heart, as the second question had something to do with Yoga. These words of course have no sense whatever. We prepared finally to depart and the astrologer noticing, our state of mind, offered to act according to our wishes. We did not however claim back the fee paid by us, but quietly took leave of him with our mind freed from all doubts regarding these notorious Nadigranthams.

PLACES OF PILGRIMAGE IN INDIA.

THE following communication sent to me by a Student of Occult Science will throw some light on the significance attached to the ancient Hindu religious symbology as illustrated in the various places of pilgrimage abounding in India, and account for the high veneration in which these places are held by the masses of the Hindu population. Speaking of "pilgrimage as a means of spiritual education," the said correspondent writes as follows:—

"The insistance of the later Brahmanical Scriptures on pilgrimages as a means of spiritual education is well known. At the present day there is hardly a pious Hindu, of whatever sex and in whatever part of India, who considers his or her religious duties performed without visiting the principal places of pilgrimage. In this respect the modern Hindu differs so completely from his Christian contemporaries, that the latter would hardly credit what a vast number of pilgrims annually circulate over the country to fulfil their religious obligations, and to what trouble and expense they put themselves for the purpose. With the social aspect of the question, the present paper is not concerned It is proposed to examine what real good pilgrimage in India does produce in the spiritual education of the people, and what is the rationale of the institution. The places of pilgrimage are so numerous and their esoteric significance so deep, that anything like completeness must be disclaimed by the present writer. At the same time the hope is expressed that the lines of inquiry indicated herein may be followed up by competent scholars and mystics, so that the highly beneficial character of pilgrimages may be made apparent to all open-minded people, and the great wisdom of his ancestors shown to the Hindu of the present day.

"In the first place it is to be remarked that the sacred cities of the Hindus are well-organized and powerful spiritual centres, and from them there radiates an elevating influence which is not the less active because unperceived by the ordinary Philistine. Places of pilgrimage are truly spiritual seminaries which, though completely closed to the idler and the superstitious in selfish quest of personal holiness and personal salvation, are ever open to receive the earnest and devoted searcher after truth. The statement may be boldly made and the support of all true mystics confidently expected on its behalf, that there is no important place of pilgrimage in India which does not enjoy the presence, in most cases permanent, of some adept or initiate of a high order, who is ever ready to point the path to the higher life into which he himself has entered. It is a matter of common experience that people's spiritual eyes has opened in these holy cities under the benign influence of some great *Sadhu* (sinless man). But, for reasons which will be readily understood, the pious hand must not seek to withdraw the veil of obscurity which shrouds the holy men and their work. The members of the silent brotherhood will but speak to those whose Karma deserves it. Shankarácharya says :—

दुर्लभं त्रयमेवैतत् देवानुग्रहहेतुकं । मुमुक्षत्वं मनुष्यत्वंमहापुरुषसंश्रय: ॥

" These three are difficult to attain and are due to the favour of the gods* (*i. e.* the good karma of previous births) :—Humanity, desire for liberation, and contact with great spiritually-minded men."

" The holy cities were built, or at all events completed, in the later epochs of Brahmanic history. When the spirituality of mankind began to be clouded by progressive materiality consequent upon the desire of selfish enjoyment, the seclusion of the adepts became greater and the sacred Sanskrit language became daily less understood. As a remedy for this great cyclic evil, the holy ones of the earth left to the profane vulgar the symbolical architecture of the great temples, which yet serve as finger-posts to the mystical student. Very few persons are aware that as the pilgrim stands on the bridge of boats on the Ganges before Benares he is face to face with a most sublime and awful mystery, the full import of which none but the higher initiates comprehend. This mystery is

---

* This interpretation of the term " gods" is accepted by all mystics.

represented by the general aspect of the holy city, whose two Sanskrit names—Kaci and Varanaci—will yield a mine of truth to the earnest inquirer. It is not for us to elucidate the point ; for the present it will suffice to suggest to the reader a fruitful field of inquiry, where each will be rewarded according to his earnestness and spiritual penetration.

" What is Kaci ?

" The question has been answered in a well-known treatise by a celebrated mystic, Satya Gnáná Nanda Tirtha Yati. He says that Kaci is the supreme power of the great God Siva who is the undifferentiated bliss, consciousness, and being.* Siva or Peace here represents the fourth or unmanifested state of the universe. He is the Chidakaca, his other name being Vyoma or space, the small circle or dot which is placed on the top of the Sanskrit mystic, symbol *Om* (ओं). What releation it has to the force located in the human body above the eyebrows, and represented by the dot over the crescent moon, the mystic knows very well. Kaci is called the goddess who embodies consciousness and bliss, and is the same as the Sakti or power to whom the sacred verses of Shankarácharya—*Ananda lahari*—are addressed. The great teacher says that if Siva is not united to Sakti he cannot produce even a flutter of well-being. Sakti is adorable of Hari, Hara and Viranchi. By once turning the key of the symbology here adopted we find that Hari or Vishnu is the dreaming state of the universe, the first differentiated aspect of the darkness, the destroyer or remover Hara. Although Hara is usually taken as a loose synonym for Siva, it is here used with the deliberate object of implying that the transcendental state of the universe, emblematized by Siva, is beyond the state of the destroyer, as the *turiya* state is beyond the *sushupti.* Siva is Para-nirvana, while Hara is Nirvana. It is easily intelligible how to the popular mind no distinction is observable between Nirvana and Para-nirvana,

* The word *Sat* has been roughly translated " being, " as the English language does not afford a better word; Be-ness if allowed in English would be a more adequate rendering.

Hari, we have said, is the first differentiated condition realised by the human ego. He is therefore the son represented by the sign Leo on the Zodiac (see Mr. Subba Row's invaluable article on the 'Twelve Signs of the Zodiac' in the *Theosophist*, Vol. III). Viranchi or Brahma the Creator is the aggregation of the perceptible universe. Sakti is therefore above these three, and the consort of Siva. This explains why Kaci is called *Tripuraraidhzvi*, the royal residence of the destroyer of the three cities, the undifferentiated synthetic condition of the three states mentioned above. With regard to the human ego the three cities are the three bodies, gross, subtile and causal, beyond which is the spirit. From this it also becomes clear that Kaci is the eternal *Chinmatra* which has been well explained by Mr. Subba Row in his article on 'Personal and Impersonal God.'—(*Theosophist*, Vol. IV). It also becomes manifest from this that in one of its aspects Kaci is *pragnz*, in which is realized the great formula 'Thou art It.' This *pragna* is the mother of mukti or liberation, as all Vedantins know. The Trithayati says :—'I make salutation to that Kaci by whose favour I am Siva,' and I know Siva to be the spirit of all that is. Kaci is pragna, Buddhi, Sakti or Maya, the different names of the divine power which dominates throughout the universe; in fact, it is one aspect of the One Soul. The above quoted mystic states further :—'This Kaci is the power of Siva, the supreme consciousness, but not different from him. Know Kaci to be the same as Siva and the supreme bliss. . . Kaci is that by which the supreme reality of the spirit is manifested or *in* which it is so manifested. She is also sung as the Chinmatra ; I make salutiation to her, the supreme Knowledge. Elsewhere the same writer calls Kaci the darkness (Syámá).' This Darkness is the undifferentiated matter of the Cosmos, beyond which dwelleth the sun-coloured one, the spirit. In the Psalms this Asat or Prakriti is referred to in the highly poetical passage :—'There is darkness round his pavilion.'

"Krishna, the supreme spirit, is dark in his human form. No human eye can penetrate beyond this divine darkness.

In some Vaishnava work it is stated that on one occasion Krishna transformed himself into Syámá in Kali (darkness in its feminine aspect), thus hinting at the truth which reveals itself to the spiritual eye of intuition. Unconsciously guided by the higher light; the Christian church believes that Jesus Christ was "black and comely," although the passage in the Song of Solomon in which the expression occurs has no relation whatsoever to Christ.

"To return to Kaci in its aspect of Buddhi. It is to be remembered that Buddhi is the first differentiation of Prakriti. According to Kapila Buddhi is the termination (*adhyava sáya*) in nature of Prakriti to evolve egotism. Buddhi has three conditions or aspects. Its own essentially pure condition is that in which it is identical with Prakriti, in which the three substantive qualities of goodness (*satva*), passional activity (*rajas*) and delusion (*tamas*), are in a state of equilibrium and in that sense non-existent. This Buddhi is the mother of salvation ; in fact it *is* salvation. When under the influence of *rajas* the quality of *satva* predominates, four things are generated :—the practice of virtue (*dharma*), dispassion (*vairagya*), the spiritual powers (*aisvarya*), and finally salvation, when by the excess of goodness Buddhi returns to its original state of purity When under some influence *tamas* predominates, the four opposites of what is stated above are produced. *Tamas* by its enveloping power (*ávaran sakti*) makes the one reality in the universe appear as the differentiated universe of matter, and then *rajas* by its expansive power (*vikshepa sakti*) produces the passions which are the cause of bondage.

"These three conditions of Buddhi the Trithayati gives as aspects of Kaci:—*Nirvisesha* (undifferentiated), *Suddha* (pure, when the *sâtvaka* quality predominantes) and *jada* (when *tamas* predominates). One under the domination of *tamas* looks upon the geographical Kaci as the reality:—

दोत्ररूपाजडाकाशी ।

"The Suddha Kaci is the abstract consciousness still limited by forms :—

मूर्त्तिरूपातुयाकाशी शुद्धसाचिन्मयोसती ।

"One under the domination of the *satva* quality practises virtue, still ascribing good and evil to nature around him.

"In her Nirvishesha condition, Kaci is self-existent in her glory, and is the supreme God of Siva and of all liberated souls :—

पूर्णरूपा स्वमाहात्म्यं स्वयमेवविचारयेत ।
निर्विशेषांतुमुक्तानां शिवस्यचपरागतिः ॥

"We shall now understand why it is generally believed that residence in Kaci removes all sins committed elsewhere, but a sin committed in the temple of the Lord, Kaci itself, renders one incapable of receiving grace—the reference being to the spiritual evil, the sin against the Holy Ghost—for which there is no remission. The wretch who knows the truth and follows the left hand path is doomed to nameless misery in Avitchi Nirvana.

"The Tirthayati says :—'Terrible indeed is the suffering of one who commits a sin in Kaci. Alas ! the state of a Rudra pisácha that the sinner attains is more intolerable than the suffering of all the hells.'

"By the acquisition of true knowledge all sins consumed by the fire kindled in the hearth of heart (*chidagni kundam*), but there is no hope for the damned soul who murders his spirit, as far as that is possible, by the practice of black magic.

"Without prolonging the present paper, the student may be recommended to the Skanda Purana for further information on this subject ; and in conclusion, it may be stated that the practical occultist will derive great benefit from a proper study of the Trithayati's treatise, which has here been so largely quoted."

I will add a few remarks to the foregoing communication. It will be no exaggeration to say that the secrets of the ancient archaic science, for which an enquirer will search in vain the mystical books of the East, are often symbolically represented in some of the most celebrated places of pilgrimage in India. The mysterious ideas generally associated with the position of Benares (Kaci), its past history and its innumerable gods and goddesses, contain clearer indications of the secrets of final initiation than a cart-load of books on Yoga philosophy. Look again at Chidambaram and examine carefully the plan on which its celebrated temple was built by Patanjali, by the light of the Kabalistic, the Chaldean, the Egyptian and the Hindu doctrines relating to the great mystery of the Logos. You are far more likely to penetrate this mystery by such a course of study than by examining all the obscure statements of the ancient initiates regarding the sacred voice of the great deep and the impenetrable veil of Isis. Masons are searching in vain for the lost golden delta of Enoch ; but an earnest seeker of truth who has comprehended the rules of interpretation which are applicable to such subjects will not find it very difficult to discover this delta in Chidambaram. Similarly, various occult secrets find their true interpretation and explanation in Srisylam, Ramanal, Jugganath, Allahabad and other places, justly considered as sacred, owing to their various associations, by the followers of the Hindu religion. It would require several volumes to explain at length the sacred symbols connected with these places and their mystic significance, and interpret in a proper manner the Sthalapuranums relating thereto. As no writer was permitted in ancient times to divulge in clear language the secrets of occult science to the public, and as books and libraries could be easily destroyed either by the ravages of time or the vandalism of barbarous invaders, it was thought proper to preserve, for the benefit of posterity, in strong and lasting edifices of granite, some of the greatest secrets known to the designers of these buildings, in the form of signs and symbols. The very same necessity which brought into existence the Sphinx and the great pyramid led the ancient leaders of Hindu religious thought to construct these temples, and express in stone and metal the hidden meaning of their doctrines. A few explanations and suggestions will be sufficient to justify the foregoing statements, and indicate the manner in which these symbols should be interpreted.

A Sanskrit verse is often repeated by Hindus, which says that journeys to seven places of pilgrimage will secure Moksha to the devotee. These places are enumerated thus; (1) Ayodhya, (2) Mathura, (3) Maya, (4) Kaçi (Benares), (5) Kanchi (Conjiveram), (6) Avantika (Ojeen), and (7) Dwaraka. Now, these places are intended to represent the seven centres of occult energy in the human body, known as (1) Sahasram, (2) Agnya, (3) Visuddhi, (4) Anahatam, (5) Swadhisthanam, (6) Manipurakam, and (7) Mulatharam respectively. The ideas associated with these places will become intelligible when examined by the light of the doctrines connected with these force-centres by Yogis.

It is generally believed by the Hindus that death in Benares secures final emancipation from the necessity of a rebirth. This belief is so strong in the minds of the ordinary people as to lead a considerable number to resort to this place every year for the purpose of remaining there till they die.

This certainly appears to be a ridiculous superstition. But a great spiritual truth is lurking behind this strange belief. This truth will become apparent when we ascertain what death at Benares is really intended to mean. From the foregoing arrangement of the seven sacred places alluded to, it will be seen that Benares corresponds to the heart in the human body, in the centre of which the *Anahata chakram* of the Yogis is located; and the truth of this inference is further strengthened by the manner in which Kaçi is described in the *Sankalpam* (preliminary recitation before bathing or commencing any worship). It is therein said that Benares is between Asi and Varuna; that it is situated in Anandavana; that it is in Mahasmasana (or the great graveyard or burial ground); that it stands in front of Gouri; that it is held up by the three points of the trident of Siva; that it is in the midst of Brahma

Nalam (the narrow passage of Brahma), going northwards, and that it is at the end of Mani (Manikarnika means Pranavakarnika). It may be easily seen now how far this is a figurative representation of the *Anahata chakra* of the Yogis. This *chakra* is between the two Nadis. Idá and Pingalá in the human body, which are represented by the two small streams Asi and Varuna named in the foregoing description. The state of ecstacy is realized when consciousness is centred in the germ of *pragna*, which is placed in this *chakra*, and hence Benares is an Anandavan, which literally means a pleasure garden. When this centralization of consciousness in the germ of *pragna* is secured, the objective consciousness realized in the physical body and in the astral body entirely ceases; consequently before the spiritual consciousness of the regenerated spirit (the Christ after resurrection) is awakened, the condition realized may be compared to that of sound sleep or *sushupti*—the death of the incarnated Christ, the death of the individual man. This is the time of the great peace and calmness after the tempest. Hence Kaçi or *Anahata chakra*, wherein this condition is realized, is the great burial ground or burning ground, as every thing—the ego and the non-ego—seems to be dead and buried for the time being. Gouri is the Sophia of the gnostics and the Isis of the Egyptians. When this condition—that of *pragna*—is reached, the spirit is in front of the Divine light and wisdom, and ready to behold the mysterious Goddess without the veil as soon as its spiritual eyes are opened on the other side of the Cosmos.

Hence Benares is in Gourimukham. This condition again marks the termination of the three conditions of consciousness experienced by the incarnated spirit, *viz.*, the ordinary, the clairvoyant and the Devachanic conditions. These three states of differentiated *pragna* are the three points of Siva's trident. Again *Anahata chakra* is in the Sushumna nadi—a mysterious and narrow passage running through the spinal cord to the crown of the head through which vital the electricity flows, and Benares is therefore said to be in Brahmanalam, which is another name for Sushumna nadi. Further, the condition above alluded to is represented by the dot over Pranava, as our correspondent says, and hence Benares is described as Mani-karnika.

It will thus be seen that Benares is an external symbolical representation of the *Anahata chakra* of the Yogis. Death in Benares therefore means the concentration of *pragna* in the original germ consciousness, which constitutes the real individuality of the man. It must further be noticed that *Sahasram* represents the positive pole and *mulatharam* the negative pole in the body. From the mysterious union of their energies in the heart the sacred and irrepressible (*Anahata*) voice is generated in the *Anahata chakra*. This voice is heard when the tempestuous activity of conscious existence terminates in the death of Sushupti, and out of the ashes of the individual man the regenerated man springs into existence electrified by this "song of life." Hence it is stated that when a man dies at Benares, Rudra (a form of manifestation of Thoth, the initiator), communicates to him the secret of the Logos and secures moksha for him. It will be clear now that the popular belief is full of meaning to a student of occult science. Similarly the traditions connected with every other important place of pilgrimage will yield much valuable information when properly interpreted.

THE VIRGIN OF THE WORLD.

This is the title of a recent publication in English of some of the books generally attributed to Hermes. The first book, however, is the only part of the publication to which this heading is strictly appropriate. Two philosophical discourses named "Asclepios on Initiation" and "Definitions of Asclepios" and a few fragments of Hermetic philosophy are added to it, with two introductory Essays by Mr. Maitland and Dr. Kingsford, which are very interesting and instructive.

It will be a most interesting study for every occultist to compare the doctrines of the ancient Hermetic philosophy with the teachings of the Vedantic and Buddhist system of religious thought. The famous books of Hermes seem to occupy with reference to the Egyptian religion the same position which the Upanishads occupy in Aryan religious literature. As there were forty-two provinces in ancient Egypt, and the body of Osiris was cut up into forty-two pieces, so there were forty-two books of Hermes. This, however, is not the number of the Vedas nor of their sub-divisions, as Mr. Maitland seems to suppose. This number is one of the characteristic features of Egyptian mysticism, and veils a profound truth. It has nothing to do with the number of stars in any particular constellation, as some Egyptologists have imagined. So long as these investigators of the Egyptian religious doctrines erroneously believe that they are based on the signs of the Zodiac, the motions of the heavenly bodies, or the appearance of particular groups of stars, it will be impossible for them to penetrate into the profound depth of their meaning. These books of Hermes, if they can be discovered, will no doubt but an end to all such speculations. But Hermes said, "O Sacred Books of the Immortals, ye in whose pages my hand has recorded the remedies by which incorruptibility is conferred, remain for ever beyond the reach of destruction and of decay, invisible and concealed from all who frequent these regions, until the day shall come in which the ancient heaven shall bring forth instruments worthy of you, whom the Creator shall call souls."

This passage has a double meaning, applicable alike to the works of the Divine Hermes and the human Hermes; and the time is yet distant when the true Hermetic philososhy and the ancient civilization of Egypt will be revived in the natural course of evolutionary progress. The works that are now being published as Hermetic, however, do not appear to be the real Hermetic books which were so carefully concealed, though they contain fragments of true Hermetic philosophy coloured by Grecian thought and mythology, and "The Virgin of the World" was probably based on some Egyptian compilation professing to be one of the Hermetic books. It is curious to notice that in it we find Isis informing Horus that the animal signs were placed in the Zodiac after those of human form, which would be the case when the equinoctial point was at the beginning of Gemini. Moreover, as will be shown further on, the main doctrines taught by the discourse are in harmony with the religious doctrines of Ancient Egypt. But the prominent references to Zeus, Kronos, Ares, and Aphrodite unmistakably show that it can in no wise be considered as one of the ancient Hermetic books. In the context in which such names occur, Hermes would no doubt have referred to the corresponding deities of Egyptian mythology. By referring to page 9 it will be seen that the writer identifies Hermes with Mercury, which no ancient Egyptian properly acquainted with his ancient philosophy would have done. Hermes is "cosmic thought," as is stated in another part of this discourse. Strictly speaking, he is the universal mind in his divine aspect, and corresponds with Brahma in the Hindu religion. Just as the Vedas and the Upanishads are said to have originated from Brahma before the evolution of the manifested Cosmos, the Egyptians declared that their religious books originated from the Divine Hermes. Hermes, like Brahma, is represented (p. 10) as taking part in creation. Such being the case, it will be erroneous from the Egyptian standpoint to represent him as Mercury. Hermes is further spoken of as the teacher and initiator of Isis, though in one place the Great Master and the Ruler of the Universe addresses the mysterious goddess as the soul of his soul and the holy thought of his thought. Isis, the great Cosmic Virgin, is the sixth principle of the Cosmos. She is the generative power of the Universe.– not Prakriti, but the productive energy of Prakriti—and as such she generates ideation in the universal mind. Even in her human incarnation she cannot properly be placed in the position of a pupil of Hermes. The human incarnatian of Isis is not the descent of soul into matter, as is the case with the rape of Persephone. Curiously enough in referring to this incarnation in her discourse to Horus, Isis speaks thus:—"The Supreme God . . . at length accorded to earth for a season thy father Osiris and the great goddess Isis." Who then is this Isis who addresses Horus? Possibly the term Isis was applied to every incarnated soul, as the term Osiris was applied to every departed spirit in the later times of Egyptian history; but even this supposition will be found inconsistent with some portions of the dialogue under consideration. The author of the book, whoever he was, did not comphrehend in its true light the mysterious connection between Isis and Hermes, and, trying to imitate the tone and form of the real Hermetic dialogues (which were repeated during the times of initiation only) according to the traditions current in his time, wrote the dialogue under review in the form in which it is now presented to the public. Before proceeding to notice in detail the doctrines inculcated in this book it is necessary to point out that Persephone is not the Cosmic Virgin, and cannot be represented as such from the standpoint to Hermetic philosophy. This title is only applicable to the great Isis, and not to every soul which is encased in matter and which ultimately manifests itself as the spiritual intelligence of man. The Cosmic Virgin is the maiden mother of the manifested Universe and not the Virgin mother of incarnated Chirst (Spirit).

Isis occupies in the cosmos or macrocosm the same position which the soul that has fallen into the clutches of matter occupies in the microcosm. Isis is the mother of the Logos manifested in the Cosmos, as the soul is the Virgin mother of the regenerated spirit; Isis is mother of Adonais, while the incarnated soul is the mother of Christ: but the former alone is entitled to be called the Cosmic Virgin, and not the latter. In our humble opinion the Cosmic Virgin is not the Virgin manifested in the Cosmos, but the Virgin mother of the Cosmos. The contrast is not between the Virgin of the Cosmos and the "perpetual maid of heaven," but between the macrocosmic Virgin and the microcosmic Virgin. Consequently in the discourse of the Cosmic Virgin to her divine son, we find a general account of cosmic evolution, and not a mere description of the descent of soul into matter. It must be remembered in this connection that the human incarnations of Isis and Osiris should not be taken as mere allegorical representations of the incarnations of spirit. They were placed on quite a different footing by the ancient Egyptian writers; and in this very discourse Isis said that she would not and dared not "recount *this* nativity" and "declare the origin" of the race of Horus. The so-called myth of Osiris is the great central mystery of Egyptian occultism, and has probably a closer relation with the appearance of Buddha than has usually been imagined. It must further be stated here that the Greek God Dionysos has no proper position to occupy in the Egyptian Pantheon. Dr. Kingsford speaks of the " incarnation martyrdom and resuscitation of Dionysos Zagreus " in the essay prefixed to this book. She says that Dionysos was intended to mean the spirit, and adds further on that " the spirit or Dionysos was regarded as of a specially divine genesis, being the son of Zeus by the immaculate Maiden Kore-Persephoneia. . . ." If so, Dionysos is the seventh principle in man, the Logos that manifests itself in the microcosm. But we are informed at the end of the essay that "Osiris is the microcosmic sun, the counterpart in the human system of the *microcosmic* Dionysos or Son of God." This latter statement is clearly inconsistent with what has gone before, and is evidently the result of misconception—a misconception generally prevalent in the minds of the Western Hermetic students regarding the real position of Osiris—and an attempt to interpret the higher mysteries of the Egyptian religion by the mythological fables of ancient Greece, which, though elegant and refined in form, bear no comparison whatever to the allegories of the ancient Egyptian writers in point of occult significance.

There is a remarkable passage on p. 34 of the book under consideration which, if closely examined, may throw some light on the subject. Isis informs Horus that "on high dwell two ministers of the Universal Providence; one is the guardian of the Souls, the other is their conducter, who sends them forth and ordains for them bodies. The first minister guards them, the second releases or binds them, according to the Will of God." The real position and duties of Osiris may perhaps be gathered from this significant paragraph. It will not be very difficult to ascertain the name of the other minister, who has a nearer relationship with the Macroscosmic Sun than Dionysos, from a careful examination of the religious doctrine of Egypt. But as it is the business of the Sphinx to propose riddles, not to solve difficulties on such subjects, nothing more can be said in this connection. Buddha and Shankaracharya may perhaps disclose the real mystery of these two ministers.

II

Most of the important doctrines explained to Horus by his divine mother are in perfect harmony with the corresponding teachings of Hinduism and Buddhism, as will be seen from the following explanations. Horus represents the regenerated spirit of man, and it is to him that the Cosmic Virgin unveils herself and reveals the mysteries of human existence.

In tracing the evolution of the physical man Isis commences by giving an account of the origin of the spiritual monad. God, it would appear, took out of himself such essence as was necessary, and "mingling it with an intellectual flame, he combined with these other materials in unknown ways; and having, by the use of secret formulæ, brought about the union of these principles, he endowed the universal combination with motion. Gradually in the midst of the protoplasm glittered a substance more subtle, purer and more limpid than the elements from which it was generated. . . . He called it *self-consciousness*." The name given to it is very appropriate; it is the germ of pragna, the point of consciousness, the monad which ultimately evolutes the human being. This explanation is similar to that given by alchemists of the composition of the philosopher's stone. Mercury, described as Sivaviryam by the Hindus, is considered by the alchemists as the essence of God, while the intellectual flame is represented by sulphur. The mysterious salt is the other material spoken of in the above account, and it is the azoth that begins to glitter in the composition. This has a profound significance, and gives a clue to the solution of that perplexing problem—the nature and origin of consciousness. Isis points out that myriads of souls were thus formed, and that they were authorized to take part in the creation of the material world and the lower organisms, and were forbidden to transgress certain limits assigned to their action. In course of time, however, they rebelled, and with a view of imprisoning them in organisms and thereby curtailing their power and freedom, God convened a meeting of the celestials and asked them " What they could bestow upon the race about to be born ?" Sun, Moon, Kronos (Saturn), Zeus (Jupiter), Aries (Mars), Aphrodite (Venus), and Hermes (Mercury) responded to this call and promised to invest human nature with various qualities, intellectual and emotional, good and bad, peculiarly appertaining to the nature of the donors ; and Hermes constructed organisms out of the existing material for the monads to inhabit. Thus was formed the man before his fall. With the transition from simple self-consciousness to the plane of mind and its varied activities there came then a change of Upadhi also, from a mere centre of force to an astral body. While the spiritual monad is evolved by God himself, the latter Upadhi is represented at the work of subordinate powers.

There yet remained one more step of descent into matter. The souls perceived the change in their condition and bewailed their fate ; hopes of a better and happier future were held out to them, and it was further pointed out that if any of them should merit reproach they would be made to inhabit abodes destined to them in *mortal organisms*. In spite of this warning the necessity for a further degradation of the spiritual monad soon arose. Man as an astral being was in a transition stage ; and this condition was not such as could be permanently maintained. Mental faculties acting without any weight of responsibility to control and restrain their action were likely to produce evil results. The genius of the law of Karma soon arose from the earth in the form of Momos and pointed out to Hermes the evil results which would inevitably follow if mankind were allowed to remain in their then condition. The wisdom of Hermes soon designed "a mysterious instrument, a measure inflexible and inviolable, to which everything would be subject from birth even to final destruction," and which would be the bond of created entities—in short, the inexorable law of Karma. The instrument forthwith operated, it would seem, as Karmic impulses were already being generated by man, owing to the very mental qualities with which he was invested, and the consequence was that souls were incorporated. This is the summary of the account given by Isis of the gradual evolution of the Karana Sarira, Sukshma Sarira, and Sthula Sarira. The constitution of these Upadhis was also to a certain extent indicated, as well as the nature of the conscious energy and its functions manifested in and through the said Upadhis. This three-fold division of a human being is in agreement with the Vedantic classification of the various Upadhis.

Man thus left encased in matter, with his internal light altogether clouded and obscured, began to grope in the dark. Without a guide, a teacher and enlightener, mankind developed tendencies which if left unchecked would lead to a still lower level of existence. Confusion and discord reigned supreme. Even the very elements could not bear the presence of man. Loud were the complaints made by the whole of nature against the moral and spiritual chaos that prevailed. It was found that if left to himself man would be unable to liberate his soul from the trammels of matter and attain to salvation. As long as he remained a trinity merely he would remain an imperfect being. It was necessary to convert this trinity into a quaternary. This condition of things had to be remedied, and "forthwith God filled the Universe with His divine voice :—' Go,' said He, ' Sacred offspring, worthy of your father's greatness ; seek not to change anything, nor refuse to my creatures your ministry."

This divine Voice is the Logos—the seventh principle in man. He is the real Eswara of the Vedantins and the Saviour of mankind. Through Him alone can salvation and immortality be secured by man; and the end and object of all initiation is to ascertain His attributes and connection with humanity, realize His sacred presence in every human heart, and discover the means of transferring man's higher individuality, purified and ennobled by the virtuous Karma of a series of incarnations, to His feet as the most sacred offering which a human being can bestow.

God further found necessary to send a teacher and a ruler to mankind to disclose to them the laws of initiation and point out the way to reach their own Logos. In spite of the presence of Atma in his own heart, man might remain ignorant of that sacred presence unless the veil of ignorance were removed from his eyes by a spiritual teacher. To meet this necessity God thought of sending down into the world such a teacher and made the following promise to the complaining elements :—

" I will send you an *efflux* of myself, a pure being who shall investigate all actions, who shall be the dreadful and incorruptible judge of the living : and sovereign justice shall extend its reign even into the shades beneath the earth. Thus shall every man receive his merited deserts."

This efflux manifested itself as Osiris and his female counterpart Isis.

This nativity, the mystery of which Isis refuses to disclose even to Horus, does not however correspond with the nativity of Christ.

Christ or Christos is the divine voice or Logos which manifests itself in every man ; and the biblical narrative of Christ is an allegorical account of every regenerated spirit generally. It is not the historical value of the biblical account which is of importance to mankind in general, but its philosophical and occult significance, as asserted by Dr. Kingsford and

Mr. Maitland. But it will be erroneous to look upon the incarnation of Buddha or this nativity of Osiris and Isis in the same light as that of Christ. Every Buddha is also a Christ; but every Christ is not a Buddha. Every man may become a Christ and identify himself with Christ, but it is not open to every man to develope into a Buddha. Every true Kabalist knows that Christ is the son of man, and not Ennoia, the *primitive man*; or to express the same thing in Buddhist phraseology, Christ is a Bodhi Satwa and not a Buddha. It must be remembered that by the term Christ I do not refer to any particular individual, but to the spiritual entity with reference to which the Bible account has its philosophical importance. The germ of a Bodhi Satwa is in every man, but not the germ of a Buddha; hence when a Buddha is evolved by humanity in the course of its progress, his appearance will become a matter of historical importance. The appearance of Osiris was placed on the same footing, and was looked upon in the same light by Egyptian initiates. Osiris is not the Logos, but is something higher than the Logos. The Logos itself has a soul and a spirit as everything else has which is manifested; and there is nothing unreasonable in supposing that Osiris or Buddha may represent the soul of the Logos. The Sphinx cannot and dare not say anything more on the subject. The reader may find a very interesting and instructive commentary on the foregoing statements in the second volume of "*Isis Unveiled*."

We will now proceed with the account of Isis. The reign of order and justice commenced with the appearance of Isis and Osiris; who, amongst other things, taught mankind the secrets of the occult science and the sacred mysteries of initiation. After finishing their work on earth the divine couple were recalled by "the inhabitants of heaven."

After having thus traced the descent of spirit into matter and indicated the provision made by God for securing salvation to mankind, Isis proceeds to give replies to certain questions put to her by Horus. The first question relates to royal or kingly souls. The royalty herein referred to is spiritual royalty. Now and then men like Buddha, Shankaracharya, Christ, Zoroaster and others have appeared on earth as spiritual leaders and rulers of mankind. In point of spiritual development and elevation of moral character they stand at such an enormous height above the level of ordinary humanity as to lead mankind into the belief that they are special incarnation of divinity. This popular belief, however, is not endorsed by Isis, whose way of accounting for the appearance of such men is in harmony with the teachings of occult science. She explains to Horus that "souls destined to reign upon the earth descend thither for two causes, There are those who in former lives have lived blameless, and who merit apotheosis ; for such as these royalty is a preparation for the divine state. Again there are holy souls, who for some slight infringement of the interior and divine Law receive in royalty a penance whereby the suffering and shame of incarnation are mitigated. The condition of these in taking a body resembles not that of others ; they are as blessed as when they were free." If this reply of Isis is properly understood and accepted by the generality of people, sectarian strife, discord and bigotry will almost cease to exist.

There are differences, it would appear, among these royal souls, due to the nature of the angels and genii who assist them. The reader must not suppose that these powers are elementals ; they are the guardians of the souls, whose teaching and guidance the souls follow, as declared by Isis. It is this guardian angel of the soul which is the Kwan-yin of the Buddhists and the Chitkala of the Hindus.

"How are souls born male or female ?" asks Horus ; and Isis answers thus :—"There are not among them either males or females ; this distinction exists only between bodies, and not between incorporeal beings. But some are more energetic, some are gentler, and this belongs to the air in which all things are formed. For an airy body envelopes the soul......". It is hardly necessary to state that the air referred to is the anima mundi—astral light—and that the airy body is the astral body of man. The next question answered by Isis relates to the various degrees of spiritual enlightenment seen amongst men.

The real difference between a man who has spiritual vision and discernment, and another who does not possess these faculties, is not to be found in the inmost nature of the soul ; just as the clearness of vision depends, not on the latent perceptive faculty of the soul or mind, but upon the nature of the organ of vision and the tunics in which it is enveloped, the clearness of spiritual or clairvoyant perception depends, not on the nature of the soul, but on the condition and nature of the Upadhis in which it is placed.

Consequently all progressive development consists in the improvement of the Upadhis ; the soul is perfect from the beginning and undergoes no alteration during the course of evolution.

Isis further proceeds to point out differences in national character, physical, intellectual and spiritual, amongst the various races inhabiting the globe, and attributes them to differences in climate and position of their respective countries. The reference to the constellation *Ursa Major* has a mystic significance. The ancient Hindus calculated the period of one of their secret cycles with reference to the movements of the stars composing this constellation ; and this cycle is related to the evolution of the various races and sub-races on the globe.

Speaking of the agencies which cause " in living men during long maladies an alteration of discernment 'of reason' even of the soul itself," Isis points out " that the soul has affinity with certain elements and aversion for others" and that therefore its functions are sometimes disturbed and affected by changes in either the physical or astral body.

The last chapter of the treatise under review contains the explanations of Isis regarding existence in Devachan or Swarga.

Isis says that there are several regions between the earth and heaven, adapted to varying degrees of spiritual development, wherein "dwell the souls who are freed from bodies and those who have not yet been incorporated." These regions correspond to the various Devalokams (each Devagana has a separate loka) spoken of in Hindu books, and the rupa and arupa lokas of the Buddhists. The two mysterious ministers alluded to in the former part of this article exercise, it would seem, certain powers of supervision and control over the condition of the various Devachanees in accordance with the law of Karma. This law is set in motion by two energies described as memory and experience. The former "directs in nature the preservation and maintenance of all the original types appointed in Heaven." This refers to the record of Karma preserved in astral light. "The function of Experience is to provide every soul descending into generation with a body appropriate thereto." It is needless to state that this is a correct rationale of the doctrine of Karma from the Buddhist and the Hindu standpoint.

There is nothing more of importance to consider in this treatise. The points already referred to show that the same main doctrines of the ancient wisdom religion underlie every exoteric creed whether ancient or modern. It is not true, as Mr. Herbert Spencer says, that the only statement with reference to which all the nations in the world agree in the matter of religious belief is that there is an unknown and unknowable Power in the universe. The religious history of humanity shows that there are a number of doctrines regarding the origin, the nature and the ultimate destiny of the human soul, highly philosophical and complicated, which form the foundation of every exoteric religion and which have influenced the religious sentiments of mankind from time immemorial. How are we to account for these beliefs? Have they any inherent special connection with human nature as it is? Or are they the outcome of a divine revelation during the infancy of the human race, whose influence has survived the vicissitudes of so many civilizations? If neither of these hypothesis is acceptable to the mind of a modern agnostic, can the evolution of these doctrines from a few simple ideas which are common to humanity in general be explained by the operation of known psychological laws? If the latter hypothesis is tenable, how is it that these products of human experience have not undergone any change in spite of great improvements in material civilization and mental culture?

It is not my object now to undertake a discussion of the above subject and offer my own solutions of the problem; I only beg to call the reader's attention to this important question, and request him not to lose sight of it in meditating on the origin and history of religious belief amongst mankind, and the possibility of discovering a common platform on which the followers of the various religions on the globe may take up their stand with brotherly love and affection, forgetting the petty differences of their exoteric dogmatic creeds. The Sphinx does not think it necessary to say anything about the contents of the short philosphical dissertations appended to "The Virgin of the World" as they seem to contain more of Grecian speculation than of Egyptian wisdom.

Correspondence.

"THE VIRGIN OF THE WORLD."

TO THE EDITOR OF THE THEOSOPHIST.

In your remarks upon my prefatory essay to the "Virgin of the World," you assert that Persephone cannot be regarded as the Kosmic Virgin. She was, however, undoubtedly so regarded by all the neo. Platonic school, whose exponent, Thomas Taylor, in his "Dissertation of the Eleusinian and Bacchic Mysteries," quotes largely from Greek Hermetic authors to prove this very point. I wish that my reviewer, before committing himself to the statement he has made on page 97 of the November number of the *Theosophist*, had made himself familiar with this standard work, and also with certain passages of Proclus, Olympiodorus, the Orphic hymns, Claudian, Apuleias, and other accredited and classic authorities, from all of which it is abundantly clear that the mythos of the rape of Persephone, the theme of the mysteries, represented the descent into Matter, or Generation, of the Soul, and that the title "Kore

Kosmou" was throughout the whole mythos attributed to Persephone, the daughter of Demeter or supermundane Intelligence.

Isis never represented the soul or sixth Principle (third) of the universe, but the eighth sphere; not properly a Principle, but an influence. Passages from the best authors are cited in my essay to prove this fact, and many more can be adduced. If, as is certain, Isis was identified with the Moon, and wore as an ensign the double horns of Selene, it is placed beyond doubt that she symbolised the Occult Power of Increase and Decrease, Good and Evil, and cannot possibly, therefore, be identified with the Soul whom she rejoices or afflicts according to an inflexible law. I cannot in the least understand your reviewer's reference to the *Egyptian* pantheon in connection with Dionysos-Zagreus. No pretence is made in my essay or elsewhere in the work, that Dionysos occupied such a place, although, of course, he had his correspondence therein. But the whole of my exposition follows the *Greek* mysteries, and deals with their presentations. That Dionysos-Zagreus personified in these mysteries the seventh Principle (Hermetically, the Fourth) in the universe,—that is—the Divine and vitalizing Spirit, is no surmise or assumption of mine, but an undoubted fact, placed beyond controversy by the authorities already mentioned. This Dionysos-Zagreus, (*Dionusos Chthonios*) the Mystic Dionysos, must not be confounded with the later god, identical with Bacchus, the son of Semele. I will only add that there is no such inconsistency in my essay as your reviewer charges on me. Dionysos represents the Spirit or Seventh Principle (Fourth) whether macrocosmically or microcosmically, and, as such, has been identified with Osiris, the Egyptian presentation of the same Principle. And Persephone is alike, in both aspects, greater and lesser, the Soul. But the Greek Mysteries dealt ostensibly with the *macrocosmic* presentation of the divine drama, and with its individual meaning by implication only. Hence Persephone is generally taken to signify the Soul in her larger acceptation, as "Kore Kosmou," and hence also, her son Dionysos, represents rather the son of God in the World than the son of God in Man.

And, in this connexion, in order further to elucidate the function and position of Isis in the macrocosm as it is expounded by Hermetists and neo-Platonists, I may add that her counter-partal analogy in the microcosm, or individual, is found in the Genius:—the gurdain angel of Christian theosophy. This Genus is good or bad, helpful or hindering, bright or dark, favorable or hostile, according to the state of grace (Karma) which the Soul has acquired. The Genius sheds upon the Soul the light derived from her own celestial Sun. (see pp. 88 and 89 of the "Perfect Way.")

In the Discourse accompanying the allegory of the "Virgin of the World," I understand Isis to represent the Illuminatrix or Revealer; Osiris, the Saviour or Redeeming Principle; and Horos, the Initiate,—

offspring of a good "Karma" or state of Grace, and Divine Influx, by which parentage is exactly described the generation of every true "Jesus."

I must content myself with a simple expression of dissent from your reviewer's appreciation of the relation existing between the mysteries of Egyptian and of Grecian origin. No doubt I feel somewhat strongly on this point, because my own instruction and illumination in mystic doctrine have been obtained chiefly through the splendid arcana which I cannot, without regret, find characterised by your reviewer in a sentence evidently intended to disparge them, as "mythological fables."

Christmas, 1885. ANNA KINGSFORD, M. D., F. T. S.

SIR,—In thanking you for the notice of this book in the November *Theosophist*, I wish to correct a misapprehension caused by your reviewer's statement that the books now being published do not appear to be the real Hermetic books. The misapprehension in question consists in the impression that this statement is made in contradiction of the position taken up by me. Whereas, the fact is it correctly describes that position the only conclusion to which I have committed myself in the point being "that the doctrine contained in the Hermetic books is in part, at least, a survival from the times of ancient Egypt, and therein really Hermetic." I have not said a word to imply that I considered them the work of Trismegistus himself, or that the term Hermetic meant other than a certain school or system of doctrine, originating, so far as the Western World is concerned, in Egypt, and bearing tho name of Hermes Trismegistus, a name which has long been, for the Western World, a synonym for the intellectual principle.

Your reviewer's expression "misconception generally prevalent in the minds of the Western Hermetists" seems to me unfortunate as constituting an affirmation that the "Western Hermetists" are not rightly instructed concerning their own doctrine. Whereas all that your reviewer can possibly be in a position to affirm is that there is a divergency of view between his system and that of the West. That there may be and probably is such a divergency we "Western Hermetists" are quite ready to admit. But we are not ready to admit that the error, if any, lies with us. Rather do we hold, and believe, that the revival of occult knowledge now in progress will some day demonstrate, that the Western system represents ranges of preception, which the Eastern—at least as expounded in the pages of the *Theosophist*—has yet to attain.

EDWARD MAITLAND.

P. S.—Allow me to state, in **justice to** my fellow-editor and myself, that the **responsibility for the defective** title-page and table of contents **does not rest with us,** these not having been submitted to us prior to publication.

SIR,—Kindly permit me to say a few words with reference to the two letters sent by Dr. Kingsford and Mr. Maitland in connection with my review of the "Virgin of the World."

If my critics had borne in mind that the subject-matter of my review was the "Virgin of the World" and not their introductory essays or Hellenic mysteries, they would no doubt have refrained from making all the irrelevant statements which their letters contain. There were but two specific references to these introductory essays in my article. One of my objections remains altogether unanswered, and the explanation given with reference to the other throws no additional light on the real question at issue as the following remarks will show.

"The Virgin of the World" was published though not as a genuine work of Hermes himself, yet as a treatise on Egyptian mysteries. In reviewing it, therefore, I found it necessary to examine it by the light of the Hermetic science and not by that of Grecian philosophy. With reference to the title of the Hermetic Fragment under consideration, I made the following statement in my article—"......it is necessary to point out that Persephone is not the Cosmic Virgin and cannot be represented as such *from the stand-point of Hermetic philosophy.*" Dr. Kingsford objects to this statement on the authority of various writers *on Grecian philosophy.* If Grecian writers have bestowed this title on Persephone, it is no proof whatever that Egyptian writers did the same thing. Persephone might be the Kore Kosmou of the Hellenic mysteries, but she was not the cosmic Virgin of the Egyptians. It will even be difficult to find the corresponding goddess of the Egyptian Pantheon. It cannot even be contended that the "Virgin of the World" not being a genuine Egyptian book, but a work written by some Grecian author, to some extent according to Egyptian models, the title in question might have been used according to the conception of Grecian writers in general. For, under such a supposition, there would be no connection whatever between the contents of the book and the title is chosen for it. There is no special reference whatsoever to Persephone or any corresponding goddess in the treatise as we find it at present. The only female deity who figures prominently in it is Isis. Under these circumstances it would have been extremely absurd on my part if I had put on the title in question the construction now contended for by my critic and tried to force into the teachings of Isis by means of strained interpretations and far-fetched analogies any ideas relating to the position of Persephoneia in Grecian mysteries. I beg to state further that the description, when judged by itself and not in connection with the usage of any particular class of writers, is more appropriate to the Egyptian Isis than to the Grecian Persephone.

It is my humble opinion that my critic has misconceived the position of the Egyptian Isis. What is really meant by saying that Isis represented "the Eighth sphere" it is not easy to understand. She further says that Isis is not a *principle* but an *influence*. In spite of my critic's assurance to the contrary, I am unable to find any authority for these assertions in her introductory essay. Though the word principle is now rejected as inapplicable, yet I find in p. 27 of the said essay that Isis is "a *principle*" represented by the Kabbalists under the figure of Malcuth or the Moon. The reason assigned for disproving my statement that Isis represented the 6th principle of the Cosmos is stated as follows:— "If, as is certain, Isis was identified with the moon, and wore as an ensign the double horns of Selene, it is placed beyond doubt that she symbolized the occult power of Increase and Decrease, Good and Evil, and cannot possibly therefore be identified with the soul whom she rejoices and afflicts according to an inflexible Law." To begin with, what proof is there that Isis was identified with the moon by Egyptian writers? There is no use in saying that Grecian writers identified her with Diana or Artemis. When the question whether Grecian writers rightly or wrongly interpreted the Hermetic doctrines of ancient Egypt is under discussion, it is improper solely to rely on their statements. The sign of the Crescent is no proof that Isis represents the moon. This symbol, which has a profound significance to every true occultist, is associated with a very large number of male and female deities in the Hindu religious philosophy; but not one of them is on that account ever confounded with the moon. Isis has not got all the attributes of Diana or Artemis. She was never represented as a huntress, for instance with a bow and arrows in her hands. Another Egyptian goddess—the Divine Neith—had these attributes. But Neith was clearly a Solar Deity in the Egyptian doctrine. It would be extremely unsafe for a student of comparative mythology to infer the identity of two deities belonging to the mystical conceptions of two very different nationalities from the mere fact that they have some similar attributes. Even admitting that the moon was a symbol of Isis, how does it follow from it that Isis was considered by the Egyptian as "the occult power of increase and decrease, good and evil?", The description itself conveys no definite idea, and there is no evidence to show that the Egyptians attached any such significance to the moon in their writings. Even supposing that the chain of inference is so far sound and that this influence called Isis rejoices and afflicts the soul, how is it shown thereby that Isis is not the Cosmic soul or the 6th principle of the Universe? Does Isis or the law of Karma afflict and rejoice the 6th principle or the spiritual intelligence of the Cosoms. If it does, it requiries no doubt a "range of perception" which the Eastern system "has yet to attain" to comprehend the meaning of this statement. If it does not, the whole arguement is simply worthless. The law of Karma and its influence is as much a manifestation of the energies of the Cosmic 6th principle of every other all in the Universe: and the rejoicings and sufferings of the soul encased in matter do not disprove the real genuine claims of Isis to be rgarded as the spiritual soul of the Cosmos.

I did not say and did not mean to insinuate in my articles that Dr. Kingsford made any incorrect statements as regards Dionysos Zagreus as is now alleged. I simply pointed out in my article that Dionysos as contrasted with Osiris had no place in the Egyptian Pantheon to preclude the possibility of any misconception that might otherwise arise regarding the real position of Osiris from certain passages in the introductory essay: and I must further state now that if Osiris is to be left out of account Dionysos has no correspondence in the Egyptian Pantheon.

The inconsistency pointed out in my article is in no way removed by the explanation now given. I beg to call the readers's attention to the following passages in the introductory essay in this connection.

1. " . . . The incarnation, martyrdom and resuscitation of Dionysos Zagreus."

2. "For, Osiris is the *microcosmic* sun, the counter-part in the human system of the *macrocosmic* Dionysos or Son of God. So that these authors who confound Isis with Demeter, equally and quite comprehensibly confound Osiris with Dionysos . . . "

"The Hermetic books admit three expressions of Deity; first, the supreme, abstract, and infinite God, eternally self-subsistent and unmanifest; secondly, the only Begotten, the manifestation of Deity in the universe; thirdly, God in man, the redeemer, or Osiris."

Comparing these various statements with each other we find Dionysos, described as the macrocosmic sun or the only Begotten Son of God manifested in the Universe, undergoing incarnation, martyrdom and resuscitation as if he were the incarnated spirit. It is now asserted that Dionysos represents the spirit or 7th principle, whether *macrocosmically or microcosmically*. If so, he is identical with Osiris as is virtually admitted. Why then was it stated in the introductory essay that some authors confounded Dionysos with Osiris and Isis with Demeter? If one and the same principle is alike the Logos manifested in the Cosmos and the Logos manifested in man, what foundation is there for the *three* expressions of Deity above described? If the Greek mysteries dealt ostensibly with the *macrocosmic* presentation of the Divine Drama, and with its individual meaning by implication only as is now asserted this statement is altogether at variance with the following statements in the introductory essay:—"The Greek mysteries dealt *only with two subjects*, the first being the Drama of the rape and restoration of Persephone; the second that of the incarnation, martyrdom and resuscitation of Dionysos Zagreus." It cannot, surely, be contended that these form the subject-matter of the macrocosmic presentation of the Divine Drama; and we are further informed that the Hellenic mysteries dealt *only* with these two subjects. If so, the presentation is pre-eminently if not entirely microcosmic and the macrocosmic position assigned to Dionysos and the difference pointed out between him and Osiris in the introductory essay by reason of such position, is out of place in the Grecian mysteries. Any number of difficulties may be pointed out in the position assumed by Dr. Kingsford, and the explanation now offered is likely to make matters worse.

As regards the guardian angel of Christian Theosophy, I find it necessary to state that this guardian angel is not the counterpart of Isis. If Isis is not a principle but a mere influence as stated by my critic, it is difficult to understand how this influence can discharge the duties assigned to, and be invested with, the attributes of a guardian angel in the Christian doctrine.

With reference to Dr. Kingford's letter I have only to state further that I did not use the expression cited for the purpose of disparaging the Grecian mystical doctrines. According to ordinary usage the expression in question was the only one which I could use to indicate that part of the Grecian literature which dealt with mystical and occult subjects. But my convictions are equally strong that there is a greater depth of occult significance in the allegorical fables of Egypt than in those of Greece, and that it will be extremely unjust to the Egyptian doctrine to interpret it in accordance with Hellenic notions.

Mr. Maitland's letter requires but very few words in reply. He makes no attempt to justify his assertion that the number of the Vedas or their sub-divisions is 42, but raises a discussion which is altogether irrelevant and unnecessary. I do not see how he can hold me responsible for any misapprehension that might have arisen from his own words. Mr. Maitland seems to think that I have no right whatever to speak of the misconceptions regarding the Hermetic doctrine that seem to exist in the minds of the so-called "Western Hermetists," because the said doctrine is "their own doctrine," and it must therefore be presumed that they know all about it. If, by Hermetic doctrine Mr. Maitland simply means the doctrine now professed by the so-called "Western Hermetists" of the present day, there is some reason for the assertion made. But the expression is generally applied to the occult philosophy and the mystical doctrines of the ancient Egyptians, and when I spoke of the misconceptions regarding the Hermetic doctrine in my review, I had this system of philosophy in view and not any other doctrine to which my critic might apply the expression.

But if Mr. Maitland goes to the length of saying that the Hermetic doctrine of the ancient Egyptians can be claimed by the Western Hermetists "as their doctrine," I am bound to reject such a claim as simply absurd. The real Hermetic doctrine is far more closely connected with the Eastern systems of occult science than with the Western. A considerable portion of it has long ago disappeared from the West entirely. The old Hermetic doctrine dealt with various systems of initiation. There were mysteries of Isis, of Osiris, of Hermes, of Neith, of Amen-ra and various others divided into distinct groups. A few of the doctrines only belonging to the mysteries of Isis and Osiris came to the West through Hebrew, Grecian and other sources considerably modified. The other parts of the true Hermetic doctrine were altogether lost to the West.

Under such circumstances it is highly desirable that "Western hermetists" should be a little more tolerant and discreet. Mr. Maitland's reference to the Theosophist is entirely out of place in the present discussion. I must confess that I have as yet seen very little of this Western wisdom which is somewhere stored up in Europe. Possibly it has very wide ranges of perception not yet attained by Eastern systems as Mr. Maitland is pleased to state.

But as these ranges of perception have very little to do with the Virgin of World or my review of the same, or with the introductory essays appended to it, it is unnecessary to enter into any controversy with Mr. Maitland on this subject.

THE SOLAR SPHINX.

BHAGAVAD GITA.

In studying the Bhagavad Gita it must not be treated as if isolated from the rest of the Mahabharata as it as present exists. It was inserted by Vyasa in the right place with special reference to some of the incidents in that book. One must first realise the real position of Arjuna and Krishna in order to appreciate the teaching of the latter. Among other appellations Arjuna has one very strange name—he is called at different times by ten or eleven names, most of which are explained by himself in Virataparva. One name is omitted from the list, *i.e.*, Nara. This word simply means "man." But why a particular man should be called by this as a proper name may at first sight appear strange. Nevertheless herein lies a clue, which enables us to understand not only the position of the Bhagavad Gita in the text and its connexion with Arjuna and Krishna, but the entire current running through the whole of the Mahabharata, implying Vyasa's real views of the origin, trials and destiny of man. Vyasa looked upon Arjuna as man, or rather the real monad in man; and upon Krishna as the Logos, or the spirit that comes to save man. To some it appears strange that this highly philosophical teaching should have been inserted in a place apparently utterly unfitted for it. The discourse is alleged to have taken place between Arjuna and Krishna just before the battle began to rage. But when once you begin to appreciate the Mahabharata, you will see this was the fittest place for the Bhagavad Gita.

Historically the great battle was a struggle between two families. Philosophically it is the great battle, in which the human spirit has to fight against the lower passions in the physical body. Many of our readers have probably heard about the so-called Dweller on the Threshold, so vividly described in Lytton's novel "Zanoni." According to this author's

* Notes of a lecture, delivered at the Convention of the Theosophical Society, 1885, by Mr. T. Subba Row as an introduction to a set of lectures, which he had promised to give at the subsequent Anniversary.—*Ed.*

description, the Dweller on the Threshold seems to be some elemental, or other monster of mysterious form, appearing before the neophyte just as he is about to enter the mysterious land, and attempting to shake his resolution with menaces of unknown dangers if he is not fully prepared.

There is no such monster in reality. The description must be taken in a figurative sense. But nevertheless there is a Dweller on the Threshold, whose influence on the mental plane is far more trying than any physical terror can be. The real Dweller on the Threshold is formed of the despair and despondency of the neophyte, who is called upon to give up all his old affections for kindred, parents and children, as well as his aspirations for objects of worldly ambition, which have perhaps been his associates for many incarnations. When called upon to give up these things, the neophyte feels a kind of blank, before he realises his higher possibilities. After having given up all his associations, his life itself seems to vanish into thin air. He seems to have lost all hope, and to have no object to live and work for. He sees no signs of his own future progress. All before him seems darkness; and a sort of pressure comes upon the soul, under which it begins to droop, and in most cases he begins to fall back and gives up further progress. But in the case of a man who really struggles, he will battle against that despair, and be able to proceed on the Path. I may here refer you to a few passages in Mill's autobiography. Of course the author knew nothing of occultism; but there was one stage in his mental life, which seems to have come on at a particular point of his career and to have closely resembled what I have been describing. Mill was a great analytical philosopher. He made an exhaustive analysis of all mental processes,—mind, emotions, and will.

'I now saw or thought I saw, what I had always before received with incredulity,—that the habit of analysis has a tendency to wear away the feelings, as indeed it has when to other mental habits is cultivated. * * * Thus neither selfish nor unselfish pleasures were pleasures to me.'

At last he came to have analysed the whole man into nothing. At this point a kind of melancholy came over him, which had something of terror in it. In this state of mind he continued for some years, until he read a copy of Wordsworth's poems full of sympathy for nature's objects and human life. "From them," he says, "I seemed to learn what would be the perennial sources of happiness, when all the greater evils of life should have been removed." This feebly indicates what the chela must experience when he has determined to renounce all old associates, and is called to live for a bright future on a higher plane. This transition stage was more or less the position of Arjuna before the discourse in question. He was about to engage in a war of extermination against foes led by some of his nearest relations, and he not unnaturally shrank from the thought of killing kindered and friends. We are each of us called upon to kill out all our passions and desires, not that they are all necessarily evil in themselves, but that their influence must be annihilated before we can establish ourselves on the higher planes. The position of Arjuna is intended to typify that of a chela, who is called upon to face the Dweller on the Threshold. As the Guru prepares his chela for the trials of initiation by philosophical teaching, so at this critical point Krishna proceeds to instruct Arjuna.

The Bhagavad Gita may be looked upon as a discourse addressed by a Guru to a chela who has fully determined upon the renunciation of all worldly desires and aspirations, but yet feels a certain despondency, caused by the apparent blankness of his existence. The book contains eighteen chapters, all intimately connected. Each chapter describes a particular phase or aspect of human life. The student should bear this in mind in reading the book, and endeavour to work out the correspondences. He will find what appear to be necessary repetitions. These were a necessity of the method adopted by Vyasa, his intention being to represent nature in different ways, as seen from the standpoints of the various philosophical schools, which flourished in India.

As regards the moral teaching of the Bhagavad Gita, it is often asserted by those who do not appreciate the benefits of occult study, that, if everybody pursued this course, the world would come to a standstill; and, therefore, that this teaching can only be useful to the few, and not to ordinary people. This is not so. It is of course true that the majority of men are not in the position to give up their duties as citizens and members of families. But Krishna distinctly states that these duties, if not reconcilable with ascetic life in a forest, can certainly be reconciled with that kind of mental abnegation which is far more powerful in the production of effects on the higher planes than any physical separation from the world. For though the ascetic's body may be in the jungle, his thoughts may be in the world. Krishna therefore teaches that the real importance lies not in physical but in mental isolation. Every man who has duties to discharge must devote his mind to them. But, says the teacher, it is one thing to perform an action as a matter of duty, and another thing to perform the same from inclination, interest, or desire. It is thus plain that it is in the power of a man to make definite progress in the development of his higher faculties, whilst there is nothing noticeable in his mode of life to distinguish him from his fellows. No religion teaches that men should be the slaves of interest and desire. Few inculcate the necessity of seclusion and asceticism. The great objection that has been brought against Hinduism and Buddhism is that by recommending such a mode of life to students of occultism they tend to render void the lives of men engaged in ordinary avocations. This objection, however, rests upon a misapprehension. For these religions teach that it is not the nature of the act, but the mental attitude of its performer, that is of importance. This is the moral teaching that runs through the whole of the Bhagavad Gita. The reader should note carefully the various arguments by which Krishna establishes his proposition. He will find an account of origin and destiny of the human monad, and of the manner in which it attains salvation through the aid and enlightenment derived from its Logos. (Some have taken Krishna's exhortation to Arjuna to worship him alone as supporting the doctrine of a personal god. But this is an erroneous conclusion.) For, though speaking of himself as Parabrahm, Krishna is still the Logos. He describes himself as Atma, but no doubt is one with Parabrahm, as (there is no essential difference between Atma and Parabrahm.) Certainly the Logos can speak of itself as Parabrahm. So all sons of God, including Christ, have spoken of themselves as one with the Father. His saying, that he exists in almost every entity in the Cosmos, expresses strictly an attribute of Parabrahm. But a Logos, being a manifestation of Parabrahm, can use these words and assume these attributes. Thus Krishna only calls upon Arjuna to worship his own highest spirit, through which alone he can hope to attain salvation. Krishna is teaching Arjuna what the Logos in the course of initiation will teach the human monad, pointing out that through himself alone is salvation to be obtained. This implies no idea of a personal god.

Again notice the view of Krishna respecting the Sankhya philosophy. Some strange ideas are afloat about this system. It is supposed that the Sutras we possess represent the original aphorisms of Kapila. But this has been denied by many great teachers, including Shankaracharya, who say that they do not represent his real views, but those of some other Kapila, or the writer of the book. The real Sankhya philosophy is identical with the Pythagorean system of numerals, and the philosophy embodied in the Chaldean system of numbers. The philosopher's object was to represent all the mysterious powers of nature by a few simple formulæ, which he expressed in numerals. The original book is not to be found, though it is possible that it still exists. The system now put forward under this name contains little beyond an account of the evolution of the elements and a few combinations of the same which enter into the formation of the various tatwams. Krishna reconciles the Sankhya philosophy, Raja Yoga, and even Hatta Yoga, by first pointing out that the philosophy, if properly understood, leads to the same merging of the human monad in the Logos. The doctrine of Karma, which embraces a wider field than that allowed it by orthodox Pundits, who have limited its signification solely to religious observances, is the same in all philosophies, and is made by Krishna to include almost every good and bad act or even thought.) The student must first go through the Bhagavat Gita, and next try to differentiate the teachings in the eighteen different parts under different categories. He should observe how these different aspects branch out from our common centre, and how the teachings in these chapters are intended to do away with the objections of different philosophers to the occult theory and the path of salvation here pointed out. If this is done, the book will show the real attitude of occultists in considering the nature of the Logos and the human monad. In this way almost all that is held sacred in different systems is combined. By such teaching Krishna succeeds in dispelling Arjuna's despondency and in giving him a higher idea of the nature of the force acting through him, though for the time being it is manifesting itself as a distinct individual. He overcomes Arjnana's disinclination to fight by analysing the idea of self, and showing that (the man is in error, who thinks that *he* is doing this, that and the other.) When it is found that what he calls "I" is a short of fiction, created by his own ignorance, a great part of the difficulty has ceased to exist. He further proceeds to demonstrate the existence of a higher individuality, of which Arjuna had no previous knowledge. Then he points out that this individuality is connected with the Logos. He furthermore expounds the nature of the Logos and shows that it is Parabrahm. This is the substance of the first eleven or twelve chapters. In those that follow Krishna gives Arjuna further teaching in order to make him firm of purpose; and explains to him how through the inherent qualities of Prakriti and Purusha all the entities have been brought into existence.

It is to be observed that the number eighteen is constantly recurring in the Mahabharata, seeing that it contains eighteen Parvas, the contending armies were divided into eighteen army-corps, the battle raged eighteen days, and the book is called by a name which means eighteen. This number is mysteriously connected with Arjuna. I have been describing him as man, but even Prabrahm manifests itself as a Logos in more ways than one. Krishna may be the Logos, but only one particular form of it. The number eighteen is to represent this particular form. Krishna is the seventh principle in man, and his gift of his sister in marriage to Arjuna typifies the union between the sixth and the fifth. It is worthy of note that Arjuna did not want Krishna to fight for him, but only to act as his charioteer and to be his friend and counsellor. From this it will be perceived that the human monad must fight its own battle, assisted when once he begins to tread the true path by his own Logos.

THE IDYLL OF THE WHITE LOTUS.

The interesting story published under the title above mentioned has already attracted considerable attention. It is instructive in more ways than one. It truly depicts the Egyptian faith and the Egyptian priesthood, when their religion had already begun to lose its purity and degenerate into a system of Tantric worship contaminated and defiled by black magic, unscrupulously used for selfish and immoral purposes. It is probably also a true story. Sensa is represented to be the last great hierophant of Egypt. Just as a tree leaves its seed to develope into a similar tree, even if it should perish completely, so does every great religion seem to leave its life and energy in one or more great adepts destined to preserve its wisdom and revive its growth at some future time when the cycle of evolution tends in the course of its revolution, to bring about the desired result. The grand old religion of Chemi is destined to reappear on this planet in a higher and nobler form when the appointed time arrives, and there is nothing unreasonable in the supposition that the Sensa of our story is probably now a very high adept, who is waiting to carry out the commands of the Lady of the White Lotus. Apart from these speculations, however, the story in question has a very noble lesson to teach. In its allegorical aspect it describes the trials and the difficulties of a neophyte. It is not easy, however, for the ordinary reader to remove the veil of allegory and clearly understand its teachings. It is to help such readers that I proceed to give the following explanation of the characters that appear in the story in question and the events therein related.

(1.) *Sensa*, the hero of the story, is intended to represent the human soul.

It is the Kutashtha Chitanyam, or the germ of Pragna, in which the individuality of the human being is preserved. It corresponds with the higher and permanent element in the 5th principle of man. It is the ego or the self of embodied existence.

(2.) *Seboua*, the gardener, is *intuition*. "They cannot make a phantom of me," declares Seboua ; and in saying so this unsophisticated but honest rustic truly reveals his own mystery.

(3.) *Agdmahd*, *Kamen-Baka* and the nine other high priests of the temple, who are the devoted servants of the dark goddess whom they worship, represent respectively the following entities :—

(1.) *Kâma* ... ... Desire.
(2.) *Krodha* ... ... Anger.
(3.) *Lobha* ... ... Cupidity.
(4.) *Moha* ... ... Ignorance.
(5.) *Mada* ... ... Arrogance.
(6.) *Matsara* ... ... Jealousy.
(7, 8, 9, 10 & 11.) ... ... The five Senses and their pleasures.

(4.) The female characters that figure in the story are the following:—

(1.) The dark and mysterious goddess worshipped by the priests;

(2.) The young girl who played with Sensa;

(3.) The grown up girl met by him in the City;

(4.) And lastly, the Lady of the White Lotus.

It must be noticed here that the 2nd and the 3rd are identical. Speaking of the fair woman of the City, whom he met apparently for the first time, Sensa says that as he gazed into her tender eyes it seemed to him that he knew her well and that her charms were familiar to him. It is clear from this statement that this lady is no other than the young girl who ran about the temple with him.

Prakriti, say the Hindu philosophers, has three qualities, Satwa, Rajas and Tamas. The last of these qualities is connected with the grosser pleasures and passions experienced in Sthulasarira. Rajoguna is the cause of the restless activity of the mind, while Satwaguna is intimately associated with the spiritual intelligence of man, and with his higher and noble aspirations. Maya, then, makes its appearance in this story in three distinct forms. It is Vidya, a spiritual intelligence, which is represented by the Lady of the White Lotus. It is the Kwan-yin and the Pragna of the Buddhist writers. She represents the light or the aura of the Logos, which is wisdom, and she is the source of the current of conscious life or Chaitanyam. The young girl above referred to is the Mind of man, and it is by her that Sensa is led gradually into the presence of the dark goddess, set up in the holy of the holies for adoration by the priesthood whom we have above described.

The dark goddess herself is *Avidya*. It is the dark side of human Nature. It derives its life and energy from the passions and desires of the human soul. The ray of life and wisdom, which originally emanated from the Logos and which has acquired a distinct individuality of its own when the process of differentiation has set in, is capable of being transformed more or less entirely into this veritable Kali, if the light of the Logos is altogether excluded by the bad Karma of the human being, if the voice of intuition is unheard and unnoticed, and if the man lives simply for the purpose of gratifying his own passions and desires.

If these remarks are kept in mind, the meaning of the story will become clear. It is not my object now to write an exhaustive commentary. I shall only notice some of the important incidents and their significance.

Look upon Sensa as a human being, who, after running his course through several incarnations, and after having passed through a considerable amount of spiritual training, is born again in this world with his spiritual powers of perception greatly developed, and prepared to become a neophyte at a very early stage in his career. As soon as he enters into the physical body, he is placed under the charge of the five Senses and the six Emotions above enumerated, who have it as their place of residence. The human Soul is first placed under the guidance of his own intuition, the simple and honest gardener of the temple, for whom the High Priests seem to have no respect or affection, and, when it has not yet lost its original purity, gets a glimpse of its spiritual intelligence, the Lady of the White Lotus. The priests, however, are determined that no opportunity should be given for the intuition to work, and they therefore remove the child from its guardianship and introduce him to their own dark goddess, the goddess of human passion. The very sight of this deity is found repulsive to the human soul at first. The proposed transfer of human consciousness and human attachment from the spiritual plane to the physical plane is too abrupt and premature to succeed. The priests failed in their first attempt and began to devise their plans for a second effort in the same direction.

Before proceeding further I must draw the reader's attention to the real meaning of the Lotus tank in the garden

Sahasrava Chakram in the brain is often spoken of as a Lotus Tank in the Hindu mystical books. The "sweet sounding water" of this tank is described as Amritam or nectar. See p. 349 of the second volume of "Isis Unveiled" for further hints as regards the meaning of this magic water. Padma, the White Lotus, is said to have a thousand petals, as has the mysterious Sahasravam of the Yogis. It is an unopened bud in the ordinary mortal, and just as a lotus opens its petals, and expand in all its bloom and beauty when the sun rises above the horizon and sheds his rays on the flower, so does the Sahasravam of the neophyte open and expand when the Logos begins to pour its light into its centre. When fully expanded it becomes the glorious seat of the Lady of the Lotus, the sixth principle of man; and sitting on this flower the great goddess pours out the waters of life and grace for the gratification and the regeneration of the human soul.

Hatta Yogis say that the human soul in *Samadhi* ascends to this thousand-petalled flower through Sushumna (the *dath* of the Kabbalists) and obtains a glimpse of the splendour of the spiritual sun.

In this part of Sensa's life an event is related which deserves attention. An elemental appearing in the guise of a neophyte of the temple tries to take him out from his physical body. This is a danger to which a man is liable before he acquires sufficient proficiency as an adept to guard himself against all such dangers, especially when his internal perception is developed to a certain extent. Sensa's guardian angel protects him from the danger owing to his innocence and purity.

When the mental activity of the child commences and absorbs its attention, it recedes farther and farther from the Light of the Logos. Its intuition will not be in a position to work unshackled. Its suggestions come to it mixed up with other states of consciousness which are the result of sensation and intellection. Unable to see Sensa and speak to him personally,

Sebona sends him his beloved lotus flower surreptitiously through one of the neophytes of the temple.

Mental activity commences first by way of sensation. Emotions make their appearance subsequently. The opening mind of the child is aptly compared to a little girl playing with Sensa. When once the mind begins to exercise its functions the pleasures of sensation soon pave the way for the strong and fierce emotions of the human soul. Sensa has descended one step from the spiritual plane when he loses sight of the sublime lotus flower and its glorious goddess and begins to be amused by the frolicsome little girl. "You are to live among Earth-fed flower," says this little girl to him, disclosing the change that has already taken place. At first it is the simple beauty of nature that engrosses the attention of Sensa But his mind soon leads him to the dark goddess of the shrine. Avidya has its real seat in mind, and it is impossible to resist its influence so long as the mind of man is not restrained in its action. When once the soul gets under the influence of this dark goddess, the high priests of the temple begin to utilize its powers for their own benefit and gratification. The goddess requires twelve priests in all, including Sensa, to help her cause. Unless the six emotions and the five sensations above enumerated are banded together she cannot exercise her sway completely. They support and strengthen each other as every man's experience clearly demonstrates. Isolated, they are weak and can easily be subdued, but when associated together their combined power is strong enough to keep the soul under control. The fall of Sensa now becomes complete, but not before he receives a well merited rebuke from the gardener and a word of warning from the Lady of the Lotus.

Addressing Sensa, Seboua is made to utter the following words: "You came first to work; you were to be the drudge for me; now all is changed. You are to play, not work, and I am to treat you like a little prince. Well! Have they spoiled thee yet, I wonder, child?" These words are significant; and their meaning will become plain by the light of the foregoing remarks. It must be noted that the last time he went into the garden, Sensa was taken, not to the Lotus Tank, but to another tank receiving its waters from the former.

Owing to the change that has come over him, Sensa is unable to see the Light of the Logos by direct perception, but is under the necessity of recognizing the same by the operation of his fifth principle. It is in the astral fluid that he floats and not in the magic water of the Lotus Tank. He sees, nevertheless, the Lady of the Lotus who pathetically says, "Soon thou wilt leave me; and how can I aid thee if thou forgettest me utterly?"

After this occurrence Sensa becomes completely a man of the world, living for the pleasures of the physical life. His developed mind becomes his companion and the priest of the temple profit by the change. Before proceeding further I must draw the reader's attention to the possibility of eliciting from a child any desired information by invoking certain elementals and other powers, by means of magic rites and ceremonies After the soul gets completely under the influence of Avidya, it may either succumb altogether to the said influence, and get absorbed, as it were, in the Tamoguna of Prakriti, or dispel its own ignorance by the light of spiritual wisdom and shake off this baneful influence. A critical moment arrives in the history of Sensa when his very existence is merged up for the time being with the dark goddess of human passion on the day of the boat festival. Such an absorption, however short, is the first step towards final extinction. He must either be saved at this critical juncture or perish. The Lady of the White Lotus, his guardian angel, makes a final attempt to save him, and succeeds. In the very holy of the holies, she unveils the dark goddess; and Sensa, perceiving his folly prays for deliverance from the accursed yoke of the hated priesthood. His prayer is granted, and relying upon the support of the bright goddess he revolts against the authority of the priests, and directs the attention of the people to the iniquities of the temple authorities.

It is necessary to say a few words in this connection as regards the real nature of soul-death and the ultimate fate of a black magician, to impress the teachings of this book on the mind of the reader. The soul, as we have above explained, is an isolated drop in the ocean of cosmic life. This current of cosmic life is but the light and the aura of the Logos. Besides the Logos, there are innumerable other existences, both spiritual and astral, partaking of this life and living in it. These beings have special affinities with particular emotions of the human soul and particular characteristics of the human mind. They have of course a definite individual existence of their own which lasts up to the end of the Manwantara. There are three ways in which a soul may cease to retain its special individuality. Separated from its Logos, which is, as it were, its source, it may not acquire a strong and abiding individuality of its own, and may in course of time be reabsorbed into the current of Universal Life. This is real soul-death. It may also place itself *en rapport* with a spiritual or elemental existence by evoking it, and concentrating its attention and regard on it for purposes of black magic and Tantric worship. In such a case it transfers its individuality to such existence and is sucked up into it, as it were. In such a case the black magician lives in such a being, and as such a being he continues till the end of Manwantara.

The fate of Banasena illustrates the point. After his death he is said to live as Mahakala, one of the most powerful spirits of Pramadhagana. In some respects this amounts to acquiring immortality in evil. But unlike the immortality of the Logos it does not go beyond Manwantaric limits. Read the 8th chapter of Bhagavat Gita in this connection, and my meaning will become clear by the light of Krishna's teaching. The occurrence in the boat of Isis, depicted in the book under consideration, gives some idea of the nature of this absorption and the subsequent preservation of the magician's individuality.

When the centre of absorption is the Logos and not any

other power or elemental, the man acquires Mukti or Nirvana and becomes one with the eternal Logos without any necessity of rebirth.

The last part of the book describes the final struggle of the soul with its inveterate foes, its initiation and ultimate deliverance from the tyranny of Prakriti.

The assurance and the advice given by the Lady of the White Lotus to Sensa in the holy of holies marks the great turning point in the history of his career. He has perceived the light of the Divine Wisdom and has brought himself within the pale of its influence. This light of the Logos, which is represented in the story as the fair goddess of the sacred flower of Egypt, is the bond of union and brotherhood which maintains the chain of spiritual intercourse and sympathy running through the long succession of the great hierophants of Egypt, and extending to all the great adepts of this world who derive their influx of spiritual life from the same source. It is the Holy Ghost that keeps up the apostolical succession or Guruparampara as the Hindus call it. It is this spiritual light which is transmitted from Guru to disciple when the time of real initiation comes. The so-called "transfer of life" is no other than the transmission of this light. And further, the Holy Ghost, which is, as it were, the veil or the body of the Logos and hence its flesh and blood, is the basis of the holy communion. Every fraternity of adepts has this bond of union; and time and space cannot tear it asunder. Even when there is an apparent break in the succession on the physical plane, a neophyte following the sacred law and aspiring towards a higher life, will not be in want of guidance and advice when the proper time arrives, though the last Guru may have died several thousands of years before he was born. Every Buddha meets at his last initiation all the great adepts who reached Buddhaship during the preceding ages : and similarly every class of adepts has its own bond of spiritual communion which knits them together into a properly organised fraternity. The only possible and effectual way of entering into any such brotherhood, or partaking of the holy communion, is by bringing oneself within the influence of the spiritual light which radiates from one's own Logos. I may further point out here, without venturing to enter into details, that such communion is only possible between persons whose souls derive their life and sustenance from the same divine ray, and that, as seven distinct rays radiate from the "Central Spiritual Sun," all adepts and Dhyan Chohans are divisible into seven classes, each of which is guided, controlled and overshadowed by one of seven forms or manifestations of the divine wisdom.

In this connection it is necessary to draw the reader's attention to another general law which regulates the circulation of spiritual life and energy through the several adepts who belong to the same fraternity. Each adept may be conceived as a centre wherein this spiritual force is generated and stored up, and through which it is utilized and distributed. This mysterious energy is a kind of spiritual electrical force, and its transmission from one centre to another presents some of the phenomena noticed in connection with electrical induction. Consequently there is a tendency towards the equalization of the amounts of energy stored up in the various centres. The quantity of the neutral fluid existing in any particular centre depends upon the man's Karma and the holiness and purity of his life. When evoked into activity by being brought into communication with his Guru or Initiator it becomes dynamic, and has a tendency to transfer itself to weaker centres It is sometimes stated that, at the time of the final initiation, either the hierophant or the "newly born," the *worthier* of the two must die (see page 38, *Theosophist*, November 1882). Whatever may be the real nature of this mysterious death, it is due to the operation of this law. It will be further seen that a new initiate, if he is weak in spiritual energy, is strengthened by partaking of the holy communion; and for obtaining this advantage he has to remain on earth and utilize his power for the good of mankind until the time of final liberation arrives. This is an arrangement which harmonizes with the Law of Karma. The neophyte's original weakness is due to his Karmic defects. These defects necessitate a longer period of physical existence. And this period he will have to spend in the cause of human progress in return for the benefit above indicated. And, moreover, the accumulated good Karma of this period has the effect of strengthening his soul, and when he finally takes his place in the Sacred Brotherhood, he brings as much spiritual capital with him as any of the others for carrying on the work of the said fraternity.

If these few remarks are borne in mind, the incidents related in the last five chapters will soon disclose their real significance. When Sensa gains his power of spiritual perception through the grace of his guardian angel, and begins to exercise it knowingly and voluntarily, he has no occasion to rely on the flickering light of intuition. "You must now stand alone," says the gardener, and places him in possession of his beloved flower, the full meaning of which Sensa begins to understand. Having thus gained the seat of spiritual clairvoyance, Sensa perceives the hierophants who preceded him and into whose fraternity he has entered. The Guru is always ready when the disciple is ready. The initiation preceding the final struggle for liberty from the bondage of matter is pretty plainly described. The highest Chohan reveals to him the secrets of occult science, and another adept of the Brotherhood points out to him the real basis and nature of his own personality. His immediate predecessor then comes to his assistance and reveals to him the mystery of his own Logos. "The veil of Isis" is removed, White Lotus, his real Saviour, lay concealed. The Light of the Logos enters his soul and he is made to pass through the "baptism by Divine Fire." He hears the final directions given by his Queen and recognises the duty cast upon his shoulders.

His predecessor, whose soul is so "white and spotless," is commanded to give him a portion of his spiritual strength and energy. The three great truths which underlie every religion, however, disfigured and distorted, through ignorance, superstition and prejudice, are then taught to him for the purpose of being proclaimed to the world at large. It is needless for me to explain these truths here as their enunciation in the book is sufficiently plain. Thus fortified and instructed Sensa prepares for the final struggle. During these preparatory stages the passions of the physical man are, as it were, dormant, and Sensa is left alone for the time being. But they are not entirely subdued. The decisive battle is yet to be fought and won. Sensa begins to enter on the higher spiritual life as a preacher and spiritual guide to men, directed by the light of wisdom which has entered his soul. But he cannot pursue this course for any length of time before he has conquered his foes. The moment for the final struggle of the last initiation soon arrives. The nature of this initiation is very little understood. It is sometimes represented in vague terms as a terrible ordeal through which an initiate has to pass before he becomes a real adept. It is further characterized as "the baptism by blood." These general statements do not in the least indicate the precise nature of the result to be achieved by the neophyte or the difficulties he has to encounter.

It is necessary to enquire into the nature of the psychic change or transformation which is intended to be effected by this initiation before its mystery is understood. According to the ordinary Vedantic classification there are four states of conscious existence, *viz.*, *Viswa*, *Tajasa*, *Pragna*, and *Tureeya*. In modern language these may be described as the objective, the clairvoyant, the ecstatic, and the ultra-ecstatic states of consciousness. The seats or *upadhis* related to these conditions are the physical body, the astral body, the *Karana Sarira* or the Monad and the Logos. The soul is the Monad. It is, as it were, the neutral point of consciousness. It is germ of *pragna*. When completely isolated no consiousness is experienced by it. Its psychic condition is hence compared by Hindu writers to *Sushupti*—a condition of dreamless sleep. But it is under the influence of the physical body and the astral body on the one side, and the sixth and seventh principles on the other. When the attraction of the former prevails, the *Jiva* becomes *Buddha* and is subject to all the passions of embodied existence. The power of these passions grows weaker and weaker as the neutral point we have indicated is approached. But so long as the neutral barrier is not crossed their attraction is felt. But when once this is effected, the soul is, as it were, placed under the control and attraction of the other pole—the Logos; and the man becomes liberated from the bondage of matter. In short he becomes an adept. The struggle for supremacy between these two forces of attraction takes place on this neutral barrier. But during the struggle the person in whose interest the battle is fought is in a quiescent, unconscious condition, almost helpless to assist his friends or strike hard at his enemies, though the result of the fight is a matter of life and death to him. This is the condition in which Sensa finds himself in passing through the last ordeal, and the description of the said condition in the book under examination becomes clear by the light of the foregoing explanations. It can be easily seen that the result of the fight will mainly depend upon the *latent* energy of the soul, its previous training and its past Karma. But our hero passes successfully through the ordeal; his enemies are completely overthrown. But *Sensa* dies in the struggle.

Strangely enough when the enemy is defeated, the *Personality* of Sensa is destroyed on the field of battle. This is the final sacrifice which he makes, and his mother, *Prakriti*—the mother of his presonality—laments his loss, but rejoices at the prospect of the resurrection of his soul. The resurrection soon takes place; his soul rises from the grave as it were, under the vivifying influence of his spiritual intelligence, to shed its blessings on mankind and work for the spiritual development of his fellow beings. Here ends the so-called tragedy of the soul. What follows is merely intended to bring the story in its quasi-historical aspect to a proper conclusion.

NOTES ON HATA YOGA.*

The *Sushumna* is connected with the tube that runs through the centre of the spine. It is a sort of vein of magnetic electricity, and the energy passing through the *Sushumna* is a stream of vital electricity. The tube above-mentioned is connected with the ventricles of the brain.

The *Sushumna* begins with the *Muladharam* and ends in *Sahasraram*. The former *Chakram* is at the base of the spine where it forms a traingle.

The *Brahmarandhra* is put in different places in different books, it should be taken to be the top of the head.

You may know the action of *Sushumna* by feeling an accession of fire to the brain—as if a hot current of air were being blown through the tube from the bottom to the top.

Hata Yogis say that *Ida* and *Pingala* act alternately, but if you stop both of these the hot current is forced through the *Sushumna*. Also without having anything to do with *Ida* and *Pingala*—by practising *Kumbaka* alone—the *Sushumna* comes into play ; but a *Raj Yogi*, without using either of these methods, has a way of rousing the *Kundalini*. The means the *Raj Yogi* employs belong to the mysteries of initiation.

The reason why *Sushumna* is reckoned to be the chief of the *Nadis* is, because it is only through it that the *Monad* goes out in the case of a *Yogi* ; and in the case of an adept, at the time of his death, his soul goes out through the *Sushumna*. Moreover it is the seat of circulation of the soul or *Karana-sarira*.

The *Karana-sarira* is said to be in a state of sleep, but this is no ordinary sleep, it is *Yoga* sleep. It is the calm after the tempest spoken of in "Light on the Path" (Rule 21).

Samadhi includes the realization of *Yoga Anandam*, but it is a generic term used to denote several conditions.

---

* Notes of a conversation with "Solar Sphinx."

It is absurd to suppose, as stated in some of the books, that the solar system is contained in the *Sushumna*. What is meant is that when consciousness is fixed for the time being in the *Monad* circulating in the *Sushumna*, the *Yogi* becomes *en rapport* with astral light and the universal mind and thus is able to see the whole cosmos.

The six *Chakrams* are located in the *Sthula-sarira*, but they are not visible when a body is dissected, because the leaves and petals described in the books have no objective existence, but represent so many powers or energies.

For instance, *Sahasraram* is considered to have eight main petals, and the meaning of this is that the brain has eight poles. Similarly the letters, characters, symbols, goddesses, etc., said in the books to exist in these *Chakrams*, all symbolize different power.

The reason of the differences between the *Chakrams* is that in the seven centres seven powers are located, and it is said that as the *Kundalini* breaks through each *Chakram*, it causes the man to subdue that *Chakram*.

As *Kundalini* goes on breaking through the *Chakrams* one by one, it gains control over so many forces connected with the elements, the astral counterparts of which are located in the respective *Chakrams*. The location of the mind is said to be between the eyebrows by the Hata Yogis.

The *Chakra Sammalanam* mentioned in the books means that when *Kundalini* passes through one *Chakram*, it takes its essence or energy, and so on with the rest, and finally joins all into a sort of united current.

The seven *Chakrams* are connected with the seven planets in the following order, beginning with *Muladharam*: Saturn, Jupiter, Mars, Venus, Mercury, Moon, Sun. The moon is connected with the mind of man, because it is so changeable and vacillating.

The mind of man never penetrates (as sometimes asserted) into the *Chakrams*, but the *Kundalini* does so penetrate, and the mind itself will finally combine with *Kundalini* when this latter gets near the *Agna Chakram*, and then the man becomes clairvoyant.

Kundalini is a power or energy in the *Muladharam*, sometimes called the astral serpent. It has its head in the region of the navel; it can be roused by increasing the fire in the *Muladharam*. It is said to be like a serpent, because it moves in curves, it appears to move round and round in a circle, *Ida* and *Pingala* alternate on account of its motion.

Kundalini is said in the books to have three and a half circles to show that it pervades the three and half *matras* of *Pranava*. In some cases it is represented as light, because its energy runs through *Ashtaprakriti*. Sometimes it is represented as four.

Some say that, in order to attain *Raja Yoga*, one should investigate *Mahavakyam*; others that the mind must be concentrated on a point and the *Yogi* must contemplate *Parabrahm*; some say one's own *Guru* is the true subject of contemplation, and it is enough to lead a good life; some say the repetition of the *Pranava* is in itself *Raj Yog*, and others say you must cultivate will-power: which of these ways is the true one?

All these are necessary and much more—read "Light on the Path."

The end of *Raj Yog* is the attainment of immortality.

CLASSIFICATION OF "PRINCIPLES."

In a most admirable lecture by Mr. T. Subba Row on the *Bhagavad Gita*,* published in the February [1887] number of the *Theosophist*, the lecturer deals, incidentally as I believe, with the question of septenary "principles" in the Kosmos and Man. The division is rather criticized, and the grouping hitherto adopted and favoured in theosophical teachings is resolved into one of *Four*.

This criticism has already given rise to some misunderstanding, and it is argued by some that a slur is thrown on the original teachings. This *apparent* disagreement with one whose views are rightly held as almost decisive on occult matters in our Society is certainly a dangerous handle to give to opponents who are ever on the alert to detect and blazon forth contradictions and inconsistencies in our philosophy. Hence I feel it my duty to show that there is in reality *no* inconsistency between Mr. Subba Row's views and our own in the question of the septenary division ; and to show, (*a*) that the lecturer was perfectly well acquainted with the septenary division before he joined the Theosophical Society ; (*b*) that he knew it was the teaching of old "Aryan philosophers who have associated seven occult powers with the seven principles" in the Macrocosm and the Microcosm (see the end of this article) ; and (*c*) that from the beginning he had objected—not to the classification, but to the form in which it was expressed. Therefore, now, when he calls the division "unscientific and misleading," and adds that "this sevenfold classification is almost conspicuous by its absence in *many* (not *all*?) of our Hindu books," etc., and that it is better to adopt the time-honoured classification of four principles, Mr. Subba Row must mean only some special orthodox books, as it would be impossible for him to contradict himself in such a conspicuous way.

A few words of explanation, therefore, will not be altogether out of place. For the matter of being "conspicuous by its

---

* This lecture has been published in a separate book.

absence" in Hindu books, the said classification is as conspicuous by its absence in Buddhist books. This, for a reason transparently clear: it was always esoteric; and as such, rather inferred than openly taught. That it is "misleading" is also perfectly true; for the great feature of the day—materialism—has led the minds of our Western theosophists into the prevalent habit of viewing the seven principles as distinct and self-existing *entities*, instead of what they are—namely, *upadhis* and correlating states—three *upadhis*, basic groups, and four principles. As to being unscientific," the term can be only attributed to a *lapsus linguæ*, and in this relation let me quote what Mr. Subba Row wrote about a year *before he joined* the Theosophical Society in one of his ablest articles, "Brahmanism on the sevenfold principle in man," the best review that ever appeared of the Fragments of Occult Truth—since embodied in "Esoteric Buddhism." Says the author:—

"I have carefully examined it (the teaching) and find that the results arrived at (in the Buddhist doctrine) do not differ much from the conclusions of our Aryan philosophy, though our mode of stating the arguments may differ in form." Having enumerated, after this the "three primary causes" which bring the human being into existence—*i. e.*, Parabrahmam, Sakti and Prakriti—he explains: "Now, according to the Adepts of ancient Aryavarta, *seven principles* are evolved out of these three primary entities. Algebra teaches us that the number of *combinations* of things, taken *one* at a time, *two* at a time, *three* at a time, and so forth $=2n\text{-}1$. Applying this formula to the present case, the number of entities evolved from different combinations of these three primary causes amount to $2^3\text{-}1=8\text{-}1=7$. As a general rule, whenever seven entities are mentioned in the ancient occult sciences of India in any connection whatsoever, you must suppose that these seven entities come into existence from three primary entities; and that these three entities, again, are evolved out of a single entity or MONAD." (See "Five Years of Theosophy," p. 160.)

This is quite correct, from the occult standpoint, and also Kabbalistically, when one looks into the question of the *seven* and *ten* Sephiroths, and the *seven* and *ten* Rishis, Manus, etc. It shows that in sober truth there is not, nor can there be any fundamental disagreement between the esoteric philosophy of the *Trans* and *Cis*-Himalayan Adepts. The reader is referred, moreover, to the earlier pages of the above mentioned article, in which it is stated that " the knowledge of the occult powers of nature possessed by the inhabitants of the lost Atlantis was learnt by the ancient Adepts of India, and was appended by them to the esoteric doctrine taught by the residents of the sacred island (now the Gobi desert)*. The Tibetan Adepts, however, (their precursors of Central Asia) have not accepted the addition." (pp. 155-156.) But this difference between the two doctrines does not include the septenary division, as it was universal after it had originated with the Atlanteans, who, as the Fourth Race, were of course an earlier race than the Fifth—the Aryan.

Thus, from the purely metaphysical standpoint, the remarks made on the Septenary Division in the " *Bhagavad-Gita*" Lecture hold good to-day, as they did five or six years ago in the article " Brahmanism on the sevenfold principle in Man," their apparent discrepancy notwithstanding. For purposes of purely theoretical esoterism, they are as valid in Buddhist as they are in Brahmanical philosophy. Therefore, when Mr. Subba Row proposes to hold to " the time-honoured classification of four principles" in a lecture on a Vedanta work—the Vedantic classification, however, dividing man into *five* " *kosas*" (sheaths) and the *Atma* (the six *nominally*, of course),† he simply shows thereby that he desires to remain strictly within theoretical and metaphysical, and also orthodox computations of the same. This is how I understand his

* See " Isis Unveiled," Vol. I, p. 600, and the appendices by the Editor to the above quoted article in " Five Years of Theosophy."

† This is the division given to us by Mr. Subba Row. See " Five Years of Theosophy," p. 136, article signed T. S.

words, at any rate. For the *Taraka Raj-Yoga* classification is again *three upadhis*, the *Atma* being the fourth principle, and no *upadhi*, of course, as it is one with Parabrahm. This is again shown by himself in a little article called "Septenary Division in different Indian systems."*

Why then should not "Buddhist" Esoterism, so called, resort to such a division? It is perhaps "misleading"—that is admitted; but surely it cannot be called "unscientific." I will even permit myself to call that adjective a thoughtless expression, since it has been shown to be on the contrary very "scientific" by Mr. Subba Row himself; and quite mathematically so, a the aforequoted algebraic demonstration of the same proves it. I say that the division is due to nature herselt pointing out its necessity in Cosmos and man; just because the number seven is "a power and a spiritual force" in its combination of *three* and *four*, of the triangle and the quarternary. It is no doubt far more convenient to adhere to the fourfold classification in a metaphysical and synthetical sense, just as I have adhered to the threefold classification—of body, soul and spirit—in *Isis Unveiled*, because had I then adopted the septenary division, as I have been compelled to do later on for purposes of strict analysis, no one would have understood it, and the multiplication of principles, instead of throwing light upon the subject, would have introduced endless confusion. But now the question has changed, and the position is different. We have *unfortunately*—for it was premature—opened a chink in the Chinese wall of esoterism, and we cannot now close it again, even if we would. I for one had to pay a heavy price for the indiscretion, but I will not shrink from the results.

I maintain, then, that when once we pass from the plane of pure subjective reasoning on esoteric matters to that of practical demonstration in Occultism, wherein each principle and attribute has to be analysed and defined in its application to the phenomena of daily and especially of *post-mortem* life,

* See "Five Years of Theosophy," p. 185.

the sevenfold classification is the right one. For it is simply a convenient division which prevents in no wise the recognition of but *three* groups—which Mr. Subba Row calls "four principles associated with four *upadhis*, and which are associated in their turn with four distinct states of consciousness."* This is the Bhagavad Gita classification, it appears; but not that of the Vedanta, nor—what the Raj-Yogis of the *pre*-Aryasanga schools and of the *Mahayana* system held to, and still hold beyond the Himalayas, and their system is almost identical with the *Taraka Raj-Yoga*,—the difference between the latter and the Vedanta classification having been pointed out to us by Mr. Subba Row in his little article on the "Septenary Division in different Indian system." The Taraka Raj-Yogis recognize only *three upadhis* in which *Atma* may work, which, in India, if I mistake not, are the *Jagrata*, or waking state of consciousness (corresponding to the *Sthulopadhi*); the *Svapna*, or dreaming state (in *Sukshmopadhi*); and the *Sushupti*, or causal state, produced by and through *Karanopadhi*, or what we call *Buddhi*. But then, in transcendental states of *Samadhi*, the body with its *Lingasarira*, the *vehicle* of the life-principle, is entirely left out of consideration: the three states of consciousness are made to refer only to the three (with *Atma* the fourth) principles which remain after death. And here lies the real key to the septenary division of man, the three principles coming in as an addition only during his life.

As in the Macrocosm, so in the Microcosm: analogies hold good throughout nature. Thus the universe, our solar system, our earth down to man, are to be regarded as all equally possessing a septenary constitution—*four* superterrestrial and

* A crowning proof of the fact that the division is arbitrary and varies with the schools it belongs to, is in the words published in "Personal and Impersonal God" by Mr. Subba Row, where he states that "we have *six* states of consciousness, either objective or subjective. . . and a perfect state of unconsciousness, etc." (See "Five Years of Theosophy," pp. 200 and 201.) Of course those who do not hold to the old school of Aryan and Arhat Adepts are in no way bound to adopt the septenary classification.

superhuman, so to say ;—*three* objective and astral. In dealing with the special case of man, only, there are two stand-points from which the question may be considered. Man in *incarnation* is certainly made up of seven principles, if we so term the seven states of his material, astral, and spiritual framework, which are all on different planes. But if we classify the principles according to the seat of the four degrees of consciousness, these *upardhis* may be reduced to four groups.* Thus his consciousness, never being centred in the second or third principles— both of which are composed of states of matter (or rather of "substance") on different planes, each corresponding to one of the planes and principles in Cosmos —is necessary to form links between the first, fourth and fifth principles, as well as subserving certain vital and psychic phenomena. These latter may be conveniently classified with the physical body under one head, and laid aside during trance (*Samadhi*), as after death, thus leaving only the traditional *exoteric* and metaphysical *four.* Any charge of contradictory teaching, therefore, based on this simple fact, would obviously be wholly invalid ; the classification of principles as septenary or quaternary depending wholly on the stand-point from which they are regarded, as said. It is purely a matter of choice which classification we adopt. Strictly speaking, however, *occult*—as also profane—physics would favour the septenary one for these reasons.†

---

* Mr. Subba Row's argument that in the matter of the three divisions of the body "we may make any number of divisions, and may as well enumerate nerve-force, blood and bones," is not valid, I think. Nerve-force—well and good, though it is one with the life-principle and proceeds from it ; as to blood, bones, etc., these are objective material things, and one with, and inseparable from, the human body ; while all the other six principles are in their *Seventh—the body*—purely *subjective* principles, and therefore all denied by material science, which ignores them.

† In that most admirable article of his "Personal and Impersonal God" —one which has attracted much attention in the Western Theosophical circles, Mr. Subba Row says, "Just as a human being is composed of *seven* principles, differentiated matter in the solar system exists in *seven* different conditions. These do not all come within the range of our present objective

There are *six* Forces in nature : this in Buddhism as in Brahmanism, whether exoteric, or esoteric and the seventh—the *all-Force*, or the absolute Force, which is the synthesis of all. Nature again in her constructive activity strikes the key-note to this classification in more than one way. As stated in the third aphorism of "*Sankhya Karika*" of *Prakriti*—"the root and substance of all things," she (*Prakriti*, or nature) is no production, but herself a *Producer* of *seven* things, "which, produced by her, become all in their turn producers." Thus all the liquids in nature begin, when separated from their parent mass, by becoming a spheroid (a drop) ; and when the globule is formed, and it falls, the impulse given to it transforms it, when it touches ground, almost invariably into an equilateral triangle (or three), and then into an *hexagon*, after which out of the corners of the latter begin to be formed squares or cubes as plane figures. Look at the *natural* work of nature, so to speak, her artificial, or helped production—the prying into her occult work-shop by science. Behold the coloured rings of a soap-bubble, and those produced by polarized light. The rings obtained, whether in Newton's soap-bubble, or in the crystal through the polarizer, will exhibit invariably, six of seven rings— " a black spot surrounded by six rings, or a circle with a plane cube inside, circumscribed with six distinct rings, the circle itself the *seventh*. The " Noremberg " polarizing apparatus throws into objectivity almost all our occult geometrical symbols, though physicists are none the wiser for it. (See Newton's and Tyndall's experiments*).

---

consciousness, but they can be perceived by the spiritual ego in man. Further *Prâgna*, or the capacity of perception, exists in *seven different aspects*, corresponding to the seven conditions of matter. Strictly speaking there are *six* states of differentiated *pragna*, the seventh state being a condition of perfect unconsciousness (or absolute consciousness). By differentiated *pragna* I mean the condition in which *pragna* is split up into various states of consciousness. Thus we have six states of consciousness, etc., etc. ("Five Years of Theosophy," pp. 200 and 201.) This is precisely our Trans-Himalayan Doctrine.

* One need only open Webster's Dictionary and examine the snowflakes and crystals at the word "Snow" to perceive nature's work. "God geometrizes," says Plato.

The number seven is at the very root of occult Cosmogony and Anthropogony. No symbol to express evolution from its starting to its completion points would be possible without it. For the circle produces the point; the point expands into a triangle, returning after two angles upon itself, and then forms the mystical *Tetraktis*—the plane cube; which *three* when passing into the manifested world of effects, differentiated nature, become geometrically and numerically $3+4=7$. The best Kabbalists have been demonstrating this for ages ever since Pythagoras, and down to the modern mathematicians and symbologists, one of whom has succeeded in wrenching for ever *one of the seven* occult keys, and has proved his victory by a volume of figures. Set any of our theosophists interested in the question to read the wonderful work called "The Hebrew Egyptian Mystery, the Source of Measures;" and those of them who are good mathematicians will remain aghast before the revelations contained in it. For it shows indeed that occult source of the measure by which were built kosmos and man, and then by the latter the great Pyramid of Egypt, as all the towers, mounds, obelisks, cave-temples of India, and pyramids in Peru and Mexico, and all the archaic monuments; symbols in stone of Chaldæa, both Americas, and even of the Eastern Islands—the living and solitary witness of a submerged prehistoric continent in the midst of the Pacific Ocean. It shows that the same figures and measures for the same esoteric symbology existed throughout the world; it shows in the words of the author that the Kabbala is a "whole series of developments based upon the use of geometrical elements; giving expression in numerical values, founded on integral values of the circle" (one of the seven keys hitherto known but to the Initiates), discovered by Peter Metius in the 16th century, and re-discovered by the late John A. Parker.* Moreover, that the system from whence all these developments were derived "was anciently considered to be one resting in

* Of Newark, in his work *The Quadrature of the Circle*, his "problem of the three revolving bodies"—(N. Y., John Wiley & Son.)

nature (or God), as the *basis* or *law* of the exertions practically of creative design;" and that it also underlies the Biblical structures, being found in the measurements given for Solomon's temple, the ark of the Covenant, Noah's ark, etc., etc., —in all the symbolical myths, in short, of the Bible.

And what are the figures, the measure in which the sacred Cubit is derived from the esoteric Quadrature, which the Initiates know to have been contained in the *Tetraktis* of Pythagoras? Why it is the universal primordial symbol. The figures found in the *Ansated Cross* of Egypt, (as I maintain) in the Indian *Swastika*, "the sacred sign" which embellishes the thousand heads of Sesha, the Serpent-cycle of eternity, on which rests Vishnu, the deity in Infinitude; and which also may be pointed out in the threefold (*treta*) fire of Pururavas, *the first fire in the present Manvantara*, out of the forty-nine (7×7) mystic fires. It may be absent from many of the Hindu books, but the Vishnu and other Puranas teem with this symbol and figure under every possible form, which I mean to prove in the "SECRET DOCTRINE." The author of the "Source of Measures" does not, of course, himself know as yet the whole scope of what he has discovered. He applies his key, so far, only to the esoteric language and the symbology in the Bible, and the Books of Moses especially. The great error of the able author, in my opinion, is, that he applies the key discovered by him chifly to post-Atlantean and quasi-historical phallic elements in the world religions; feeling, intuitionally, a nobler, or higher, a more transcendental meaning in all this —*only* in the Bible,—and a mere sexual worship in all other religions. This phallic element, however, in the older pagan worship related, in truth, to the physiological evolution of the human races, something that could not be discovered in the Bible, as it is absent from it, (the Pentateuch being the latest of all the old Scriptures.) Nevertheless, what the learned author has discovered and proved mathematically, is wonderful enough, and sufficient to make our claim good: namely, that the figures ○ △ ▭ and 3, 4 = 7, are at the very basis, and are the soul of cosmogony and the evolution of mankind.

To whosoever desires to display this process by way of symbol, says the author speaking of the *ansated cross*, the *Tau* T̂ of the Egyptians and the Christian cross—"it would be by *the figure of the cube unfolded in connection with the circle whose measure is taken off on to the edges of the cube.* The cube unfolded becomes in superficial display a *cross proper*, or of the *tau* form, and the attachment of the circle to this last, gives the *ansated cross* of the Egyptians with its obvious meaning of *the Origin of Measures.** Because this kind of measure was also made to co-ordinate with the idea of *the origin of life*, it was made to assume the type of the *hermaphrodite*, and in fact it is placed by representation to cover this part of the human person in the Hindu form..." [It is "the hermaphrodite Indranse Indra, the nature goddess, the *Issa* of the Hebrews, and the *Isis* of the Egyptians," as the author calls them in another place.] "... It is very observable, that while there are but six faces to a cube, the representation of the cross as the cube unfolded as to the cross bars displays one face of the cube as *common to two bars*, counted as belonging to either; then, while the faces originally represented are but six, the use of the two bars counts the square as four for the upright and three for the cross bar, making seven in all. Here we have the famous four, three and seven again, the four and three on the factor members of the Parker (quadrature and of the "three revolving bodies") problem" ... (pp. 50 and 51.)

And they are the factor members in the building of the Universe and MAN. Wittoba,—an aspect of Krishna and Vishnu —is therefore the "man crucified in space," or the "cube unfolded," as explained (See Moore's *Pantheon*, for Wittoba).

---

* And by adding to to the cross proper ✛ the symbol of the four cardinal points and infinity at the sam time, thus 卐, the arms pointing above, below, and right, and left, making six in the circle—the Archaic sign of the Yomas—it would make of it the Swastika, the "sacred sign" used by the order of "Ishmael masons," which they call the Universal Hermetic Cross, and do not understand its real wisdom, nor know its origin.

It is the oldest symbol in India, now nearly lost, as the real meaning of *Vishvakarina* and *Vikkarttana* (the "sun shorn of his beams") is also lost. It is the Egyptian *ansated cross*, and *vice versa*, and the latter—even the *sistrum*, with its cross bars—is simply *the symbol of the Deity as man*—however phallic it may have become later, after the submersion of Atlantis. The *ansated cross* ☥ is of course, as Professor Seyfforth has shown—again the *six* with its head—the *seventh*. Seyfforth says: "It is the skull with the brains, the seat of the soul with the nerves extending to the spine, back, and eyes and ears. For the Tanis stone thus translates it repeatedly by *anthropos* (man); and we have the Coptic *ank*, (*vita*, life) properly *anima*, which corresponds with the Hebrew *anosh*, properly meaning *anima*. The Egyptian *anki* signifies "my soul."*

It means in its synthesi, the *seven principles*, the details coming later. Now the *ansated cross*, as given above, having been discovered on the backs of the gigantic statues found on the Easter Isles (mid-Pacific Ocean) which is a part of the submerged continent; this remnant being described as "thickly studded with cyclopean statues, remnants of the civilization of a dense and cultivated people;"—and Mr. Subba Row having told us what he had found in the old Hindu books, namely, that the ancient Adepts of India had learned occult powers from the Atlanteans (*vide* supra)—the logical inference is that they had their septenary division from them, just as our Adepts from the "Sacred Island" had. This ought to settle the question.

And this *Tau* cross is ever *septenary*, under whatever form—it has many forms, though the main idea is always one. What are the Egyptian *oozas* (the eyes), the amulets called the "mystic eye," but symbols of the same? There are the *four* eyes in the upper row and the *three* smaller ones in the

* Quoted in "Source of Measures."

lower. Or again, the *ooza* with the *seven luths* hanging from it, "the combined melody of which *creates one man*," say the hieroglyphics. Or again, the *hexagon* formed of six traingles whose apices converge to a point—thus  the *symbol of the Universal creation*, which Kenneth Mackenzie tells us "was worn as a ring by the Sovereign Princes of the Royal Secret" —which they never knew by the bye. *If seven* has nought to do with the mysteries of the universe and men, then indeed from the Vedas down to the Bible all the archaic Scriptures —the Puranas, the Avesta and all the fragments that have reached us—have no *esoteric* meaning, and must be regarded as the Orientalists regard them—as a farago of childish tales.

It is quite true that the *three upadhis* of the *Taraka Raj Yoga* are, as Mr. Subba Row explains in his little article "The Septenary Division in different Indian Systems," "the best and the simplest"—but only in purely *contemplative* Yoga, and he adds: "Though there are *seven* principles in man there are but *three* distinct *upadhis*, in each of which his *Atma* may work independently of the rest. These three *upadhis* can be separated by the Adept without killing himself. He cannot separate the seven principles from each other without destroying his constitution" ("Five Years of Theosophy," p. 185). Most decidedly he cannot. But this again holds good only with regard to his lower three principles—the body and its (in life) inseparable *prana* and *linga sarira*. The rest can be separated, as they constitute no *vital*, but rather a mental and spiritual necessity. As to the remark in the same article objecting to the fourth principle being "included in the third *kosa* as the said principle is but a vehicle of will-power, which is but an energy of the mind." I answer: Just so. But as the higher attributes of the fifth (*Manas*), go to make up the original *triad*, and it is just the *terrestrial* energies, feelings and volitions which remain in the Kama-loka, what, is the vehicle, the *astral* form, to carry them about a *bhoota* until they fade out—which may take centuries to accomplish? Can the "false" personality, or the *pisacha* whose ego is made up precisely of all those terrestrial passions and feelings, remain in *Kamaloka*, and occasionally appear, without a substantial vehicle, however ethereal? Or are we to give up the seven principles, and the belief that there is such a thing as an *astral body*, and a bhoot, or spook?

Most decidedly not. For Mr. Subba Row himself once more explains how, from the Hindu standpoint, the *lower* fifth, or Manas, can re-appear after death, remarking very justly, that it is absurd to call it a *disembodied spirit.* "Five Years of Theosophy," p. 174.) As he says; "It is merely a power, or force, retaining the impressions of the thoughts or ideas of the individual *into whose composition it originally entered.* It sometimes summons to its aid the *Kamarupa* power, and creates for itself some particular, etherial form."

Now that which "sometimes summons" *Kamarupa*, and the "power" of that name make already two principles, two "powers"—call them as you will. Then we have *Atma* and its vehicle—*Buddhi*—which make *four.* With the three which disappeared on earth this will be equivalent to *seven.* How can we, then, speak of modern Spiritualism, of its materalizations and other phenomena, without resorting to the Septenary.

To quote our friend and much respected brother for the last time, since he says that "our (Aryan) philosophers have associated seven *occult* powers with *the seven principles* (in men and in the kosmos), which seven occult powers correspond in the microcosm with, or are counterparts of, occult powers in the macrocosm."*—quite an esoteric sentence,—it does seem almost a pity, that words pronounced in an *ex tempore* lecture, though such an able one, should have been published without revision.

H. P. Blavatsky.

---

* "Brahmanism on the Sevenfold Principle in Man."

THE CONSTITUTION OF THE MICROCOSM.

The few remarks which I have made in my first lecture on the Bhagavad Gita published in the February issue of *Theosophist*, on the septenary classification of the various principles in man hitherto adopted in theosophical publications, have elicited a reply from Madame H. P. Blavatsky, which appeared in the last issue of this Journal under the heading of "Classification of Principles." The reply was apparently intended to explain away the remarks which fell from my lips and justify the classification hitherto advocated. I feel extremely thankful to the writer for the friendly tone of criticism which she has adopted. I cannot, however, fail to see that the line of arguments which she had followed is likely to create a wrong impression in the minds of her readers regarding my real attitude in the matter without a few words of explanation on my part. And moreover the important question raised by the controversy which is set on foot by the article under consideration deserve a thorough investigation. I think it necessary therefore to define clearly the position taken up by me, and examine how far the arguments now advanced in defence of the septenary classification are calculated to remove the objections raised against the said classification and weaken the force of my criticism. Looking at the tenour of the reply it becomes necessary to decide at the outset whether my remarks were intentional or whether they were due to a *lapsus linguæ* as my critic is pleased to assert, and formulate the real question at issue in case there should be found a serious difference of opinion between us. I cannot but confess that my remarks were deliberate and intentional. I thought it fit to condemn the seven-fold classification after serious and anxious consideration, and I duly weighed my words in using them. It will be easily conceded that my evidence is the best and the most direct evidence available as regards my own states of consciousness which accompanied the expressions used. The term unscientific is characterized as a thoughtless expression.

Whether the epithet was rightly or wrongly applied is the very issue to be settled between us; but it was certainly not due to any negligence or carelessness on my part. It is further alleged in the article under examination that when I said that the seven-fold classification was conspicuous by its absence in many Hindu books, I must have meant "some special orthodox." This allegation has no foundation whatsoever. I was not speaking from the standpoint of any special orthodox system and could not have referred therefore to any special orthodox books. The word 'many' is taken advantage of by my critic for the purpose of attributing to me an intention which I never had I could not very well have said that the classification was absent in the whole range of Sanskrit mystic literature unless I had examined *every* book on the subject. I did not come across this classification in *any* book that I have read, though I have perused many of these books. If my learned critic means to assert that it would be found in some book which I have not read, she ought to name the book and the author. A classification like this should not be allowed to rest merely on the basis of a theoretically possible inference without some clear and definite proof of its existence. And, again, I really cannot see what authority my critic has for asserting that, in making the remarks commented upon, I desired to remain strictly "within theoretical and metaphysical and also orthodox computations" of the microcosmic principles. For the purposes of this controversy a distinction is drawn between occult theories which are theoretically and metaphysically good, and those which are good for "practical demonstration" whatever the expression may mean. This is simply absurd. Occultism is both a science and an art. Its scientific principles, if they are correct, must be consistent with the rules of their practical application which are, as it were, but matters of inference from the said principles. Any system of occultism which has got one set of principles for its theory, and another set of principles inconsistent with the former for its practice, would be but an empirical system which could hardly be called scientific.

Fortunately for the occult science of the ancients such a distinction does not exist. I am obliged therefore to repudiate the specific motives and intentions attributed to me and frankly confess that the difference of opinion between us is not merely apparent but real. Such being the case I am fully prepared to justify my assertions.

Any further discussion of the subject will of course be out of the question if it is asserted that I am not at liberty to question the correctness of the so-called "original teachings." Some have argued, it would appear, that a slur was thrown on "the original teachings" by my remarks, thereby implying that I had no business to make them and contradict these teachings. The author of the article probably endorses this view, as she virtually informs her readers in the footnote on page 450, that they must either adopt the seven-fold classification or give up their adherence "to the old School of Aryan and Arhat adepts." I am indeed very sorry that she thought it proper to assume this uncompromising attitude.

It is now necessary to examine what these "original teachings" are and how far they must be considered as conclusive on the subject. The "original teachings" on the subject in question first made their appearance in an editorial headed "Fragments of Occult Truth" published in the issue of the *Theosophist* for October 1881. They were subsequently referred to in various articles written by the Editor, and additional explanations have been given from time to time. These teachings were also embodied in Mr. Sinnett's "Esoteric Buddhism," which has been put forth as an authoritative book. They were further alluded to in "Men," which has been considered equally authoritative, but whose teachings are materially inconsistent with those of "Esoteric Buddhism."

As far as I am in a position to see, these are the authorities on which these so-called "Original teachings" have their foundation.

In my humble opinion it would be highly dangerous for the future well-being and prosperity of the Theosophical Society, if it were to evolve, so early in its career, an orthodox creed from the materials supplied by the above mentioned sources and raise the publications above named to the dignity of an originally revelation. Most of the members of Theosophical Society know full well the circumstances under which these teachings were given. Their fragmentary character has been repeatedly acknowledged. Their defective exposition is apparent on their very face; and their imperfection can be easily detected by a careful examination. It was also pointed out, I believe, that these teachings were derived from teachers who could not and would not reveal their real secrets, and *fully* explain their doctrines except to real initiates. The writers of these various publications had to work according to their own lights on a few hints thrown out to them. It was often pointed out that the real teachings of the ancient Arcane Science had to be approached very gradually and that the line of exposition followed was of a tentative character. It will be found on examination that the teachings connected with the sevenfold classification have gone through various changes since the appearance of the first article on the subject; and it is in my humble opinion premature to say that we have arrived at the end of our labours in this direction and ascertained the true constitution of the Microcosm. Under these circumstances it will be inconsistent with the policy which has been hitherto adopted to declare now that these "original teachings," which have already gone through so many transformations, should be accepted as an infallible revelation. Such a declaration will effectually prevent all further progress in the work of investigation which the Society has undertaken and perpetuate the blunders already committed. The introduction of anything like an orthodox dogmatic creed at this stage of our progress will simply be ruinous to the cause of our Society. It is submitted that under such circumstances it will be no crime on my part to maintain the correctness of my remarks regarding the unsatisfactory nature of this seven-fold classification, and I am not in the least afraid that by doing so I shall forfeit my right to follow the teachings of " the old school of Aryan and Arhat adepts." I am yet to be convinced that the seven-fold classification we have adopted was the real seven-fold classification of this ancient school of occultism.

I have characterized this seven-fold classification as misleading and unscientific. It is admitted in the reply that the classification is really misleading, but the blame is thrown on Western Materilaism. This is putting the blame on the wrong party. If the classification has misled no less a person than its original exponent herself, and made her change her conceptions about the nature of the various principles from time to time, it is pretty nearly certain that the classification itself must be held responsible for all the confusion it has created.

I must now invite the attention of my readers to the " Fragments of Occult Truth " (p. 17, *Theosophist*, Oct. 1881) which contains the " original teaching " on the subject, and the other articles and publications herein referred to. I shall take up principle after principle in the order of enunciation, and point out what new ideas have subsequently been introduced into the conception of these various principles.

The first principle is here described as the physical *body*. It is made to correspond to *Rupa* or *form* in "Esoteric Buddism " (p. 21). It will perhaps be said that both mean the same thing. But a distinction is drawn in the original article between the astral *body* and the astral *shape*. They are counted as two *distinct* principles.

The second principle is here called the vital principle or Jiva-Atma. It is differentiated from the *astral elements* in the human constitution and is described as a "form of force." It is however identified in an article headed " Transmigrations of Life Atoms" (p. 535, "Five Years of Theosophy") written by the same author, with *anima mundi* which is equivalent to *astral light* (See p. 301, Vol. I, Isis Unveiled). And again the same author has identified this very principle with *kàrana sarira* in an article on "The Septenary Principle in Esotericism" (p. 193, "Five Years of Theosophy"). Here then we have a mysterious principle which was at first described as an indestructible force different from astral light, which was afterwards identified with the astral light itself, and which was ultimately transformed into *karana sarira.* And yet we are bound to accept the classification, it would appear, as thoroughly scientific and correct.

The third principle of the original classification is stated to be the astral body, otherwise called therein Linga Sarira. It is considered as *sukshma sarira* in "The Septenary Principle in Esotericism" above referred to; in another place (p. 197), however, in the same article, it is considered as a part of the *manomaya kosa.* The "original teaching" places this principle in the *second group* which represents the Perisprit of man. It is apparently transferred to the first group representing the physical man in the "Transmigrations of life Atoms" (p. 538). It is brought back into the second group subsequently (see p. 235, *The Path*, November 1886, and p. 70, *The Theosophist*, Nov. 1886). In the present article it is again retransferred to the first group (p. 451, l. 23). It will be interesting to notice further in this connection that this principle is described as something different from the astral body in "Esoteric Buddhism." More than five years have elapsed since the appearance of the "original teachings," and yet we are not quite certain whether this third principle is a part of the physical man or of the astral man. Moreover the "original teaching" says that this principle dies with the body. "Esoteric Buddhism" repeats the same lesson. But this principle is made to survive the dissolution of the physical body in "The Theories about Reincarnation and Spirits" (paras. 3 and 4, p. 235, *The Path,* Nov. 1886). My critic, however, reverts to the original view in her present article (p. 451, lines 3, 4, 5). In spite of all these contradictions we are assured that thus sevenfold classification is the right one for explaining the phenomena "especially of *post-mortem* life"

The *fourth principle* is described as the astral *shape* in the "Fragments" and as something different from the astral *body*. The reason for this distinction is not yet clear. It has subsequently usurped the place of the astral *body*. The original teaching seems to imply that it is *astral* in its constitution. Curiously enough, however, the present article divides the seven principles into two groups ; the three principles of the first group are described as "objective and *astral*," and the four principles of the second group as "Superterrestrial and Superhuman." Is this fourth principle then to be removed from the plane of astral light ? If not, what is the reason for drawing a line of demarcation between the third principle and the fourth principle which are so intimately connected with each other according to the "Fragments"? In this connection a strange blunder has been committed by my critic. The following statement occurs in an article by me published in "Five Years of Theosophy" (p. 185):—"It will also be seen that the fourth principle *is included* in the third Kosa (sheath) as the said principle is but the vehicle of will-power, which is but an energy of the mind. Now see what my critic says in present article : "As to the remark in the same article (the one above referred to) *objecting* to the fourth principle being included in the third Kosa, as the said principle is but a vehicle of will-power which is but an energy of the mind, I answer : Just so." In saying so, she is misquoting my statement and contradicting the assertion which she made in her article on "The Septenary Principle in Esotericism" (p. 19, "Five Years of Theosophy") to the effect that this fourth principle was a part of the third Kosa. This is sufficient to show how ready she is to change her opinions about these "original teachings" which are declared to be almost infallible.

The fifth principle of the classification originally occupied but a very humble position. It was nothing more than the animal or physical intelligence of man not far removed from "reason instinct, memcry, imagination, &c.," of the brute creation. No part of it was then allowed to go to Devachan. It was simply a part of the animal soul which was ultimately dissolved in Kamaloka (See Fragments, pp. 18, 19 and 20). The real ego of man—the permanent element in him which runs through the various incarnations,—had not its basis in this principle originally or any part of it. The "Elixir of Life" assigns to it more or less the same position as the following passage shows:—" Each of these (seven principles) has in turn to survive the preceding and more dense one and then die. The exception is the 6th when absorbed into and blended with the 7th." It is partly mixed up with Ananda-Maya Kosa and partly with Vignanamaya Kosa according to the "Septenary Principle" (p. 197, *Five Years of Theosophy*), these two Kosas being described as the "*illusion of supreme bliss*" and the "*envelope of self-delusion*" respectively. It is also to be inferred from the "Replies to an English F. T.S." (p. 274, "Five Years of Theosophy") that it is not the ego or the human monad. It is further declared in the Transmigrarion of Life-atoms (p. 539, "Five Years of Theosophy") that the particles composing this principle disperse after death and "reform after going through various transmigrations to constitute over again" the fifth principle of the next incarnation. The nature of this principle has gradually changed. Though originally it was but the animal consciousness of man, it has subsequently been represented as the fully developed human mind. The whole of it used to perish originally, but subsequently a part of it has been allowed to remain in existence. The whole of it was originally destined for Kamaloka, but a portion has been subsequently lifted up to Devachan. In this connection it must be noticed that it has not up to this time been explained whether after death this principle is physically split up into two parts, or whether the principle merely leaves impressions of its mental activity on the fourth principle taking its physical constitution to Devachan, or whether the sixth principle in conjunction with the 7th takes with it to Devachan the mere *vasana* (aroma) of this fifth principle leaving its material constitution behind with the fourth principle in Kamaloka. If the first view is accepted it must be admitted that the material constitution of this principle is something peculiar and unintelligible. No other similar phenomenon is presented to us by Nature. In case we accept the second view, we shall be placing the Devachanee in a very uncomfortable position as, according to "The Transmigrations of Life-atoms," the particles composing his fifth principle will have to undergo the process of disintegration before the next incarnation. The third view will require us to have the sixth principle for the real seat of the Ego. But it has been declared in an article published in *The Path* (p. 235 November 1886) that Manas or the fifth principle should be considered as the seat of the Ego. The first view is inconsistent with the original teaching, the second view with the philosophy of "Esoteric Buddhism," and third view with the later developments of the occult theory. And to make our difficulties worse there is no other view possible. The latest change in the doctrine is yet to be noticed. According to the present article this principle is a mere "*correlating state*"—a condition of existence—and not a physical *upadhi*. It will be very interesting to enquire whether "correlating state" or composed of particles which disperse and reform as originally taught. It is further declared in this article that this principle is in its nature "superterrestrial and superhuman." The change from animal consciousness to something that is superhuman is indeed very vast; but it has queitly been effected within the last five years.

Now taking the whole of this teaching into account this principle may be described as follows:

The fifth principle of man is his "animal or physical consciousness" composed of particles subject to *post-mortem* disintegration which is under certain conditions "the illusion of supreme bliss" and under other conditions the "envelope of self-delusion," but which must be conceived as the seat of the Ego, and "a superterrestrial and superhuman" "correlating state" corresponding to the dreamy condition.

Let us now turn our attention to the *sixth principle.* It was originally described as the higher or spiritual intelligence or consciousness in man, and the main seat of consciousness in the "*perfect man*" ("Fragments," p. 19, *Theos.*, Oct. 1881). It must be noticed that the expression "perfect man" used in this connection does not mean the perfected man or an adept, but a human being who has fully reached the level of humanity in the course of evolutionary progress from the animal kingdom.

According to the original teaching of the "Fragments" the *post-mortem* career of this principle is something very peculiar. It is stated that if this principle—"spiritual ego" —"has been in life material in its tendencies," it clings blindly to the lower principles and severs its connection with the 7th (p. 19, para. 3). It is further stated that its severance from the 7th principle brings about its dissolution. The author of the "Fragments" writes thus on the subject, "Withdraw the oxygen and the flame ceases. Withdraw the spirit and the spiritual Ego disappears." It is further declared that in such cases the 7th principle passes away "taking with it no fragment of the individual consciousness of the man with which it was temporarily associated." It is also pointed out on the next page that under certain peculiar conditions this principle may remain in combination with the fifth as an elementary. Is Madame H P. Blavatsky prepared to adhere to this original view at present? If so a considerable portion of the subsequent theosophical literature will have to be thrown to the winds. If the spiritual ego, the main seat of consciousness in the so-called "perfect man," is liable to be destroyed whenever the man's tendencies in life happen to be material; if the fifth principle is likewise to be dissolved in Kamaloka, and if the 7th principle carries nothing connected with the individual with it, how is the chain of incarnations kept up and sustained?

What becomes of the doctrine of karma then? Now see what changes have been introduced into the conception of this principle by subsequent articles and other publications. According to "The Elixir of Life" the 6th principle does not perish in the manner stated. "The Replies to an English F. T. S." speak of it in conjunction with the 7th principle as the permanent monad which runs through the whole series of incarnations. The teachings of "Esoteric Buddhism" are utterly inconsistent with the original view as may be easily perceived. In the present article my critic identifies it with *Karanopadhi* and calls it at the same time a "correlating state." This very Karanopadhi she has some time ago identified with the 2nd principle, as above shown. She has thus contradicted the original teaching any number of times in her subsequent writings. It must also be remembered that in writing these "Fragments" she has made the following distinct declaration: "These are no speculations—we speak what we do know." And yet she herself has treated them as if they were something worse than mere speculations. Nevertheless with all these contradictions and all this confusion people must accept, it would appear, these teachings as gospel truths, and not utter a single word to criticize them.

There is not much difficulty perhaps about the 7th principle as nothing very definite has ever been said about it. One fact about it is pretty nearly certain. It must be considered as the Logos, there being no other entity in the Cosmos which possesses the attributes assigned to it. It has been often declared, as far as my recollection goes, that the ancient occultists regarded this principle as something existing out of the body and not in the body. It was once loosely stated that this principle should be considered as a principle running through the other principles (p. 197, "Five Years of Theosophy"). This might be true as regards its light or aura; but the Logos itself is never present in the microcosm except when it finally enters into a man before his final emancipation from the trammels of incarnate existence. It is erroneous in my humble opinion to name the Logos as a principle in man. It will be quite as proper to name Parabrahmam itself as a principle in man.

In tracing the course of evolution it is stated in "Esoteric Buddhism" and some other writings, that each succeeding planetary round is calculated to bring about the development of one of the seven principles. But to avoid certain difficulties which are obvious, it is further asserted that the germs of the higher principles in man are present in him at every stage of his evolutionary progress. These various statements when put together are apt to give rise to the belief that the 7th principle is subject to a course of evolutionary development. This difficulty has long ago been pointed out by one or two writers, but received no consideration from the propounders of the original doctrine. My critic calls even this principle "a correlating state." There is no use quarrelling about the nature of this principle when so little has been or can be said about it.

From the foregoing remarks it will be seen that this unfortunate seven-fold classification is misleading, not on account of western materialism as my critic asserts, but on account of its own inherent defects. Its unscientific nature is equally clear from all that has been said about it. A Classification which has brought about such a state of things, and required so many alterations in the conceptions associated with it to keep it in existence, must be supported, if it can be supported at all, by clear definitions and powerful arguments. On the other hand my critic virtually evades the real question at issue and undertakes to establish a proposition which I have never denied.

RE-CLASSIFICATION OF PRINCIPLES.

In the May *Theosophist* (1887,) I find the first part of a long explanatory article, by Mr. T. Subba Row, in which the able author has gone to the trouble of dissecting almost everything I have written for the last ten years, upon the subject under review.

My first thought was, to leave his "answer" without reply. Upon reading it carefully over, however, I have come to the conclusion that perhaps it would not be safe to do so. The article in question is a manifesto. I am not allowed to labour any longer under the impression that it was only an apparent disagreement. Those members and ex-members of our Society who had *rejoiced* at Mr. Subba Row's remarks were consequently right in their conclusions, and I—wrong. As I do not admit—in our case, at any rate—that "a house divided against itself" must fall, for the Theosophical Society can never fall so long as its foundation is very strong, I regard the disagreement, even if *real*, as of no great or vital importance. Yet, were I to fail to answer the strictures in question, it would be immediately inferred that I was silenced by the arguments; or, worse, that I had expounded a tenet which had no basis.

Before I say anything further upon the main subject, however, I must express my surprise at finding the learned author referring to me continually as his "critic." I have never criticized him, nor his teachings, whether orally, or in print. I had simply expressed regret at finding in the *Theosophist* words calculated, as I then thought, to create false impressions. The position assumed by the lecturer on the Gita was as unexpected as it was new to me, and my remarks were meant to be as friendly as I could make them. Nor am I actuated even now by any other feelings. I can only regret, and nothing more, that such new developments of ideas should occur just now, after nearly seven years of *tacit*, if no actual, agreement.

Nor do I find on page 450 of the April *Theosophist* in my foot-note anything that should imply, even remotely, least of all "probably," that I endorse the views that "a slur was thrown on the original teaching." I had said that "some (Theosophists) argued that it looked like a slur." As for myself I have too much reverence for the "original" TEACHERS to ever admit that anything said or done, could ever be "a slur" upon their teachings. But if I, *personally*, am made out "the original expounder," there can be no slur whatever. It is, at the worst, a disagreement in personal views. Everyone is free in the Theosophical Society to give full expression to his own ideas,—I among the rest; especially when I know that those views are those of *trans*-Himalayan esotericism, if not of *cis*-Himalayan esoteric Brahmanism, as I am now told squarely—for the first time. The words written by me in the foot-note, therefore—" Of course those who do not hold to the old school of Aryan and Arhat adopts are in no way bound to adopt the septenary classification"—were never meant for Mr. Subba Row. They applied most innocently, and as I thought liberally, to every and each member of our Association. Why my friend, Mr. T. Subba Row, should have applied them to himself is one of those mysterious combinations—evolved by my own *karma* no doubt—which pass *my* comprehension. To expect a Brahmin, a Vedantin (whether an occultist or otherwise) to accept *in their dead-letter* the tenets of Buddhist (even if Aryan) adepts, is like expecting a Western Kabbalist, an Israelite by birth and views, to adhere to our Lord Buddha instead of to Moses. To charge me on such grounds with dogmatism and a desire to evolve " an orthodox creed" out of tenets I have tried to explain to those who are interested in Buddhistic occultism, is rather hard. All this compels me to explain my past as well as my present position. As the second portion of Mr. Subba Row's *reply* can hardly contain stronger charges than I find in the first, I ask permission to state that :—

I. Neither the original " Fragments of Occult Truths" nor yet " Esoteric Buddhism" were ever meant to expound

Brahminical philosophy, but that of the *trans*-Himalayan Arhats, as very correctly stated by Mr. Subba Row in his "Brahminism on the Seven-fold Principle in Man"—"it is extremely difficult to show (to the profane H. P. B.!) whether the Tibetans derived their doctrine from the ancient Rishis of India, or the ancient Brahmans learned their occult science from the adepts of Tibet; or again, whether the adepts of both countries professed originally the same doctrine and derived it from a common source. However that may be, the knowledge of the *occult power of nature* possessed by the inhabitants of the lost Atlantis, was learnt by the ancient adepts of India, and was appended by them to their esoteric doctrine taught by the residents of the sacred island (Shambhala). The Tibetan adepts, however, have not accepted this addition to their esoteric doctrine". Thus, the readers of the *Theosophist* were told from the first (in 1882) that they "should expect to find a difference between the two doctrines." One of the said "differences" is found in the *exoteric exposition*, or form of presentation of the seven-fold principle in man.

II. Though the *fundamental* doctrines of Occultism and Esoteric philosophy are one and the same the world over, and that is the secret meaning under the outward shell of every old religion—however much they may conflict in appearance—is the outcome of, and proceeds from, the universal Wisdom-Religion—the modes of thought and of its expression must necessarily differ. There are Sanskrit words used—"Jiva," for one—by *trans-Himalayan* adepts, whose meaning differs greatly in verbal applications from the meaning it has among Brahmans in India.

III. I have never boasted of any knowledge of Sanskrit, and, when I came to India last, in 1879, knew very superficially the philosophies of the six schools of Brahminism. I never pretended to teach Sanskrit or explain Occultism in that language. I claimed to know the esoteric philosophy of the *trans*-Himalayan Occultists and no more. What I knew again, was that the philosophy of the ancient *Dwijas* and Initiates did not, nor could it, differ *essentially* from the esoterism of the "Wisdom-Religion," any more than ancient Zoroastrianism, Hermetic philosophy, or Chaldean Kabbala could do so. I have tried to prove it by rendering the technical terms used by the Tibetan Arhats of things and principles, as adopted in *trans-Himalayan* teaching (and which, when given to Mr. Sinnett and others without their Sanskrit or European equivalents, remained to them unintelligible, as they would to all in India)—in terms used in Brahmanical philosophy. I may have failed to do so correctly, very likely I have, and made mistakes,—I never claimed infallibility—but this is no reason why the seven-fold division should be regarded as "unscientific." That it was *puzzling* I had already admitted, yet, once properly explained, it is the right one, though, in transcendental metaphysics, the quarternary may do as well. In my writings in the *Theosophist* I have always consulted learned and (even *not* very learned) Sanskrit speaking Brahmans, giving credit to everyone of them for knowing the value of Sanskrit terms better than I did. The question then is not, whether I may or may not have made use of wrong Sanskrit terms, but whether the occult tenets expounded through me are the right ones—at any rate those of the "Aryan-Chaldeo-Tibetan doctrine" as we call the "universal Wisdom-religion." (See *Five Years of Theosophy*, 1st note, to Mr. Subba Row's "Brahminism on the seven-fold Principle in Man," p. 177-9).

IV. When saying that the seven-fold classification of principles is *absolutely* necessary to explain *post-mortem* phenomena, I repeat only that which I had always said and that which every mystic will understand. "Once we pass from the plane of pure subjective (or methaphysical, hence purely *theoretical*) reasoning on esoteric matters to that of practical demonstration in occultism, wherein each (lower) principle and attribute has to be analised and defined in its application . . . to *post-mortem* life (that of spooks and *pisachas*), the seven-fold classification is the right one." These are my words, which every spiritualist will understand. Vedantin metaphysicians, denying as they do objective reality or importance even to our physical body, are not likely to lose their time in dividing the lower principles in man, the compound *aspects* and nature of the *phantom* of that body. *Practical* occultism does; and it is one of the duties of those Theosophists who study occultism to warn their brethren of the dangers incurred by those who know nothing of the real nature of those apparitions: to warn them that a *shell* is not "*spirit*." This statement of mine I find qualified as "simply absurd." Having never regarded as *absurd* anything said or written by Mr. Subba Row, I could not retaliate even if I would, I can only pronounce the epithet, let us say—*unkind*, and demur to the qualification. Had the author to face "practical demonstration" in spiritual phenomena and "*materializations* of spirits," so called, he would soon find that his four principles could never cover the ground of this kind of phenomena. Even the *lower aspect* of the principle of *manas* (physical brain, or its *post-mortem* auric survival)and of *kamarupa* are hardly sufficient to explain the *seemingly* intelligent and spiritual principles (*bhuta* or elements) that manifest through mediums.

V. It is not consistent with fact and truth to charge me, "the original (?) exponent herself" with changing my conceptions about the nature of principles. "I have never changed them, nor could I do so." In this I claim my right, too, as Mr. Subba Row does, to my evidence being "the best and the most direct evidence available as regards *my own states of consciousness*." I may have used wrong Sanskrit expressions, (and even wrong and clumsily put English sentences, for the matter of that)—while trying to blend the Arhat with the Brahminical occult tenets. As to those conceptions, my "four principles" have to disintegrate and vanish in the air, before any amount of criticism can make me regard my ten fingers as only four; although *metaphysically*, I am fully prepared to admit that they exist only in my own *mayavic* perceptions and states of consciousness.

VI. Mr. Subba Row, taking hold of "Esoteric Buddhism," the "Elixir of Life" and "Man," is pleased to father all their sins of omission and commission on the "Original Expounder." This is hardly fair. The first work was written absolutely without my knowledge, and as the author understood those teachings from letters he had received, what have I to do with them? The *Elixir of Life* was written by its author under direct dictation, or *inspection*, in his own house, in a far way country, in which I had never been till two years later. Finally "Man" was *entirely rewritten* by one of the two "chelas" and from the same materials as those used by Mr. Sinnett for "Esoteric Buddhism"; the two having understood the teachings, each in his own way. What had I to do with the "states of consciousness" of the three authors, two of whom wrote in England while I was in India? He may attribute to the lack of *scientific* precision in the "original teachings," there being "a jumble." No one would accuse Mr. Subba Row's *Bhagavat Gita* lectures of any such defects. Yet, I have already heard three or four intelligent persons among our members expounding the said three lectures (those which have already appeared)—*in three different and diametrically opposite ways*.

This will do, I believe. The *Secret Doctrine* will contain, no doubt, still more *heterodox* statements from the Brahminical view. No one is forced to accept *my* opinions or teaching in the Theosophical Society, one of the rules of which enforces only mutual tolerence for religious views. Our body is entirely unsectarian and "only exacts from each member that toleration of the beliefs of others which he desires . . in regard to his own faith."

Most of us have been playing truants to this golden rule as to all others: more's the pity.

H. P. Blavatsky.

THE CONSTITUTION OF THE MICROCOSM.

I shall now proceed with the continuation of my article on the Constitution of the Microcosm. Madame H. P. Blavatsky has sent a reply to the previous portion of my article for publication in this issue, and to avoid the necessity of writing another article on the subject, I find it necessary to take this reply also into consideration in this very article.

The real question at issue between us is after all a very simple one; but it has been obscured and unnecessarily complicated by the line of argument which Madame H. P. Blavatsky has chosen to adopt. I have nowhere denied the importance of number seven in the processes of natural evolution or the interpretation of cosmic phenomena. On the other hand it will be clearly seen from my first lecture that I fully admitted its importance while rejecting the seven-fold classification hitherto adopted as unsound and unscientific. I have not even denied the possibility of a seven-fold classification in the case of the microcosmic principles, or the existence of a seven-fold classification recognized by the ancient occult science. My remarks and criticism were strictly confined to the particular classification which has hitherto been explained and commented upon in Theosophical publications. It must further be noted in this connection that my criticism did not proceed from the necessity of maintaining any orthodox Brahminical dogma. I found it necessary to condemn this classification on account of its own inherent defects, and not because it emanated from a trans-Himalayan source. I found fault, not with Madame H. P. Blavatsky, or her use of Sanskrit terms, or her exposition of Brahminical philosophy, but with the incorrect and misleading classification which has introduced so many contradictions and so much confusion into Theosophical writings. If these few facts are borne in mind, it will be found that a considerable portion of Madame H. P. Blavatsky's argument is altogether irrelevant to the real question at issue. The whole argument, from the commencement of page 452 to the end of the second paragraph on page 455, can only establish the fact that the number seven is of great importance in nature and the arrangements of occult symbology. Even if this fact is admitted, it does no necessarily follow that in every case we are bound to adopt a seven-fold classification. The only inference that can fairly be drawn from it is, that in all probability there are seven principles which enter into the composition of a human being. But this inference can by no means establish the correctness of the particular classification under consideration. Otherwise the truth of any seven-fold classification we may choose to adopt can be equally proved by this process of reasoning. Any person can name any seven principles in the complex structure of man and claim the sanction of nature for his classification, as is now done by my critic.

It is pointed out in the reply that the seven-fold classification is essential for "practical demonstration in Occultism," and that the four-fold classification, though "metaphysically" and "theoretically" sound, is incapable of any practical application to "the phenomena of daily and especially of *post-mortem* life." The same argument is repeated in various forms throughout the reply. This is one of those vague general arguments which seem to mean a good deal, and which take easy possession of the minds of people who are not generally in the habit of scrutinizing or analyzing their own ideas. I fail to understand what kind of pratical demonstration it is which necessitates the adoption of this classification. My critic is silent on the point. I know for certain that this seven-fold classification will be an obstacle in the way in a considerable number of occult process which an initiate has to pass through in seeking that final union with the Logos, which is to be the ultimate result of his labours. This inconvenience results from the fact that the mystic constitution of the Logos itself, as represented by the sacred Tetragram, has not a septenary basis. If the assertion, however, does not mean anything more than that the septenary classification is required for explaining the so-called spiritualistic phenomena, I am fully prepared to account for everyone of these phenomena from the stand-point of the classification I have adopted. I have in fact dealt with the general aspects of spiritualism in my lectures from this very stand-point. The very fact that this four-fold classification was found sufficient for all practical purposes by occultists who investigated these phenomena for thousands of years and examined the workings of nature on all its planes of activity, will be an unanswerable reply to this argument. I am quite certain that Pisachas and Bhutas will never succeed in disproving my classification. I think that this defect is the result of a serious misapprehension in my critic's mind regarding the nature of this four-fold classification. At the end of page 450, Madame H. P. Blavatsky points out that the three *Upadhis* of the Raja-yoga classification are Jagrata, Swapna and Sushupti, and continues as follows :—" But then, in transcendental states of Samadhi, the body with its *linga sarira*, the vehicle of the life principle, is entirely left out of consideration; the three states of consciousness are made to refer only to the three (with Atma the fourth) principles which remain after death. And here lies the real key to the septenary division of man, the three principles coming in as an addition only during his life." This real key unfortunately breaks in our hands the moment we begin to apply it. The whole mistake has arisen from confounding *Upadhi* with the state of Pragna associated with it. Upadhi is the physical organism. The first Upadhi is the physical body itself, and not merely Jagrata Avastha. And again how is Jagrata to be identified with the fourth principle ? If, as my critic says, the three states of consciousness—Jagrata, Swapna and Sushupti—are made to refer only to the three principles which remain after death in addition to Atma, Jagrata must necessarily be identified with the fourth principle. But sure enough the fourth principle is not the physical body. The four principles of my classification can by no means be superadded to the first three principles of the seven-fold classification, seeing that the physical body is the first principle of the four-fold classification. Even if Upadhi is mistaken for a state of consciousness, the seven-fold classification cannot be deduced from the Raja-yoga classification. Jagrata Avastha is not the condition of Pragna associated with the fourth principle. The whole argument thus ends in nothing; and yet on the basis of this argument Madame H. P. Blavatsky has thought it proper, in the fourth argument of her present reply, to pronounce an opinion to the effect that the Vedantins have denied the objective reality and the importance of the physical body, and overlooked its existence in their classification, which has thereby been rendered unfit for practical purposes. My critic would have done better if she had paused to ascertain the real meaning of Upadhi and of Jagrata before using such a worthless argument in defence of her own classification and giving expression to such an erroneous view regarding the Vedantic theory.

The whole argument about the comparative merits of the two classifications rests on a series of misconceptions, or arbitrary assumptions. The first Upadhi is identified with Jagratavastha, and then it is assumed that the latter is the same as the fourth principle of the septenary classification. I must here call the reader's attention to another curious mistake in the reply. It is stated in the second para, on page 456, that the four-fold classification is the "Bhagavad Gita classification," "but not that of the *Vedanta.*" This statement is apparently made for the purpose of somehow or other discrediting the four-fold classification. It has, however, no real foundation in fact, and is altogether misleading. Madame H. P. Blavatsky has probably ventured to make this assertion on account of the headings given to the five-fold and the four-fold classifications in my note on the "Septenary Division in different Indian Systems." I called the five-fold classification, the Vedantic classification, and the four-fold classification the Raja-Yoga classification, merely for convenience of reference and not because the two classifications refer to two different systems of philosophy. Though both the classifications are used in Vedantic philosophy, the four-fold classification is the one frequently referred to. Tharaka Raja-Yoga is, as it were, the centre and the heart of Vedantic philosophy, as it is decidedly, in its higher aspects, the most important portion of the ancient Wisdom-Religion. Very little of it is known at present in India. What is generally seen of it in the books ordinarily read, gives but a very inadequate idea of its scope or importance. In truth, however, it is one of the seven main branches into which the whole of the occult science is divided, and is derived according to all accounts from the "children of the fire-mist" of the mysterious land of Shamballah.

It is necessary to state further in this connection that the four-fold classification I have used is not the only classification to be found in this magnificent system of philosophy. It has also a seven-fold classification, which will hereafter be noticed.

Attention has been called to some of my former articles in the *Theosophist*, and it is argued that I have already admitted the truth and the correctness of the classification which I am now criticizing, and that I am now estopped from denying the same. This kind of argument is altogether out of place in the present case. The only article in which I had seriously considered the question, is the one referred to as the article on "Brahminism on the Seven-fold principles in man." I must explain the circumstances under which this so-called article was-written. While yet an utter stranger to me, Madame H. P. Blavatsky, after seeing my article on the Zodiac, asked me certain questions by letter about the classification of the various powers and forces recognised by occultism, and further, calling my attention to the "Fragments of Occult Truth," enquired of me whether *as regards spiritualistic phenomena* my views harmonized with those put forward in the said article. I sent her a letter in reply, not having the slightest notion at the time of writing the same that it would ever be published as an article for the information of the public. This fact was acknowledged by the editor in her preface to the said article, when it was originally published in the columns of the *Theosophist,* and it was the editor who selected the title. It will be clearly seen that the article is divided into two parts. The first part is confined to the questions put regarding the classification of the "powers of nature," while the second part deals with the spiritualistic phenomena. Madame H. P. Blavatsky has, however, thought it proper to quote a passage from the first part, which has nothing to do with the classification of the microcosmic principles, or the spiritualistic phenomena, for the purpose of drawing an unwarranted inference in support of her contention, and for the purpose of making a disagreeable insinuation against the ancient occult science of India.

The passage in question is as follows :

"However that may be, the knowledge of *the occult powers of nature* (the italics are in the original, see p. 155, "*five Years of Theosophy*") possessed by the inhabitants of the lost Atlantis was learnt by the ancient adepts of India, and was appended by them to the esoteric doctrine taught by the residence of the sacred island. The Tibetan adepts, however, have not accepted this addition to their esoteric doctrine; and it is in this respect that one should expect to find a difference between the two doctrines."

There is nothing ambiguous in this passage. It clearly refers to the Tantras and Agamas which were originally cultivated and developed by the Atlanteans. In course of time their doctrines and ritual gradually crept into the Brahminical doctrine, as the Dugpa doctrines crept into Tibetan Buddhism before the time of Song-ka-pa. And just as the last named adept undertook to weed out these doctrines from the Tibetan religion, Shankaracharya attempted to purify the Brahminical faith. The assertion made in the article does not in the least justify the assumption that the ancient Brahminical occult science was derived from the Atlantean. Tantras and Agamas have little or nothing to do with the classification of the microcosmic principles; and the statement quoted has not the remotest reference to the seven-fold or the four-fold classification. My critic was more or less of the same opinion when she wrote her first article on the "Classification of Principles," published in the April issue of this Journal. After quoting the above-mentioned paragraph from my article, she makes the following observation on p. 442:—"But this difference between the two doctrines does not include the septenary division ... " But this poinion seems to have changed subsequently. For, in the present article, after citing the same passage, she makes the following remark: " Thus, the readers of the *Theosophist* were told from the first (in 1882) that they 'should expect to to find a difference between the two doctrines; One of the said ' differences' is found in the *Esoteric Exposition* or form of presentation of the seven-fold principle in man. As might naturally be expected, this statement is a little obscure. This " Exoteric Exposition" cannot possibly refer to the seven-fold classification, because in her opinion this classification " was always esoteric" (p. 448). It must therefore refer to the four-fold classification which is looked upon as the exoteric form of the esoteric seven-fold classification. The statement now made amounts to this then. The seven-fold classification was esoteric and was derived by the Tibetan adepts from Shamballah; the four-fold classification was exoteric and was derived by the ancient adepts of India from the Atlanteans. This difference was noticed and admitted by the article on " Brahminism and the Seven-fold principles in man."

This is the gist of the present agrument. This argument is sufficiently refuted by what she herself wrote in the April article. She then thought that my statement did not refer to the classifications, and alleged that both the parties derived the seven-fold classification from the Atlanteans (see page 449). It will be a mere waste of time to dissect this argument any further. I can only regret that my critic should stoop to such arguments and insinuations for the purpose of defending her position.

The second part of my article deals with the seven-fold classification only *incidentally.* It was not necessary to discuss the merits of the seven-fold classification of the "Fragments" in that article. And I did not think it proper to go out of my way and criticize the said classification. It would have been foolish on my part to have done so when my correspondent was a stranger to me, and when I was assured that in her opinion it was a correct classification. I therefore followed the classification of the "Fragments" as far as it was convenient, introducing such changes into it as were absolutely necessary. The following passage at the commencement of the second part of my article will show what I undertook to establish in the said article, and why I adopted the seven-fold classification:— "I have carefully examined it (The Fragments) and find that the results arrived at do not differ much from the conclusions of our Aryan philosophy, though our mode of stating the arguments may differ in form. I shall now discuss the question from my own stand-point *though following, for facility of comparison and convenience of discussion*, the sequence of classification of the seven-fold entities, or principles constituting man which is adopted in the 'Fragments.' The questions raised for discussion are—(1) whether the disembodied spirits of human beings appear in the seance rooms and elsewhere, and (2) whether the manifestations taking place are produced wholly or partly through their agency." The conclusions referred to herein do not refer to the classification adopted, but to the views expressed on the questions raised. The reason given for following the seven-fold classification is clearly stated and cannot possibly mislead anybody. The so-called mathematical demonstration of the evolution of seven entities from three can only establish, if correct, the probability of a seven-fold classification, but is utterly insufficient to establish the truth of the seven-fold classification therein adopted. It will be further seen that the seven-fold classification I adopted in that article is different in many important respects, *viz.*, the position of Prana and the nature and importance of the 5th and the 6th principles, from the classification of the "Fragments," in which the so-called "original teachings" was embodied. Curiously enough my alterations were quietly accepted in subsequent expositions in spite of the "original teachings," to which so much importance is now attached. I was not then pretending, and I have never pretended subsequently, that I was teaching occult wisdom to the members of the Theosophical Society. Under such circumstances it is altogether unreasonable to lay so much stress on the importance of my article in discussing the important question now formally raised for final decision. It is quite true that I refrained from pointing out fully the defects and the unsoundness of the seven-fold classification in my note on the various classifications while I was the acting editor of the *Theosophist*, though I stated that, in some respects, it would be more convenient to follow the four-fold classification. I did not then think it proper in the interests of theosophical investigation to raise an important issue about the correctness of the seven-fold classification, as I thought it would be premature to do so. The seven-fold classification, though incorrect, was a step in advance. It did serve some purpose in its own way towards the investigation of the ancient systems of occult psychology. And I did not think it prudent to disturb it when matters were hardly ripe for taking another step in the right direction. My article on the "Personal and Impersonal God" does not, in fact, touch the question at issue. It does speak no doubt of seven states of matter, of seven principles in man, and seven aspects of Pragna. But the article does not adopt the seven-fold classification under consideration. It is based on Mandukyopanishad which enumerates seven phases of consciousness, while it accepts the four-fold classification. These articles therefore do not settle the point in dispute, and there cannot be a better proof of the weakness of my critic's position, than the fact that, instead of attempting to justify the seven-fold classification on its merits, she is trying to find a support for it in the articles above alluded to.

Madame H. P. Blavatsky says that she is certain that the classification in dispute is the real esoteric seven-fold classification. I am very sorry she is so positive in her statements. In my humble opinion it is not the real esoteric classification. There is but one source from which all the various writers on occult science have derived their classification. It is one of the oldest directions of the ancient Wisdom-Religion that the macrocosm should be interpreted according to the plan revealed by *Malchuth*, and that *Shechinah* should be accepted as a guide to the interpretation of the constitution of the microcosm. I use the Kabbalistic names, though not precisely in the Kabbalistic sense, as I am not at liberty to use the Sanskrit equivalents. This Shechinah is an androgyne power, and is the Thureeya Chaitanyam of the cosmos. Its male form is the figure of man seen on the mysterious throne in the vision of Ezekiel. Its mystic constitution gives us, as it were, the equation to the microcosm. It is the eternal model of the perfected microcosm. The universal life copies this model in its work of evolutionary construction. This equation can be interpreted in nine ways, and it has been so interpreted by the ancient teachers. There are nine stand-points from which the microcosm can be looked at, and in nine ways has the constitution of the microcosm been explained. The real esoteric seven-fold classification is one of the most important, if not the most important classification, which has received its arrangement from the mysterious constitution of this eternal type. I may also mention in this connection that the four-fold classification claims the same origin. The light of life, as it were, seems to be refracted by the treble-faced prism of Prakriti, having three Gunams for its three faces, and divided into seven rays, which develop in course of time the seven principles of this classification. The progress of development presents some points of similarity of the gradual development of the rays of the spectrum. While the four-fold classification is amply sufficient for all practical purposes, this real seven-fold classification is of great theoretical and scientific importance. It will be necessary to adopt it to explain certain classes of phenomena noticed by occultists ; and it is perhaps better fitted to be the basis of a perfect system of psychology. It is not the peculiar property of "the trans-Himalayan esoteric doctrine." In fact it has a closer connection with the Brahminical Logos than with the Buddhist Logos. In order to make my meaning clear I may point out here that the Logos has seven forms. In other words, there are seven kinds of Logoi in the cosmos. Each of these has become the central figure of one of the seven main branches of the ancient Wisdom-Religion. This classification is not the seven-fold classification we have adopted. I make this assertion without the slightest fear of contradiction. The real classification has all the requisites of a scientific classification. It has seven distinct principles, which correspond with seven distinct states of Pragna or consciousness. It bridges the gulf between the objective and subjective, and indicates the mysterious circuit through which ideation passes. The seven principles are allied to seven states of matter, and to seven forms of force. These principles are harmoniously arranged between two poles, which define the limits of *human* conciousness. It is abundantly clear from all that has been said in this controversy, that the classification we have adopted does not possess these requisites. It is admitted by Madame H. P. Blavatsky, that in her classification there are not *seven distinct seats* of consciousness (see p. 451). The arrangement of the principles also is not regular. The life principle, for instance, which is alleged to have for its vehicle the *linga sarira*, is made to precede the latter instead of following it. Such defects show that the classification we have hitherto used is not quite sound and scientific. It was to pave the way for the adoption of the real classification that I ventured to criticize the old classification, and I hardly expected that my remarks would give rise to such a controversy. It will be a mere waste of time at present to explain the real seven-fold classification. There is not the slightest chance of my being heard. Time will show whether I was justified in my criticism or not. Personally I am not in the least interested whether the members of the Theosophical Society adhere to or reject the seven-fold classification. I have no desire of having a following of my own in the Society, or starting a separate branch for enforcing my own views on the matter. There is but one statement more in the reply to which it is necessary for me to advert. I have not held Madame H. P. Blavatsky responsible for the mistakes of "Man" and "Esoteric Buddhism," as she and some of her friends seem to think. I merely grouped together all the various inconsistent statements found in prominent theosophical publications about the classification under enquiry, and in giving my quotations I referred to the various books and articles by name. I nowhere alleged or insinuated that Madame H. P. Blavatsky should be held responsible for the blunders committed by others. The scope of my argument will be clear if my article is carefully perused. But before the heat of advocacy subsides there is no chance of preventing people for raising unnecessary side issues for the purpose of quarrelling. I am extremely sorry that I have entered into this unpleasant controversy. I hope Madame H. P. Blavatsky will kindly excuse me if I have in any way wounded her feelings by my remarks or criticism.

T. Subba Row.

THE BHAGAVAD GITA

AND

THE MICROCOSMIC PRINCIPLES.

Mr. T. Subba Row has thrown a new light on the study of the Bhagavad Gita by the very learned lectures delivered by him at the last anniversary of the Society. The publication of these in the *Theosophist* has afforded the opportunity to numerous students of philosophy to have something like a clear introduction to some of the teachings of the Vedanta. There are several points, however, which need some further elucidation before they become quite explicable to the reader, and as these difficulties have been felt by a large number of Theosophists and non-Theosophists, I shall try to state some of them as shortly as possible in the hope that Mr. Subba Row will be good enough to add some more information and thus make his notes as useful and instructive as possible.

Mr. Subba Row says:—" Now creation or evolution commenced by the intellectual energy of the Logos." Is the *intellectual energy* the same as the *Light of the Logos ?* Again, " What springs up in the Logos at first is simply an image, a conception of what it is to be in the cosmos." Whence springs this image?

The four principles of the whole of the infinite cosmos are said to be—

1. The manifested solar system in all its principles and totality constituting the *Sthula sarira.*

2. The Light of the Logos, the *Sukshma sarira.*

3. The Logos which is the one germ from which the whole cosmos springs, and which contains the image of the universe, stands in the position of the *Karana sarira.*

4. Parabrahm.

The four principles of the *manifested* cosmos are enumerated as follows:—

1. *Vishwanara* or the basis of the objective world.

2. *Hiranyagarbha* or the basis of the astral world.

3. *Eshwara* or rather *Sutratma.*

4. Parabrahm.

It is said that regarding this 4th principle "differences of opinion have sprung up, and as for this principle we ought to have, as we have for the cosmos, some particular entity out of which the other three principles start into existence, and which exist in it, and by reason of it, we ought no doubt to accept the *Avyaktam or Mulaprakriti* of the Sankhyas as this 4th principle." "You must conceive without my going through the whole process of evolution that out of these three principles, having as their foundation *Mulprakriti*, the whole manifested solar system with all the various objects in it has started into being." Now Mulprakriti is said to be, "*veil of Parabrahmam* considered from the objective stand point of the Logos." And yet, in the above passages, it is said to be the foundation out of which the three first principles of the manifested solar system, including the Logos, start into existence. Parabrahm would be the proper 4th principle and not *Mulaprakriti,* out of which the Logos does not and cannot arise. These passages therefore require to be explained.

"By the time we reach man this one light (the light of the Logos) becomes differentiated into certain monads and hence individuality is fixed."

The term "human monad" has not yet been properly explained, and a great deal of confusion therefore arises in speaking about it, and in reference to the four principles that have been enumerated in the notes, a clear conception of the human monad is necessary.

The four principles in man are said to be—

1. The physical body.

2. Sukshma sarira.

3. Karana sarira, which can only be conceived as a centre of *pragna,*—a centre of force or energy into which the 3rd

principle (*or sutratma*) of the cosmos was differentiated by reason of the same impulse which has brought about the differentiation of all these cosmic principles, and "now the question is, what is it that completes this trinity and makes it a quaternary ?"

4. "Of course this light of the Logos."*

Again it is said : " In the opinion of the Vedantists and in the opinion of Krishna also man is a quaternary. He has first the physical body or *Sthula sarira;* secondly, the astral body or *Sukshma sarira*; thirdly, the seat of his higher individuality, the *Karana sarira*; and fourthly and lastly, his *atma*†."

Is the human *atma* then the light of the Logos ? The word *atma* is used several times in the lectures, and it seems that the term *atma* is applied to the Logos. What does the word "*atma*" mean in reference to the four-fold classification ?

The word human soul is also used in several places, and it is not clear what is meant by the word "soul" as applied to the four-fold classification of man.

"The *Sukshma sarira* or the astral body is simply said to be the seat of the lower nature of man. His animal passions and emotions, and those ordinary thoughts which are generally connected with the physical wants of man, may no doubt communicate themselves to the astral man, but higher than this they do not go."

"The *Karana sarira* is what passes as the real ego which subsists through incarnation after incarnation, adding in each incarnation something to its fund of experiences and evolving a higher individuality as the resultant of the whole process of assimilation. It is for this that the *Karana sarira* is called the *Ego* of man, and in certain systems of philosophy it is called the *Jiva*."

---

* *Theosophist*, page 309, vol. VIII. † *Ibid*, page 310.

"It must be clearly borne in mind that this *Karana sarira* is primarily the result of the action of the light of the Logos, which is its life and energy, and which is further its source of consciousness on that plan of *Mulaprakriti*, which we have called *Sutratma* and which is its physical basis."

The word *Sutratma* has been applied to Eshwara or the Logos. What then is meant by the plan of *Mulaprakriti* called *Sutratma*? The Logos is certainly not a plane of *Mulaprakriti*.

In rejecting the septenary classification and adopting the four-fold classification, it has been said that this latter classification divides man into so many entities as are capable of having separate existences, and these four principles are further associated with four *Upadhis*.

Now what are the four *Upadhis* of the four principles mentioned above?

The two principles, *Karana sarira* and *Sukhshma sarira*, are in no way more intelligible than the 3rd, 4th, 5th, and 6th principles of the septenary classification. The description given of these two will have to be considerably amplified and brought home to the mind of the ordinary reader before the existence of these principles as separate entities is recognized. Under what principles are the human mind, the will, the emotions, passions, desires, intuitions, &c., to be classified, and by what means or in what way are these two principles to be known as separately existing entities in man? Again, as to the 4th principle called the light of the Logos, does it simply show itself as the *Karana sarira*, or besides acting as the *Karana sarira* does it separately act as a 4th principle, and what function does it then fulfil and how is it to be recognized? According to this classification the Logos does not form one of the human principle but is something higher towards which the human monad must ultimately go. In the cosmic principles as well as in those of the solar system the Logos forms the 3rd principle, while in man the Logos forms no principle at all. The doctrine of correspondence shifts here a great deal. The Logos, which is the 3rd in the cosmos, become something beyond the 4th in man. Some explanation as to this difference is necessary.

Regarding the Logos it is said that "it is a centre of energy, but that such centres of energy are innumerable in the bosom of Parabrahm, and there may even be difference even in this one centre of energy." "Maha Vishnu is a representative of the Logos, but it must not be inferred that there is one Logos in the cosmos or even that but one form of Logos is possible in the cosmos." ... "Maha Vishnu seems to be a Dhyan Chohan that first appeared on this planet when human evolution commenced during this Kalpa." Owing to there being innumerable Logoi in the cosmos, the Logos is said to be considered in the abstract.

As the doctrine of the Logos is the very basis of the teachings of the Bhagavad Gita, and as almost every reader of the " Notes " has been startled by hearing of innumerable Logoi, a good deal of explanation is necessary to make this portion of the teaching as clear as possible. What are the innumerable Logoi and what relation do they bear to each other ? Are they the same as the Dhyan Chohans as the hint regarding Maha Vishnu would lead one to suppose ?

In the introductory lecture* to the Bhagavad Gita, Mr. Subba Row says, " Krishna may be the Logos, but only a particular form of it. The number 18 is to represent this particular form." Krishna is the 7th principle in man, and his gift of his sister in marriage to Arjuna typifies the union between the 6th and the 5th. What is meant by the *form* of the Logos ? Again, in this, Mr. Subba Row speaks of the Logos as the 7th or highest principle in man: while in his four-fold classification the Logos has no place. Again, what would be meant in terms of the four-fold classification by the words " the union between the 6th and the 5th ?"

* *Theosophist*, Vol. VII, page 235.

In this review* of the "Virgin of the World," it is said that Osiris is not the Logos, but something higher than the Logos. The Logos itself has a soul and a spirit as everything else which is manifested, and there is nothing unreasonable in supposing that Osiris or Buddha may represent the soul of the Logos."

What is meant by saying that the Logos has a soul and a spirit, and if the Logos is the very first emanation from Parabrahm, how is Osiris higher than the Logos?

In another place† Mr. Subba Row says: Where Videha Kaivalyam (the union of the disembodied monad with the absolute Parabrahm) is reached by any monad, the sum total of its Karma goes to enrich the universal mind, wherein lie the archetypes of all that is, was, or will be. In the "Notes" the union of the monad with the Logos is spoken of. Is the Videha Kaivalyam the same as the union with the Logos, or is it different? What again is the universal mind? From the words used above the universal mind seems to correspond with the Logos.

It is said that "the four-fold classification is amply sufficient for all practical purposes, and that there is another and a real seven-fold classification (different from the one that has hitherto been put forward) which is of great theoretical and scientific importance, fitter to be the basis of a perfect system of psychology. It has a closer connection with the Brahmanical Logos than with the Buddhistic Logos. There are seven kinds of Logoi in the cosmos. Each of these has become the central figure of one of the seven main branches of the ancient Wisdom-Religion.

Mr. Subba Row complains that "it was to pave the way for the adoption of the real classification that he ventured

---

* *Theosophist*, Vol. VII, page 156.

† Observations on a letter addressed to the Fellows of the London Lodge.

to outrage the old classification, and he hardly expected that his remarks would give rise to such a controversy." He says again, "It will be mere waste of time at present to explain the real seven-fold classification. There is not the slightest chance of my being heard."

Mr. Subba Row takes here a very gloomy view of the short controversy that was quite inevitable when for years he kept quite silent and tacitly allowed the readers of the *Theosophist* to suppose that he agreed in the truth of the septenary classification that has hitherto been given out. The year before last Mr. Subba Row gave an introductory lecture on the Bhagavad Gita, and in that lecture, as quoted above, he distinctly spoke of the 7th principle, and the union between the 5th and 6th. When he commenced his notes at the last anniversary there was a short and sudden attack on the septenary classification, and no reasons were given for taking up what seemed a hostile attitude.

Had he in the introductory lecture to the Bhagavad Gita said somewhat as follows:—"In explaining the philosophy of the Bhagavad Gita, I shall not adopt the septenary classification of man, which has hitherto been put forward, as that classification has not yet been properly explained as having a scintific basis, neither have the seven principles been accurately defined. I shall adopt and explain to you hereafter the Vedantic four-fold classification, which is far more scientific and practical. I might tell you here that there is another and a real seven-fold classification which is fitted to be the basis of a perfect system of psychology. I shall try and explain that septenary classification also, and then you will be able to judge for yourself which classification appears to be the true one."

Some such calm remarks, coupled with a promise to explain clearly what he meant, would have saved a great deal of useless controversy.

From Mr. Subba Row's notes, it appeared to many as if he meant to urge that there was no septenary classification of any kind, the intuitions of numerous students of philosophy led them to suppose that there was a septenary classification somewhere, and Mr. Subba Row has at last confirmed that belief. We are almost all of us quite aware that the septenary principles as explained at present do create a good deal of confusion in the mind, and we are unable to form a clear conception of several of these principles. We do not at all go, however, upon the supposition that the theory of these principles ought to be an accepted truth.

In the same manner we must with all due deference say that we do not as yet clearly understand what Mr. Subba Row means by his four microcosmic principles. There seems to be a Brahminical Logos and Buddhistic Logos, and there are innumerable Logoi and so forth. All the statements puzzle the mind ; not because we cannot comprehend what is said, but because short statements are made here and there and no explanation is given of them.

Mr. Subba Row is very much mistaken when he says that "It would be a mere waste of time at present to explain the real seven-fold classification, and that there is not the slightest chance of his being heard." Every thing that Mr. Subba Row has hitherto written has been read and studied with care by almost all the educated Theosophists, and however much he may differ upon certain points of esoteric philosophy from Madame Blavatsky and other writers on the same subject, whatever more he has to say will very readily and thankfully be received by all learned Theosophists. Hypothesis, theories and truths are not studied and accepted because they emanate from A or B, but on their own intrinsic merits, and this is just the time when Mr. Subba Row will find many readers and hearers. The letter of Mr. W. Q. Judge in the August number of the *Theosophist* will show that even in the far West he is not likely to be misunderstood neither will he be here.

Since Mr. Subba Row has boldly pointed out the defect of the septenary classification as given out at present, and he also asserts that a four-fold and also a septenary classification on a different basis are the true classification recognized in Brahminical occultism, and that he knows them, it will be a great pity to refuse further explanation. The grounds on which Mr. Subba Row tries to keep silence have, as I have said before, no existence. He will have numerous hearers fair and impartial, and now that the difference has been proclaimed in somewhat large language, all unnecessary disagreements could only be ended by Mr. Subba Row's clearly explaining his four principles as well as the *real* seven-fold principles of which he is aware. There is clearly no other way out of the difficulty.

NAVROJI DORABJI KHANDALAVALA.

THE FORMS OF VAK.

With reference to Mr. Subba Row's lectures on Bhagavad Gita, published in the Theosophist for April 1887, page 446, where he says, "I would here call your attention to the 1st Anhika of Mahabhashya, where Patanjali speaks of three forms manifested, Pasyanti, Maddhyama and Vaikhari vach; the way he classifies is different. . . . ," I have to state that the 1st Anhika of Mahabhashya does not contain any such particular divisions. Patanjali quotes a verse from Rig Veda "Chatvarivak parimitapadam," &c., and interprets "Chatvarivak" nama, akyata, upasarga, and nipata. The same verse of Rig Veda is interpreted by Yaska in his Nirukta, chapter 12, in the same way as by Patanjali, and he adds some other explanations than those quoted by Mr. Subba Row; nor does Kaita, the well-known commentator of Mahabhashya, give them in his Bhashyapradipa. But Nageshabhatta, a commentator of Bhashyapradipa, gives Mr. Subba Row's sub-divisions in detail, in his Bhashyapradipothyota, referring to Harikarika, or Vakyapadiya of Bhartrihari. This Nageshabhatta speaks of the same sub-divisions in the Sphotavada of his Manjusha and some modern grammarians give the same sub-divisions quoting from Mahabharata: Annambhatta, a commentator on Bhashyapradipa, who lived before Nageshabhatta, did not interpret the passage in question in the way that Nageshabhatta did.

I would therefore ask you to draw Mr. Subba Row's attention to the above facts, and to explain the thing in a more acceptable way. I have herewith enclosed extracts from Mahabhashya, Kaita, and Nirukta on this point.

Yours fraternally,

N. BHASHYACHARY.

I have to thank Mr. Bhashyachary for having called my attention to the wrong reference given in my third lecture. Instead of referring to Nageshabhatta's Bhashyapradipodyota and Sphotavada, I referred to the Mahabhashyam itself through oversight. I had especially in my mind Nageshabhatta's remarks on the four forms of Vak in his Sphotavada when I made the statements adverted to in your learned correspondent's letter. Patanjali had to interpret the original rik of the Rig Veda from the stand-point of a grammarian in his Mahabhashya : but he certainly recognised the importance of the interpretation put upon it by Hatayogis and Rajayogis as might be easily seen by the symbols he introduced into the mystic arrangements of the Chidambaram temple. Apart from mystic symbology, Nageshabhatta had very high and ancient authorities to guide him in interpreting this risk. Nearly seven interpretations have been suggested for this rik by various classes of writers and philosophers. The four forms of Vak enumerated by me are common to the interpretation of Hatayogis and Mantrayogis on the one hand and Rajayogis on the other. I request your learned correspondent to refer to Vidyaranya's commentary on the 45th rik of the 164 Sukta of the 22nd Anuvaka of the first Mandala of Rig-veda. Most of these various interpretations are therein enumerated and explained. The learned commentator refers to Para, Pasyanti, Madhyama and Vaikhari and indicates the order of their development as stated by Mantrayogis and Hatayogis. It will be useful to refer to Yoga Sikha and other Upanishads in this connection. There is still higher authority for the views expressed in my lecture and the statements made by Nageshabhatta in Shankaracharya's commentary on Nrisimhottara Tapani (see page 118, Calcutta edition, from line 14 to the end of the para). These four forms of vak are therein explained from the stand-point of Tharaka Rajayoga. I would particularly invite the reader's attention to the explanation of Madhyama. Madhyama is so called because it occupies an intermediate position betwaen the objective form and the subjective image. On carefully perusing this portion of the commentary, it will be seen that the explanations therein given form, as it were, the foundation of the various statements made by me in my lectures regarding these four forms of vak. Whether this commentary is attributed to Shankaracharya as many have done, or to Goudapatha as some have stated, its authority is unimpeachable. I do not think it necessary to refer to any works on Mantra Shastra in this connection, as the authorities cited above are amply sufficient to justify my statements. I may perhaps have to refer to the mystic philosophy of vak at greater length in another connection.

T. S. R.

THE OCCULTISM OF SOUTHERN INDIA.

SOUTHERN India has always produced the greatest Aryan philosophers. Madavâchârya came from Southern India, and Shankarâchârya was born in Malabar; and at the present day there are high adepts and schools of occultism in Southern India. In the adept hierarchy, there are always seven classes of adepts, corresponding to the seven rays of the Logos. Two of these classes of adepts are so mysterious, and their representatives on earth are so rare, that they are seldom spoken of. Perhaps one or two adepts of these two mystrious orders appear every two or three thousand years.

It is probable that Buddha and Shankarâchârya come under this category.

But of the other five classes of adepts, representatives are always to be found on earth.

All five classes are represented in the Himâlayan school.

At present, it is unlikely that all five classes are represented in Southern India: though all the adepts of this and every other school must belong to one of these five classes.

It is a doctrine of the Southern Indian school that, though belonging to one of these five classes, and falling into one of these five rays, all of which are represented in the Himâlayan school, adepts in India, for example, need not be correlated to the Tibetan school,—need not dovetail, so to speak, into the *Guruparampara* chain of the Himâlayan school,—and need not therefore owe allegiance to one of the five *Chohans*, or chiefs of the five classes of adepts in Tibet.

When a great adept has passed away from incarnated life, his spiritual self may select some suitable person on whom to impress his teachings, who thus becomes his unconscious medium and apostle: this chosen exponent of the adept's wisdom may not recognise the source of his knowledge and power; to recognise their source is almost impossible, since these ideas are instilled into the inmost spirit of the man, the deep, secret place of his nature, from whence arise moral leadings and spiritual ideals. Such apostles have often found that their wisdom left them even in life, when their work was done the overshadowing adept then withdrawing his inspiration thus overshadowing by a high adept is what is called a divine incarnation, an *avatâr*.

It is probable that Shankaracharya was such an incarnation.

He was already a great adept when he was sixteen years old; at which time he wrote his great philosophical works.

It seems that Gautama Buddha was not such an incarnation as we see in him the actual life struggle of man striving to perfection, and not the fruition of a great soul who had already reached its goal. But in Shankarâchârya we see no such struggle; this is why we say he is a divine incarnation.

The seven rays we have spoken of represent the outflowing energy from the seven centres of force in the Logos; represent seven forces, so to speak, which must enter into every thing in the universe. No object can exist without the presence of each of these seven forces.

A man's past Karma determines which of the seven, or, practically speaking, five rays of occult wisdom he shall take his place in; but it is impossible to say that the fact of belonging to one of these rays indicates the presence in a man of any particular moral or mental quality; such as patience, honesty, or courage, on the one hand; or the poetic or artistic faculty, on the other.

The Southern Occult school divides the states of consciousness into three:—(1) *jagrat*, or waking consciousness; (2) *swapna*, or dream consciousness, and (3) *sushupti*, or the consciousness of dreamless sleep. As this classification stands, however, it is purposely obscure: to make it perfect, it must be understood that each of these three states is further divided into three states.

Let us take these in their order beginning with the lowest.

The *jagrat* concionsness is divided into three; (1) the *jagrat* of *jagrat*, which is ordinary waking consciousness; (2)

the *swapna* of *jagrat*, the ordinary dream state; (3) the *sushupti* of *jagrat*, which is dreamless sleep.

Similarly, the *swapna* state has three divisions; (1) the *jagrat* of *swapna*, which is the consciousness of waking clairvoyance; (2) the *swapna* of *swapna*, or somnambulic clairvoyance ; and (3) the *sushupti* of *swapna*, the consciousness of *Kamâ Loka*.

The *sushupti* state is also divided into three states: (1) the *jagrat* of *sushupti*, the conciousness of Devachan; (2) the *swapna* of *sushupti*, the consciousness in the interval between two planets ; and (3) the *sushupti* of *sushupti*, the true *arupa* (formless) consciousness which exists between two planetary rounds.

To make this clear, the following table may be useful:

Jagrat.	*Jagrat.*—Waking consciousness. *Swapna.*—Dreaming. *Sushupti.*—Dreamless sleep.
Swapna.	*Jagrat.*—Waking clairvoyance. *Swapna.*—Somnambulic clairvoyance. *Sushupti.*—Kama Loka.
Sushupti.	*Jagrat.*—Devachan. *Swapna.*—Between planets. *Sushupti.*—Between Rounds.

Above these nine stages, come the true mystical states of consciousness, to which the adepts have access.

These different states of consciousness mean simply this, that the one observer, the *atma*, or self, observes nine classes of objects ; the fact that the *atma* observes one class of objects is indicated by saying that such and such a state of consciousness is active.

In each of these classes of objects, which are on the different planes, there are five elements, each corresponding to one of the senses. In the view of the occultists of Southern India, it is erroneous to speak of seven senses, two being considered still undeveloped. It is true that there are seven factors in each plane of consciousness; but only five of these are senses, nor, in the view of this school, will there ever be two additional senses analogous to these.

The sixth factor is the mind, which rules and guides the senses, and draws deductions from their impressions when collected and arranged. The seventh factor is the *atma*, which is the observer of the generalization which the mind makes from the impressions of the senses. It is the self, the sense of "I," in us, behind which it is impossible to go, either in logic or in observation. The seven factors must be present on every plane: in dreaming, for example, objects corresponding to the senses of sight, touch, taste, smell and hearing, pass before the dreamer: his mind classifies these impressions and he feels the sense of "I," the observer which is the subject of these subjects. There is the sense of "I" on each plane, but it is not quite identical, only the kernel, or basic notion of "I" remained unchanged.

Corresponding to the five senses are the five classes of objects on each plane; or, as we may call them, the five qualities of impression, or five elements.

These are (1) earth, corresponding to the sense of smell; (2) water, corresponding to the sense of taste; (3) air, corresponding to the sense of touch; (4) fire, corresponding to the sense of sight; (5) ether, or Akash, corresponding to the sense of hearing. Each of these has its psychic counterpart; the counterpart of earth is magnetism; the counterpart of water is electricity; the counterpart of air is perhaps the forces discovered by Keely; while the counterparts of the other two are mystical forces the names of which it is useless to give.

When the seven rays we have spoken of proceed from the *logos*, they are separate, and subsequently co-mingle in the formation of all beings. When an individual begins his course of evolution, these rays are equally balanced in him, none preponderating more than another. In the course of time the man's actions, his *karma*, cause him to come particularly under the influence of one or other of the rays. Up this ray he must make his further progress, till he has succeeded in merging his life in the life of the Logos,—the grand fountain-head of light and power.

When this mergence takes place, the man does not suffer loss of individuality; rather he enjoyes an almost infinite extension of individuality. Each of the seven classes of *Logoi* has its own peculiar consciousness, and knows that this is so; that is to say, each *Logos* recognises its own light; but each *Logos* also participates in the life of all the other classes of *Logoi*; that is to say, the peculiar quality of their life is represented in it also; so that an individuality, in merging in a particular *Logos*, is not cut off from the consciousness of the other *Logoi*, but shares in, and experiences, their consciousness also.

We have said that the *Âtma* is represented on every plane, and the *Logos* is related to the *Âtma* on each of the planes. It is however, useless to attempt to understand the relation between the *Âtma* on any plane, and the Logos.

This relation must be known, however, after the last initiation, when man will thoroughly understand his spiritual nature.

After the last initiation, the adept thoroughly comprehends the relation of *Âtma* with the *Logos*, and the method of merging himself in the *Logos*, by which he obtains immortality: but it is a mistake to suppose that the life of the *Logos* rises up within the man at the last initiation, or that its light enters into him.

He understands his spiritual nature, and sees the way to the Logos; but it may take him several incarnations after the last initiation before he can merge in the Logos.

This philosophy recognises two paths, both having the same end, a glorified immortality.

The one is the steady natural path of progress through moral effort, and practice of the virtues. A natural, coherent, and sure growth of the soul is the result, a position of firm equilibrium is reached and maintained, which cannot be overthrown or shaken by any unexpected assault. It is the normal method followed by the vast mass of humanity, and this is the course Shankarâchârya recommended to all his Sannayasis and successors. The other road is the precipitous path of occultism, through a series of initiations. Only a few specially organised and peculiar natures are fit for this path.

Occult progress, growth along this path, is effected by the adept directing through the chela various occult forces, which enable him to obtain prematurely, so to speak, a knowledge of his spiritual nature: and to obtain powers to which he is not morally entitled by degree of his progess.

Under these circumstances it may happen that the chela loses his moral balance, and falls into the *dugpa* path.

From this it must not be concluded that the Southern Indian school of occultism regards adeptship and initiation as a mistake, as a violent and dangerous usurpation of nature's functions.

The adept hierarchy is as strictly a product of nature as a tree is: it has definite and indispensable purpose and function in the development of the human race : this function is to keep open the upward path, through which descend the light and leading without which our race would require to make each step by the wearisome, never ending method of trial and failure in every direction, until chance showed the right way.

In fact the function of the adept hierarchy is to provide religious teachers for the stumbling masses of mankind.

But this path is eminently dangerous to those who do not hold the talisman which ensures safety; this talisman is a perfectly unselfish, self-forgetting, self annihilating devotion to the religious good of mankind, a self-abnegation, which is not temporal, but must have no end for ever, and the object of which is the religious enlightenment of the human race. Without this talisman, though the progress of the chela may be very rapid for a time, a point will come when his upward advance will be arrested, when real moral worth will tell; and the man who progressed along the slow and steady path may be first to merge himself in the light of the *Logos*.

This school recommended as the best path for all, a devotion to virtue, a gradual withdrawal from the grosser material concerns, a withdrawal of the life forces from the outward world and its interests, and the direction of these forces to the inner life of the soul, until the man is able to withdraw himself within himself, so to speak, and then, turning round to direct himself towards the Logos and the spiritual life and away from the material plane; passing first into the astral life, and then into spiritual life, till at last the Logos is reached, and he attains *Nirvana*.

It is therefore wiser not to seek the path of chelaship; if the man is fit for it, his Karma will lead him to it imperceptibly and infallibly; for the path of occultism seeks the chela and will not fail to find him, when the fit man presents himself.

[The foregoing is a summary of a discussion with Mr. T. Subba Row, B.A., B.L., at the Adyar Library, on the 1st December 1888. *Ed.*]

To

MADAME H. P. BLAVATSKY,

Corresponding Secretary to the
Theosophical Society.

MADAME,

After a careful examination of the private and confidential "Letter" addressed to the Fellows of the London Lodge by its President and one of the Vice-Presidents, I could not help coming to the conclusion that the writers of the letter have greatly misunderstood the relations of the Himalayan Brotherhood to the Theosophical Society, and the peculiar circumstances under which Mr. Sinnett's book on Esoteric Buddhism was written. Their criticism, moreover, of the doctrines contained in that work seems to me illogical, and quite uncalled for, as I have attempted to show in the accompanying observations.

In accordance with the order of the Mahatmas and the desire of the Council, I have in every case given full reasons for the conclusions I have arrived at. Now I have the honor to request you to forward these observations to the London Lodge for the consideration of its members, with such additional remarks as you may think proper.

Yours, &c.,
T. SUBBA ROW, C. T. S.

Forwarded to the London Lodge Theosophical Society, for the consideration of its Fellows.

HEAD-QUARTERS OF THE
THEOSOPHICAL SOCIETY,
ADYAR (MADRAS), INDIA,
January 27, 1884.

By order,
H. P. BLAVATSKY,
Corresponding Secretary to the
Theosophical Society.

Observations on "a letter addressed to the Fellows of the London Lodge of the Theosophical Society, by the President and a Vice-President of the Lodge."

BY T. SUBBA ROW.

THERE is nothing said in the Rules of the Theosophical Society which is likely to induce one into the belief that the Society, as such, has any particular religious doctrines, or owes exclusive allegiance to any definite school or system of philosophy, or to any fraternity of religious teachers. On the other hand, the Rules clearly indicate that the Society is at full liberty to investigate any philosophical system, ancient or modern, with a view to ascertain the broad fundamental principles which form the basis of every school of religious philosophy, properly so called, and thereby "promote the principle of a Universal Brotherhood of humanity, without distinction of race or creed." It is, no doubt, expected that, after carefully inquiring into the doctrines of every such existing system, the Society will be able to "reconstruct religion on a scientific, and science on a religious, basis, and elaborate a perfect system of thought and rule of life;" just as a body of jurists may construct a perfectly scientific system of jurisprudence after investigating and comparing the various codes of law which are in force in all the civilized countries of this world. Before this grand object can be accomplished, every member is expected to study, to the best of his abilities, *any* system of religious philosophy which he may select, and place the result of his investigations before his fellow-members for comparison and discussion. But no member is allowed, by the Rules of the Association, to force his own individual opinions or beliefs on his fellow-members, or insist on their being accepted by them. The Society does not constitute a body of religious teachers, but is simply an association of investigators and inquirers.

These are the principles that are definitely laid down for the guidance of the Theosophical Society, with the approval and approbation of the great Himalayan Initiates, who are its real founders. Now as our Mahatmas have not offered themselves as the sole instructors of the members who join our Body, nor have they claimed "to monopolise for themselves their exclusive allegiance," therefore, no intention can be said to exist on their part to swerve from the above principles, or to interfere, in any way, with the work of any branch, so long as it acts within its prescribed limits. A doctrine, or fragments of a doctrine, although professedly emanating from the Mahatmas, has to rest on its own merits, and no other considerations are ever urged in its favour. Under such circumstances, there cannot be any valid reason for supposing that the system set forth in Mr. Sinnett's book "was intended by its compilers to supplant every other, and monopolise for themselves the exclusive allegiance of the Theosophical Society." It thus seems hardly necessary for Mr. E. Maitland to complain that the "choice of instructors" involved no exercise of judgment or that he was compelled to accept any one as an instructor, as nobody has yet, so far as we know, offered himself in this capacity. If Mr. Sinnett has *positively prohibited* any expression of dissent from, or criticism of, his book, or "of its supreme authority," as is alleged in the letter under examination, he is, no doubt, acting against the Rules of the Society; and it is fully competent for the London Lodge to prevent him from doing so, without any necessity for an appeal to the Head-quarters. But if Mr. Sinnett has merely refused to accept the view taken of the doctrines, embodied in his book, by Mrs. Kingsford and Mr. Maitland, and has urged in their favour such reasons as he has thought proper, his position is unimpeachable. Mr. Sinnett has as much right to explain his Esoteric Buddhism to the members of the London Lodge as Mrs. Kingsford and Mr. Maitland have to explain their esoteric significance of Christian symbology. The latter are no more entitled to interpret Mr. Sinnett's book in their own way, and claim the sanction of the head-quarters, or of the Mahatmas, for so doing, than the former is, to put his own construction on the "Perfect Way" and appeal to an authority from the same source to be regarded as the apostle alike of Eastern and of Western Theosophy. Nevertheless, Mrs. Kingsford and Mr. Maitland hold that the doctrines contained in Mr. Sinnett's book are atheistic, illogical, unscientific, incongruous and non-Buddhistic,—if accepted as literally true; and they are under the impression that those doctrines are presented in an allegorical or figurative garb, with the intention of testing the powers of discernment of the Western Theosophists, between truth and falsehood. They feel indignant, moreover, that Mr. Sinnett has been pertinaciously insisting on the correctness of his own interpretation, when that interpretation is such as to bring discredit upon the Himalayan Brotherhood, and their philosophy. This is the gist of their complaint and "the head and front" of Mr. Sinnett's offending. The gifted President of the London Lodge may, no doubt, imagine that she has discovered "the true solution of the Sphynx's riddle". The Sphynx in question, however, not being a Christian but a Hindu-Buddhistic Sphynx, may not be altogether prepared to commit suicide, in the manner indicated by the talented "writers of the 'Perfect Way.'" Rejecting four out of the five distinct hypotheses, proposed by Mr. Maitland, we may admit, with certain limitations, hypothesis the 3rd (page 25); namely, "that the system, as presented, is but a portion (or rather several portions picked out at random) of a system which, as a whole, is perfect ; and that, when received, it will prove complete and harmonious."

The Egyptian Sphynx propounded riddles, and Œdipus solved them ; while now the Buddhist Sphynx speaks the sober language of fact and the Œdipus of the 19th century is grievously misled: perhaps, because "truth is stranger than fiction." Mr. Sinnett's book has, indeed, served the purposes of "a test," but in a direction quite unexpected.

I may be now permitted to examine, in detail, the adverse criticism to which this work has been subjected. It is necessary, however, that I should preface my remarks with a few words regarding the circumstances under which Mr. Sinnett came to write his book, and the sources from which the doctrines, therein embodied, were derived.

After Messrs. Hume and Sinnett were introduced to, and put in communication with, the Mahatmas, they commenced asking them questions on various subjects, first to satisfy their own curiosity, and probably also to gauge the depth of the knowledge, possessed by them, respecting religious and scientific subjects. It was not, and could not have been, their intention, at first, to construct a complete system of philosophy from the meagre answers elicited.

The questions were first asked through Mme. Blavatsky, who, fearing to commit herself by treading upon forbidden ground, submitted them to our Guru, Mahatma M—, who checked off most of the questions proposed, as subjects to be explained only to regular Chelas at later initiations, and permitted very little information to be given upon most of the queries. This restriction and secrecy provoked much discontent. Neither Mr. Sinnett nor Mr. Hume could understand such a "policy of selfishness" that allowed them only "painfully doled out glimpses of the hidden higher knowledge," it was "a *sin* in the Teachers not to communicate to the world all the knowledge they possess. . .' which "they are *bound* to give. . ." &c., &c., as Mr. Hume thought. Such accusations expressed publicly in the *Theosophist* (see Sept. 1882, p.324-6), raised, from the first, a great discontent among the Hindu Chelas; and called forth a PROTEST from them, in the same number of our Magazine. After much solicitation, Mahatma K. H., who had nothing to do with the instructions at first received, promised to give Mr. Sinnett such information and explanation as would be permitted by the strict rules of the Brotherhood. The idea of publication being an after thought, questions were often put at random. They were not certainly such as to elicit complete and connected instructions on any particular subject; nor were the answers given, calculated to enable one to obtain a faultless, systematic, and complete exposition of department of the Esoteric doctrine, or of the knowledge possessed by the Esoteric Teachers. The Himalayan Adepts have never professed to instruct any particular section of the Theosophical Association. The Simla Theosophical Society was distinctly informed by one of them that it would be highly unadvisable, if not altogether impracticable, to depute one of the Adepts, or even an advanced Chela, to become the direct instructor of that Anglo-Indian Society. And when permission was subsequently granted to Mr. Sinnett to publish the *Fragments* (fragments, indeed !) of information obtained by him, it was left entirely to his discretion to present the philosophy embodied therein in the manner he thought proper. It is necessary also to give some idea of the materials that Mr. Sinnett possessed for writing his book, and the difficulties he had to encounter, before deciding upon the proper course to be adopted. Mr. Sinnett, I may here state, had from the Mahatmas, in addition to their lettters bearing on the planetary evolution, the Law of Karma, the nature of Devachanic Existence, the Seven Principles in Man, and other cognate subjects discussed by him as fully and as clearly as he was able, a few letters or communications touching the nature of Purusha and Prakriti, the commencement of cosmic evolution, the septenary constitution of the manifested Cosmos, the nature and evolution of the germs of the primary elements in nature (Mahabhutams), and some isolated subjects connected with physical science. But not one solitary subject among the last named class had he ever received, except in bare outlines. As to the details and their direct bearing upon other and far more important subjects, closely connected with the rest they have never been even remotely approached by the Masters—*revelations of this nature belonging strictly to the mysteries of Initiation.* Thus, the contents of some of the letters, owing to distinct prohibition, were introduced in a very incomplete form, while other subjects of vital importance, for the correct understanding of the whole, were not even mentioned in the book so severely criticized by Mr. E. Maitland—simply because they could not be given to Mr. Sinnett.* With these meagre materials, he undertook to write a book, and give the public in general, and the Theosophists in particular, an approximately correct conception of the system of Esoteric Science and Philosophy in the keeping of the "great Teachers of the Snowy Range." That he did as well as he has, is as surprising as it is highly creditable to his acute intelligence. But a complete system of Esoteric Philosophy which may be accepted as "a perfect system of thought and rule of life" must not only be able to explain fully and clearly the nature of the primal causes in the Cosmos and their ultimate effects in the manifested system, and to trace the whole current of evolution, in all its aspects, from its commencement up to the time of Pralaya, but also supply every individual with such a

* The specification implied in the second word of the title is itself misleading to all those who are not aware that "Buddhism" in this application refers entirely to the universal secret Wisdom,—meaning *spiritual enlightenment*—and not at all to the religion now popularly known as the philosophy of Gautama Buddha. Therefore, to set off Esoteric *Christianity* against Esoteric *Buddhism* (in the latter sense) is simply to offer one part of the whole against another such part—not one specified religion or philsophy the world over, having now the right to claim that it has the *whole* of the Esoteric truth. Brahmavidya (which is not Brahmanism or any of its numerous sects) and *Guptavidya*—the ancient and secret WISDOM-RELIGION, the inheritance of the Initiates of the *inner* Temple—have alone such a right. No doubt, Mrs. Kingsford, the gifted author of "The Perfect Way," is the most competent person in all Europe—I say it advisedly and unhesitatingly—to reveal the hidden mysteries of real Christianity. But, no more than Mr. Sinnett is she an initiate, and cannot, therefore, know anything about a doctrine, the real and correct meaning of which no amount of natural seership can reveal, *as it lies* altogether beyond *the regions accessible to untrained seers.* If revealed, its secrets would, for long years, remain utterly incomprehensible even to the highest physical sciences. I hope, this may not be construed into a desire of claiming any great knowledge for myself; for I certainly do not possess it. All that I seek to establish is, that such secrets *do* exist, and that, outside of the initiates, no one is competent to prove, much less to *disprove*, the doctrines now given out through Mr. Sinnett.—*H. P. Blavatsky.*

system of physical, intellectual, moral, and spiritual training, as would enable him to reach the highest condition of development possible; it must furnish mankind with such a code of morals and such a system of political and social organization as would enable them *en masse*, to move on rapidly and smoothly with the current of progressive evolution, and to reach the desired goal—the condition of spiritual perfection. Such a system, when it reaches the maximum of elaboration, assumes the form of a deductive science in common with every particular branch of science. And just as every branch of science, entitled to the dignity of that name, has to adopt the inductive method in its infancy, so Esoteric Science must also pursue a similar method in the preliminary stages of its progress to be able to construct religion on a really scientific basis. As Mr. Sinnett had neither the knowledge nor the materials that would have enabled him to construct a complete system of Esoteric Science and Philosophy, he had to content himself with simply presenting, in a comprehensible form, to the members of the Theosophical Society and the intelligent public, a collection of interesting and useful information. This he did with regard to the nature and direction of planetary evolution and the constitution of man, and such kindred subjects as are calculated to throw some light, at least, on a few of the profoundest questions of religious philosophy, and indicating, in some measure, the lines on which further enquiry would prove profitable. He thought it prudent to abstain from recording in his book any decisive opinions regarding the real nature of the primal causes, operating in the Cosmos, the highest spiritual principle in man, and the first beginnings of cosmic evolution, or any other subject, equally momentous to religious metaphysics and dogmatic theology. Such isolated remarks as are to be found in his book touching them, are merely intended to convey to the reader's mind some conception, however imperfect, which it is necessary to realise for the purpose of clearly understanding the operation of particular laws, or the nature of a particular group of phenomena. But none of these are intended to supply the place of a complete exposition of the Esoteric Philosophy connected with those subjects ; nor do they amount to a denial of the possibility of any other conception, or the correctness of any other view, which may be entertained with respect to other phases of the Cosmos. In elucidating Esoteric Philosophy, it is not seldom necessary to adopt the same course, that is almost always adopted, for the sake of convenience, by a teacher of astronomy, in explaining to the student the relation between the zenith, the pole, the equator, the ecliptic and the horizon; the definitions of right ascension and declination, latitude and longitude; the causes of the change of seasons, the application of spherical trignometry for the solution of astronomical problems, and various other subjects, with reference to the *geocentric* system. The assumption that the Earth is the fixed centre, and that all the heavenly bodies revolve round it, is doubtless wrong; but such a conception is found necessary for the easier explanation of the subjects above enumerated. Again, when at a further stage of progress the heliocentric system is expounded, the sun is assumed to occupy in space a fixed position. This assumption is equally erroneous, as it is now ascertained that the sun has a proper motion in space. Suppose, a professor of astronomy, taking into consideration all these motions, and ascertaining the complicated and peculiar curve which a given point on the Earth's surface traces in space, were to begin to account to his pupils for these most ordinary phenomena: is it not evident that he and his students would soon get into a terrible state of confusion? Can it be contended, under such circumstances, that every teacher of astronomy, at the present time, who places the geocentric system before his students, for the purpose of giving certain explanations, is ignorant of the heliocentric system and the proper motion of the so-called fixed stars in space? or that he is giving a wrong explanation of the phenomena dealt with; or that he is speaking in riddles which require an Œdipus for their solution; or that he is employing allegorical language for the purpose of wilfully misleading his students and testing their powers of discrimination between fact and fancy? It will be easily conceded that all such suppositions must be equally unreasonable, the preliminary conception in question being introduced merely for the sake of convenience. This possibility, however, is entirely left out of consideration by Mr. Sinnett's critics. To exclude every ground of misapprehension, it is necessary for me to state, at this point, that the foregoing remarks are applicable only to the particular class of observations in Esoteric Buddhism to which reference is already made.

While on the subject, I may as well point out that Mr. Sinnett has not given in his book as much explanation as he might have given even with the scanty information in his possession, regarding cosmogony, the nature of Purusha and Prakriti, the germs out of which the elements were evolved, and some other subjects above alluded to. But, besides the very good reason that his limited knowledge prescribed imperatively such a prudential policy, the following reasons may also be assigned for the course adopted by him. They will, I trust, be found satisfactory when closely and impartially examined:

I. Almost every religion, every dogmatic system of theology, and every sectarian doctrine has some decisive opinions to offer regarding these subjects, and it is in connection with these questions that sectarian strife and casuistry have always raged with unmitigated fury, for thousands of years. In these days of inquiry and investigation, such controversy can be set at rest not by appealing to the authority of this or that religious book, or religious teacher, but by introducing into the discussion the same scientific method which is found so very useful in other departments of human inquiry. It is necessary for such a course, that all the phenomena which may throw light on these subjects should be clearly observed and closely examined. The nature of the effects must be scrutinised before any valid inferences can be drawn regarding the nature of their cause. This is the only way open to the public at large. An initiate may be able to perceive the eternal verities by his developed spiritual power, and those who rely upon his statements may take them on trust. But it is impossible to expect the secrets of initiation to be made public, or even if made public, to be accepted unchallenged, in these days, simply on the authority of even the highest adept. Under such circumstances, when religious prejudices are yet so very strong, and when the public is not scientifically prepared to test the correctness of the views of the Himalayan Mahatmas—it is not desirable to publish them in any other but a fragmentary form.

II. As already pointed out, the Mahatmas have no intention whatsoever of assuming the attitude of world-instructors; nor are they in any way anxious that the public, or any portion of it, or even any of our own members, should relinquish their own settled religious opinions, and accept their views without inquiry. As any explanation regarding the subjects in question is likely to come directly into collision with the religious doctrines prevalent in various parts of the civilized world, it will be premature to give out any such explanation, until the public is prepared to test the correctness of their respective religious dogmas, in the same manner in which the validity of a scientific hypothesis is tested. In a word, they must wait until humanity has evolved up to the plane of spiritual intuitiveness, or take the crushing responsibility of trying to force artificially such a preternatural psychic growth. Very slight occult experience is sufficient to show how futile would be the task, how disastrous the failure, how direful the reaction in its consequences, were the MASTERS to adopt any other policy!

III. It is impossible to give *complete explanations* regarding most of the subjects touched upon in "Esoteric Buddhism," *without disclosing some of the secrets of initiation.*

IV. It is extremely difficult to express in English the abstract and metaphysical ideas connected with these subjects. Until many of these ideas are gradually made familiar to the mind of the Western reader, any attempt at a general explanation of these questions in the language of ordinary life, is likely to be resented, to provoke failure, and may even lead to some very dangerous misconceptions.

V. It must be frankly admitted that Mr. Sinnett himself has not thoroughly understood much of the information given to him by the Mahatmas on several subjects, (as for instance the part played by the 8th sphere in the scheme of evolution, and the opprobrium thrown upon the *visible* moon,)—he, having no time to obtain the required additional explanations, during his short stay at the Head-quarters, on his way to England. For these reasons, Mr. Sinnett was obliged to refrain from introducing into his work anything like a systematic discussion of more than one subject from the stand-point of the Esoteric Philosophy of the Himalayan Mahatmas. The plan, however, that he has adopted is in perfect accordance with the intentions of the MASTERS, and is well adopted to the programme laid down for the guidance of the Theosophical Society. "Esoteric Buddhism," in short, is not intended to be a complete and systematic exposition of the religious philosophy of the Initiated Fraternity, or an authoritative declaration to Theosophists in general of our Teachers' views which they are called upon to accept "as necessarily final and beyond appeal." It is merely intended to be an important contribution to the mass of information, which, it is the object of the Theosophical Society to accumulate, for the purpose of leading ultimately to the evolution of a complete system of philosophy. If any member of the London Lodge was led to anticipate, from the publication of Mr. Sinnett's book, "a formal communication to the world, in a crisis of the gravest description, and for the first time in the world's history, *of (all) the most sacred mysteries of existence*"—he was entirely mistaken; and if any member expected that the publication in question would supply the requirements of "a prefect system of thought and rule of life" and is now disappointed, no one is responsible for his disappointment. It is altogether unfair to condemn Mr. Sinnett's book as wholly misleading or allegorical, and undervalue the important services rendered by him to the Theosophical Association, on the ground that his work does not satisfy the unwarranted expectations of a few Theosophists who are more sanguine than prudent.

In order to show the correctness of my assertions, I shall endeavour to point out how far the criticisms of Mrs. Kingsford and Mr. Maitland are justified, and how far they are misdirected and erroneous.

For the sake of convenience, I shall arrange the remarks of Mrs. Kingsford and Mr. Maitland on "Esoteric Buddhism" with reference to the subjects to which they relate. That part of their criticism which refers to the views put forth by Mr. Sinnett regarding Purusha and Prakriti claims our attention first.

Mr. Maitland's first and most important objection against "Esoteric Buddhism" is, that its doctrine is distinctly atheistic, and that its statements regarding the nature and attributes of Parabrahma are inconsistent with each other. It is admitted, however, that a considerable number of the passages, quoted by the critic from Mr. Sinnett's writings are not atheistic in their tone; and that the existence of a universal spiritual principle prior to "any organized or derived entities," is distinctly postulated therein, under the same of Parabrahm, which is spoken of as "the motion, that animates Cosmic matter" and as "the energy of the universe." It is, I believe, an acknowledged canon of interpretation, that, when a large number of dispersed statements regarding a particular subject are to be found in any book, the author's views on that subject should be gathered from a careful comparison of all such statements, and a critical examination of the contexts in which they appear, and not from the literal meaning of particular words or phrases. When metaphysical or philosophical difficulties are involved in any subject, and the phraseology in which it has been discussed by various writers has been rendered extremely vague and uncertain by the different connotations attached to the words used, it becomes absolutely necessary to proceed according to this method. And this necessity is considerably enhanced in the case of "Esoteric Buddhism"

—as a complete discussion of the subjects involved is not undertaken by the author. But Mr. Sinnett's critic has thought it proper to depart from this principle, for the not overkind purpose of detecting contradictions and absurdities where there are really none. It now remains to be seen, how far he has gained his object even by the false cannon of criticism adopted. We are informed by him that the doctrine "openly avowed" in "Esoteric Buddhism" is "distinctly atheistic." So far as I can see, there is no such *open avowal* in any part of the book; nor are we informed on what page we are to search for it. The assertion made by the critic is, therefore, a mere matter of inference; and a very painful and circuitous process of reasoning is adopted to establish the strange proposition. It is stated that the epithet "atheistic" is used "not reproachfully but descriptively." But the required description is not given by the plaintiff though it is so very essential for a just appreciation of the correctness of his reasoning and the validity of his *inference.* It is left to his readers to ascertain the bearing of his conclusions by an examination of the reasons assigned for them. This is by no means an easy task; and the reasons for, and against, his inferences are, moreover, left in a tangled maze of confusion. When extricated from it, the reasons which are intended to support the position may be enumerated in the following order:—

I. "The Parabrahm or spirit of matter is motion," we are told,—from the stand-point of "Esoteric Buddhism."

II. "Elsewhere (p. 153) it is called Energy."

III. It is declared (p. 182) that the end of all existence is the "merging by man of his glorified individuality in that sum total of all consciousness, which Esoteric Metaphysicians treat as absolute consciousness, which is non-consciousness."

IV. "Objection is taken (by Mr. Sinnett) to the being of

God, on the ground that it would be incompatible with freedom of will on the part of man."

I shall examine these reasons *seriatim*.

I. The first reason for the inference involves a misstatement of the author's view. Mr. Sinnett says that the unmanifested basis of the manifested cosmos is "matter *animated* by motion, its Parabrahm or spirit" (p. 183). Motion that *animates* Cosmic matter is not equivalent to motion in general. The motion of a cricket ball, for instance, is not to be considered as motion that *animates* matter. Molecular motion, in the particles of a decomposing body, is, no doubt, motion, but it is not motion that *animates* the dead body. The qualifying clause is used by Mr. Sinnett with a definite object. Parabrahma is often spoken of as "the One Life" by the Buddhist philosophers, and is considered as the Mahachaitanyam (an equivalent expression) by the Adwaitees. And even Kabalists have described En-soph as "The life that is no life." The word "animates" is calculated to draw the reader's attention to this aspect of Parabrahma. I fail to see the incongruity really involved in further investing Paramatma with the attributes of motion. When heat, light, and electricity are the manifestations, or effects, of particular kinds of motion, the material plane of action being the same in the opinion of modern science, there is nothing very ridiculous in the assertion that the life existing in Mulaprakriti and manifesting itself in various forms in differentiated and organized Prakriti, is but the effect of a mysterious kind of motion. Perhaps, we shall be informed by Mr. Maitland that the *First Cause* cannot have the essential attributes of motion, as some pre-existing force or energy is required to produce this motion. But there is no necessity for any such supposition. Every force or energy in nature, when properly examined, will be found to have in itself some kind of motion or other. When correctly stated, the author's assertion amounts to saying that Parabrahma pervades the infinite expanse of cosmic matter—Mulaprakriti—and consequently every differentiated and organized form in it; that it has the essential attributes of motion, and that the peculiar characteristic of this motion is, that the life existing everywhere throughout the Cosmos, whether in its primary or secondary aspects, is its manifestation or effect. It is not pretended that this amounts to a *complete* description of Parabrahma. But it is maintained that it is a *correct* representation of one of its phases. The critic is welcome to show, if he can, that this description is wrong; but why should he cover the main question with a cloud of irrelevant matter? If this amounts to atheism in his opinion, so be it; Mr. Maitland is fully entitled to have his own definition of the word.

II. The second reason for the inference is likewise based upon a misconstruction of the author's views. On p. 153 of his work, Mr. Sinnett has defined Parabrahma from the stand-point of Adwaita philosophy, and in the following words: "Brahma or Parabrahma, is thus a passive, incomprehensible, unconscious principle, but the essence, one life, or energy of the universe," and here, Mr. Maitland asserts again that Parabrahma is called energy (in any form apparently) by the author! He further contends that a principle, or entity, possessing the attributes of motion cannot be considered as the "energy of the universe"; evidently forgetting that motion *in the abstract* is one thing, and the object in motion—quite another. Energy is defined by him as the cause of motion, and if motion is not energy under any circumstances, in that gentleman's opinion, one kind of motion can never be the cause of another kind of motion. For instance, it will be wrong, in his opinion, to say that the motion of the particles composing a certain quantity of steam caused by its inherent tendency to expand, produces the motion of the steam engine! This, I believe, will make clear that Mr. Sinnett's statement involves no such absurdity. Energy is but the statical aspect of motion, and motion is but the kinetic aspect of energy. Parabrahma has both these aspects. During Pralaya it is the sum total of the energy of the Infinite Universe, and during the peroid of Cosmic activity it manifests itself as the motion in Cosmic matter, which is the basis of Life, in all its forms and aspects. And this, again, is atheistic in Mr. Maitland's opinion.

III. It is more difficult to perceive how the third reason is intended to prove the charge of atheism. The author has stated that the consciousness realized in Nirvana is "absolute consciousness," which is "non"—consciousness. It is absolute consciousness, because the soul is fully *en rapport* with the universal mind—the Adam Kadmon of the Kabalists, and the Adonai of the Jews ;—and it is non-consciousness, because it is not consciousness in any way similar to the consciousness realized by us in any of the conditions with which we are familiar. But we are once more informed that this also is an atheistical doctrine. In Mr. Maitland's opinion, therefore, a doctrine is said to be atheistical when it declares that the consciousness realized in Nirvana, or the highest paradise,* is not similar to the consciousness realized by man in his objective condition of existence, because, according to our opponent's Esoteric Philosophy, the case is entirely different. In his ideas, it seems, even in Heaven we are not going to be deprived of our enjoyments and amusements of our picnics, theatres and fashionable dress-parties.

IV. The fourth and the last reason, in support of the allegation made, has no foundation whatever, except in the imagination of the learned Vice-President of the "London Lodge." On p. 185 of his work, the author merely points out that the doctrines propounded therein are free from the difficulties generally raised in connection with the doctrine of free will and pre-destination, in the ordinary theological sense. To this Mr. Sinnett's opponent replies that the Esoteric Buddhist

---

* It is very unfortunate that the English language has no word to indicate a higher state of existence than what is realized in *Swaraga, or Devachan*.

doctrine has contrived to get rid of the idea of God (Mr. Maitland's "idea" probably) for the purpose of avoiding these difficulties. This is clearly fallacious. In the Esoteric doctrine, Parabrahma is not a matter of inference. If the necessities of logic and theoretical metaphysics have not led the students of Esoteric science to adopt any particular view regarding the "first cause," it is because their knowledge is derived by a more direct method ; and thus, they being most pronounced gnostics, it becomes the more ridiculous to suspect them of agnosticism. Highly developed spiritual powers, and a keen sense of intuitive perception have enabled them to arrive at the truth without any reference whatever to the difficulties of theoretical religious philosophy, as conceived by Western minds. Mr. Maitland is simply trying to throw discredit on "Esoteric Buddhism" by the dint of far fetched and strained constructions, in direct connection with those interminable and meaningless controversies regarding free will and pre-destination, which occupy such a prominent place in the arena of Western religious speculation, and are so happily conspicuous by their absence from the plane of Hindu and Buddhist religious thought.

From this it becomes quite clear, that, *(a)* in our critic's opinion, the denial of a personal God is synonymous with rank atheism; and *(b)* that the teachings of "Esoteric Buddhism," as really stated by the author, are, in no way, inconsistent, *illogical*, or unscientific; but that simply Mr. Maitland has run away with a very hazy idea of what those teachings are, in truth. Whatever those teachings may be, one thing is certain: they are neither atheistic nor even materialistic in the ordinary sense of the words; for, if anything, they are *pantheistic*. Mr. Maitland's definition of atheism seems to be one of a very complicated character. From his stand-point, an atheist is to be defined as one who believes the doctrines of Esoteric Buddhism, or entertains the same opinions as Mr. Sinnett regarding Parabrahma; and this is to be considered as the outcome of the whole discussion !

The second part of Mr. Maitland's objection is to the effect that expressions are used in Esoteric Buddhism, which imply "a conscious, intelligent and, therefore, personal being as subsisting prior to any organized or derived entities," and are, therefore, inconsistent with the statements examined above. The reasons assigned for this new objection are equally unsatisfactory, as I shall presently show.

Such expressions as "the purposes of nature," "the continuous effort made by nature," and others, similarly worded, do not imply the existence of a "personal" God. I am surprised to find that an argument of this nature is introduced into a serious philosophical discussion. Every man who believes in the diurnal rotation of the earth, ordinarily speaks of sunrise and sunset. Can it be advanced as a serious argument against the existence of this rotation that the very language used disproves the theory? The argument brought forward is precisely similar to the baseless objections advanced against Mills' Cosmological theory, on the ground that the ordinary language in use supports the realistic theory. The English language is no more, than any other language, the special creation of philosophers against whose authority there is no appeal. For, it is developed by the national common sense of England and the usages of every day life; and certainly no great philosophical acumen can be claimed for it under these circumstances. If Mr. Maitland's objection is admitted, all figurative language will have to be studiously eschewed from philosophical writings. If there is, however, any real foundation beneath the objection, it is tantamount to saying that the existence of a definite method in the order of Cosmic evolution necessitates the admission of a personal God. This question, however, will be more fully discussed further on, in connection with Mr. Maitland's inferences from the existence of Cosmic laws.

We are informed by the critic that Theism finds expression in the statements made regarding the 7th principle in man, and thus shows Mr. Sinnett's inconsistency.

Now, Mr. Maitland's endeavours to catch Theism "under yet another mode" of expression are very unsuccessful. Although," it is urged, "the name [of Theism] is repudiated, the idea is retained under the term "Seventh Principle" (p. 179) or "Universal Spirit," which is described as "existing everywhere and operating on matter, provoking the existence of man himself, and the world in which he lives, and the future conditions towards which he is pressing." "The Seventh Principle, indefinable for us in our present state of enlightenment, is," we are further assured, "the only God recognized by Esoteric knowledge, and no personification of this can be otherwise than symbolical. It is, we are told, "the all-pervading Judge, to whom men have to give account." Unfortunately, Mr. Maitland has omitted to define the term Theism, and thus prevented us from examining the process by which he has evolved that faith out of the above quotations from "Esoteric Buddhism." All that, under the circumstances, remains for us to do is, to show that Mr. Sinnett's statements, although the word "God" occurs therein, do not warrant the acceptance of a personal God. It is not certainly justifiable to convert the "Seventh Principle" or "Universal Spirit" into a Jehovah, from what has been said of it in one place, utterly regardless of the reiterations about it, in other connections. In one passage, for instance (p. 176), we find Mr. Sinnett saying:—"The one and chief attribute of the Universal Spiritual principle, the unconscious but ever active life-giver, is to expand and shed; that of the Universal Material Principle is to gather in and fecundate." Then on the same page and the following *creation* is denied *in toto*. Without endorsing the phraseology adopted by Mr. Sinnett, which is, however, that of all the Kabalists and may be even found in Eliphas Levi's "Dogme et Rituel de la Haute Magie," as in the great book of Khiu-ti, I may safely assert that no Theist would be over-anxious to claim the author of "Esoteric Buddhism" as a fellow-worshipper. The argument founded upon Mr. Sinnett's use of such words as "God" and "Judge" has already been disposed of. In fact, such criticism only reminds one of

Lamb's North Briton friend, whose sense of propriety was outraged by the commonest figures of speech.

The tenour of the whole argument on theistic or atheistic character of "Esoteric Buddhism," most unmistakably betrays a great want of comprehension on the part of the critic of Buddhism in general, and *esoteric* Buddhism especially. A system, of which one part appears as theistic and another part atheistic, ought certainly not to be placed in either of the categories and then condemned as self-contradictory, so long as a third course remains open. And unless he has shown that the division of religious philosophy, as above, into theism and atheism, is a division by dichotomy, it is unreasonable for him to talk of Mr. Sinnett's wholly untenable "radical inconsistencies and contradictions;" and at the same time, it shows him hardly acquainted with the subtle monism of the pantheistic philosophy as taught in our great schools. Mr. Maitland seems to have endeavoured to lay the doctrines contained in "Esoteric Buddhism" on the Procrustean bed of his own ideas, and, failing in the attempt, is now seeking to discredit them as inconsistent with themselves. As well call Shankaracharya, the greatest Occultist and adept of all the ages, the founder, of the *Adwita* school, the master whose followers are to this day referred to as *Prachanna Bauddhas* (Buddhists in disguise), so identical are the two teachings—one day an atheist, and a theist the next.

The next argument that Mr. Maitland brings forward (p. 15), comes to this: since law implies a person, the expression of whose will the law is, therefore, Mr. Sinnett by speakig of "the law of evolution" tacitly admits the existence of a personal God, whose impressed will is the law of the Universe. This is a very extraordinary argument. I could hardly believe that the talented Vice-President of the London Lodge would have failed to recognize the difference between the command of the sovereign power in a political body, and the sequence of causation implied in a natural law, especially after such a masterly exposition of the subject by such thinkers as Mill and Austin. My surprise becomes greater still to find Mrs. Kingsford, with her splendid natural gifts, standing sponsor to such an intellectual deformity! It is now pefectly clear that Mr. Maitland's statements that "these citations imply theism," and that they "describe precisely that which the theist means by a personal God," are merely gratuitous assumptions.

Then comes a point, the objection to which involves a *totally* inaccurate presentation of Mr. Sinnett's statements. "This Eternal Something," says Mr. Maitland, "it is further declared, although there is nothing but Matter, Motion, Space, and Duration, consists of two principles, the Universal Spiritual Principle and the Universal Material Principle, which, when separate, are unconscious and non-existing, and only when brought together (by whom or from whence, it is not said) become consciousness and life."

Before proceeding to answer the objections arising out of what Mr. Sinnett is represented to have said above, it is necessary to tally it with what Mr. Sinnett actually says. On page 176 of "Esoteric Buddhism" we read:—"The one eternal, imperishable thing in the Universe which Universal Pralayas themselves pass over without destroying, is that which may be regarded indifferently as Space, Duration, Matter and Motion, not as something having these four attributes, but a something which *is* these four things at once, and always. And evolution takes its rise in the *atomic polarity which motion engenders.* In cosmogony the *positive and the negative*, or *the active and the passive, forces* correspond to the *male and female principles.* The spiritual efflux enters into the veil of Cosmic matter; the active is attracted by the passive principle; and if we may here assist imagination by having recourse to old occult symbology—the great Nag—the serpent, emblem of eternity, attracts its tail to its mouth, forming thereby the circle of eternity, or rather cycles in eternity. The one and chief attribute of the Universal Spiritual Principle the unconscious but ever active life—giver, is to expand and shed; that of the Universal Material Principle to gather in and fecundate. Unconscious and non-existing when separate, they become consciousness and life when brought together. " If this is not sound, orthodox Kabalistic and " Hermetic Philosophy " to which Mrs. Kingsford confesses she feels herself " especially attracted, " then Eliphas Levi has written his *theistic* " dogmas and Ritual of High Magic " in vain ? Let the Fellows of the " London Lodge " open his Vol. I ; and see what this great master of *Christian* Esoteric Doctrine says on the subject, on pages 123–26 *et seq*, and then draw their conclusions. Mr. Sinnett's language is that of every occultist, who refuses to substitute his own personal fancy for the accepted theories of the ancient Hermetic Philosophy.*

Now, from an examination of Mr. Maitland's citations with the original, with special reference to the passages italicised, it will appear that what Mr. Sinnett does say is not that the Eternal Something does " consist " of the two principles named, but that the latter are the two force-emanating poles engendered by Parabrahman, considered the animating motion of the Universe (Purusha), in itself, the exhaustless fountain of

* I would draw the attention of Mrs. Kingsford, Mr. Maitland, and the other Members of the London Lodge to that whole chapter in the work cited, and ask them to compare its grossly materialistic language with the explanation offered on the same subject by Mr. Sinnett. If Eliphas Levi's "number of *gnosis*"...this "Adam, the human tetragrammaton resumed in the mysterious *jod*, the image of the Kabalistic *phallus* ...the insertion of the verticle phallus in the horizontal cteis forming the *stauros* of the gnostics, or the philosophical cross of the Masons, in the mysterious language of the Talmudic Kabalists"—as he calls it--can be preferred to the chaste images offered by the Eastern Esotericism, it is only by those who are unable to divorce their thoughts from an anthropomorphic God and his *material* progeny, the Adam of the Old Testament. Withal, the idea and substance, if not the language, are identical; for Elphas Levi expounding the true Hermetic Philosophy, in the course language of the Jewish Seers and for the benefits of a Christian born public says neither more nor less than what was given to, and written by, Mr. Sinnett in the far more philosophical phraseology of "Esoteric Buddhism."—*H. P. Blavatsky*.

material existence (Prakriti). Bearing this explanation in mind, many of Mr. Maitland's difficulties will entirely disappear. The Universal Spiritual Principle or Purusha does not certainly exist as a separate entity at the time of the Mahapralaya, but is interblended with Prakriti (the Material Principle) and both exist in their eternal and ineffable state of Parabrahman.* When by the operation of the chain of causation, which is embodied in Parabrahman, the emanating impulse is awakened, the two principles spring forth into Being, and by their mutual action produce the manifested Cosmos. Some reflection might give us a glimpse of the grand fact that prior to the moment when the emanation takes place no duality can possibly exist. The primal duality, Prakriti and Purusha are each the necessary condition of the other's existence. This fact is sufficiently well implied by what Mr. Sinnett says of the "atomic polarity which motion engendered." One pole cannot exist without the other. And now will be thrown into bold relief what Mr. Sinnett means when he says:—"Unconscious and non-existing when separate, they become consciousness and life when brought together"—by their inherent quiddity, the *Swabhavat* of the Buddhists.† The next objection of Mr. Maitland comes to this:—If Purusha is "unconscious" and Prakriti is "unconscious," how can consciousness evolve at all? The first idea to be clearly grasped, is the

---

* In the *Rigveda* it is said that prior to the period of evolution in the celebrated Mantra beginning, *Násadasit nasadasit* (X. 129)—" neither *asat* or Prakriti nor *sat* or Purusha was " but the one Life latent in the one Element, " was breathing without breath."

† The entire chain of Mr. Maitland's reasoning is vitiated by a false assumption. He seems to think that Prakriti and Purusha existed prior to the period of Cosmic activity as to separate entities and required some motor to bring them together to interact on each other, just as oxygen and hydrogen are caused to combine chemically by the agency of electricity. But the real fact is that Prakriti and Purusha are separate entities to us *only subjectively*. We can only *imagine* that they are separate and then try to comprehend their nature from that stand-point. In point of fact neither of them can exist by itself.

nature of Prakriti and Purusha. This subject, however, need not be pursued at length, as it has been pretty fully treated by me in an article in the *Theosophist* for July last (Vol. IV, No. 10.), to which reference may be made for fuller information.

Now to turn to the evolution of conscious existence. If it is maintained that the great first cause—Parabrahman —is unconscious, in the sense that it is the negation of all consciousness—it is a great fallacy. If, on the other hand, it is imagined to be conscious in our sense of consciousness—it is equally fallacious. If words are to have any meaning, conscious existence involves three elements—the Knower, the Knowledge and the Known. Now Parabrahman is "Only One without a second"—*ekamevadvitiyam*,—or, in other words, the unification of the three elements of conscious existence, mentioned above—the break-up of the three receptacles as it is technically called—*triputi bhangam.* Therefore there can be no conscious existence in Parabrahman. On the other hand, if Parabrahman is regarded as absolute unconsciousness violence will be done to the first principles of our philosophy. Unconsciousness is the negation of every form of consciousness, and therefore, without any relation thereto; to derive the latter from the former is to establish some sort of relation between the two, which, as we have seen is impossible. Therefore, Parabrahman is not unconsciousness, and as has been showed before, it is not conscious, in the sense the word must always be used. We are, therefore, reduced to the conclusion that Parabraman is *absolute* consciousness, or *nirupadhikam maha-chaitanyam,* as the Upanishad says. This, again, is verified by the experience of practical occultists. The emanations of Mulaprakriti become conscious by the reflection of this absolute consciousness. By the interposition of the veils of Maya, this absolute consciousness gives rise to conditioned *Sopadhikam*—consciousness, or conscious existence. The details of the process cannot be entered into here, as they touch many grand secrets of initiation.

The next thing I notice, shall be Mr. Maitland's criticism with regard to the position assigned to the Dhyan Chohans in the scheme of Cosmic evolution. His objection relates first to the question—how the first Dhyan Chohans could evolve, if there be no personal God to produce them consciously? and then urges, "if the assistance of the Dhyan Chohans be indispensible to the production of the universe" how came "the universe to reach such perfection as to produce Dhyan Chohans in the first instance, when there were no Dhyan Chohans to aid it?" If Mr. Maitland has brought forward these objections for the purpose of eliciting further information, all I have to say is, that such information will be forthcoming when the ground is prepared for it by the doctrines which he now criticises. But if there are intended to imperil the position taken up by Mr. Sinnett, I have only to point out that Mr. Maitland puts entirely out of calculation the agency involved in the ideation of the Universal Mind, the Demiurgos of Western Mystics. It must not, however, be here understood, that the ideation of the Universal Mind is set in motion by an act of that mind's volition; quite the contrary. The ideation of the Demiurgos is governed by an eternal chain of causation, and is absolutely involuntary. A flood of light will be thrown on this subject by letter from one of the Mahatmas, now in the possession of Mr. Sinnett. Then, again, it must be remembered that all Dhyan Chohans are not evolved in one and the same way. It may as well be here remarked, that to talk of the first Dhyan Chohans—is slightly illogical. The chain of Manvantara and Pralaya—"Cosmic Day and Night"—is an endless one. As there can be no beginning of eternity, so there can be no first Dhyan Chohans.

I shall now pass to a question of great importance. The gifted President maintains that the septenary constitution of man is the same as the seven productive *vikaras* or products of Prakriti, as given by Kapila, in his Sankhya philosophy: only inverted and more materialized. I regret to have to point out that the talented lady is here entirely in the wrong. If she takes the last of the seven *vikaras* she would find that it is a subtile element as far removed from the gross outer human body, *the first* principle in Mr. Sinnett's classification —as can possibly be imagined. In the system of Kapila, whatever relation it may bear to the system adopted in "Esoteric Buddhism" the *tatwas* (or principles) are not certainly those mentioned in Mr. Sinnett's book. The true relation has, to a certain extent, been shadowed forth in an article on the "Septenary Principle in Esotericism," published in the *Theosophist* for July last (Vol. IV, No. 10). But the best exposition of the subject will be found in another letter from the Mahatma to Mr. Sinnett, where, if one will but look for it, the order is correctly given, and special attention is drawn to the difference in the two classifications. The sevenfold division, that appears in "Esoteric Buddhism," is not given by Kapila in the same form. I am sorry to have to come to the conclusion, that the gifted lady has, besides misunderstanding Kapila, hardly bestowed on Mr. Sinnett's book that degree of attention that should be given to a work, before it is subjected to the fiery ordeal of such merciless criticism.

Further on, the President finds fault with Mrs. Sinnett for having degraded, as she thinks Kapila's Prakriti by calling it "molecular matter,' which, according to her, has the effect of charging it with divisibility. I have carefully gone through Mr. Sinnett's book and have to confess my inability to identify the passage where the peccant expression occurs. But apart from that, it is impossible to conceive how the word "essence," which she proposes as a better substitute, can be freed from the charge of materialistic degradation attaching to the phrase against which her own criticism is directed; the more so as ultimate "molecular," hence, "motion" is entirely unknown to modern science, from which alone Mrs. Kingsford can derive her conception of molecules. She will feel the force of this argument, if she only tries to frame a scientific definition of the word "essence." Her strictures on Mr. Sinnett's use of the words "matter" and "motion," clearly show that she has woefully misconceived the nature of both, and that all her animadversions in this connection hang—like those of her co-worker—upon her own misconceptions.

There is no portion of Mrs. Kingsford's and Mr. Maitland's objections which is so full of erroneous notions, as that relating to the Dhyan Chohans. Mrs. Kingsford, on page 7 of the pamphlet under notice, says:—"There is no doctrine in his (Mr. Sinnett's) book which is more repugnant to common sense, and to the intuitive perception of the fitness of things, than that which attributes the physical creation of the worlds to perfected men or Dhyan Chohans. We are told that they and they alone, are the artificers of the planets and the re-constructors of the Universe." Here, if nowhere else, we find the gifted President unable to rise entirely above the peculiarities of her sex. This is, indeed, an instance of what Shakespeare calls a "lady's reason." Before dealing with that lady's statement, I shall correct a slight inaccuracy into which she has fallen. Mr. Sinnett does not attribute "physical creation" to the Dhyan Chohans. His words are perfectly unequivocal:—"All things are accounted for by law, working on matter in its diverse forms, *plus* the guiding and modifying influence of the highest intelligences associated with the Solar System, the Dhyan Chohans." Does this endow the Dhyan Chohans with the privilege of creation, physical or otherwise? Further on, Mr. Sinnett says, "they (the Dhyan Chohans) can only work through the principle of evolution," &c. This certainly shows that the Dhyan Chohans are not creators at all, at any rate, not in the ordinary sense of that word. Nevertheless, the first objection that she levels against the doctrine is its repugnance "to common sense." Common sense is, no doubt, a very elastic word, as deceitful as the Greek god Proteus, but I have never yet heard it being appealed to as an arbiter, on the transcendental plane, where admittedly our every day experience has no room to stand upon. The only other argument against the position is, that it is opposed " to the intuitive conception of the fitness of things." The doctrine presents a distinct line of cleavage, and I shall endeavour to find out, which of the divisions objection is taken to, on the aforesaid ground. Does it militate against Mrs. Kingsford's notion of the fitness of things that Dhyan Chohans should be allowed to have a hand in the fashioning of the planets, or that human entities should be allowed to rise to the height of Dhyan Chohans ? The former can scarcely be objectionable. The offending doctrine then is that which teaches that the state of Dhyan Chohans is not beyond the reach of humanity. But a little reflection will show the perfect consonance of the doctrine with reason--and justice. If the Dhyan Chohans were free from the necessity of passing through all the different stages of evolutionary progress and thus appearing as men, at some time or another, where will be the dominion of absolute justice in the world ? Such a monstrous doctrine, in fact, would be but the restatement of the horrid Clavinistic dogma of salvation by election and damnation by predestination. I would request the gifted lady to consider whether the doctrine as presented by Mr. Sinnett is so much opposed to the fitness of things as she imagines. Mrs. Kingsford lays down that the doctrine of Dhyan Chohan is common alike to Buddhism and Christianity, and then goes on to explain it from her own stand-point. "It is taught" she says, " by the former of these religions [*i. e.* Buddhism] that whenever a Buddha passes into Nirvana, his Karma is poured out through the worlds as a living moral energy whereby a fresh influx of spiritual life is developed." To this she offers as a parallel the Christian doctrine embodied in the saying of Christ—" If I go not away, the Paraclete will not come to you; but if I go, I will send him to you."

With all deference, I must here submit that Mrs. Kingsford has taken an entirely wrong view of the nature of the energy, evolved by a Monad in the state of *mukti* (freedom from the wheel of births and deaths), and also of the *Nirvanic* condition. Every human being, on attainment of a certain stage in his spiritual development, begins to shed on the world "a living moral energy, whereby a fresh influx of spiritual life is developed," and for this, passage into Nirvana (in the sense in which she understands it) is not necessary. The Paraclete that descends has nothing to do with the Dhyan Chohans, who are not Monads in the *Nirvanic* condition, contemplated above. When *Videha Kaivalyam* (the union of the disembodied Monad with the absolute Parabrahman) is reached by any Monad, the sum total of its Karma goes to enrich the Universal Mind, wherein lie the archetype of all that is, was, or will be. The fresh influx of realised ideas thus brought in, is showered by the Cosmic energy, called *Fohat* by Buddhist Occultists and the Initiates. This is how the Paraclete (or the manifested *Buddhi*) is made to descend, in the *true* Esoteric doctrine. But the Dhyan Chohans are not in that state of Nirvana from which the *Buddhi* or the *Pragna* (the Sophia of the Gnostics, or again the Christian Paraclete) descends. As all Eastern Occultists know, there are fourteen gradations in Nirvana, exclusive of two others (which are but one, the manifested and the unmanifested), some of which, in truth nine, are attained by the adepts even while alive, and others reached only when in the Dhyan Chohanic state, and so on. This explanation will clearly show that the doctrine of Dhyan Chohans, whether repugnant or not to Mrs. Kingsford's "common sense," is certainly not what she takes it to be.

I shall now pass to Mr. Maitland's objections on this head. The first exception that he takes is, that the presence of the Dhyan Chohans interferes with the freedom of the human will. The subject of free-will and predestination is one which has been a bone of contention among Western theologians and metaphysicians, time out of mind, and as such, no doubt, possesses a peculiar charm for the Western intellect; but it must not be forgotten that the metaphysical problem of free-will and predestination has very little importance outside of a religious system which rests upon an almighty and omniscient

God, who brings into existence beings from the realms of absolute nothingness by an act of his volition. The Dhyan Chohans, as has been already shown, are no more creatures or creators, than we are ourselves. With us, all will is free, because there is no overruling Power to interfere with its exercise. At the same time, it must be borne in mind that there is a law which every will has to obey, because the nature of the ONE and only Substance in the Universe is the embodiment of that Law. I have stated the doctrine quite plainly, I believe, and will now leave it to the reader to find out if it agrees with his notions of free-will and predestination, or not. The objection under notice seems to have arisen from a mistaken apprehension of the nature of the Dhyan Chohans ; and, when once explained, the doctrine contained in "Esoteric Buddhism" will be found more scientific than the objectors imagine. The two passages in that book which, according to Mr. Maitland, conflict with human "free-will," have thus been, again, very strangely misunderstood. It is said on page 189 that the Dhyan Chohans "reign in a divine way over the destinies of the world." Here, perhaps, the word "divine" has led Mr. Maitland to imagine that Mr. Sinnett has invested the Dhyan Chohans with all the attributes of the God of the *hoi polloi*. But to any ordinary reader it naturally appears that Mr. Sinnett's intention was simply to show what is the nearest approach, in truth, to the common idea about God. The other passage (p. 177) runs thus :—" [The Dhyan Chohans] exercise a guiding and modifying influence throughout the whole progress of evolution, all things being accounted for by law working on matter in its diverse forms, *plus* the guiding and modifying influence of . . . the Dhyan Chohans." No more in this, than in the previous passage, is there anything said which would support Mr. Maitland's position. All that Mr. Sinnett asserts here is, that a certain amount of the evolutionary energy of the universe operates through the endeavours of a host of exalted beings, the conscious agents of the Immutable Law, inherent in the One Life, which is *non*-conscious, only because consciousness is limited and conditioned.

This does by no means show that the Dhyan Chohans can, like the so-called personal God, be charged with having created the iron-chain of causation which produces results, to some—pleasurable, to others—painful.

Mr. Maitland is not more fortunate in his next objection against the doctrine of Dhyan Chohans. Stated shortly, his argument comes to this : Esoteric Doctrine and Occultism are perfectly useless, since " the highest, or rather only, objects offered us for worship, are our own perishable selves –in an advanced stage of evolution, it is true, but a stage, which is so far from involving our perpetuation, so far from securing to us that ' gift of God which *is* eternal life'—that the attainment of it is but the prelude to inevitable extinction,—extinction not of mere existence of manifested being but or being itself. " After reading the above, one feels inclined to drop the pen in despair ! Evidently, Mr. Sinnett has written his book in vain for readers of his Vice-President's stamp ! Is the idea, expressed above, that Nirvana, the final goal of man, is nothing but annihilation justified by the teachings of " Esoteric Buddhism ? " For, it is stated on page 163 :—" All that words can convey is that Nirvana is *a sublime state of conscious rest in omniscience.*" Is the state of Nirvana which is attempted to be shadowed forth by Mr. Sinnett, in the above words, nothing but annihilation ? If so, the sooner it is recognised that language has ceased to be the medium of communication between man and man,—the better. It is perfectly plain that Mr. Maitland has opened his critical volley on Mr. Sinnett's devoted head, without even taking the trouble to acquaint himself sufficiently with the subject of his criticism, and must, therefore, submit to the censure which such reckless conduct deservedly calls for.

Considering the cloudy mist which seems to surround the subject of Dhyan Chohans, it may not be out of place to subjoin a few observations thereon from the Hindu. or rather the Adwaita, stand-point—the latter being identical with Esoteric " Buddhism. " I wish it, however, to be distinctly understood that my views are not at all compulsory on any Fellow of the Theosophical Society, in this country or abroad; my object being simply to offer food for reflection, and to lead our Brother-members to more active and independent investigation.

The Dhyan Chohans are referred to by a variety of names in the Hindu sacred writings. The Dhyan Chohan when incarnating himself as a man, at the first appearance of humanity on our planet, is referred to as Manu Swayambhu (the self-existent) who begets the seven Rishis uncorporeally, they being known as his *manasaputras*—the children of *manas* or mind—and who, therefore, represent the 5th principle of the planet. These are referred to as 7 × 7 in Occult treatises; and it is they again, who are appointed, we are taught, to hold in trust for the nascent human race the sacred Wisdom-Religion. These Rishis beget, *i. e.*, take under their charge, the seven Pitris, the first evolved men on this planet, and ancestors of all the human family. This is one aspect of the thing. As the offspring of Aditi or the "Measureless," the Infinite (Prakriti) the Dhyan Chohans are known as the Adityas, who are said to be twelve in number, with reference to the different grades among them. These Dhyan Chohans, as the guardian spirits of this world, are known also as *Dikpalas* (the keepers of the different points of the compass), a name under which, it will be found, they are constantly referred to in the earlier Buddhist writings. As agents of destruction of our system, when it comes to its proper termination, they are the twelve Rudras ("burning with anger,"* erroneously translated as "Howlers" by Max Müller), who reduce everything back to its undifferentiated

* This has reference to the fiery consummation which our system must undergo at the time of the *Solar* Mahapralaya. Twelve Suryas (suns) will arise, it is *exoterically* taught, to burn up the solar universe—and bring on the Pralaya. This is a travesty of the esoteric teaching that our end will come from the exposure of the *real* sun "by the withdrawal of the veil"—the chromo and photo sphere, perhaps, of which the Royal Society thinks, it has learnt so much—H. P. BLAVATSKY.

state. Mr. Maitland represents Mr. Sinnett to have said that the Dhyan Chohans perish like everything else. But, as has been shown before, no entity that has once reached Paranirvana can be said to perish ; though the state of existence known as the Dhyan Chohanic, no doubt, merges into, or assimilates itself with, the state of Absolute Consciousness for the time being, as the hour of the Mahapralaya strikes, but to be propelled again into existence at the dawn of the following Manvantara.* This, by no means, shows that the entities, who existed as Dhyan Chohans, *perish*, any more than the water converted into steam perishes. The Dhyan Chohans are, in fact, the gods mentioned allegorically in our Puranas. These exalted beings, in common with all the other classes of the Devi (god) kingdom are of two types—one consisting of those who *have been* men, and the other of those who *will be* men at some future period. It is distinctly mentioned in our books that those who are now gods lived once on this earth as men. The Dhyan Chohans are the Elohim of the Western Kabalists. I was obliged to make this somewhat lengthy digression to show that the doctrine of the Dhyan Chohans as taught in the Esoteric doctrine, and faintly delineated in " Esoteric Buddhism, " is essentially the same as taught by the ancient Rishis, by Shankaracharya, and even *by* the present Brahmanical authorities—however distorted the modern forms. Those who consider this doctrine " as repugnant to common sense, " and yet would, in the face of " the urgency of the demand in the West for fuller enlightenment from the East, " " invite teaching from yet other schools of Occult Science " would only fall from the frying pan into the fire. There is not a school in India, whether esoteric or exoteric, that teaches any other doctrine as regards the Adityas or the Dhyan Chohans--unless, indeed, it be the world-famed Vallabhacharya or the " Black

---

* The word *Manvantara* literally means a " different Manu, " or incarnate Dhyan Chohan. It is applied to the period of time intervening between two successive appearances of Manu on this earth, as the word *Manu-antara* shows.

Tantrika "—school, to whose philosophical tenets Mr. Maitland and his followers are quite welcome to address themselves.

I shall now deal with Mrs. Kingsford's objection to the whole system of evolution as given by Mr. Sinnett. "The mathematical precision," it is argued, "of the clockwork arrangement invoked by Mr. Sinnett's mechanical system" shows its disaccord with "the suggestions of scientific and spiritual thought."

Whatever may be the merits or demerits of the system in question, it is very hard to see how any system can be condemned as "unscientific" merely because of its mathematical precision. If everything in the universe is subject to a rigorous chain of causation, then, it cannot be denied that all natural facts are capable of being represented "with the mathematical precision of a clockwork arrangement," although the official science of the day may not acquire the capacity of so representing them. But, it cannot, for a single moment, be denied that the more precision any science acquires, the closer does it approach its abstract ideal—immutable Law. The only thing that seems to me unscientific in the whole matter is—Mrs. Kingsford's objections.

Attack is next directed by the gifted lady against the physical existence of the seven planets, which form the planetary chain spoken of in Mr. Sinnett's book. On the authority of some exoteric Buddhist dogmas, Mrs. Kingsford asserts that the seven planets in question are only "an allegory," and really indicate so many "spiritual states." But elsewhere she admits the reality of a diversity of spiritual states, and then with a strange forgetfulness of one of the fundamental axioms of Occult Science—"as it is above, so it is below"—denies diversity to material conditions of existence. If there are several conditions of Devachan, and several states of Nirvana, why should then material existence be limited to only one? I find, however, from a foot-note on page 6, that Mrs. Kingsford does not question the fact of "planetary evolution and transmigration;" and I infer therefrom, that her objections apply only to matters of detail. But, as it does not appear what her objections really are, they cannot be examined any further. With regard to the submergence of Atlantis, Mr. Maitland's idea seems to be (p. 22) that although the sinking of continents is a well-proved geological fact, yet "the tale of Atlantis is a parable" which has a meaning purely spiritual. Although this is no new idea of his, and was only recently expounded at length by another Spiritualist, Mr. Gerald Massey, it is nevertheless as purely fanciful. The author of *Surya Siddhanta* lived, in spite of the attempts of Western Sanskritists, to assign to him quite a modern date, in the lost Atlantis, as all our traditions and chronicles declare. In the geographical system given in the above-mentioned astronomical work, mention is made of the seven Islands of Atlantis—Plakshadvipa and others, and their position is indicated with scientific precision. So much, as regards a work in the possession of European Sanskritists. As to the numerous works in which the subject of the lost continents and the *third* and *fourth* races that inhabited them is fully treated, but which no European eye has ever beheld—no need of mentioning them since they would only give rise to a very impolite denial. The celebrated astronomer "Asura Maya" (whom Prof. Weber has transformed into the Greek Ptolemaios) was another, a native of Atlantis. The submergence of this island is also spoken of in *Uttara Ramayana*, if people would but understand it, and various other works of unquestionable authority. The real fact, therefore, is, that the disappearance of Atlantis is a geographical, and will soon become an historical fact, although I do not deny that it has also been made to serve as an allegorical represenation of certain spiritual truths.

The next point that I notice shall be Mr. Maitland's most extraordinary travesty of Mr. Sinnett's view of Buddha. I do not consider myself justified to speak publicly of the real Esoteric Doctrine of Buddhaship. So, all I can here say is, that Mr. Sinnett's presentation of the doctrine though incomplete, is correct so far as it goes. The first thing I have to emphasise is, that Christ and Buddha do not signify one and the same thing : Christ *is a principle*, and Buddha *is a state.* It is not necessary for every Monad to pass through Buddhahood in its progress towards Nirvana.* Every man who passes through the last state of initiation does not necessarily become a Buddha. The historical view of the case is after all the correct one, and no confusion has been made by Mr. Sinnett between "similarity" and "identity" as suggested by Mr. Maitland on page 22.

I shall now conclude my review of the misconceptions charged on, and arguments urged against, the teachings contained in "Esoteric Buddhism," by calling attention to Mr. Maitland's sarcastic reference to the "chief inspiring adept himself," as he calls the MASTER. Mr. Maitland considers it "worthy of note that although the being of God, or of any absolute good, is strenuously denied, that of "absolute evil" is . . . maintained, the phrase being used by the chief inspiring adept himself of the book." The phrase quoted by him is so completely separated from the context of what the said "adept" really asserts, that to draw inferences from such an isolated expression without having it more clearly defined by what precedes and what follows it—is not far removed from misrepresentation. Begging Mr. Maitland's pardon, it is distinctly stated on page 61, "that when your race, the fifth, will have reached the zenith of its physical intellectuality and developed its highest civilization . . . unable to go on any higher in its own cycle, its progress towards absolute evil will be arrested (as its predecessors . . . were arrested in their progress toward the same)." Strange, indeed, must be the construction by which, from the above citation, the Vice-President's proposition can be extracted "that the existence

* It must be here borne in mind that no man,—Gautama Buddha, Christ, or any other is here referred to. The state which Siddhartha Gautama attained by placing himself in direct *rapport* with a particular ray of the Absolute Wisdom is called—Buddha.

of 'absolute evil' is asserted by the adept!" On the contrary, the implication is plain that no such thing "as absolute evil" is ever realised by humanity. If, however, still further elucidation of the subject is sought, I have but to point out another passage, on the same subject, on page 84, and by the same "inspiring adept;" which will render Mr. Maitland's--I love to think *unconscious*--misrepresentation as clear as day to everyone. "There is *more apparent and relative than actual evil even on earth*, and it is not given to the *hoi poloi* to reach the fatal grandeur and eminence of a Satan every day"--writes the venerated Master on the said page. It is, indeed, very hard to conceive how a person of Mr. Maitland's undoubted fairness and ability could have so hopelessly sunk in such a slough of serious errors!

To crown the list of voluntary and involuntary mistakes and misconceptions, we must mention his ascription to Madame Blavatsky of certain statements that, considering her relation to the holy personage to whom they refer, could never have been, nor were they made by her. The internal evidence, in the absence of any signature to the article (Replies to an English F. T. S.), in which the sentence occurs (see *Theosophist*, October 1883, p. 3), is strong enough to warn off all careful readers from the unwarranted assumption which Mr. Maitland has made. But it is certainly curious that the gentleman should have never missed a single chance of falling into blunder! The "Replies"--as every one in our Society is aware of--were written by three "adepts" as Mr. Maitland calls them--none of whom is known to the London Lodge, with the exception of one--to Mr. Sinnett. The sentence quoted and fathered upon Madame Blavatsky is found in the MSS. sent by a Mahatma who resides in Southern India, and who had alone the right to speak, as he did, of another Mahatma. But even his words are not correctly stated,* as

* I here deny most emphatically of having ever caused to be printed—let alone to have myself written it—the sentence as it now stands quoted by Mr. Maitland in his "Remarks". The *Theosophist* of October is, I believe, available in England and the two sentences may be easily compared.

shown in the foot-note. With this remark, I may begin to wind up this already too prolonged controversy.

To sum up. Our rather lengthy examination of the strictures contained in the joint papers by the President and a 'Vice-President of the London Lodge' will now clearly show to our fellow members, and to any impartial reader of "Esoteric Buddhism," that its doctrines are neither unscientific, nor are they entirely allegorical. If, owing to their extremely abstruse character, they are misleading, or rather difficult of comprehension,—the author should hardly be blamed for it. He has done his best; and, as the system of philosophy explained by Mr. Sinnett comes assuredly from the highest sources of esoteric knowledge known to us in the East—he has deserved, on the contrary, the best thanks, for even the little he has done. His book forms part of a complete system of Esoteric Science and philosophy which is neither Hindu nor Buddhist in its origion, but which is identical with the ancient Wisdom-Religion itself, and which forms the basis or foundation of every system of religion conceived by the human mind since the time when the first Dhyan Chohan appeared on this planet to plant the germ

---

When the writer of Reply No. 2, referring to "Greeks and Romans," jocularly remarked that their ancestors might have been mentioned by some other name, and added that "besides the very plausible excuse that the names used were embodied *in a private letter*, written (as many unimportant letters are) in great haste, and which (*this* particular letter,) "was hardly worthy of the honour of being quoted *verbatim* with all its imperfections"—he certainly never meant his remark to yield any such charge as is implied in Mr. Maitland's incorrect quotation. Let any one of the London Lodge compare and decide whether the said sentence can lead any person to doubt "the accuracy of the adept Brothers," or infer "that they are frequently given to write in great haste things which are hardly worthy of the honour of being quoted, etc." And since the word "frequently" does not occur in the alleged quotation, and alters a good deal the spirit of the remark, I can only express my regret that, under the present serious circumstances, Mr. Maitland should have become himself (inadvertingly, no doubt,) guilty of such an *inaccuracy*.—H. P. BLAVATSKY.

of Esoteric Wisdom. Its form may appear indistinct, and the conceptions put forth may be under the necesssity of being expanded or modified, when the whole system in its completeness is given out. Until then, it would be extremely improper to form any hasty ideas as regards the highest aims and objects of the said system, or its insufficiency to serve as "a perfect system of thought and rule of life." To realise such an expectation, we have to wait till it is presented to us in its most perfect form, not assuredly from the fragmentary doctrines put together in Mr. Sinnett's work; and it appears equally unreasonable to criticize the doctrines now before the world from the isolated stand-point of Esoteric Christianity. If any of the members of the London Lodge are of opinion that there are higher and purer doctrines in the East, they are at full liberty to investigate them. But the fullest freedom given to them in their option can never justify the many uncalled for remarks, scattered over the two "Letters" against the "inspirers" of Mr. Sinnett's "Esoteric Buddhism." To hint at length, as Mr. Maitland has done, "that nothing would be more likely than that . . . we (the members of the L. L.) should . . . be pledging ourselves to an obscure and outlying sect . . . with but a fragment of the truth, . . . so perverted, as to represent no longer truth but error" is surely, in the absence of final proof, neither Theosophical, Buddhistic, nor even *Christian*, but simply very uncharitable, and as unjust to our Society at large.

As to the proposal made to split the London Branch into two sections, to be called the Tibetan and the Catholic, in our humble opinion, it is hardly calculated to promote the cause of Theosophy in the West. There may be, as the revered Mahatmas have suggested, two distinct groups in the London Lodge Theosophical Society; but these groups must be on a footing of *perfect equality*. To adopt Mrs. Kingsford and Mr. Maitland's views in their entirety—excepting so far as they coincide with the views of the Master—would be fatal to the Society's Catholic policy, and as such, the Parent Society would not give to its sanction. According to the rules of the Association, every Theosophical Society *is* "Catholic" in its aims and intentions, and we do not see the propriety of calling any particular section of the Society Catholic or Universal—in contrast with any other section, to limit it, after all, only to one particular person's views. I gather further, from Mrs. Kingsford's letter, that the object of the Catholic section is to proclaim Esoteric Christianity to the Western world. If this is to be its sole object, and if Esoteric Christianity is to be interpreted, agreeably to the authority of two individuals, and every other system of Esoteric doctrine is to be treated in the same manner in which Mr. Sinnett's book has been, then the section in question will be as much entitled to the distinctive appellation proposed, as an obscure Hindu sect to identify itself with the Ancient Wisdom-Religion. As for all practical details of administration, the President-Founder, who will be in London within a short time of the receipt of the present, will be best competent to deal with them, in accordance with instructions received by him from the MAHATMAS—his, and our guides and MASTERS.

ENGLISH SERIES.

	Rs.	a.
Bhagavad-Gita Translation of, with notes and annotations by the late Mr. Tukaram Tatya	0	6
The Jivanmuktiviveka or the path to liberation in this life by Swami Shri Vidyaranya Saraswati rendered into English by Manilal N. Dvivedi, B. A.	1	4
Lectures on the Study on the Bhagavad-Gita being a help to students of its philosophy by T. Subba Rao, B. A., B. L., F. T. S. ...	0	10
Tatva-kaumudi (Sankhya) *of Wachaspati Misra* with an English Translation of the Sanskrit Text by Ganganath Jha, M. A., F. T. S.	1	8
The Ishavasyopanishad, translated into English with the commentaries of Shri Shankaracharya and Shri Anantacharya and notes from the Tikas of Anandagiri, Uvatacharya,, Shankarananda, Ramchandra Pandit and Anandabhatta by Shrisa Chandra Vasu, B. A., F. T. S.	0	8
Gheranda Samhita being a Treatise on the Hatha and Raja Yogas, printed with Sanskrit Text and an appendix containing extracts from English works of authority, describing the Samadhi taken by the Sadhu Haridas at the Court of Ranjitsingha in Punjab.	0	8
The Twelve Principal Upanishads, translated into English by Raja Rajendralal Mitra and other Oriental Scholars, with notes from the Bhashya of Shankarscharya, and the Glossary of Anandgiri, being a reprint of the translations published by the Royal Asiatic Society of Bengal.	4	0
The Mandukyopanishad, with Gaudapàda's Kàrikâs and the Bhàshaya of Shankara, translated into English, by Manilal N. Dvivedi, B. A.	1	8
The Yogsara-Sangraha, or the Philosophy of Yoga-shàstra, being one of the rare Treatises by Vidnyànabhikshu, the greatest authority on the Sankhya and Yoga-Shastras with English translation by Gangânàth Jhâ, M. A., F. T.S.	0	12
A Compendium of The Raja-Yoga Philosophy, comprising principal Treatises of Shankaràchàrya Swàmi; such as the Aparokshânubnti, the Atmànâtma-Viveka, the Viveka Chudamani, the Charpatpanjari and the Vâkyasudhà with the Vedàntasàra of Sadànand Swàmi. Some of these Treatises are printed with Sanskrit Texts, 2nd Edition....	1	4
The Yoga Sutras of Patanjali, translated by Professor Manilàl Nabhubhài Dvivedi, B.A., F.T.S., with nots, explaining fully the meaning of each Sutra with the help of Vyâs's Commentary and other works by subsequent writers. He has also brought to bear on the subject the light of modern research, wherever necessary.	1	0

		Rs.	a.
12.	*Bhagavad-Gita*, translated by Mr. Charles Wilkins, New Edition, revised and enlarged, with two learned Introductions by Professor Manilal N. Dvivedi and Mr. Nobinchandra Banarji...	0	12
13.	*Prabodha Chándrodaya Nataka*, a drama on the conflict between the higher and lower Nature of Man, ultimately ending in the triumph of the former; and Shrimat Shankaracharya's Atmabodha, translated by Mr. Taylor.	0	8
14.	*The Purpose of Theosophy*, by Mrs. A. P. Sinnett. Cheap Edition	0	4
15.	*Sankhya Karika*, a Treaties on the Sankhya Philosophy, with Gaudapada's Commentary, translated into English, with introduction and notes by Professor H. H. Wilson and T. Colebrooke.	1	8
16.	*Yoga Philosophy*, explained with the help of the modern sciences by Dr. Paul.	0	6
17.	*Letters to an Indian Raja*, by an Indian Recluse...	1	0
18.	*Hath-yoga-Pradipika*. English translation with the Sanskrit Text and Commentary and an able Introduction, proving that the Yoga is a compliment of the Dnyana (knowledge) and *vice versa*.	1	0
19.	*The Uttara-Gita*, being the Initiation of Arjoona by Shri Krishna into Yoga and Dnyana.	0	4
20.	*The Philosophy of Brahmanical Sandhya and Gayatri*.	0	6
21.	*The Mahimnastotra*, or a Hymn to Shiva with the Sanskrit Text.	0	2
22.	*The Higher Life*, or Rules of Raja-Yoga, by Bhagwan Buddha...	0	2
23.	*An Introduction to the Study of the Yoga Aphorisms of Patanjali* ...	0	4
24.	*An Introduction to the Mantra-Shastra*.	0	6
25.	*Aparkshyanubhuti or Direct Cognition of the Unity of Jiva and Brahma*.	0	4
26.	Atmanatma-Viveka.	0	6
27.	Shree-Vakya-Sudha-	0	6
28.	Crest-Jewel of Wisdom.	0	8
29.	*The Mental Cure* with Notes, by Dr. W. F. Evans.	1	8
30.	*The Mental Medicine* do.	2	0
31.	*The Divine Law of Cure* do.	2	0
32.	*Soul and Body*. do.	1	0
33.	Yoga Darshana by Ganganâth Jhâ....	1	8

IN PRESS—

1. Panchdashi translated by Rao-Saheb Raoji B. Pavagi.

Intending purchasers should get their names registered as early as possible.

☞ These Books can be had from *Mr. Rajaram Tukaram Tatya*, 21, Hummum Street, Fort, Bombay; also from the Manager, "*Theosophist*", Adyar, Madras; and from the Theosophical Publishing Society, Benares City.

BOMBAY:—Printed by Bhiva Hari Shinde, at the "TATVA-VIVECHAKA" PRESS, Nos. 1-2-3, Khetwadi Back Road.

Published by

Facsimile Publisher
Ashok Vihar, Delhi-110052 (India)
Website: www.facsimilepublishers.com

Distributed by

Gyan Books Pvt. Ltd.
5, Ansari Road, Daryaganj, New Delhi-110002 (India)
E-mail: books@gyanbooks.com, Website: www.gyanbooks.com

8 888000 965824